UNDERSTANDING ETHNIC MEDIA

Producers, Consumers, and Societies

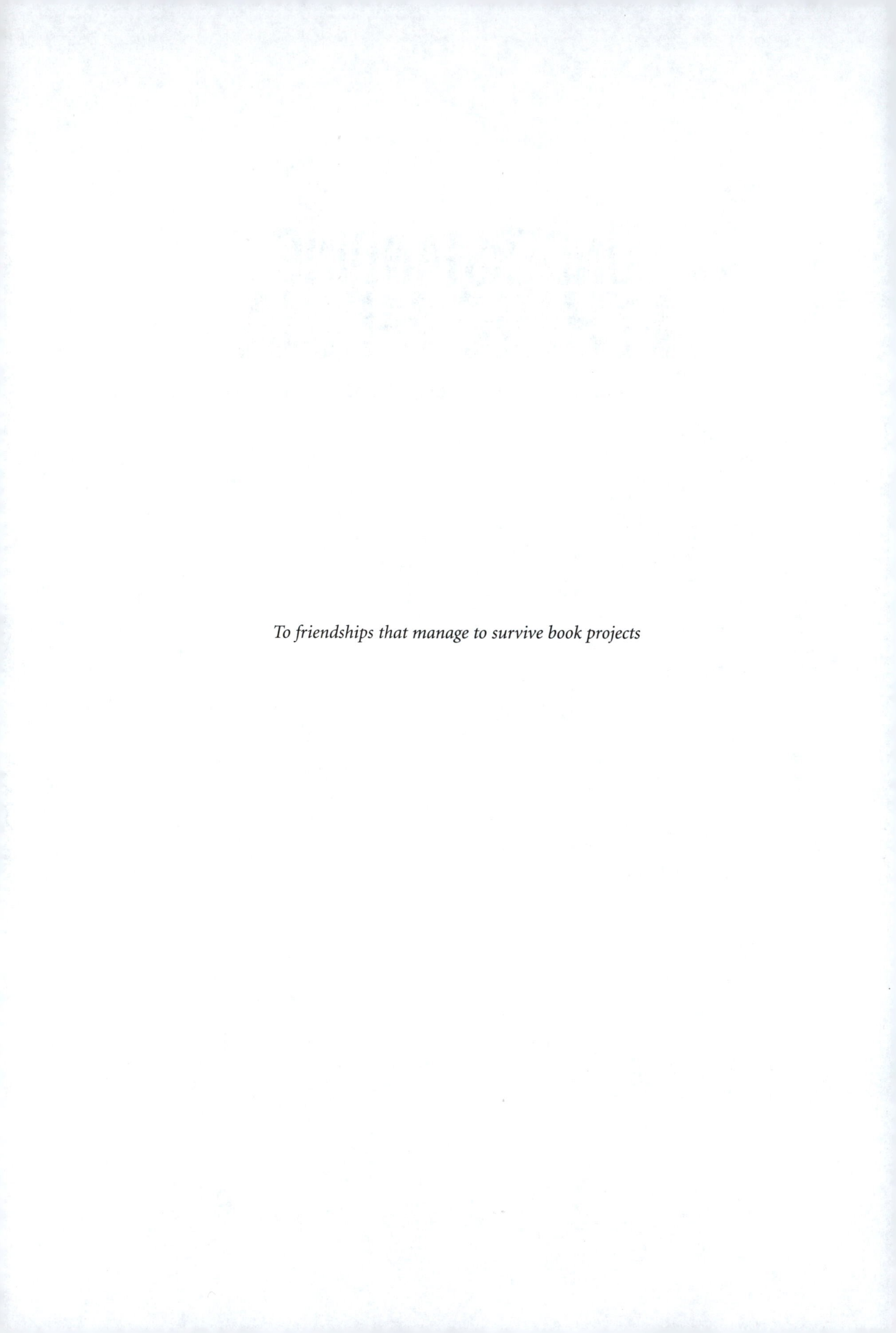

To friendships that manage to survive book projects

UNDERSTANDING ETHNIC MEDIA

Producers, Consumers, and Societies

Matthew D. Matsaganis
University at Albany, State University of New York

Vikki S. Katz
Rutgers, the State University of New Jersey

Sandra J. Ball-Rokeach
Annenberg School for Communication and Journalism, University of Southern California

Los Angeles | London | New Delhi
Singapore | Washington DC

For information:

SAGE Publications, Inc.
2455 Teller Road
Thousand Oaks,
California 91320
E-mail: order@sagepub.com

SAGE Publications Ltd.
1 Oliver's Yard
55 City Road
London EC1Y 1SP
United Kingdom

SAGE Publications India Pvt. Ltd.
B 1/I 1 Mohan Cooperative
Industrial Area
Mathura Road, New Delhi 110 044
India

SAGE Publications Asia-Pacific Pte. Ltd.
33 Pekin Street #02-01
Far East Square
Singapore 048763

Printed in the United States of America

Library of Congress Cataloging-in-Publication Data

Matsaganis, Matthew D.
Understanding ethnic media : producers, consumers, and societies / Matthew D. Matsaganis, Vikki S. Katz, Sandra J. Ball-Rokeach.
p. cm.
Includes bibliographical references and index.
ISBN 978-1-4129-5912-4 (cloth)—ISBN 978-1-4129-5913-1 (pbk.)
1. Ethnic mass media. 2. Mass media and minorities. I. Katz, Vikki S. II. Ball-Rokeach, Sandra. III. Title.

P94.5.M55M38 2011
302.2308—dc22 2009050796

This book is printed on acid-free paper.

10 11 12 13 14 10 9 8 7 6 5 4 3 2 1

Acquisitions Editor: Todd R. Armstrong
Editorial Assistant: Nathan Davidson
Production Editor: Astrid Virding
Copy Editor: Jovey Stewart
Typesetter: C&M Digitals (P) Ltd.
Proofreader: Carole Quandt
Indexer: Jean Casalegno
Cover Designer: Gail Buschman
Marketing Manager: Jenny Raven

Brief Contents

Preface xiii

PART I: ETHNIC MEDIA IN CONTEXT 1

1. What Are Ethnic Media? 3
2. Ethnic Media in History 25

PART II: THE CONSUMERS 49

3. Immigrants and Their Media 51
4. Ethnic Minorities and Their Media 69

PART III: THE PRODUCERS 91

5. Ethnic Media Audience Trends and What Lies Behind the Numbers 93
6. Ethnic Media Organizations and Competition 117
7. Globalization and the Ethnic Media Organization 147
8. Policy and Ethnic Media Development 173

PART IV: ETHNIC MEDIA AS CIVIC COMMUNICATORS 205

9. Ethnic Media as Local Media 207
10. Professional Challenges for Ethnic Media Journalists 227

PART V: THE FUTURE OF ETHNIC MEDIA 251

Conclusion: What Does the Future Hold for Ethnic Media? 253

Detailed Contents

Preface **xiii**

PART I: ETHNIC MEDIA IN CONTEXT **1**

Chapter 1 What Are Ethnic Media? **3**

Introduction 3
Defining Ethnic Media 5
Ethnic Media Contrasted With Other Types of Media 8
Ethnic Media Versus Mainstream Media 10
The Role of Geographic Context 11
The Roles of Ethnic Media 12
Defining Culture, Ethnicity, and Race 12
The Roles of Ethnic Media 15
The Ethnic Community: Ethnic Media as Mobilizing Forces 16
Ethnic Media as Indicators of Social Change 17
Ethnic Media Change the Landscape, Make Markets More Competitive 17
Globalization and the Ethnic Media 18
Social Changes That Make Studying Ethnic Media Necessary 19
Chapter-by-Chapter Book Overview 21

Chapter 2 Ethnic Media in History **25**

Emigration, Immigration, and the Ethnic Media 25
Indigenous Media as Ethnic Media 26
Migration Trends and the Emergence of Media 26
Beginnings of the Ethnic Press in Europe 27
Ethnic Media in Europe in the 19th and Early 20th Centuries 28
Ethnic Media in Europe in the Post-War Era 29
European Public Broadcasting Reluctantly Opens Its Doors to Ethnic Minorities 30
From "Pirates" to Legal Ethnic Media Broadcasters 30
Ethnic Media in the United States 31
The Beginnings of Ethnic Media in the United States 31
The Black Press Before 1900 31
The Beginnings of the Native-American Press 32

The Early Latino Press 34
The Chinese Press in the 19th and 20th Centuries 34
The Immigrant Press and the "Old" Immigrants 35
Ethnic Media and Politics of Loyalty: World Wars I and II 35
Ethnic Media for "New" Immigrants in the Post-1965 Era 37
Ethnic Media in Canada 37
First Nation Media in Canada 37
The Rise of Third Language Media 38
Ethnic Media in Mexico 40
Indigenous Media in Mexico 40
Ethnic and Immigrant Media in Australia 42
Aboriginal Media in Australia 42
Moving Toward Interactive and Visual Media 43
Immigrants, Their Descendents, and Their Media 43
How the Past Affects Present Ethnic Media Trends 45

PART II: THE CONSUMERS **49**

Chapter 3 Immigrants and Their Media **51**
Why Immigration Matters 51
Defining Immigration 52
Context of Reception 54
Ethnic Media as Resources for Immigrants 58
Understanding What Is Happening in the Settlement Community 58
Finding Jobs 60
Understanding Their Rights 60
Connecting to Immigrants With Similar Experiences 63
Keeping Up With Developments in the Home Country and Community 64
Online Ethnic Media Resources for Immigrants 65

Chapter 4 Ethnic Minorities and Their Media **69**
What Is an Ethnic Minority? 69
Racial Versus Ethnic Identities 70
Developing Ethnic Identities 71
Developing Hyphenated Identities 72
Developing Conglomerate Identities 73
Developing Hybrid Identities 74
Ethnic Media and Identity Formation 75
Ethnic Media's Roles in Ethnic Minority Communities 75
An Independent Voice 76
Covering Content of Interest 78
Ethnic Media as a Platform for Social Equality 78
Ethnic Media as a Social Institution 82
Ethnic Media and Family Life 83

Language Development and Maintenance 83
Ethnic Media as a Cultural Teacher 84
The Challenge for Ethnic Media to Remain Viable 85
Local Content 85
Language of the Ethnic Media 87
Exclusivity and Authenticity 88

PART III: THE PRODUCERS **91**

Chapter 5 Ethnic Media Audience Trends and What Lies Behind the Numbers **93**
Ethnic Newspapers: The Importance of Circulation Audits 94
Ethnic Television and Radio: Trends and Politics Behind the Ratings 99
How Television and Radio Audiences Are Quantified 99
The Audience of Electronic Ethnic Media: Two Examples From the United States 100
Challenges in Measuring Electronic Ethnic Media Audiences 101
Two Alternative Models for Sustainable Ethnic Television and Radio 103
Trends in Print Media Circulation 105
Latino and African-American Print Media: Two Different Stories 105
Decreases in Latino Print Media Numbers and Circulation 107
The Impact of the Larger Industry Context 108
The Effects of the 2008 Economic Crisis 109
The Audiences of Ethnic Television and Radio 110
Ethnic Television 110
Ethnic Radio 112

Chapter 6 Ethnic Media Organizations and Competition **117**
Surviving Competition, Achieving Sustainability 117
Competing for Advertising Revenue 118
Competition Among Ethnic Print Media 119
Circulation Elasticity of Demand 119
Circulation Spirals 119
Ethnic Newspapers and Market Dynamics 119
"Umbrella" or Intercity Competition 122
Challenges and Opportunities for Ethnic Print Media 124
The Downside of Success Hypothesis 124
Return Migration and the Ethnic Media Audience 126
The Internet Challenge 126
The Internet as a Substitute for Ethnic Print Media 126
The Cannibalization Dilemma 128
To Lead or to Follow? 135
Competition in Ethnic Television and Radio 135
Ethnic Television, Ethnic Radio, and the Internet 136
Online-Only Ethnic Media 137

The 2008 Global Economic Crisis: Catalyst for Innovation or Demise? 137
Satellite Broadcasting Networks 138

Chapter 7 Globalization and the Ethnic Media Organization 147
The Structure of Ethnic Media Organizations 147
What Is Globalization? 148
Three Different Approaches to Globalization 148
Forces of Globalization 153
Technological Innovation 153
New Communication Technologies and the Ethnic Media Consumer 153
New Communication Technologies and the Ethnic Media Producer 154
Economic Globalization 155
Regulation 156
Six Types of Ethnic Media Organizations 158
Small Scale, Local Operations 158
Large Ethnic Media Corporations 160
The Multinational Media Enterprise 161
Transnational or Global Ethnic Media 162
Public and Non-Profit Broadcasters 163
Virtual Ethnic Media Organizations 164
Who Owns the Ethnic Media? 164
Ownership Consolidation Among Ethnic Media Serving Similar Communities 165
Ethnic Media Acquisitions by Transnational and Multi-National Enterprises 166
Acquisitions of Ethnic Media by Mainstream Media Organizations 167
Decrease in Number of Owners of Media Who Are Members of a Minority Group 168

Chapter 8 Policy and Ethnic Media Development 173
Governance and Ethnic Media 173
Policymaking in a Globalizing World 174
Policymaking at the Global and International Level 175
Intergovernmental Organizations 177
International Nongovernmental Organizations 178
Policymaking at the Nation-State Level 180
Public Sector Policymakers 180
Nongovernmental and Nonprofit Organizations 181
Sub-State Policymaking and Ethnic Media 182
Local Authorities 182
Nongovernmental Organizations 183

The Broader Policy Context of Ethnic Media Development 184
State Approaches to Immigration, Citizenship, and Their Impact on Ethnic Media 184
Australia, Canada, and the United States: Multicultural at Inception 186
Belgium, Finland, and Sweden: Born Multicultural and Multilingual 187
United Kingdom and the Netherlands: Challenges in the Post-Colonial Era 188
Germany and Austria: Facing Up to the Challenges of Immigration 189
France: Ethnic Diversity in a "Color-Blind" Society 190
Greece, Italy, Spain: The Hard Realization of Becoming an Immigrant-Receiving Country 191
Media Policy Provisions and the Ethnic Media 191
Models of Media Policies Pertaining to Ethnic Media 192
Integrationist Model 192
Economic Model (or Shallow Multiculturalism) 193
Divisive Model 194
Preemptive Model 195
Proselytism Model 196
Immigrant Versus Indigenous Ethnic Communities 197
Public Service Broadcasting and Ethnic Media 198
Public Access to the Airwaves, Open Channels, and Restricted Service Licenses 199
Deregulation and the Internet 199

PART IV: ETHNIC MEDIA AS CIVIC COMMUNICATORS 205

Chapter 9 Ethnic Media as Local Media 207
Ethnic Media and the Communities They Serve 207
Geo-Ethnic Media as Part of a Community Communication Ecology 208
Ecological Approaches as a Departure From Traditional Media Measures 212
Ethnic Media and Other Community Institutions 214
Geo-Ethnic Media and Civic Engagement 216
Geo-Ethnic Media and Community Health 219
Geo-Ethnic Media Challenges 223

Chapter 10 Professional Challenges for Ethnic Media Journalists 227
The Ethnic Media Journalist in the 21st Century 227
Who Are the Ethnic Media Journalists, Editors, and Staff? 228
Journalists as Conduits to the Larger Community 229

Challenges Ethnic Media Producers, Editors, and Reporters Face 231
Attrition and "Poaching" From the Mainstream Media 231
Access to Sources and Resources 232
Professionalization: Objectivity and Social Responsibility 236
The Objectivity Standard 236
Ethnic Media as Ethnic Community Advocates 238
The Professional Modus Operandi: How Formal Standards Impact Ethnic Media Content 239
Professionalization and Elitism 240
When the Ethnic Community Turns Against Its Ethnic Media 241
Ethnic and Mainstream Media Collaborations: Experiments, Possibilities, Challenges 244
The Role of Professional Journalism Education in the Future of Ethnic Media 246

PART V: THE FUTURE OF ETHNIC MEDIA **251**

Conclusion: What Does the Future Hold for Ethnic Media? **253**
How the Experts See the Future of Ethnic Media 253
Ethnic Media and Emerging Technologies: Opportunity or Risk? 254
The Future of Ethnic Media: The Consumers 259
The Future of Ethnic Media: The Producers 262
Gaps in the Research: What Do We Still Need to Know to Understand Ethnic Media? 265

References **267**

Author Index **293**

Subject Index **299**

About the Authors **313**

Preface

History tells us that ethnic media have been part of our media landscape for centuries. The *Gazette de Leyde*, which was one of the very first ethnic newspapers published, dates back to the late 1600s. The *Gazette de Leyde* was published in Holland and its audience was French Protestants who had fled the Catholic Crown of France. This example prompts us to explain what we mean when we speak of ethnic media. In this book, we define ethnic media broadly to include media *by* and *for* (a) immigrants, (b) ethnic, racial, and linguistic minorities, as well as (c) indigenous populations across different parts of the world.

Fast forwarding from the 17th century to today, ethnic media have become an enduring feature of everyday life. The evidence suggests a fascinating proliferation of ethnic media particularly over the past two decades; proliferation both in terms of numbers of media outlets and a variety of media forms. This growth has been one of the main motivations for us to write this book. In this volume, we strive to present a far-reaching review and analysis of how ethnic media affect ongoing negotiations of self-identity, perceived lines of division between "us" and "others," and how the production and consumption of ethnic media affects the character of the larger media and societal landscape. In doing so, we address historical, policy, cultural, organizational, professional, social relations, community, migration, and globalization dimensions of the study of ethnic media.

The growth we have seen in recent years in the ethnic media sector is inextricably linked to processes we have come to identify as forces of globalization: technological innovation, international migration, the integration of world economies and policymaking intended to abolish many of the barriers that hinder activities of individuals and organizations across nation-state borders. Things are changing, but for a long time and despite the sustained focus of research on globalization, ethnic media remained largely invisible to mainstream media producers, advertisers and marketing professionals, policymakers, and last, but not least, many academic researchers. This is not entirely surprising. It can be attributed to a variety of reasons, including the following:

- For years, advertisers and marketers overlooked or undervalued the purchasing power of minority populations who connect to ethnic media.
- Mainstream media, which are produced by and targeted largely to the majority population, have underestimated the significance of ethnic media as rivals in their markets.

- The visibility and recognition of ethnic media as equal actors in the media system is contingent upon the status of the audiences they serve. In countries that have resisted acknowledging their increasingly large immigrant populations, ethnic media have been more likely to remain invisible.
- Policymakers at local and national levels have often avoided engaging ethnic media producers to the same degree as mainstream media producers. This may be motivated by uncertainties about the ethnic media, the audiences that they serve, and a desire to continue with "politics as usual."
- Ethnic media producers are often small outfits, and may not have the resources to increase their visibility by commissioning special audience studies or auditing and rating agencies that would document their impact.

The tides are shifting though. The effects of increasing population diversity—a manifestation of globalization—are becoming more obvious. The composition of the audience in many media markets around the world, and particularly in large urban centers today, is significantly different from what it was 10 or 20 years ago. This has given reason enough to mainstream media, advertisers, and marketing experts to pause and think seriously about how to connect to this new audience. In reassessing their approach, they are looking to ethnic media for cues. They are also looking at ethnic media because ethnic media outlets have grown significantly in size and have succeeded, in some cases, in capturing a larger percentage of the audience than mainstream media do. This is the case in a small number of media markets like Los Angeles, in California, where Latinos are now a majority. Mainstream media, however, can no longer afford, quite literally, to avoid the pressure of competition coming from ethnic media. Producers of mainstream media are quickly realizing that their ability to connect to a diverse market is vital for their survival, especially as the buying power of many ethnic populations is on the rise. The buying power of Latinos in the U.S., for example, is expected to top $1 trillion in 2010. The purchasing power of other ethnic communities is also increasing. For example, the buying power of African-Americans is expected to reach $921 billion by 2011, while in 2008, Asian-Americans had the highest incomes of any other ethnic group in the U.S (Nielsen, 2008).

Like mainstream media, policymakers are also realizing that they may be less in touch with the social environment they are called upon to shape. Several studies over the past few years have signaled this quite clearly. In one study, for instance, that focused on Asian and Latino communities in Southern California, researchers found that "both county and city government agencies. . . are not providing culturally sensitive disaster preparedness education in languages that reflect the demographics of the populations being served" (Mathew & Kelly, 2008, p. 6). The same study found that Chinese, Vietnamese, and Latino residents felt that the ethnic media available to them would be a much better source of information in case of an emergency than mainstream, English-language media. In addition, policymakers at all levels of government, in the U.S., Canada, Australia, and a few European countries are recognizing that they need to connect to ethnic media if they want to get their message across to increasingly multi-ethnic constituencies. Slowly, but surely, local and national government officials are also becoming more responsive to ethnic media journalists.

Often this newfound "openness" to ethnic media is the result of the persistent pressure applied by ethnic media producers and ethnic community leaders, but it remains a positive sign of change in the attitude and behavior of policymakers towards ethnic media. In 2008, for instance, Barack Obama, as the new President-elect of the U.S., chose to put legacy media, like *The New York Times,* on hold and to give his first interviews to ethnic media, starting with two African-American magazines, *Ebony* and *Black Enterprise,* but also popular Spanish-language radio talk show hosts "El Pistolero" and "El Piolin" of Radio La Que Buena 105.1 FM and Radio La Nueva 101.9 FM, respectively. His first television interview was on the Arab-language channel al-Arabiya (MacLeod, 2009; Rainey, 2009).

Globalization is also changing the classrooms in communication, media and journalism schools, sociology, anthropology, political science, and race and ethnicity departments across the world. Numerous publications have appeared over the past decade intended to help faculty respond, for example, to the needs of an ethnically and culturally diverse student body. Academic institutions are necessarily rethinking and changing their curricula to address issues pertaining to ethnic diversity.

Today, communication and journalism schools, in particular, are called upon to prepare a generation of journalists and communication industry professionals that faces a new set of tests. Many of these challenges are related to the emergence of new media, while a number of others are tied to the changing population dynamics in the workplace and broader society. They will need, for instance, to know how to engage the ethnic media (e.g., because they are running a political campaign, a public relations or an advertising campaign) to reach a particular population that may not have or may not choose to access mainstream television, radio, or newspapers. With these challenges, however, new opportunities present themselves, too. The new generation of journalists, for example, is more likely than even before to seek and take a position on the editorial staff of ethnic media organizations.

This reality has created new challenges and has put new pressures on instructors to formulate appropriate course syllabi and to select the most suitable textbooks. However, their options have been limited. The extant literature is fragmented. Many good books address only a few aspects of the new media environment; for example, portrayals of ethnic minorities in the media, African-American-targeted marketing and advertising, Latino news production, electronic ethnic media, or the media of diasporic populations. Due to the rapidly changing landscape, previous works may also be outdated.

Our hope is that this volume will be used as a primary text particularly for upper division undergraduate and graduate courses in journalism and communication, but also classes in other fields that focus on the relationship of media and society, in general, and issues of ethnic identity, race, and gender, in particular. Because these issues are (a) addressed from the vantage point of the individual (the audience) and that of the producers, and (b) they are considered in context (e.g., historical trajectories, media policy framework, and immigration laws), this book is likely to be especially valuable to communication, media, and journalism faculty, and students.

The three of us came to this project motivated by some of the same, but also several very different questions. Long before we met each other, one of us worked as a journalist. The last position Matthew took on as editor was at a Greek-American publishing house based in New York City. His individual migration to Astoria, in

Queens, was precipitated by a corporate one: a former employer, one of the largest publishing companies of Greece, had bought a majority stake in that same Greek-American publishing operation. In the new position, he faced challenges he had not confronted in any other job as a journalist; that is, challenges that had to do with his role as a journalist, the role of the organization he worked for in the community it served, the pressing questions pertaining to how to ensure the organization's long-term security. While in New York, some answers were found, but the number of questions still outweighed the number of answers. That is what led him to Los Angeles to study at the University of Southern California's Annenberg School for Communication and Journalism and eventually to the Metamorphosis Project. There, he met Vikki and Sandra.

Vikki came to USC to study immigrant family dynamics, and particularly the ways that children initiate and contribute to connections with media resources that help their families integrate into their new communities. Having come to the Annenberg School to work with Sandra and the Metamorphosis Project, this interest in children and families developed into a larger interest in the consumption side of ethnic media, and how ethnic media content prompts negotiations in immigrant and ethnic minority families about how to connect with needed resources in their local communities. Having grown up in South Africa as apartheid was dismantling, she also had a deep interest in the roles that ethnic media have played in promoting social change in different parts of the world.

When Matthew and Vikki arrived at USC, Sandra had been at the helm of the Metamorphosis Project for several years already, studying the ways that globalization, new communication technologies, and increasing population diversity were transforming the urban communities of Los Angeles. Ethnic media have figured prominently in Metamorphosis Project inquiry; time and again, ethnic media are found to play a complex repertoire of roles in the lives of the communities they serve. The work done by the Metamorphosis Project over the years and the research the three of us have done with each other and other colleagues on the Project spurred an initiative to teach a class on ethnic media at USC, and subsequently sparked the idea of writing this book.

We have made a self-conscious effort to give comprehensive coverage of ethnic media production and consumption in as many countries and societies around the world as possible. By searching databases and consulting knowledgeable colleagues, we were able to include materials about ethnic media including Australia, Austria, Belgium, Britain, Canada, China, Denmark, France, Finland, Germany, Greece, Ireland, Israel, Mexico, the Netherlands, South Africa, Spain, Sweden, the Philippines, as well as the United States.

In trying to produce a volume that will be useful not only to researchers and policymakers, but as a classroom resource as well, we have included questions and ideas for further discussions or student projects in each chapter of the book. Each chapter is formatted for clarity with introductory bullet points identifying the main concepts and issues to be discussed, the use of sidebar examples, and summaries. The bibliography is likely to be a resource for researchers, teachers, and students alike.

In a book about ethnic media across the world, language capacity is essential. The fact that the literature on ethnic media is relatively limited and fragmented makes one's ability to access sources and actual ethnic media in a variety of different languages vital. This was our first major challenge. Through our collective effort, and thanks to the help of colleagues, family members, and friends, we were able to access media and sources in Chinese, English, French, Greek, Korean, and Spanish. It is very likely that there are sources and media we have missed entirely due to our language limitations. Such limitations make collaborations across countries and fields of inquiry all the more important for the future.

In addition, awareness around ethnic media is quite variable across countries. In many cases, because immigration is either a new concern or a controversial issue (often both), there is very little research on the audiences of ethnic media, the communities they serve, number of ethnic media organizations, and so forth. Here is an example of how data limitations affected our work: For our chapter on policy and ethnic media development (see Chapter 8), we sought data that could help us investigate the extent to which the actual number of ethnic media available is determined by how open or closed a country's immigration policy is and by the orientation of that country's immigrant and minority social integration policies (i.e., oriented towards assimilation or multiculturalism).

This endeavor quickly proved complicated for three reasons. First, as we expected, there are very few data sources available on the number of ethnic media in different countries. Second, even when figures are available, often the individuals or the organizations that generated the data define ethnic media differently. In some cases, for example, media targeted to indigenous ethnic minorities are included, while in others they are not. Programs produced for different ethnic communities by one broadcaster are sometimes counted as individual ethnic media offerings and other times they are counted as one media organization. Moreover, imported media (e.g., satellite programs or newspapers produced in a particular country of origin) are occasionally included in the list of available ethnic media; often, however, they are not. Third, in trying to determine the impact of policy on ethnic media, it is important to consider the year during which data were collected and to keep in mind that policy changes may not have immediate effects. Therefore longitudinal data are necessary, but even harder to find.

Taking these limitations into consideration, we compiled a database that captures the number of ethnic media in Austria, Belgium, Canada, France, Finland, Greece, Italy, the Netherlands, Spain, Sweden, the United Kingdom, and the United States. Unfortunately, we were not able to find or generate a comprehensive list of ethnic media offerings in Australia, and therefore we excluded it from further analysis. We analyzed the data available and examined whether countries with more open immigration and more multiculturalism-oriented integration policies had a larger number of ethnic media per one million inhabitants compared to countries with more closed immigration and more assimilation-oriented integration policies. As we expected, Belgium (9.13), Canada (10.54), the Netherlands (12.14), and Sweden (21.01) have the most ethnic media per one million inhabitants, while Germany (0.51), Greece (2.42), Italy (1.57), and Spain (0.54) have the least. Of course, any conclusions drawn from these results should be stated with caution; much more data are required and from a much greater number of countries.

Finally, as we put a tentative end to the journey that *Understanding Ethnic Media* represents, we realize that we are in a very challenging, quickly changing social, economic, and technological environment. Traditional (or legacy) mainstream media are in decline or in a process of radical reorganization as more and more people incorporate Internet-based media forms into their everyday lives. Old models of increasing revenue streams are being severely challenged, and while new models continue to be discussed and tested, we have yet to see a major breakthrough. In addition, in 2008–2009, the world economy entered a profound period of crisis. In late 2009, there were some signals of hope, but recovery by all accounts will be slow. The ethnic media sector has been growing in the past 10 years, but it remains unclear how the crisis and the changes in the media environment attributed to the emergence of new communication technologies will affect them in the mid and long term.

Completing this book would not have been possible without the help of many people and, first of all, our colleagues on the Metamorphosis Project at the University of Southern California's Annenberg School for Communication and Journalism. We are particularly indebted to Yong-Chan Kim, Wan Ying Lin, Jack Linchuan Qiu, and Hayeon Song, now at Yonsei University in Seoul, the City University of Hong Kong, the Chinese University of Hong Kong, and the University of Wisconsin in Milwaukee, respectively, for their original work in the Korean and Chinese ethnic communities of Los Angeles and for helping us to better understand the ethnic media to which these communities connect. Holley Wilkin, now at Georgia State University, Carmen Gonzalez, who is currently working on her dissertation at USC, and Antonieta Mercado, who is working on her dissertation at the University of California in San Diego, have also informed our work with respect to the roles ethnic media play in the lives of new immigrant communities (and particularly Latino communities).

It is hard to imagine being able to develop this project without the generous financial and moral support of former Annenberg School Dean Geoffrey Cowan and his successor, Dean Ernest Wilson III. Both have supported the Metamorphosis Project's mission over the years and provided necessary funding for research assistantships, postdoctoral fellowships, and, last but not least, office space, which allowed us to continue to work together without major interruptions. First 5 Los Angeles, the California Endowment, and the Annenberg Foundation Trust at Sunnylands have also provided much needed funding support for our work over the years.

Starting out to write a book with a fair amount of ambition can be daunting, but we have been fortunate to be able to talk through data and findings, exchange ideas, try out concepts, and debate approaches to the study of ethnic media and communities, with colleagues like Roger Silverstone and Myria Georgiou from the London School of Economics and Political Science in London. Sadly, we cannot share this final product and continue our discussions with Roger Silverstone, who passed away in 2006. Roger and Myria led a large-scale effort with a network of researchers to map the ethnic media across 15 member-states of the European Union at the turn of the millennium. That research has been a tremendous source of information and insight for us. Further, we thank Myria for reviewing and commenting on earlier versions of a number of chapters in this book, as well as pointing us to sources we may not have found on our own. Félix Gutiérrez from the University of Southern California has also supported us greatly in this effort. Through his pioneering work on ethnic media (and particularly Latino media in the U.S.), but also by making himself available over the past couple of years to read drafts of chapters and provide feedback and perspective, he has helped us improve our work. Likewise, we thank Jessica Retis, now at California State University at Northridge, for agreeing to serve as a reviewer and for taking our calls and questions over the phone at odd hours of the day while she was still living in Madrid.

We also want to thank Catherine Murray, Daniel Ahadi, and Sherry Yu (Simon Fraser University, Canada), for introducing us to the ethnic communities of Vancouver and their media. In addition, we would like to thank Catherine and Daniel especially for reading earlier versions of book chapters and their enlightening comments.

We are also indebted to Donald R. Browne (University of Minnesota); Gene Burd (University of Texas at Austin); Simon Cottle, (Cardiff University, UK); Susana Kaiser (University of San Francisco); Charlotta Kratz (Santa Clara University); Cinzia Padovani (Southern Illinois University, Carbondale); Barbara Straus Reed (Rutgers University); and Indira Somani (Washington and Lee University) for serving as reviewers at various stages of this book project. No doubt, their comments, criticisms, and suggestions have helped us deliver a higher quality manuscript than what we would have without them. Of course, we are solely responsible for all mistakes and omissions.

For being able to include the rich voices of journalists and publishers of ethnic media, we owe tremendous gratitude to New America Media and especially Julian Do, the organization's director in Southern California. It was with his help that we were able to host roundtable discussions, in 2007 and 2008, with ethnic media journalists serving a diverse set of ethnic communities from across California. Of course, we also thank all those journalists and ethnic media producers who over the past 2 years took time out of their busy schedules to attend these roundtable discussions, and to talk to us over the phone and via e-mail.

In the final chapter of this book, we have asked a number of scholars, researchers, and professionals that work on, with, or in ethnic media in the United States, Canada, Europe, Israel, and Australia, to help us look ahead to the future of ethnic media. For their contributions we would like to thank people we have not yet mentioned, including: Susan Brink (Mira Media and Radboud University, Nijmegen, the Netherlands); Sandy Close (New America Media); John Downing (Southern Illinois University, Carbondale), Augie Fleras (University of Waterloo, Canada); Nelly Elias (Ben Gurion University, Israel), Jon Funabiki (San Francisco State University), Frank Herron (University of Massachusetts, Boston); James Ho (Mainstream Broadcasting Corporation and the *Chinese Canadian Times* in Vancouver, Canada); Kira Kosnick (University of Frankfurt, Germany); John Hartley (Queensland University of Technology, Australia); Edward Schumacher-Matos (Rumbo Newspapers/Meximerica Media, now at Harvard University); and Paulo Rogério Nunes (Instituto Mídia Étnica, Brazil).

Others helped by providing information about different countries and places that would otherwise have remained out of reach; for this, we thank Hannah Adoni (Hebrew University of Jerusalem), Dan Caspi (Ben Gurion University, Israel), Antoni Castells-Talens (University of Veracruz, Mexico), Akiba Cohen (Tel Aviv University), Larry Gross (University of Southern California), Ellen Hume (University of Massachusetts in Boston), Lucy Montgomery (Queensland University of Technology,

Australia), and Roger Waldinger (University of California, Los Angeles). We also thank Michelle Hawks for her photographs, which appear in Chapter 3.

Of course, behind every ambitious book project like this one there must be an excellent editorial team. We thank Todd Armstrong, our editor, Aja Baker, Nathan Davidson, Astrid Virding, Jovey Stewart, and the rest of the SAGE team that helped us turn an idea into an actual book.

Finally, it is hard to imagine that this book would be completed without the surplus of patience and unwavering support of our families and friends. To Meg and Dimitris Matsaganis, Christopher Matsaganis, Marc Douaisi, Ian and Cheryl Katz, Jeff Katz, Ailsa Ball, and Jenny—we could not have done it without you.

Matthew Matsaganis, Vikki Katz, and Sandra Ball-Rokeach

PART I

Ethnic Media in Context

CHAPTER 1

What Are Ethnic Media?

CHAPTER OBJECTIVES

This chapter is an introduction to ethnic media. By the end of this chapter you will:

- Be able to define ethnic media.
- Gain a basic understanding of key terms related to the study of ethnic media.
- Learn about the roles ethnic media play in everyday life.
- Understand how globalization is changing the media landscape as we know it, as well as the opportunities globalization creates for the founding and longevity of ethnic media.
- Understand what historical, social, political, and economic conditions make studying ethnic media timely and necessary.
- Have a map to how this book unfolds.

Introduction

The National Directory of Ethnic Media, which is compiled every year by New America Media, contains information on over 2,500 ethnic media organizations in the United States (New America Media, 2009).[1] These media tell the stories of vibrant African, African-American, Asian, European, indigenous, Latino, and Middle Eastern communities that comprise much of American society today. A study released in June 2009 indicated that nearly 60 million Americans of African, Latino, and Asian background get their news and other information regularly from ethnically targeted television, radio, newspapers, and Web sites. Just 4 years earlier, that figure was 16% lower (Allen, 2009).[2] Many of these ethnic media publish or broadcast their stories in languages other than English. In New York alone, a Ford Foundation report indicated that the circulation of Chinese language dailies has grown from about 170,000 in 1990 to more than half a million in 2006. One in three New Yorkers is Hispanic,[3] and four Spanish-language dailies serve this population. In other major cities in the U.S., Canada, the European Union (EU), and Australia, the growth of ethnic media is equally impressive. In 2007, there were more than 250 ethnic newspapers in Canada that represent over 40 ethnic communities and 40 television channels that provide programming to a variety of ethnic groups. Additionally, more than 60 Canadian mainstream radio stations offer ethnically targeted programming. CHIN Radio in Toronto, for example, broadcasts in over 30 languages (Media Awareness Network, 2007).[4] Across the Atlantic, from 2001 to 2004, a number of reports that captured the vitality of ethnic media in Europe were released by the Diasporic Minorities and Their Media project housed at the London School of Economics and Political Science. In the Netherlands, there are more than 150 ethnic broadcasting organizations (Bink, 2002), while there are more than 90 print and broadcast media produced in Germany (Raiser, 2002). The ethnic media in Germany serve 15 different ethnic communities, including people who identify as Albanian, Bosnian, Chinese, Greek, Russian, Turkish, and Vietnamese. In Europe, the United Kingdom is perhaps the country that has witnessed the largest explosion in the numbers of ethnic media. British citizens and residents read over 100 ethnic daily and weekly newspapers and periodicals, and they tune in to over 15 ethnic radio and 30 television channels (Georgiou, 2002b). In the southern hemisphere, in Australia's New South Wales, the regional Community Relations Commission for Multiculturalism has recorded the presence of more than 115 ethnic media organizations, which serve 39 different ethnic communities, including Armenians, Dutch, Egyptians, Fijians, Greeks, Indians, Indonesians, Koreans, Nepalese, Filipinos, Polish, Sri Lankan, and Turks.[5]

While these figures are compelling enough to warrant research,[6] there are a number of other considerations that make studying ethnic media particularly salient today. However, before discussing the roles ethnic media play in the everyday lives of millions of people worldwide, we must first explain what we mean by the term *ethnic media*.

Profile 1.1 Diasporic Minorities and Their Media in the EU (EMTEL II)—London

The project's goal was to map the diasporic communities living in European Union member-states and to examine how these communities develop their own media. Researchers on the project were particularly interested in understanding how ethnic media contribute to the integration of ethnic minorities into broader society or to their exclusion from civic life in the countries of the EU. Project affiliates also devoted their attention to how national policies on immigration and media impact social inclusion of ethnic minorities, as well as the development of ethnic media. The Diasporic Minorities and Their Media Project was housed at the London School of Economics, in Britain. The 12 national reports produced by the project provide a wealth of information about ethnic media in Austria, Belgium, Denmark, Finland, France, Germany, Greece, Ireland, Italy, the Netherlands, Portugal, Spain, Sweden, and the United Kingdom. The project was funded through the 5th Community Structural Funds Framework Program of the European Union and it ended in 2003.

Defining Ethnic Media

Ethnic media are media produced *for* a particular ethnic community. The *Haitian Times,* for example, is a newspaper published in New York. It aims to cover all the news that Haitian-origin people living in the city care about. The paper's staff may write about developments in the political situation in Haiti, but they may also cover the campaign of Haitian candidates running for a seat on the City Council of New York. The *Haitian Times* is an ethnic medium. It is produced *for* the 200,000 Haitians who live in New York. But it is also produced *by* that ethnic community. The editor-in-chief of the *Haitian Times,* former *New York Times* journalist Gary Pierre-Pierre, is Haitian (Akst, 2003). There are numerous such media: newspapers, radio, and television stations, as well as Internet-based media.

However not all ethnic media are produced by the ethnic community they serve. The *Korea Times,* for instance, reaches Koreans in New York City, Washington DC, Chicago, Atlanta, Seattle, San Francisco, and Los Angeles. It is produced *for* an ethnic community. But, about half the stories that appear in its pages are written by staff writers located in the American cities mentioned, while the other half are written by journalists who live in South Korea. Antenna Satellite claims to be the first Greek radio and television network in North America. While the network targets Greeks in the U.S. and Canada, it is based thousands of miles away from its audience, in a suburb of Athens. SAT-7 is a Christian Arab channel based in Nicosia, Cyprus, but its audience is spread out across the Middle East and North Africa. The same holds true for the audience of Chinese satellite network TVBS-Europe, which is based in Middlesex (in Britain) and Paris. These media produce programming *for* people who self-identify as Greek, Arab, and Chinese respectively. However, the Chinese station TVBS-Europe, for example, does not target the Chinese living in Britain or in Paris in particular. It covers 48 European countries. Its programming is also not produced by any one of the Chinese communities found throughout Europe. Most of the programming comes from TVB-Hong Kong and other affiliates, and it is broadcast in both Mandarin Chinese and Cantonese.

The previous examples indicate that there is a large variety of ethnic media. They vary, first of all, with regard to who produces them. Producers may be members of one ethnic community living in one city or town, but producers can also be big media organizations whose activities span the globe. The audience of ethnic media can be co-ethnics living in a neighborhood of a huge metropolis, but it may also be comprised of all people with the same ethnic background living in various countries around the world. The content of ethnic media may be focused on the life of a particular ethnic community, the news from a home country, or both. And while there are many ethnic newspapers, magazines, radio stations, and television channels, ethnic media producers are also making use of cable networks, satellite network technology, and the Internet to distribute their stories and programs (Karim, 1998): For example, the Web site *www.ayrinti.de* is an Internet magazine that addresses cultural issues, literature, and the arts, for Turks in Germany. It is published in Turkish (Raiser, 2002).

Figure 1.1 indicates eight important dimensions across which ethnic media may vary. Every dimension includes multiple categories. Arguably, there are at least as

Figure 1.1

Defining ethnic media

Ethnic media are media that are produced *by* and *for* (a) immigrants, (b) racial, ethnic, and linguistic minorities, as well as (c) indigenous populations living across different countries.

Who are the PRODUCERS?

- Members of an ethnic community in a particular geographic area of a country (e.g., city or region)
- One or more media organizations based in an ethnic community's country of origin
- A media firm (or firms) in a home country with production units located in the ethnic communities of a host country or countries
- A collaborative effort of one or more media organizations located in a home country and organizations based in ethnic communities outside the home country

Who are the FUNDERS?

- Entrepreneurs of the ethnic community in one or more countries of settlement
- Entrepreneurs from a home country
- Entrepreneurs from a home country and entrepreneurs of ethnic communities in host countries

What is the SIZE of the organization?

- Small, family-owned, "mom-and-pop" type businesses
- Medium-size organizations: relatively small number of employees, few levels of hierarchy, fairly formalized relationships and job descriptions, and clearly defined audience
- Large corporations, organizations resembling major publishing organizations and broadcast networks
- Multinational organizations

Where is the organization LOCATED?

- A neighborhood where many members of an ethnic community live
- Anywhere in a host country with a significant number of people who self-identify as members of a particular ethnic community
- In a home country
- In a "home" country or a country of settlement, but with offices in more than one place around the world. They target audiences in more than one country

Diversity in the Ethnic Media Landscape

Our definition of ethnic media allows for the inclusion of a variety of different ethnic media. In this figure, there are eight piles of puzzle pieces. Think of every pile as a particular characteristic of ethnic media. The puzzle pieces in every pile represent the variations we find in the universe of ethnic media. There are many unique ways to combine pieces and create the full picture of any of these media. If you had to describe the ethnic media available where you live, what puzzle pieces would you use?

What is the target AUDIENCE?

- An ethnic community in a particular geographic space (i.e., city or region)
- Distinct ethnic communities residing in multiple locations within a particular country or across different countries
- Ethnic communities outside a home country and audiences within the home country
- People who may not have origins in the same home country, but who share a variety of cultural characteristics (e.g., language, religious traditions)

What LANGUAGE is used?

- Language or dialect spoken in the home country
- In the language of the host country and the language (or dialect) of the home country
- Language spoken in the host country

What is the CONTENT focused on?

- The local ethnic community
- Members of the ethnic community who live anywhere in a host country (in multiple ethnic communities across a country)
- The host country (country of settlement)
- The home country (or country of origin)
- People identified as members of one ethnic community living in multiple countries of settlement
- Individual ethnic communities, the country of origin, and the country or countries of settlement

How is the content DISTRIBUTED?

- Print media may be distributed door-to-door or to newsstands by the owners, journalists, or employees of the media
- Local distribution agencies
- Mail service
- Independently owned radio and television broadcasting networks
- Public radio or television broadcasting networks
- Cable networks
- Satellite networks
- Internet-based networks

many types of ethnic media as there are combinations of categories. Figure 1.1 is not comprehensive. It does not account, for instance, for different choices ethnic media make to target the older or younger generations of an ethnic community. These issues will be discussed at greater length as the book unfolds. Despite this variability, however, all these media are targeted to people who belong to a particular ethnic group.

¤ For Further Discussion

Select two different ethnic media available in your community, a print medium and a television or radio station, for example, and create their profiles using the dimensions and categories presented in Figure 1.1. You may not have noticed these media before, but unless you live in a completely ethnically homogeneous community, you will find many of them canvassing the television or radio dial, street corner stands, and the shelves of your local grocery store alongside other newspapers and magazines.

Are there additional dimensions or categories you would add to Figure 1.1 that would help you better describe the media you chose?

Ethnic Media Contrasted With Other Types of Media

Even a cursory look at the bibliography on ethnic media would reveal that there are many different terms used to describe similar things. *Minority media, immigrant media, diasporic media,* and *community media* are terms often used along with or instead of the term *ethnic media.*

Term preferences are often related to how different countries understand differences between people based on their ethnic or racial background. In some countries, like France for example, there is no official recognition of ethno-racial differences among people. No one has to describe themselves as White or Caucasian, African-American or Black, Hispanic or Latino, Asian, Native-American, Pacific Islander, or indigenous, as people often have to do in the United States, Canada, Britain, and elsewhere. Individuals in France are identified only as citizens or non-citizens. In such cases, therefore, researchers rarely speak of ethnic media. They prefer the term *minority media* (e.g., Georgiou, 2001b; Malonga, 2002).

Sometimes, the choice of the term "minority" seems most appropriate because the group of people these media are produced for are in fact a minority among the general population. The term is limiting, however, because many groups that are referred to as "minorities" are actually the majority in particular cities or communities. The 2000 U.S. Census showed that Los Angeles had become a "plurality" city, with almost identical numbers of Whites and Hispanics. When one or more "minority" groups are such a large percentage of a city, referring to them as "minorities" would be misleading.

The term minority in some contexts also conveys a power differential in which one ethnic group is contrasted against another more powerful group. In much of the western world, minorities have been thought of as "non-White," while the dominant group (and presumed majority) is identified as Caucasian or White. Some scholars choose to use the term *ethnic minority media*, because they study media produced for a particular ethnic group but, more specifically, they study the roles these media play in the negotiation of minority-majority or minority-dominant group relations (Riggins, 1992). A fair amount of research in Canada, for example, has looked at the creation of Inuit broadcast media as the result of this Native population's determination to represent and speak for themselves. The success of these media is considered an indicator of the "minority" population's empowerment (e.g., Alia & Bull, 2005; Valaskakis, 1992) in relation to the "majority" White population. These "minority" media are included in our definition of ethnic media.[7]

Other researchers refer to *immigrant media* (Waters & Ueda, 2006), as many ethnic media are focused on the concerns and interests of immigrant populations. This definition, however, is restrictive. It would not cover the media of Native populations in North, Central, and South America, Canada, and Australia. It also does not include African-American media, which represent an extremely vibrant segment of the ethnic media in the U.S., and Black media that have a long history in Canada and Britain. Additionally, the term has an expiration date: It refers to media that are created for newly arrived immigrants. When the majority of an ethnic magazine's audience is young Algerians born in Southern France, and not their parents who moved from an Algerian village on the Mediterranean coast, is it still an immigrant medium? The goals this magazine serves are distinctively different from those a purely immigrant print medium would serve. One of the key roles of immigrant media is to help introduce new arrivals to the host country and a new way of life. That is not the role ethnic media that target younger demographics perform. The young Algerians in France were born into the French way of life. They do not require an introduction. What they may seek in ethnic media instead is a link to others who are like them; those who have similar family histories, similar family traditions, similar problems and dreams, and a common language.[8]

The term *diasporic media* (Georgiou, 2006) is common in European research on ethnic media. However, the term *diaspora* does not fit many immigrant or ethnic communities. Greek, Jewish, Indian, and Chinese origin communities are the most prominent diasporas. The term literally means to "to sow over." Scholars generally agree that the idea of diaspora is qualitatively different from the idea of migration (e.g., Faist, 2000). Cohen (1997) has studied extensively some of the most well-known diasporas, such as Jews, Armenians, and African-origin, while Van Hear (1998) has focused on the evolution of diasporic communities from the 1960s onwards, including Kuwaiti Palestinians, Bulgarian ethnic Turks, Saudi Arabian Yemenis, and Dominican Republic Haitians. Common characteristics of diasporas are found in the extensive research of Cohen, Van Hear, and others:

- A diaspora entails movement of a large population from one or more points of origin. This is often connected with traumatic events, such as a massacre or expulsion of a particular ethnic group. This creates a common history of a shared injustice, and this common history binds the group together (Chaliand & Rageau, 1995; Cohen, 1997; Safran, 1991).[9]

- Out of this common tragedy comes a shared identity and sense of "home" that the diasporic community remembers positively. The definition of diaspora is usually related to maintaining or restoring a homeland. When an independent homeland does not or has not existed, the diaspora may bond over the desire to create a homeland. Such was the case of the Jewish diaspora, which culminated in the establishment of the state of Israel.
- The term diaspora was originally used to describe the movement of people from the city-states of the Greek mainland to Asia Minor and the rest of the Mediterranean coastline, especially from 6th century BC and through the years of Alexander the Great. The Greek diaspora established itself primarily through trade and conquest, but also through voluntary migration and settlement. The establishment of a diaspora requires extended periods of time, often centuries. That is a third characteristic of diaspora, which makes it qualitatively different from migration (Marienstras, 1989).

As many groups do not fit the definition of a diaspora, diasporic media is too narrow a term for our purposes. However, diasporic media are included in our definition of ethnic media.

Since ethnic media generally serve people in a particular local space, some researchers refer to these as *local media* (e.g., Kaniss, 1991), *locative media* (Cherubini & Nova, 2004; Nova, 2004; Rheingold, 2002), or *community media* (Howley, 2005; Jankowski & Prehn, 2002). While the focus on geography is important, we feel that these terms do not capture the ethnic focus of the media in question. This is very important, since ethnicity is commonly a guiding motivation for the development, production, and consumption of these media.

Ethnic Media Versus Mainstream Media

We have defined ethnic media broadly to include media produced *by* and *for* (a) immigrant, (b) ethnic, racial, and linguistic minorities, as well as (c) indigenous groups living in various countries across the world. Throughout this chapter and the ones that follow we often compare ethnic media to *mainstream media*. It is a commonly used term, but it is important to define it more formally, so that the differences between ethnic and mainstream media are clear.

The mainstream, say sociologists Alba and Nee (2003), is "that part of society *within* which ethnic and racial origins have at most minor impacts on [an individual's] life chances or opportunities" (p. 12); that is to say that being in or outside the mainstream matters, with respect to how others, individuals, and institutions, treat a person. It affects, for example, the kinds of jobs a person gets offered or how he or she is treated by the authorities at an airport's passport and border control checkpoint.

The mainstream includes the ethnic majority in a society, but the mainstream and the ethnic majority are not identical. The boundaries of mainstream society are broader. In the United States, for instance, individuals with European heritage are considered part of the mainstream. Through multiple waves of immigration, particularly during the first half of the 20th century, European cultures mixed to create a composite culture that people started to identify as American. As new groups of people arrived in the country from other parts of the world, their cultures influenced and slowly changed that composite culture. Hence, the boundaries of the mainstream expand over time. For example, Alba and Nee (2003) suggest that at the turn of the 21st century intermarriage between Whites and Asian-Americans had become more widely accepted and that many Asian cultural practices and Asian cuisine had become part of the American mainstream. These trends, they argue, will eventually erode the notion that being part of the mainstream in the United States is synonymous to being White.

In this context, we define mainstream media as those media that are produced *by* and are produced *for* the mainstream of society; however that is defined in a specific country and at a particular point in time.

The Role of Geographic Context

Until this point, we have hinted at ethnicity and geography being related to each other in important ways. Geography and ethnicity shape each other. For example, an immigrant from a small town in Turkey might move to Berlin, while his cousin moves to Nierenberg, a more rural community in southern Germany. These two migrants may have grown up in the same house and left home with similar goals. However, having settled in different communities may mean that their migration outcomes are very different. They will face different challenges and opportunities in terms of the resources available in their local area. This will also mean that their needs for information might be different, and the content of locally produced ethnic media would (or should) be different for this reason. Therefore, after a period of years, these two cousins might compare and realize that the characteristics of the communities where they settled (geography) have resulted in very different migration experiences. Of course, the common point of origin and shared ethnicity will mean that these cousins still have a great deal in common.

Metamorphosis Project researchers (see Profile 1.2) have found that geography-based differences are even visible within a single city of settlement. For example, migrants from Mexico who settle in different communities within the city of Los Angeles have different settlement experiences. Even though these communities may be no more than a few miles or kilometers apart, the daily life experiences and challenges in those two spaces can be very different. One community, for example, may have a number of health care or social service resources, where employees speak Spanish and are in tune with the needs of the community. This community might also be more resource rich in terms of ethnic media produced in the area and in the information that these media provide about the local area to the residents. The other community may lack these resources, making everyday life a different and more difficult experience (Cheong, Wilkin, & Ball-Rokeach, 2004; Wilkin, Ball-Rokeach, Matsaganis, & Cheong, 2007).

Ethnicity and geography clearly affect and are affected by each other. We refer to this relationship as *geo-ethnicity* (Kim, Jung, & Ball-Rokeach, 2006). This term emphasizes that no two communities can be assumed to be the same, even if they seem very similar from the outside. Ethnicity cannot be considered without geography, and geography cannot be considered without ethnicity. The *interaction* of geography and ethnicity is the key to understanding the daily experiences and needs of ethnic minorities and immigrants, and the media that serve them.

The Roles of Ethnic Media

The reasons for studying ethnic media are directly related to the multiple roles they play in the everyday lives of immigrants, ethnic minorities, and the larger society, more generally. Before discussing these roles, however, we need to understand what we mean by *ethnicity,* how it is related to *culture,* and how ethnicity is different from *race.*

Defining Culture, Ethnicity, and Race

Culture is a learned, shared, and interrelated set of symbols whose meanings guide members of a society in solving everyday problems (Hofstede, 1984; Parker, 2000). Culture is revealed in our language, values, norms, and practices. Differences between cultures are captured by observing and comparing these symbols, values, and behaviors. What is more difficult to assess is why particular cultural practices have emerged. It takes a much deeper look into the traditions, beliefs, priorities, and values of a society to fully understand what is on the surface (Prosser, 1978; Rokeach, 1973; Schwartz, 1992). In this sense, Hofstede (2001) says, culture resembles an iceberg.

Ethnicity is a much debated term. Its roots lay in the Greek word *ethnos,* which means nation or people. Ethnicity generally refers to a community of people who have a common culture, history, language, and religion. Commonality along all these dimensions, however, is not a prerequisite for someone to belong to a particular ethnic community (Riggins, 1992). For many Basques,[10] for instance, being able to speak the language will suffice to acknowledge someone as a member of the ethnic community (Browne, 2005). Within a particular country, we may find more than one ethnic group. In Belgium, for example, two distinct ethnic groups with different cultural backgrounds co-exist: the Flemish and the French-speaking Walloons. In countries that have been, are, or are becoming destinations for immigrants (e.g., United States, Germany, United Kingdom, Italy, Portugal, and Ireland), ethnicity frequently overlaps with a minority status (U.K. NHS, 2006).

What Is Culture?

Culture is a set of traditions, customs, norms, beliefs, and values shared among members of a society.

Ethnic identity is a form of social identity. It is a way individuals put themselves and others into categories

(Turner, 1982), and it has three distinct dimensions: (a) self-identification as a member of a particular ethnic group, (b) knowledge of the ethnic culture, and (c) feelings about the behaviors that demonstrate belonging to the ethnic group. Knowledge of the ethnic culture means that someone has an intimate understanding of all those traditions, beliefs, priorities, values, and norms we described earlier. People develop their ethnic identity in the process of everyday life, as they come into contact with people who speak a different language, have a different cultural and historical background, and (or) have different religious beliefs. Ethnic identity, therefore, is a social construction that is the result of a dynamic process played out through communication (Anderson, 1991; Lieberson, 1985; Staino, 1980). As social constructions, ethnic identities are fluid. They change over time. They may disappear, fade, and resurge. Upheaval in the Persian Gulf and continued warfare in Iraq (in the early 1990s and again from 2003 onwards), for example, have accentuated the differences between Kurds living in Northern Iraq and Sunni and Shi'a Arabs who live in the center and south of the country. The increased friction between the three ethnic groups has strengthened the sense of common identity among Kurds who spread across the northern territories of Iraq, and parts of Turkey, Iran, and Syria, and who continue to pursue their goal of a unified, independent Kurdistan (O'Leary, 2002).

Profile 1.2 The Metamorphosis Project–Los Angeles

The Metamorphosis Project is an in-depth examination of the transformations of urban community, under the forces of globalization, new communication technologies, and population diversity. From 1999 to 2010, Metamorphosis studied 11 ethnically diverse Los Angeles communities, which include African-American, Armenian, Chinese (from mainland China and Taiwan), Hispanic (of Mexican and Central American origin), Korean, and White populations. Project findings highlight the significance of ethnic vis-à-vis mainstream media in the lives of individuals and communities. Metamorphosis research has also engaged ethnic media producers through interviews, joint audience studies, and market analyses. More recently, the project has focused attention on the instrumental role ethnic media play in the hands of policymakers and health service providers for communicating with populations that generally do not read mainstream newspapers or watch English-language television. Project researchers have also analyzed the content of ethnic newspapers and broadcast media to gain a better understanding of why ethnic media, in certain communities, focus primarily on producing stories about the country of origin (e.g., about current events in South Korea), while others seem more invested in the everyday life of the local community (e.g., Mexican-origin residents of East Los Angeles).

In some countries, race is considered as an element of ethnicity. In Canada, for instance, the concept of *race* is based primarily upon genetically determined features. Skin color is usually a dominant, but not the sole, attribute (Statistics Canada, 2006). Ethnic identities and racial identities can be heavily intertwined in many communities. Despite the difficulties in separating ethnicity and race, there is one key difference. Race is a label applied to individuals and groups by others. By contrast, we actively construct our own ethnic identities. We negotiate and debate the meaning of symbols, the importance of particular values, and the behaviors that are appropriate in a given situation. In 1992, for instance, Barcelona held the summer Olympic Games. Barcelona is the capital of Catalonia, a region of Spain that has a distinct culture, language, and identity. Catalans thought of the Olympiad largely as a Catalonian event, not Spanish. The regional government at the time launched an advertising campaign in the international press to present the Barcelona Olympics as a symbol of Catalonia's cultural vitality and economic vigor. They did not see the success of the Olympics as a reason to be proud that they were Spanish. The text in the two-page advertisement published in newspapers, including *The New York Times,* read: "In which country would you locate this point (Barcelona)? In Catalonia, of course. A country inside Spain which has its own culture, language and identity" (Ladrón de Guevara, Còller, & Romaní, 1995, p. 7).

Italian immigrants in the United States are a good example of the difference between racial and ethnic identities. In the early days of Italian migration to America, the Italian state had not been formed as we know it today. The differences between regions, especially northern and southern regions of Italy were much more pronounced than they are today, and there was no common Italian identity. In fact, immigrants from Northern Italy, who were lighter-skinned, loudly proclaimed that the darker complexion immigrants from Southern Italy were Black and therefore racially distinct from the northerners (Guglielmo, 2003). Over time, however, immigrants from cities all over Italy realized that they had more in common with each other than with immigrants from other parts of Europe. Slowly, these immigrants came to live in the same neighborhoods, and shared and exchanged traditions and celebrations. In many ways, Italian "ethnicity" was born in the United States before it emerged on the Italian peninsula (Conzen, Gerber, Morawska, Pozzetta, & Vecoli, 1992; Orsi, 1992). In addition, Southern Italians eventually came to be seen as White. Their case shows the arbitrary nature of racial categorizations.

What Is Ethnicity?

Ethnicity is a category we construct in the process of our everyday interaction with other people, to identify with or differentiate ourselves from others we perceive as having a common culture, history, language, and religion.

For Further Discussion

What are the traditions, customs, norms, beliefs, and values that define your culture? Make a list and then ask a family member, a friend, and a colleague to do the same. Do you see any differences across these lists? If so, explain why.

In what ways do mainstream media, like the Australian Broadcasting Corporation (ABC) or the British Broadcasting Corporation (BBC), or *The New York Times* influence how we define ourselves and others with regard to ethnicity? Do you believe that ethnic media have a similar or qualitatively different impact?

The Roles of Ethnic Media

Ethnic media are at the heart of the everyday practices that produce and transform ethnic identity, culture, and perceptions of race. Numerous studies document mass media impacts on public opinion and the agenda of policymakers (Dearing & Rogers, 1996; McCombs & Reynolds, 2002). People depend on the media for vital information that will help them understand what is going on around them and to make informed decisions about their lives. This is especially true when they feel that a situation is ambiguous or there is a crisis of some sort (Ball-Rokeach, 1985; Ball-Rokeach, 1998). Both in times of crisis and otherwise, ethnic media can be "teachers." Ethnic media can educate and orient newcomers to their new community and its resources, and can also teach more subtle rules about correct behaviors and what the new society values.

 **What Is Race?**

Race is an artificial category ascribed to people based, primarily, on genetically determined features, such as skin color and facial characteristics.

Mainstream media, however, by their very nature are less sensitive to the ongoing negotiation of ethnic identity, culture, and race. In making decisions about content, managers of mainstream media have to be more inclusive. The number of channels available via cable or satellite continues to grow to satisfy particular tastes (e.g., news-only channels, channels that broadcast historical documentaries exclusively, sports channels, channels with only children's programs), indicating that the audience is becoming more and more segmented (Alexander, Owers, & Carveth, 1998). Even so, a language barrier continues to exist for those viewers or readers whose first language is not English, in the U.S., Britain, and Australia; or French and English in Canada; or German in Germany and Austria.

Therefore, individuals are more likely to connect to ethnic media to achieve goals that have to do with understanding what makes them Chinese-American, for example, and not just American, to negotiate conflicts in cultural values (e.g., the importance of family), but to also find ways to "fit in" and to co-exist with others who have a different cultural background. Ethnic media contribute to larger social processes as well, such as the negotiation of what it means to be a citizen of a country. Additionally, ethnic media also participate in policy

Profile 1.3 Cultural Diversity and Ethnic Media in British Columbia–Vancouver

The project aimed to develop a map of third language media—meaning non-English and non-French language media—in Vancouver. Project investigators also analyzed the content of international, national, and local media in the Vancouver area to better understand how different media form their news agenda. Moreover, researchers interviewed the prominent stakeholders in the ethnic media sector (e.g., publishers, journalists, marketing and advertising professionals) and delivered policy recommendations to the regional department of Canadian Heritage; these recommendations were meant to encourage further development of ethnic media and help the communities these media represent to address their needs. The project, which was housed at the School of Communication at Simon Fraser University, concluded in 2008.

discussions affecting ethnic communities. The founding of ethnic media companies that operate across national borders linking diasporas and their homelands (i.e., *transnational media*), and the emergence of many ethnically targeted satellite television channels worldwide, for instance, has forced policymakers to consider the implications of ethnic media for the larger society. In some cases, state officials have concluded that granting television or radio station licenses to ethnic communities will negatively impact their adherence to a national identity and core cultural values. This was the case in France in the mid-1990s, where licenses were refused for the establishment of cable channels by Muslim ethnic communities with origins in Morocco or Algeria (Hargreaves & Mahdjoub, 1997).

Ethnic media perform other important roles as well, including the following: (a) They can become mobilizing forces for the ethnic community; (b) they are indicators of larger social change; and (c) they can redefine the media market and introduce new organizational structures. We will examine these roles in turn.

The Ethnic Community: Ethnic Media as Mobilizing Forces

Ethnic media provide newly arrived immigrants as well as members of more established ethnic communities a kind of social barometer. They offer an understanding of the current relationship between the ethnic community and the broader society. They identify points of contention, and they offer a venue for the ethnic community to debate the issues at hand and come to a consensus about the best course of action. In the issue resolution process, ethnic media can also serve as mobilizing agents. For example, in the spring of 2006, the U.S. Congress considered passing a law that would change the country's immigration policy. Immigrants and other supporters took to the streets to protest the proposed bill. Ethnic radio was where Hispanic-origin immigrants debated how they would deal with the changes to the immigration law introduced in Congress. Ethnic radio disk-jockeys moderated these debates and played a key role in orchestrating the rallies across the country (Baum, 2006; Félix, González, & Ramírez, 2006; González, 2006; Starr, 2006; Watanabe & Beccera, 2006). The 2006 immigration protests caught the mainstream media off guard. Many of them discovered that the proposed

Profile 1.4 The Ethnic Media Project, University of Massachusetts–Boston

The Center on Media and Society, located at the University of Massachusetts–Boston, launched a project in 2004 to support ethnic media and to build bridges across ethnic boundaries in Greater Boston. The Ethnic Media Project has created a free online directory of ethnic media organizations that are active in the region. The project's programs and initiatives are shaped by a core group of media organizations, representing the Haitian, Russian, Latino, Irish, Indian, Chinese, African, African-American, and other ethnic communities in Boston. Apart from the ethnic media directory, project participants are also working on an online news digest service, story exchanges, newsmaker press conferences, and "best practice" type of workshops for ethnic media journalists.

change to the law had been discussed in the ethnic media for months before it actually became headline news in every major media outlet in the United States. In general, ethnic media have the capacity to raise awareness about issues not addressed in mainstream media. Immigration reform, citizenship rights, and the role of immigrants in the economy and the military are only a few of these issues.

Ethnic Media as Indicators of Social Change

Ethnic media can offer people who do not belong to the intended and ethnically defined audience insights into changes that are taking place around them. In recent years, major media associations, such as the Newspaper Association of America (NAA), have urged mainstream media journalists to follow the agenda of ethnic media and to collaborate with them. Workshops and conferences have been organized by the NAA to help mainstream media professionals to get better acquainted with ethnic communities' issues and to help ethnic media journalists to get their voices heard. Similar initiatives, including the Ethnic Media Project (see Profile 1.4) developed by the Center on Media and Society at the University of Massachusetts in Boston and the Mediam'Rad Project developed by the Panos Institute in Paris (see Profile 1.5) have been launched recently by academic institutions and non-profit/ non-governmental organizations in the U.S. and Europe.

Ethnic Media Change the Landscape, Make Markets More Competitive

Dramatic worldwide changes in population diversity have created the potential for many ethnic media to grow into major and profitable operations. Their successes have prompted mainstream media, marketers, and advertisers to research ethnic audiences. They want to know how to appeal to these audiences. In the United States, Spanish-language media, like the Univisión network and the newspaper *La Opinión,* have grown to the point where they compete against established English-language media. Ethnic media,

Profile 1.5 Mediam'Rad: Ethnic and Diversity Media in Europe/Panos Institute–Paris

Mediam'Rad is a program of the Paris-based Institute Panos that promotes collaboration and partnerships between ethnic media and mainstream media. The project members assert that ethnic media can provide mainstream media with expert knowledge necessary to address issues that are increasingly challenging in Europe. By fostering ties between ethnic and mainstream media, Mediam'Rad hopes to broaden the range of perspectives Europeans have on issues related to the integration of immigrants into European societies, and ethnic and racial discrimination. Major collaborators of the Panos Institute in Paris include the Italian non-governmental organization COSPE (Cooperation for the Development of Emerging Countries) and Mira Media, based in the Netherlands. COSPE projects focus on human rights issues, combating racism, and promoting equal opportunity policies for ethnic minorities in Italy. Mira Media is an independent cooperative founded in 1986 by the major national migrant organizations in Holland. The organization works closely with Dutch national and private broadcasters to promote the participation of immigrant professionals in radio, television, and interactive media.

therefore, are redefining media markets and bringing ethnic communities out of invisibility.

Moreover, thanks to new communication technologies and the capacity they give to organizations for joint ventures, even if they are a world apart, numerous transnational ethnic media corporations and satellite-based ethnic broadcast channels have been founded worldwide. The emergence of this type of media operation has altered the way we view the media landscape. It is no longer constrained by national borders and it is more diverse in organizational structure (e.g., from mom and pop to transnational operations; see Figure 1.1.).

Globalization and the Ethnic Media

Ethnic media lay at the nexus of globalization forces that are felt by all of us. We experience increased population diversity, the emergence of more hybrid or hyphenated identities (e.g., Mexican-American, French-Algerian, Japanese-Brazilian), fewer restrictions on travel, more affordable telecommunication-services, and new organizational forms (e.g., transnational ethnic media organizations).

The idea behind pre-globalization "melting-pot" theories (e.g., Gordon, 1964; see also Alba & Nee, 2003) was that, over time, immigrants sever their ties to the culture of their home country and get assimilated into the culture of their new country. According to this line of thought, ethnic media, over time, should perish, losing their audience to mainstream media. However, today, people can continue to be connected to their home country long after they have moved away. This is because traveling is cheaper, telecommunication systems are less expensive and more efficient, and new modes of communication have been developed (e.g., e-mail, instant messenger applications, IP telephony). Being able to be linked to both "home" (i.e., the home country) and "here" (i.e., the country of settlement) enables people to forge new, dual, or hyphenated identities. I am not just American or just Chinese, but rather Chinese-American. I am not just Vietnamese, but also German. This ability to preserve elements of multiple cultural identities makes it likely that members of ethnic groups will continue to connect to ethnic media long after they set foot in their new country. Ethnic media, therefore, may survive their founders. However, the roles these media play may change. For example, people may, over time, rely on ethnic media more for negotiating bicultural identities and for social networking, as they are already acquainted with the social norms of their host country.

The impact of globalization is not uniform across the world (Scholte, 2000). Most schools in the United States, for example, provide access to the Internet for their students, while in many African countries, access to a telephone line is an unaffordable luxury. Therefore, we should expect that the opportunities afforded by globalization to ethnic media will not be the same worldwide (Castells, 2000a). Such differences across national contexts will be explored in more detail in subsequent chapters.

☒ For Further Discussion

The volume of letters that crossed the Atlantic around the turn of the 20th century is astounding. Approximately five million letters were sent to Russia and Hungary by American sojourners from 1900 to 1906 (Morawska, 2001). Letters were more than a monthly update of family affairs. Morawska observes that

> The back and forth flow of migrants and the density of this correspondence created an effective transnational system of communication, social control, household management, and travel and employment assistance that forward from the immigrant's native places in Europe into the United States and backward from America to their original homelands. (p. 182)

The five volumes of letters studied by Thomas and Znaniecki (1918–1920) and reported in their book *The Polish Peasant in Europe and America,* provide similar evidence. On February 4, 1909, for instance, Tomasz, Antonina, Aleksander, and Marya Barszcewksi write to their brother Stanislaw who is in the United States:

> We beg your pardon, don't be angry with us if we offended you about this ship-ticket because we did not know at whose expense you counted it, and now we thank you for explaining to us how it ought to be. Aleksander says that he will give us 100 rubles [of the debt he owes you] and we thank you for it. (Vol. 2, p. 114)

Think about what would be different and what would be the same had Stanislaw moved to the U.S. in the past year.

In the early 1900s, letters were a way of staying on top of what was happening in the family, but also getting news about what was new in the neighborhood, city, or country left behind. Do you believe that a Polish newspaper published in the city Stanislaw settled in could perform the same roles that letters did? What do you think the stories published in such a paper would be about? What sources would journalists have at their disposal at the time?

What sources would Stanislaw be able to rely on for information if he migrated from Poland to the U.S. today? How would these sources be different compared to the letters and early 20th century ethnic newspapers?

Social Changes That Make Studying Ethnic Media Necessary

The sheer number of new ethnic media founded in recent years is impressive enough to warrant intensive research on the subject. But marketing professionals and advertisers have also increased their interest in ethnic media, as they promise access to a large, diverse, and vibrant market. Latino media have been of particular interest in the United States. That is because the already significant spending power of Hispanics is expected to grow even more in the coming years. Hispanic spending power was estimated at $736 billion, while it is expected to reach $1 trillion by 2010 (Selig Center, 2006). Similar growth trends are observed with regard to other ethnic groups in the U.S. According to the University of Georgia Selig Center reports (2006), Asian spending power in the U.S. is expected to be 434% larger in 2011 than it was in 1990. There are a number of reasons why these trends are likely to persist. The most important reasons are (a) increased population diversity, (b) a higher degree of interaction and communication across national borders, (c) the development of new communication technologies that make this possible, and (d) the rekindling of ethnicity as an important dimension of identity.

Societal transformations are also felt in university and college classrooms around the world. In the U.S., over the past 10 to 15 years, a number of publications have surfaced to help teachers and students respond to the needs of ethnically and culturally diverse schools (see, for instance, Banks, 1991; Chism, Cano, & Pruitt, 1989; Marchesani & Adams, 1992). University faculty around the country are rethinking and changing their curricula to address issues pertaining to ethnic diversity. Instructors are participating in programs to learn how to create more inclusive classrooms and how to tailor the content they teach to the needs of an ethnically diverse student body (Castañeda, 2004). In some institutions, students must complete at least one diversity course in order to graduate. A recent survey conducted by the Association for Education in Journalism and Mass Communication (AEJMC) yielded a database consisting of approximately 460 scholars, researchers, and investigators of diversity issues in media and mass communication courses in U.S. colleges and universities.

In the rapidly changing education environment, communication and journalism schools are charged with the added responsibility of preparing a new generation of journalists and communication professionals. This new generation needs to be trained to deal with a number of new challenges, many of which are related to the emergence of new media. Young professionals in communication and media-related fields of work will also need to be able to deal with the challenges of working in an increasingly multi-ethnic society. They will need, for instance, to know how to engage the ethnic media when asked to run a political campaign, a public relations or even an advertising campaign. It will be necessary, because particular segments of the population cannot or choose not to access mainstream television, radio, or newspapers.

With the challenges, however, new opportunities present themselves, too. The new generation of journalists is also more likely than ever before to seek and take a position on the editorial staff of ethnic media organizations. This is due to the tremendous growth of the ethnic media as a sector of the media industry and the emergence of certain ethnic newspapers (e.g., Spanish-language *Hoy* in New York), radio (e.g., 102.9 FM/La Nueva in Los Angeles), and television channels (e.g., Univisión in the U.S.) as serious competitors of the mainstream media in local, regional, and national markets. For those journalism graduates who choose not to seek a position in one of the many ethnic media organizations, knowing more about these media is imperative. There is a growing consensus that mainstream media need to pay more attention to ethnic media, as they often capture a side of reality that eludes mainstream media journalists (Mira Media, 2006; NAA, 2005, Panos Institute–Paris, 2006).

Mainstream media, their audiences, and policymakers are often unaware of important unfolding events. In 2004, the mainstream media in the U.S. not only failed to capture the impact of the tsunami disaster on the local communities in Southeast Asia, but also the broader effects of the disaster. A story that appeared soon after the tsunami struck the region contemplated how the disaster might divert funding from other areas of the world in need of aid (Rodis, 2004). The article was published in the San Francisco-based newspaper the *Philippine News* on December 30, 2004, and it suggested that United Nations aid, meant initially for reconstruction in typhoon-stricken provinces of the Philippines, would, most likely, be redirected to Indonesia. The author calls upon the overseas Filipino community to cover the expected drop in international relief sent to their home country. This story was not told in the mainstream media in the United States. For days, the focus of the major television networks and print media was primarily on Americans who lost their lives or had miraculously survived.

A decade into the 21st century, it seems that there is more than ever an understanding that mainstream media can no longer ignore the ethnic media that are emerging and growing around them. Mainstream media are coming to terms with the idea that ethnic media are real competitors in their markets. In addition, though, both mainstream and ethnic media are realizing that there are concrete reasons for pursuing collaborations with each other. Out of such collaborations, ethnic media may, for example, gain access to resources they do not have (e.g., investments in new productions, online ventures). For the mainstream media, building bridges to ethnic media offers a clearer view of aspects of society they have not been able to (and possibly cannot) otherwise access. The co-presence of ethnic and mainstream media in our communication environment is critical for individual citizens and society as a whole. Society needs to be able to see itself in its media and reflect on the changes it is undergoing due to globalization and increasing population diversity. Moreover, individuals should understand that a rich, ethnically diverse media landscape helps us better understand and build bonds to each other, despite and ultimately because we are different.

Chapter-by-Chapter Book Overview

Understanding Ethnic Media: Producers, Consumers, and Societies is organized into 5 parts:

Part I, "Ethnic Media in Context," provides the historical and geographical context needed to grasp the content discussed in later chapters of this volume. **Chapter 1** begins by defining ethnic media, identifying the roles they play in the lives of millions of people worldwide and discussing social changes that make understanding ethnic media essential today. **Chapter 2** introduces the history of ethnic media, beginning with their origins in Europe and then tracing their development in Europe, the Americas, Australia, and elsewhere.

Part II, "The Consumers," identifies the individuals, families, and groups who connect with media in a variety of local and national contexts. In Part II, we also consider the reasons and goals that might motivate individuals to connect with ethnic media. In **Chapter 3**, we detail the particular roles and goals that ethnic media can serve in various migrant contexts, while **Chapter 4** traces the relationships between ethnic minorities and their media in different parts of the world and at different times in history. This chapter documents the range of ways in which media have been a forum for the development of and questioning of ethnic identities and group solidarity. In addition, this chapter discusses how the children of immigrants and later generations start to develop ethnic rather than immigrant identities and how their media facilitate this development and their negotiations of the meaning of "home."

In **Part III**, "The Producers," ethnic media are treated as organizations. In **Chapters 5** and **6,** we discuss major trends that are reflected in the circulations and ratings of print and electronic ethnic media, the politics behind these audience statistics, the dynamics of competition among ethnic media, and strategies these media employ for survival and growth.

Much has been written about ownership of the mainstream media, but little has been written about ethnic media ownership. In **Chapter 7**, we take a closer look at who is at the helm of ethnic media organizations and why. The impact of globalization on the structure of ethnic media organizations, the processes of production, and the people who work in these media is examined.

In **Chapter 8,** we focus on the effects of policies pertaining to immigration, citizenship, and the rights of ethnic minorities on ethnic media production. We examine differences across multiple countries. Immigrant-receiving nations have different laws and customs that govern media production. Government policies and how ethnic minorities are defined vary from place to place, as do definitions of legal and illegal immigration. These definitions have wide-ranging consequences for immigrant and ethnic minority institutions, including ethnic media.

Part IV, "Ethnic Media as Civic Communicators," focuses on the role of "place." In **Chapter 9**, we look at ethnic media's role in local communities and how ethnic media are connected to the local residents they serve. This chapter presents examples from local communities that illustrate the role of ethnic media in building civic engagement, in mobilizing residents, and ultimately, in community change. The discussion on ethnic media as local community advocates continues into **Chapter 10.** In this chapter, we detail the challenges for ethnic media journalists and producers, who are often expected to play a number of disparate roles. The complications of "speaking for the community," questions of advocacy versus journalistic "objectivity," and concerns around ethnic-mainstream media relationships are considered in this chapter.

Part V, "The Future of Ethnic Media," looks at current trends in ethnic media, and projections of future development and growth. In the Conclusion, we continue our discussion on ethnic media viability, paying particular attention to how the present media landscape might foretell continuing trends in the ethnic media sector. In addition, we hear from a number of ethnic media researchers and professionals from

Australia, Brazil, Britain, Canada, Germany, Israel, the Netherlands, and the United States, about how they see the future of ethnic media. The book concludes with suggestions for future research into the study and practice of ethnic media, as these outlets come to merit increased attention across a breadth of disciplines, including, but not limited, to communication, media, and journalism studies.

Notes

[1]New America Media is a collaboration of ethnic media founded in 1996 by the non-profit organization Pacific News Service.

[2]Interviews for this study were conducted in English, Spanish, Cantonese, Mandarin, Korean, Vietnamese, Hindi, and Tagalog.

[3]We use the terms Hispanic and Latino interchangeably throughout the book, although the meaning of the two words is not identical. Hispanic is a broader term that may be used to refer to individuals whose native language is Spanish, whereas the term Latino may be reserved for individuals of Latin American origins.

[4]The Media Awareness Network is a Canadian non-profit organization based in Ottawa. Its activities focus on developing media literacy among teenagers.

[5]For more information, see the Web site of the Community Relations Commission of New South Wales, Australia: http://www.crc.nsw.gov.au/ethnic_media

[6]It should be noted that the actual numbers of ethnic media available in any country are likely higher, as many are small-scale operations that often elude the radar of researchers and policymakers.

[7]We should add that in much of the Canadian literature, the designation "ethnic" is reserved for media that are not produced in English or French (i.e., "third-language" media) and not targeted to indigenous communities.

[8]For similar reasons, European ethnic media professionals who met in Paris in 2005 and subsequently in Strasbourg, France, in June 2006 rejected the term *immigrant* media. As an alternative, they offered the term *media of diversity* (*media des diversités*). According to the Panos Institute in Paris that organized these meetings in the context of the Mediam'Rad Project (see a profile of the project later in this chapter), "*These media have an editorial policy that is mainly focused on the diversity of the components of European society. Albeit not exclusively, they address an audience that is linked to one or more of the groups that comprise this diversity, are produced and mainly disseminated within the European Union, and have an editorial staff that is representative of the diversity within our societies" (Mediam'Rad, April 2007, pp. 1–2).*

[9]According to Chaliand and Rageau (1995), "A diaspora is defined as *the collective forced dispersion of a religious and/or ethnic group* [italics added], precipitated by a disaster, often of a political nature" (p. xiv).

[10]The Basque people inhabit a region around the western end of the Pyrenees. The region spans the border between France and Spain, on the Atlantic coast.

CHAPTER 2

Ethnic Media in History

CHAPTER OBJECTIVES

By the end of this chapter, you will have learned more about:

- The development of ethnic media in context of major developments in communication technologies, such as the creation of the printing press.
- The social conditions and historical events that gave rise to ethnic media in different parts of the world.
- How ethnic media have contributed to key historical periods for immigrant, ethnic minority, and indigenous populations in different national contexts.

Emigration, Immigration, and the Ethnic Media

As we discussed in the last chapter, there has been a lot of debate about the terms that are used to describe what we call "ethnic media." We said that ethnic media are media produced *for* members of a particular ethnic group. These media are often also produced *by* members of the same ethnic group, but not always. In this chapter, we will look at the development of media that have served indigenous, ethnic minority, as well as immigrant groups in different parts of the world. Ethnic media date as far back as the 17th century in Europe (Censer, 1994; Starr, 2004), and there is evidence of ethnic media in Australia and North America beginning in the 19th century (Rose, 1996; Wilson, Gutierrez, & Chao, 2003).

However, ethnic media did not develop at the same time and at the same pace in every part of the world, because they emerged in countries or regions experiencing different social, political, and economic conditions. Moreover, the development of ethnic media has always depended on technological innovations. Ethnic newspapers would not be possible without the invention of the printing press, nor would we be talking about ethnic broadcasting if radio and television had not been invented. The diffusion of these innovations, however, did not happen uniformly across the world, and therefore there are differences from country to country with respect to when certain types of ethnic media emerged. For these reasons, although we have made a concentrated effort to include the history of ethnic media from as many places as possible, most information is available on the United States, Canada, Europe, and Australia. Despite these limitations, research conducted on immigrants to North America, Europe, and Australia reveals a diverse media history that, at least in part, reflects the regions from which these immigrants have moved.

A comprehensive history of the differences in socio-political, economic, and technological conditions that have affected ethnic media development across the world would require several volumes of writing. Therefore, in this chapter, our goal is to account for the beginnings of ethnic media production in as many countries as possible, to discuss the conditions that supported the rise of these media, and to examine the impact of these early productions on later developments in ethnic media.

Indigenous Media as Ethnic Media

Most regions of the world were inhabited long before they were settled by outsiders, who generally came from Europe. Some of the most prominent examples of indigenous peoples are the United States' Native-Americans, Canada's First Nations, and Australia's Aboriginal populations. These groups endured physical resettlements, as well as discrimination in access to social power and rights. The ethnic media that developed to serve these groups have reflected the needs and interests of indigenous peoples at different points in their histories.

Migration Trends and the Emergence of Media

Evidence of people moving from one part of the world to another can be traced back to the earliest recordings of human history. However, the boundaries between "here" and "there" were not very clearly defined for much of that time. The rise of formalized boundaries between countries officially dates back to 1648, when the Treaty of Westphalia ended a series of European wars. The balance of power this treaty created depended on clearly defined, independent entities that we call *nation-states.* While many groups had long, shared histories and considered themselves a unified people long before 1648, the rise of the nation-state began to put borders around the people (the nation) and the physical boundaries that they inhabited (the state). The nation-state depends on a central system of power, generally controlled by the majority group of that nation. Therefore, the establishment of nation-states also affected how ethnic minority groups defined themselves in relation to the new system of governance.

The development of nation-states with clear and enforced borders also affected the ways that people moved. The nation and the state do not always clearly overlay each other. People who moved to a different state often still considered themselves part of the nation from which they originated. We can still see this trend today, where immigrants may live in a host country, but still consider themselves tied to their home country. Migration across nation-state borders has become increasingly regulated over time, including the development of passports and official documentation as requirements for entry and exit

(Torpey, 1999). Media systems have also developed greater complexity over time. This chapter details the distinct histories of ethnic media in different regions, showing how developments in different places were related to the larger social conditions in the nation-state where indigenous, ethnic minority and immigrant communities lived.

Beginnings of the Ethnic Press in Europe

A German goldsmith named Johannes Gutenberg is credited with the development of the printing press around 1439. The diffusion of the new technology and increased literacy levels across Europe created a surge in demand for books across the continent over the next two centuries. Until the advent of the printing press, booksellers offered relatively few and costly handwritten manuscripts produced in monasteries and by commercial stationers. Thanks to the printing press, more books could be produced at a lower cost, making them accessible to a broader public. Publishers and booksellers across Europe saw the potential to increase their profits and eagerly adopted the new technology (Starr, 2004).

Major cities in England, Germany, Italy, and Holland became important book publishing centers and would later become the centers of newspaper development as well.[1] These cities became publishing centers for minority groups within Europe. Persecution resulted in religious and ethnic minorities, including Jews and France's Protestant Huguenots, moving from one country to another. Underground routes developed to spread news and stories between those who had left and the communities they had left behind. Amsterdam became a refuge for many of these ethnic minorities, and ultimately a major center for Jewish and Huguenot publishing (Starr, 2004).

The development of the press in France was slow before the Revolution in 1789, due to pre-publication censorship and a book police that kept publishers in check. Tensions between the Catholic royal family and the country's Protestant Huguenot minority erupted into a series of eight holy wars between 1562 and 1598. In 1598, Huguenots were guaranteed some protection by the Crown, but in 1685, Protestantism was declared illegal and large numbers of Huguenots fled to England, Holland, and the Scandinavian countries. Their arrival led to a considerable proportion of French books being published outside of France, mainly in Holland and Switzerland. These books circulated, says Starr (2004), through clandestine networks into France, where Protestants were not able to publish materials on their faith. Over time, it was not just books that were published outside of France, but also newspapers. One of the most well-known newspapers of the time was the *Gazette de Leyde* (Popkin, 1989), which was first published around 1677.

The *Gazette de Leyde* and other similar newspapers may not only be the first examples of transnational journalism, but also the first ethnic newspapers published in Europe. Their audience included both the French who lived in France, but also the French who had fled their country of origin in years past. The *Gazette de Leyde* was founded by the De la Fonts, a family of Huguenot refugees to Holland. In 1738, the newspaper was bought by another French Protestant family, the Luzacs, and it remained a family business up until it ceased publication in 1811 (Censer, 1994; Van Vliet, 2003).

Ethnic Media in Europe in the 19th and Early 20th Centuries

In Europe during the 19th and early 20th century, most newspapers were published in Latin and other "high culture" languages, not in the vernacular, or spoken languages, of the people. In areas under German, Austro-Hungarian, Ottoman, and Russian control, authorities also banned publications in minority languages for fear that these publications would strengthen nationalist movements. This was certainly the case in Bulgaria. After centuries of occupation by the Ottoman Empire,[2] Bulgarians who sought higher education in Europe during the mid-1800s returned filled with ideas of liberty and equality, and began to advocate for Bulgarian independence. The first Bulgarian periodical was printed in 1844 and the first newspaper in Liepzig, Germany in 1846 (Zotova, 1995). These and other publications were smuggled into Bulgaria after being printed in Romania, Germany, and other places where content was not subject to Ottoman censorship (Kaplan, 1993; Zotova, 1995).

These publications contributed to the nationalist movement, as did the establishment of reading rooms, which provided communal spaces for lectures, performances, political debates, and education about Bulgarian history (Glenny, 1999). Western literature and political texts were translated into Bulgarian and spread through the secret press and at these reading rooms, keeping Bulgarians up-to-date with the social and political changes occurring in the rest of Europe. Nationalist efforts ultimately led to a series of uprisings against the Turks in 1835, 1841, 1850, and 1851 in efforts to gain Bulgarian independence (Glenny, 1999; Kaplan, 1993).

By the early 20th century, nationalist movements had achieved their aims in many parts of Europe, and restrictions on newspaper publications had eased. Radio also opened doors to new opportunities for ethnic media development. However, these opportunities were often hindered by national policies promoting immigrants' assimilation into European majority populations. These policies led to restrictions on media production in minority languages. In 1923, the British Broadcasting Corporation (BBC) started to broadcast some programming in Welsh and in Scots Gaelic, while in 1934 Norway's public service broadcaster, Norsk Rikskringkasting (NRK), began to offer very limited programming for the Sami, who are the indigenous populations living in northern Norway. However, programming in Sami languages only became a regular feature of Norwegian broadcasting in 1946. Similar programming was offered to Sami populations living in Sweden and Finland for the first time in 1948 (Browne, 2007; Heatta, 1984).

During World War II, many ethnic media were viewed with suspicion by the majority population in the countries in which they operated. In Britain, for example, Welsh broadcasters were severely scrutinized and were almost abolished. The BBC controller of "home broadcasting" indicated that scrutinizing Welsh programming was necessary to make sure "they did not make for national disunity" (Davies, 1994, p. 133). The underlying assumption was that Welsh language programming was "inherently subversive" (Davies, 1994, p. 133). German and Japanese media were treated with similar suspicion in the United States during World Wars I and II, as we will discuss later in this chapter.

Ethnic Media in Europe in the Post-War Era

European societies changed rather rapidly in the eras following World Wars I and II. To boost their industrial production after World War II, western European countries required greater labor power. Countries including France, Belgium, and Germany recruited "guest-workers" from southern European countries as well as Turkey and Yugoslavia. Many of these "guests," however, did not return to their home countries, choosing instead to settle where they had sought work. In the aftermath of World Wars I and II, Britain saw its empire shrink and experienced large influxes of South Asian, Caribbean, African, and other immigrants from its former colonies (Hussein, 1994).

The countries of southern Europe were generally emigrant-sending rather than immigrant-receiving nations until the late 1980s and 1990s. At that time, Portugal, Spain, Italy, and Greece began to acknowledge that large numbers of immigrants were crossing their borders and intending to settle permanently. In Spain and Portugal, many of these immigrants came from Africa and Latin America. In Italy and Greece, immigrants arrived from Balkan countries, such as Albania and Yugoslavia, but also Turkey and African states including Sudan, Ethiopia, Zaire, and Ghana (King, Fielding, & Black, 1997; Mardakis, Parsanoglou, & Pavlou, 2001).

The changing demographics across most European countries, however, did not necessarily lead to the development of ethnic media—at least not very quickly. Ethnic print media developed faster than ethnic broadcast media due to (a) the lower costs involved in production, (b) the less demanding infrastructure required, and (c) less government regulation imposed on their production.

Moreover, in countries with indigenous ethnic minority communities, like Britain (e.g., Welsh, Scots, and Northern Irish), France (e.g., Bretons, Alsatians, and Provençal communities), Norway, Sweden, and Finland (i.e., Sami communities), as well as federal states like Belgium and Switzerland, which have historically identified themselves as multi-ethnic societies where ethnic communities have equal standing (Ormond, 2002), media serving new immigrants developed faster, for two reasons:

1. The successful struggles that indigenous ethnic minorities had waged to produce media in their own language had already changed the will of policymakers and broadcasters. The issues that production of Welsh-language media in Britain had experienced, for example (Davies, 1994), had made policymakers more accepting of diversity in media and, consequently, less apprehensive about allowing circulation or broadcasting in new immigrants' languages that they could not necessarily understand.

2. The development of media for ethnic minority groups had also helped to create an infrastructure that supported the development, and sometimes funding, of media that served new immigrant groups. Within Belgium, for instance, the Walloon, Flemish, and German communities have separate authorities that have some autonomy in a variety of policy areas, including media policy. This experience made it easier for Belgian authorities to implement specific plans to support new public, community, and commercial broadcasters that wanted to provide multilingual programming for new immigrant and other ethnic minority groups (Ormond, 2002).

Although ethnic media emerged more quickly under these conditions, social constraints were certainly still a factor in many of these countries. Racism and xenophobia spiked in many European countries in the late 1980s and early 1990s in the economic crisis that followed the fall of the Berlin Wall and collapse of the Soviet Union. These social trends undoubtedly constrained the development of ethnic media in some instances (Ormond, 2002; Raiser, 2002), but in other contexts, unsettling social conditions may have been a catalyst for the development of ethnic media. While each social context is unique, countries with established multicultural media frameworks are more likely to foster ethnic media development and diversity than countries that do not have such frameworks in place.

European Public Broadcasting Reluctantly Opens Its Doors to Ethnic Minorities

With few exceptions, many ethnic communities did not have access to the airwaves until the 1980s, or even the 1990s. Until that time, broadcast services in most European countries were licensed as public broadcasting monopolies. In Britain, the BBC had a monopoly until 1954, when the parliament dictated the creation of a commercially supported television service, Independent Television (ITV), a conglomerate of 14 companies (Browne, 2007). And while indigenous ethnic minorities, like the Welsh, saw the first programs in their language air in 1953, it took 14 more years and the launching of BBC local radio to see development of programming targeting other ethnic communities within Britain. Local stations in cities with large communities of South Asian and Caribbean-origin immigrants started to provide programming that targeted those groups. These cultural programs featured mostly the popular music of ethnic groups living in a particular city. Starting in 1973, the Independent Local Radio system began to air similar programming. Ethnic communities were actively involved in developing this programming, although content was "subject to BBC and ILR [Interagency Language Roundtable] control" (Browne, 2007, p. 112).

The national public broadcasting services in France remained monolingual into the 1970s. The French public broadcasting service began to carry programming in regional minority languages (e.g., Breton, Alsatian) in the mid-1970s, but "even by 1998 there were only 265 hours of television programming *per year* in the six regional languages" (Browne, 2007, p. 177, emphasis in original; see also Guyot, 2002). Programming for the large North African-origin communities in France began around the same time, with a television program called *Mosaïque* that was aired on Sunday mornings and aimed to increase immigrants' familiarity with French culture. In 1981, Radio Soleil and Radio Beur began broadcasting in Arabic and French from Paris to serve France's North African-origin communities (Echchaibi, 2001; Karim, 2007).

From "Pirates" to Legal Ethnic Media Broadcasters

While public service broadcasting was slowly opening its doors to ethnic minorities, a number of unlicensed ethnic broadcast media appeared in many countries across Europe, including the U.K., Germany, and Italy in the 1970s, 1980s, and 1990s (Browne, 2007). The proliferation of these unlicensed stations was an important force that pushed state authorities to grant local, lower power broadcasting licenses. In Britain, in particular, several unlicensed radio stations broadcast for South Asian, Caribbean, and African listeners, either in English or in a particular mother tongue. These groups pushed British authorities for the creation of a community radio sector. The prospects were positive early in the 1980s, but "opposition within the Conservative government halted the effort, in part due to suspicion that linguistic minorities might use their 'linguistic invisibility' to criticize the government" (Browne, 2007, p. 116). It was not until the early 1990s that Caribbean, South Asian, and other ethnic stations became legal residents of the British airwaves.

Ethnic Media in the United States

The first printing press in the Americas appeared in Mexico City in 1535 or 1536, a full 100 years before the English colonists' first press arrived in 1638 (Wilson, Gutierrez, & Chao, 2003, p. 266). These presses provided colonists in Mexico with news from Europe and were also used by the Catholic Church to print materials employed in efforts to convert Mexican and Central American indigenous populations to Christianity. It would take a great deal of time before printing presses, which had been under the control of the elites, came to be used by ethnic minority groups.

The Beginnings of Ethnic Media in the United States

The earliest ethnic media in the Americas are believed to have been published in the early 1800s, and as in the case of Europe, ethnic media generally began in response to events or social conditions that threatened a particular immigrant, indigenous, or ethnic minority group. For African Americans, those conditions were slavery and segregation.

The Black Press Before 1900

The African American press began almost 40 years before slavery was officially abolished in the United States and almost a century and a half before comprehensive civil rights legislation would guarantee real protections against racial discrimination. *Freedom's Journal* began in New York in 1827 and ran until 1829, carrying local news as well as news from countries that African Americans were most interested in, including Sierra Leone and Haiti (La Brie, 1977). *Freedom's Journal* was the first newspaper to publish detailed reports of lynchings. The editors also ran fundraising campaigns to purchase and free slaves and to provide them with support to move north (Barrow, 1977). Historians believe that the audience for these initial publications was the small population of literate, Northern African-Americans, as well as sympathetic White readers (Murphy, 1974).

The same dual audience read Frederick Douglas' *North Star,* which was published from 1847 to 1851 in Rochester, New York. As the editor and publisher of the first openly abolitionist media outlet in the U.S., Douglas called for an immediate end to slavery. The content of the paper provided detailed instructions and support for Southern Blacks, both free and escaping slaves, making their way northward (La Brie, 1977). The open advocacy of these early African-American media "not only covered Black history as it happened, but also made it happen" (Page, 2006, p. xii). In the period around the Civil War, there was an explosion of African-American newspapers. These were usually short-lived, but provided essential news and support for African-Americans learning to navigate their rapidly changing environment.

The Beginnings of the Native-American Press

Native-American tribes began publishing newspapers in 1828 to address a number of rising concerns in their communities. According to Murphy and Murphy (1981), newspaper publication developed in response to the growing unease of tribal leaders as the U.S. government began to clear the way for removing the tribes from their ancestral lands and resettling them in the West. The best known of these resettlements was the Trail of Tears, the forced relocation of the Cherokees from their lands in Georgia to the Indian Territory (now Oklahoma), in 1838. The relocation resulted in the deaths of approximately 4,000 Cherokees (for more details, see Anderson, 1991; Ehle, 1988).

The first newspapers among the Cherokee, Chickasaw, Choctaw, and Creek tribes were financed by tribal leaders, which released them from the pressures of finding enough advertising revenue to stay in business, but also made these papers the official voice of the elders and chiefs. The concerns of these initial publications were primarily educational: as the U.S. government increasingly encroached on the tribes' legal rights, leaders became concerned about educating their young to be successful in their encounters with Whites (Murphy & Murphy, 1981, p. 16). This involved learning to read and write. Initially, Cherokee newspapers like the *Cherokee Phoenix*[3] were published bilingually, with some content in English and the rest published in the 86-character Cherokee alphabet invented by Sequoyah in 1812 (see Figure 2.1).

According to records from that period, it took most people less than a week to learn to read with this alphabet (La Course, 1979). For many young Cherokee, learning to read in Cherokee was a stepping stone to becoming literate in English (Murphy & Murphy, 1981). The tribal newspapers closely followed the passage of laws that systematically stripped their members of their rights to petition U.S. courts and covered the internal debates of the tribes over plans to resettle the tribes in the Western states. The disruptions of resettlement and the Civil War effectively halted production of Native American ethnic media during that time (Murphy & Murphy, 1981, p. 38). After the Civil War, new newspapers began to publish and circulate, covering local community events, as well as news from the larger U.S. society that affected life on the reservations.

Figure 2.1 Cherokee Alphabet, Created by Sequoyah in 1812

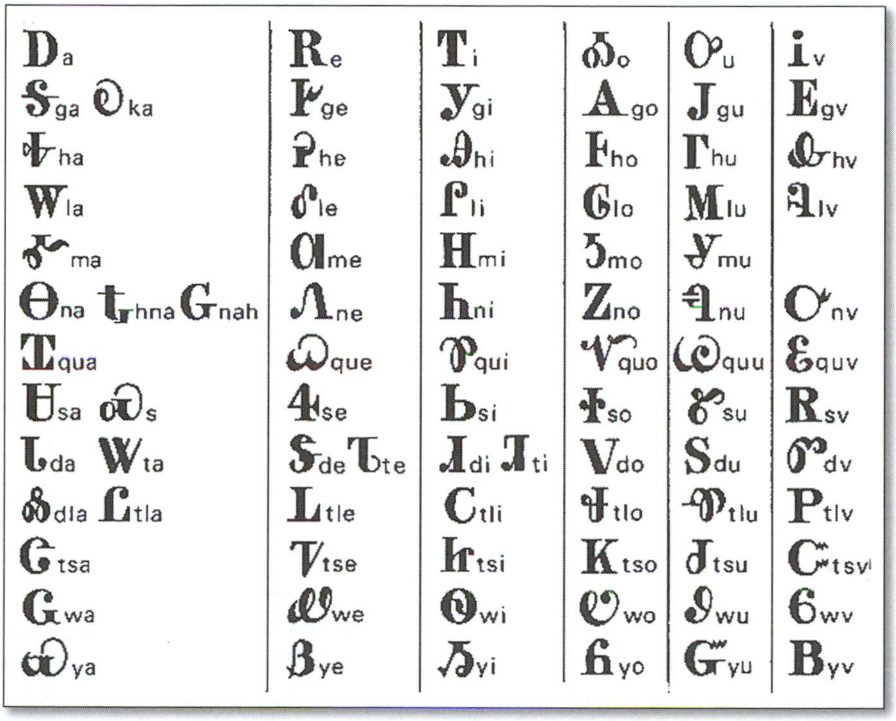

Ꭰ a	Ꭱ e	Ꭲ i	Ꭳ o	Ꭴ u	Ꭵ v
Ꭶ ga Ꭷ ka	Ꭸ ge	Ꭹ gi	Ꭺ go	Ꭻ gu	Ꭼ gv
Ꭽ ha	Ꭾ he	Ꭿ hi	Ꮀ ho	Ꮁ hu	Ꮂ hv
Ꮃ la	Ꮄ le	Ꮅ li	Ꮆ lo	Ꮇ lu	Ꮈ lv
Ꮉ ma	Ꮊ me	Ꮋ mi	Ꮌ mo	Ꮍ mu	
Ꮎ na Ꮏ hna Ꮐ nah	Ꮑ ne	Ꮒ ni	Ꮓ no	Ꮔ nu	Ꮕ nv
Ꮖ qua	Ꮗ que	Ꮘ qui	Ꮙ quo	Ꮚ quu	Ꮛ quv
Ꮜ sa Ꮝ s	Ꮞ se	Ꮟ si	Ꮠ so	Ꮡ su	Ꮢ sv
Ꮣ da Ꮤ ta	Ꮥ de Ꮦ te	Ꮧ di Ꮨ ti	Ꮩ do	Ꮪ du	Ꮫ dv
Ꮬ dla Ꮭ tla	Ꮮ tle	Ꮯ tli	Ꮰ tlo	Ꮱ tlu	Ꮲ tlv
Ꮳ tsa	Ꮴ tse	Ꮵ tsi	Ꮶ tso	Ꮷ tsu	Ꮸ tsv
Ꮹ wa	Ꮺ we	Ꮻ wi	Ꮼ wo	Ꮽ wu	Ꮾ wv
Ꮿ ya	Ᏸ ye	Ᏹ yi	Ᏺ yo	Ᏻ yu	Ᏼ yv

For Further Discussion

Imagine yourself as the editor of a Cherokee newspaper in the period leading up to the Trail of Tears. Some leaders in your community support resettlement, arguing it will result in a more peaceful life in a new place. Other leaders argue that the tribe cannot leave the land of their ancestors. There are additional pressures from the U.S. government that will try to suppress any moves by your newspaper that incite rebellion, ranging from withholding information from your staff about proposed laws to outright censorship.

As the editor, what would you do? How would you present the different sides of the argument? Would you aim for objectivity, or advocate for the position you believe to be right? Explain your reasons.

How would you deal with pressures from the U.S. government to curtail the content of your newspaper? What strategies would you employ to produce a newspaper under these conditions?

The Early Latino Press

Spanish-language ethnic media also have long histories in the United States. The first Latino newspaper, *El Misisipí,* was founded in New Orleans in 1808. The city was a major transit point for people traveling between Europe, Central, and Latin America, and a landing point for Spanish refugees from European and Latin American wars. The text in one of the surviving issues quotes a paper called *Diario de New York (New York Daily),* which Wilson, Gutierrez, and Chao (2003) believe is evidence that communication between ethnic media occurred even during this early period of production (p. 270). Wilson, Gutierrez, and Chao also point out that *El Misisipí* had many of the hallmarks that have been characteristic of ethnic media since that time: (1) it served Spanish-speaking immigrants who were escaping the turmoil of war; (2) it was bilingual, recognizing the importance of the home and host country languages; (3) *El Misisipí* covered local New Orleans events, as well as news from the home countries and major world events; and (4) a full quarter of the newspaper (one full page) was devoted to advertising, indicating that *El Misisipí* was a business venture (p. 271).

In the southwestern part of the United States, a large percentage of Mexico became part of the U.S. when the Treaty of Guadalupe Hidalgo was signed in 1848. Initially, newspapers in this region targeted to Mexican-Americans were funded by the U.S. government. Newspaper content was written by government employees and presented official views of ways that Mexicans could become "good Americans" (Rodriguez, 1999). With the printing of *El Clamor Público* (The Public Clamor or Shouting), which began in 1857, a new era in Mexican-American media was born.

El Clamor Público was independent, and opposed attempts to assimilate Mexicans without affording them rights associated with full citizenship (Gutiérrez, 1977; Rodriguez, 1999). Although *El Clamor Público* was only published for a few years before closing due to insufficient funds, this newspaper marked the beginning of a long tradition. The many hundreds of newspapers that have followed *El Clamor* in the southwestern United States have continued to document the travails of migration from Mexico, exploitation of workers, and otherwise agitate for social rights for Latinos at particular turning points in American history.

The Chinese Press in the 19th and 20th Centuries

Just as Spanish-language media like *El Clamor Público* were a response to their community's needs and an advocate for better social conditions, *The Golden Hills News* began printing in San Francisco in 1854 in response to the poor treatment that many Chinese miners experienced during the Gold Rush. The newspaper documented violent incidents that Chinese miners suffered and protested ongoing discrimination in housing, payment, and other interactions between U.S. mining companies and their workers (Lai, 1987). The *Golden Hills News* folded in 1855 but was replaced that same year by *The Oriental,* which was the first Chinese-language newspaper to include an English-language section, "aiming to increase the non-Chinese reading public's understanding of China and the Chinese in America" (Lai, 1987, p. 28).

Most newspapers from this time forward were published exclusively in Chinese. These publications covered local issues, U.S. legislation related to immigration, as well as news from China. Because the Chinese were a relatively small and long-standing ethnic community who published their newspapers in a language few other Americans could read and therefore censor (Zhao, 2002), they were able to express a wider range of viewpoints than newspapers being published in China. For example, in the 1920s and 1930s, Chinese-American newspapers denounced Japanese encroachment on Chinese territory and successfully advocated for a public boycott of Japanese goods in the United States. In this same period, Chinese-American newspapers openly criticized America's limitations on Chinese immigration (Lai, 1987; Viswanath & Lee, 2007), freely publishing opinions that editors in China could not.

The Immigrant Press and the "Old" Immigrants

In the 18th and 19th centuries, large populations of Europeans left their home countries to settle in the United States. Some, like the Huguenots, left fleeing religious persecution; others came simply to create a better life. In the United States, ethnic presses to serve these populations developed without much restriction through the 19th century and until World War I. For many of the French, German, Italian, Polish, Bohemian, Norwegian, Yiddish, Slovak, Hungarian, Slovenian, Ukrainian, and other immigrants who read these ethnic newspapers in the U.S., it was the first time they had ever picked up a publication in their own language. "The reason was not just that more of them [i.e., the immigrants] became literate after coming to America; in their native countries, the language of the press frequently did not match the spoken vernacular," as we discussed earlier in this chapter (Browne, 2007; Morawska, 2001; Park, 1922; Starr, 2004, p. 253). The majority of these media were short-lived due to struggles for economic viability, but failed efforts were quickly replaced with new publications.

Ethnic Media and Politics of Loyalty: World Wars I and II

The United States' participation in World Wars I and II left an indelible mark on the ethnic media. When the U.S. entered the war against Germany in April 1917, anti-German sentiment led to restrictions that banned speaking German in classrooms, public settings, and even on the telephone. German-language materials could not even be sent through the mail. Needless to say, this meant an effective ban on German-language ethnic media for the duration of the war, a blow from which these ethnic media never fully recovered (Crawford, 1999; Gerd 2003). Less than half of the German-language newspapers survived the war, and most local ethnic media outlets ended up closing their doors. German-speaking newspaper editors in Philadelphia were convicted of espionage, and others were interned as enemy aliens for the duration of the war. Given the public suspicion of all things related to Germany, many readers grew afraid to connect with ethnic media and started for the first time to turn to the mainstream press (Bergquist, 1987, p. 150).

After peace was established with the Treaty of Versailles in 1919, some of the German presses resumed publication. As Hitler rose to power in the 1930s, the leader of the Nazi movement in America went to the editor of *Staats-Zeijung und Herold,* the largest German-language daily in the U.S., to order him to support the Nazi cause. The Nazi leader was "summarily thrown out of [the editor's] office" (Bergquist, 1987, p. 152). Fear of triggering World War I-era restrictions lay heavily on editors and readers' minds, but all the same, the German ethnic presses were slow to oppose the rise of Nazism; "the failing of the German press during the 1930s was not so much in giving support to Nazism, but rather in being tardy in opposing what was happening within Germany" (p. 152).

The exceptions to this trend were the German-Jewish presses, which were staunchly anti-Hitler from his first appearance on the international scene. The Jewish press became a lifeline for refugees and immigrants from Europe, who followed the deteriorating situation in their hometowns in the kind of detail that was never reported in the mainstream press (Bergquist, 1987; Goren, 1987).

The Japanese-American media suffered major setbacks during WWII as a result of Japan's involvement with Nazi Germany (Kitano, 1987). After Japan's attack on Pearl Harbor in December 1941, the U.S. government suspended publication of all Japanese media. Later, these media were allowed to resume, but under military censorship. As U.S. involvement in the war progressed, Japanese-Americans were removed from their homes and settled in internment camps. These movements brought Japanese-American ethnic media to a halt, although it is now known that in some of the internment camps, detainees set up their own ethnic media publications to serve their communities for the duration of the war (Soga, 2008). When Japanese-Americans were released from their internment, they reestablished their ethnic media as best they could. Internment, however, had separated many American-born youth from their language and culture for a number of years, resulting in their being less likely to connect with Japanese-language media (Kitano, 1987).

For other immigrant and ethnic communities, ethnic media served as a lifeline for men serving in the armed forces. During World War II, Chinese-American men, like other minority servicemen, experienced discrimination while serving in racially integrated units. "Writing from Texas, Ling Ling told his friends that 'Whites Only' signs were displayed outside the day room" (Zhao, 2002, p. 111). Chinese-language newspapers responded to servicemen's need for connections to members of their own communities. Several newspapers created "Self Introduction" columns, where soldiers could write about themselves to connect with other Chinese-Americans serving overseas. In addition, since these newspapers did not have the funds to send correspondents overseas, they recruited talented soldiers to write about their wartime experiences (Zhao, 2002). The *Chinese Times* and *China Weekly* in San Francisco and the *Chinese American Weekly* and *China Daily News* in New York all had dedicated sections that published soldier's reports from the battlefields (Zhao, 2002, p. 111).

Chinese-language newspaper subscriptions actually increased during the war, as soldiers who had previously been able to pick up newspapers and magazines from businesses in their communities could no longer do so, and therefore, began to subscribe in order to get news from home while abroad. "One of the *Chinese Pacific Weekly*'s longtime readers, Harry Wong, recalled that even during the two and a half years he was stationed in West Germany, he received every single issue of the paper" (Zhao, 2002, p. 115).

The very different experiences of the German, Japanese, and Chinese-language presses highlight the impact that policy has on the development of ethnic media. The German and Japanese-language presses were adversely affected by a restrictive set of social policies that targeted these groups during wartime. We discuss the impact of policy on ethnic media development in more detail in Chapter 8. However, the experience of the Chinese-language media during this period demonstrates that conditions of threat also have the potential to be opportunities for growth. In the post-war era, changes in immigration policy would dramatically alter the demographics of America's new arrivals and provide new opportunities and challenges for the development of ethnic media.

Ethnic Media for "New" Immigrants in the Post-1965 Era

In 1965, Congress signed into law a new immigration bill that radically altered the immigrant composition of the United States. The Hart-Cellar Act lifted restrictions on immigration from Latin America, Asia, and Africa, which was a major shift from the predominantly European immigration patterns that had been maintained until that point. Increased movement from Asia reinvigorated the ethnic media that had long histories in the U.S., including the Chinese-language media, as these new immigrant communities created renewed demand for Chinese-language resources (Viswanath & Lee, 2007; Zhou, 2009). For groups that did not have such long settlement histories in the U.S., including immigrants from Korea and Southeast Asian nations like Vietnam, the need for ethnic media created opportunities for enterprising community members from these communities to set up media outlets to serve immigrants like themselves. Similar patterns of reinvigoration and new media establishment also characterized communities from Latin America and Africa (Viswanath & Lee, 2007). Ethnic media that have developed to serve these immigrants are discussed in more detail in Chapter 3.

Ethnic Media in Canada

Canada has a long multicultural history which has led to a diverse media environment. Unlike the United States, Canada has two official languages, English and French, and media produced in both these languages serve mainstream audiences. Restrictions on non-White immigration were lifted in the late 1960s, and since that time, most immigrants to Canada have been from non-European countries. Media serving these immigrant groups have benefited from policy changes that were first created to serve Canada's indigenous peoples.

First Nation Media in Canada

The first North American indigenous radio station began broadcasting in Alaska in the 1930s. Although it would be almost 30 years before Canada's indigenous populations, who call themselves First Nations, began their own radio broadcasts, Canada is arguably "the world leader in indigenous broadcasting . . . There are about thirty Native American radio stations [in the United States] as compared to several hundred in Canada" (Alia & Bull, 2005, p.107).

The major challenge for First Nation media has been the tremendous distance between communities in more remote provinces of Canada, and long winters that make travel back and forth with regular deliveries of newspapers and other print media unfeasible. Historically, radio has been the medium that best overcomes these challenges, even though reception in bad weather can be intermittent (Valaskakis, 1992, p. 68). Radio has also been the preferred medium in northern First Nation communities because start-up costs on the production side are more modest than other options, such as satellite television. On the consumer side, radio requires only the relatively minor financial investment of purchasing a radio in order to connect with ethnic programming.

Ethnic satellite television was made possible for First Nation communities only through substantial government support. The Aboriginal People's Television Network (APTN), launched in 1999, was unique among ethnic media outlets as the world's first broadcast network "developed, run and produced by minority people for a nation-wide audience" (Alia & Bull, 2005, p. 93). Rather than operating as a specialty station that only reaches First Nation groups, APTN is included in Canada's basic cable package, which makes it available to all Canadians. As such, APTN has two primary goals: first, to develop programming for First Nation peoples in several indigenous languages, as well as in French and English; and second, to increase cross-cultural understanding among members of different ethnic minority groups and between ethnic minority and majority viewers (p. 93).

¤ For Further Discussion

The launch of the Aboriginal People's Television Network was a unique development within ethnic media, as it aims to address the needs of First Nations, but also to act as a platform for developing intercultural understanding between First Nations and other racial/ethnic groups in Canada.

- Make a list of the three primary challenges you think a media outlet with this dual purpose would face. Then, explain in detail how you think APTN could overcome or deal with these challenges.

The Rise of Third Language Media

In the United States, media in languages other than English are thought of as "second language" media. Since English and French are the two mainstream languages in which government and other business is conducted, media produced in languages other than English or French[4] are generally referred to as "third language" media. Many parts of Canada, particularly large cities like Toronto and Vancouver, have long been home to diverse immigrant populations.

Legislative changes in 1991 increased the obligation for the broadcast system to reflect the diversity of Canadian society by setting legal provisions for groups speaking languages other than English, French, or First Nations languages. In 1999, the Canadian Radio-television and Telecommunications Commission (CRTC) announced an explicit ethnic media broadcasting policy that licensed domestically produced multilingual and language-specific channels, and allowed for the broadcasting of internationally produced channels via satellite.[5] These policy changes have encouraged dramatic growth in the ethnic media markets of Canada's major cities (Axelrod, 2006).

A census of ethnic media in Vancouver revealed that the South Asian (particularly Punjabi) print media environment was highly developed and changing rapidly, and that Korean and Iranian-language media were the fastest growing in the ethnic media sector (Murray, Yu, & Ahadi, 2007). These recent findings complement an earlier study of 46 ethnic newspapers in Vancouver, which found that the total circulation of these ethnic newspapers is larger than the combined figure of Vancouver's two largest English-language papers (Grescoe, 1994/95, p. 82).

These legislative changes have also encouraged growth in ethnic broadcasting. For example, the Fairchild Group took over broadcasting licenses previously held by Chinavision Canada and Cathay TV in 1993. The Fairchild TV station broadcasts in Cantonese, and now has locations in Vancouver, Toronto, and Calgary. Fairchild Radio has stations in the same three cities. Fairchild TV has become the largest Chinese-language broadcaster in Canada. Recent market research indicated that 39% of Vancouver residents and 40% of Toronto respondents had "watched Fairchild TV yesterday"[6] (Ipsos Reid, 2007a, p. 13; Ipsos Reid, 2007b, p. 16), indicating the largest market share overall. The Fairchild Group now also owns Talentvision, which is the largest Mandarin-language broadcaster in Canada. In the same survey, 37% of Vancouver respondents and 15% of Toronto respondents had "watched Talentvision yesterday" (Ipsos Reid, 2007a, p. 23; Ipsos Reid, 2007b,

Figure 2.2 Fairchild Television/Talentvision News Desks and Production Spaces, Fairchild Group, Vancouver

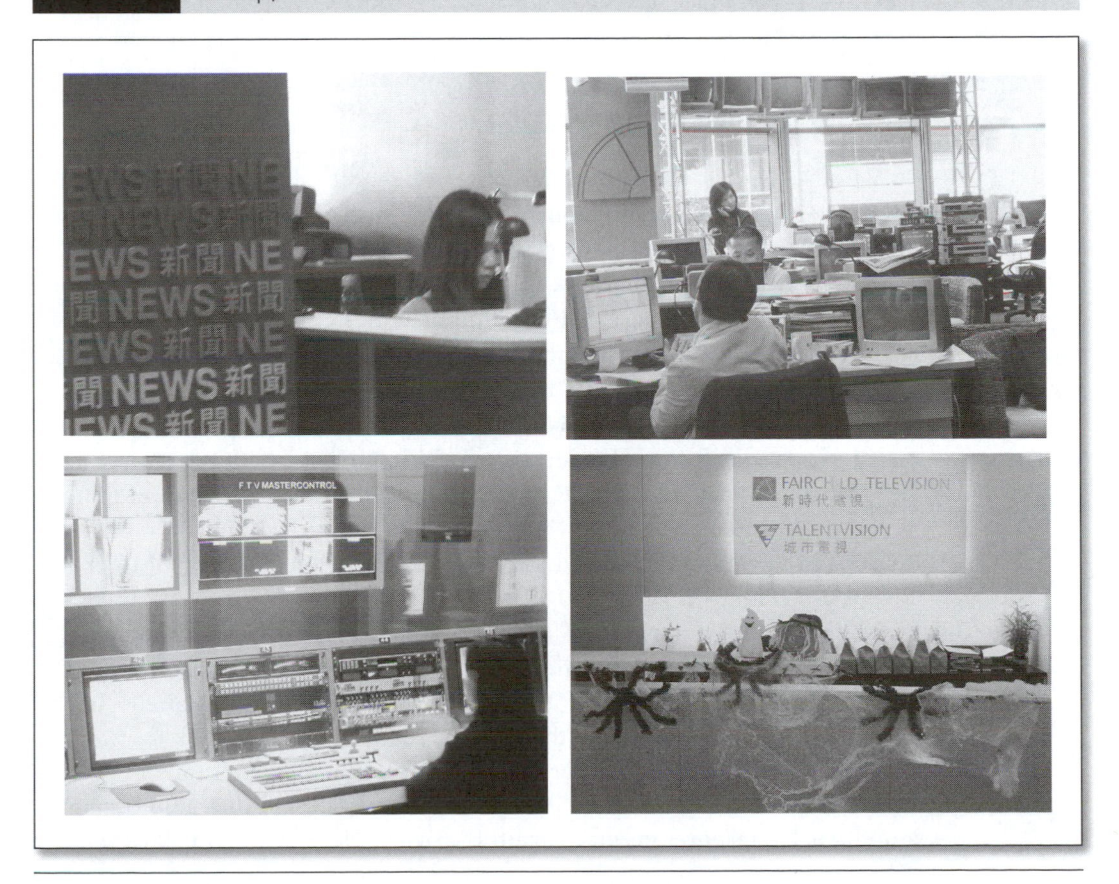

Photos: Vikki Katz.

p. 24). Overall, this survey concluded that 90% of the Chinese audience connects with Talentvision or Fairchild TV each week (Ipsos Reid, 2007). As Figure 2.2 shows, the two broadcasting groups operate side-by-side, sharing offices and even the space where they produce the evening news.

Ethnic Media in Mexico

Mexico, the United States' southern neighbor, has a very different ethnic media tradition from Canada, its neighbor to the north. Although Mexico City was home to the first printing press in the Americas, little has been written about ethnic media in Mexico. Because Mexico has traditionally been an emigrant-sending nation, rather than an immigrant-receiving one (Fitzgerald, 2008), little researcher attention has been paid to the small communities of immigrants and their descendents who settled in Mexico. There are small communities of Jewish and other European-origin groups who have lived in Mexico City for many generations, but the only online evidence of media serving these groups is *Kesher,* which has served Mexico City's Jewish community since 1987. There is also a sizeable community of American expatriates (about 1 million) who are served predominantly by the *Gringo Gazette,* which began in 1994 and prints 15,000 copies on a bimonthly basis. This newspaper, which serves additional readers online, covers local Baja California news as well as news from the United States.

Indigenous Media in Mexico

Because Mexico tends to be an emigrant-sending rather than immigrant-receiving country, the term "ethnic media" in Mexico generally refers to indigenous media. Mexico has the largest indigenous population of any country in Latin America—an estimated 12 million people belonging to nearly 60 ethnic groups distinct by language and/or culture (Ramos & Díez, 2003). In 1979, the Mexican government launched the first of what would become a network of indigenous-language radio stations, which were overseen by the National Indigenous Institute (Instituto Nacional Indigenista [INI]). This network consisted of 20 radio stations' broadcasts on AM frequencies with broadcast ranges between 50 and 120 kilometers (30 and 72 miles), and four low-power FM stations run by indigenous schoolchildren on the Mayan Peninsula. The 24 radio stations in this network targeted 5 million people belonging to 30 distinct ethnic groups (Ramos & Díez, 2003).

Although indigenous group members were key producers of content for these radio stations, the fact that the stations were 100% funded by the INI sometimes limited the content and nature of the broadcasts (Castells-Talens, 2004). In 1994, when rebels in the Chiapas region of Mexico took over an INI station and broadcast from it for a number of hours, the government began to be more restrictive, even installing devices that would kill the radio transmission if such a takeover occurred again (Castells-Talens, 2004). In 2003, the INI was dismantled, and responsibility for the radio stations was handed over to the National Commission for the Development of Indigenous Peoples (CDI). Aside from the 24 stations overseen by the CDI, a number of illegal radio stations continue to broadcast from indigenous communities in remote locations (Castells-Talens, personal communication, March 5, 2008). Because of the need to discreetly remain under the government's radar, many of these illegal signals are weak and erratic (McElmurry, 2009). In January 2009, the government shut down two of these stations, Radio Eiámpti and Radio Uékakua, operating in the state of Michoacán (McElmurry, 2009), but such closures are not common or consistent events.

Radio is a natural choice for Mexico's indigenous communities because broadcasts can carry over long distances, and because the high rates of illiteracy in indigenous communities make indigenous press virtually non-existent (McElmurry, 2009). The remoteness of many of the mountainous indigenous regions of Mexico means that communities may have intermittent or no access to telephone lines, and roads may not be accessible to the postal service. In these communities, radio broadcasts have become a way for people who have migrated to Mexico's urban areas or to the United States to deliver messages to their friends and family that would ordinarily require a phone call or letter (Vargas, 1995). Ramos and Díez (2003) provide an example of these messages:

> *From Chicago, USA, Luis Ramírez sends this message for his brother Arnulfo, in San Juan Puerto Montaña. Luis has the money for the musicians and wants Arnulfo to go to the phone booth in Metlatonic in the morning of Friday, the eleventh. Luis will call then to get the number of the bank account where the money should be deposited.* (p. 1)

Each day, INI radio stations set aside time in their daily programming to broadcast these kinds of free *avisos,* or messages, which can be requested by individuals, organizations, or institutions. In a survey conducted among Mixtecos in the state of Oaxaca in 1990, 20% of respondents indicated that these *avisos* were their favorite part of their station's programming. This percentage was superseded only by the 29% of respondents who indicated that music was their favorite part of the broadcasts (Cornejo, 1990).

As new communication technologies slowly infiltrate these outlying communities, *aviso* requests are now also being made by e-mail as the INI stations increasingly have access to the Internet, even though the connections may be intermittent and expensive. Whether by e-mail or through phone calls to the radio station, these *avisos* have become an essential part of the service these radio stations provide to the community. Daniel Cardona, director of the Tlaxiaco, Oaxaco-based radio station XETLA-AM, "La Voz de la Mixteca" (The Voice of the Mixteca) said, "What we do is put the notice on the air, but it's not just his family that hears it; the whole community hears it" (in McElmurry, 2009). In these ways, indigenous radio stations not only provide news and entertainment to residents about their local community, but a shared line to family and friends now living far away.

Ethnic and Immigrant Media in Australia

Like North America's indigenous peoples, Australia's Aboriginal populations long preceded the arrival of Europeans on the continent. European colonization began in the late 1700s, and has increased in diversity since restrictions on non-European immigration were officially lifted in 1975. As was the case in Canada, progress on media policy and inclusion achieved by Australia's Aboriginal populations have helped pave the way for immigrants' ethnic media development on the continent.

Aboriginal Media in Australia

Although indigenous peoples like Australian Aboriginals are often thought of as "oral cultures," Aboriginal communities have a long history of ethnic media production and consumption, stretching back more than 150 years. The development of print media, and later of broadcast media, arose in response to colonization (Rose, 1996). These media also served to bridge people who were separated over long distances by forced resettlements. In recent times, broadcasting through radio or television has been particularly attractive to Aboriginal communities, because visual and audio formats do not require high levels of literacy.

The early stages of Aboriginal media did, however, employ print media. The first Aboriginal newspaper, *The Aboriginal or Flinders Island Chronicle* (1836–1837) was produced by Aboriginal clerks as a handwritten, hand-copied English publication. All content had to be approved by the English commandant of the Flinders Island settlement (Rose, 1996).[7] Gale (1993) characterizes this first stage of Aboriginal publications as the "Christianizing phase," since many early newspapers were overseen by missionaries who employed these publications in their efforts to convert Aboriginal peoples.

Not until 1938 is there a clear record of another paper, the *Australian Abo Call: The Voice of the Aborigines.* As a professional quality, tabloid newspaper with content overseen by an Aboriginal editorial board, the *Abo Call* was markedly different from the publications that began a century earlier. The *Abo Call* was also the first recorded instance of Aboriginal media agitating for social rights for Aborigines (Rose, 1996). In the 1950s, a clear and consistent print presence began. Although individual papers folded, they were replaced quickly with other publications. In the 1960s and 1970s, these publications were often militant in their call for Aboriginal rights and opposition to the discriminatory actions of Whites. This more militant tone also reflected changes in education policy at the time. In 1973, Australia instituted a bilingual education policy that allowed for instruction in English and local Aboriginal dialects. These media became a resource for Aboriginal youths' language development by connecting young people to news about their people in their ancestral languages.

By the late 1980s, by building on groundwork laid in the 1960s and 1970s, Aborigines began to gain access and control over literature production centers: "As a result, the production of written materials emanating from the printing presses and photocopiers . . . now reflect what Aboriginal people themselves see as worthy of production" (Gale, 1993). The launch of the *Koori Mail* in 1991 was among the most significant indicators of Aboriginal ownership. The *Koori Mail* was the first commercially viable national Aboriginal newspaper, and continues production today.

Moving Toward Interactive and Visual Media

As new communication technologies developed, Aboriginal media began to move away from print to include broadcast technologies, particularly radio. In 1985, the first all-Aborigine station began broadcasting in Alice Springs. By 2000, there were radio stations operating in Brisbane and Townsville, as well as a community television station headquartered in Alice Springs. Men and women involved in the production of Aboriginal media established the National Indigenous Media Association of Australia (NIMAA) in 1993 to more effectively respond to the needs of indigenous communities in Australia's cities and rural areas and to represent these needs nationally. NIMAA's main goal is to bring Aboriginal media to an equivalent position with mainstream, national media organizations, and to maintain language and cultural programming in various types of media outlets (Hartley & McKee, 2000, p. 168). By 2005, NIMAA had 136 member stations (Alia & Bull, 2005, p. 107).

In 1996, Australia established the National Indigenous Radio Service (NIRS), a satellite service of NIMAA designed to reach outlying communities more effectively. The goal of NIRS is to support the outreach efforts of 160 community and 120 Aborigine radio broadcasters (Hartley & McKee, 2000, p. 170). Leading figures in NIRS, however, aimed to increase the visibility of Aborigine-produced radio content beyond their own community. According to Jim Remedio, then chair of NIMAA, the hope was that NIRS' support would bring Aboriginal music and news into the larger national consciousness, and that White Australians would be "twiddling with the dial and hearing something new" (Hartley & McKee, p. 171). In essence, NIRS was attempting to achieve the same aims as Canada's Aboriginal People's Television Network by providing content primarily for an ethnic audience, but with crossover appeal to the mainstream consumer as well.

Indigenous media are the fastest growing media in Australia, "and include print, radio, film, video and television, multimedia and online services. As elsewhere, radio is the most advanced" (Alia & Bull, 2005, p. 112) for the same reasons that radio has been successful with Canadian and Mexican indigenous media: Many Aboriginal communities are remote and difficult to reach physically with print media. Despite these difficulties, interest in developing and sustaining Aboriginal media has grown alongside the developments of ethnic media that serve other ethnic minorities in Australia, namely immigrants and their descendents.

Immigrants, Their Descendents, and Their Media

Australia is home to large immigrant communities from all over the world. Some of these groups have long histories, particularly European groups such as Greeks, Italians, and Germans, while other groups have settled since Australia liberalized their immigration laws in 1975 (Jayasuriya, Walker, & Gothard, 2003). These newer groups of immigrants are primarily from China and from Southeast Asian countries.

Communities with longer histories in Australia have more developed ethnic media systems, although newer groups are benefiting from legislation initially designed to encourage media development for ethnic minorities and indigenous peoples. Clyne (2001) indicates that the larger ethnic newspapers generally have nationwide circulation regardless of the city in which the outlet is located (see Figure 2.3). There is also a government-run network of ethnic radio stations and a television station called Channel 31 that reaches over 1 million viewers. Channel 31 is a multicultural network that serves a variety of ethnic groups, and was established to serve communities with ethnic content in 19 languages. The station has offices in Sydney and in Melbourne, with separate divisions for national content and for local content (Clyne, 2001). There are also smaller, local radio and TV stations located in Adelaide, Melbourne, and Sydney that serve large populations of Arabic, Chinese, Croatian, Farsi, Greek, Italian, Indian, Portuguese, and Turkish speakers. Some of these stations run bilingual programs in an effort to attract second and third generation youths to connect with ethnic media (Clyne & Kipp, 1999).

Greek-language media are among the most sophisticated and organized ethnic media in Australia, reflecting their long history of settlement in the country. Greeks began settling in Australia in large numbers in the 1880s, and today, Australia is home to the largest population of Greeks living outside of Greece. Half of the Greek-Australian community lives in Melbourne, which is also the center of Greek-language media production. Greek migration has continued fairly consistently over the last 130 years, meaning a steady influx of new immigrants to revitalize home language needs and tastes. Melbourne's Greek Media Group owns 3XY Radio, TV Hellas, and *TA NEA* newspaper. 3XY Radio was Australia's first 24-hour Greek-language commercial radio station. Broadcasting began in October 1994, and 3XY Radio services the major

Figure 2.2 Ethnic Media Diversity on Sydney (left) and Melbourne (right) Newsstands, Australia

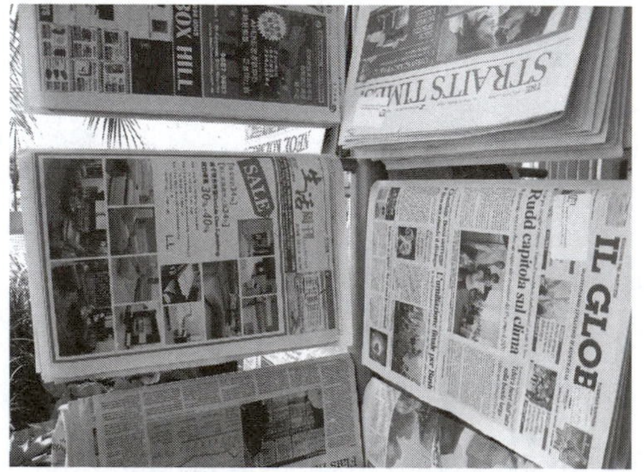

Photos: Vikki Katz.

Greek residential centers: Melbourne, Sydney, and the province of Victoria, generally. TV Hellas provides free Greek-language broadcasting to over 400,000 Greek Australians in the province of Victoria for 7 hours each week via Channel 31.

TA NEA Newspaper began in March 1994 and is one of the largest Greek-language newspapers available in Victoria and Melbourne. In August 1997, *TA NEA* merged with *Greek Beat,* an English-language ethnic outlet. *TA NEA* acquired this English-language publication in order to provide an English-language lift-out supplement in its all-Greek publication, likely as an acknowledgment of limited language proficiency in the third and later generations of Greek Australians.

How the Past Affects Present Ethnic Media Trends

The histories of ethnic media in different countries point to the importance of the nation-state's legal and social attitudes toward diversity in the media. As we have discussed, some countries take a hands-off but benign approach to ethnic media development. Other countries take an active role in supporting the development of ethnic media for their indigenous, ethnic minority, and/or immigrant communities. We can see, for example, that Canada's media policies have actively supported the development of First Nations media. Those legislative decisions have in turn encouraged the creation of media that serve Canada's immigrant communities. On the other hand, we can see that in countries that have not historically been immigrant-receiving, such as Mexico, little attention has been paid to immigrants' ethnic media production, either by the government or by researchers. In addition, the Mexican government's tolerance for indigenous media development has generally been restricted to those outlets they officially fund and control. Past decisions on media and social policy have been big contributors to the current differences in the media environments of these two countries.

There are three major forces that shape media production generally; they are particularly helpful for understanding how national contexts affect newly emerging ethnic media:

- State policies toward minorities
- Regulatory frameworks for media
- Market demand (Franchon & Vargaftig, 1995; Riggins, 1992)

As discussed in this chapter, liberal *state policies toward minorities* can provide a real boost to the development of ethnic media. In countries that receive immigrants in very small numbers or do not make active attempts to integrate immigrants, little attention is consequently paid to recording the developments of these communities, including their media. This is a major reason for the discrepancies in the amount of research that has been conducted on ethnic media in different parts of the world.

The development of ethnic media takes place within the country's *regulatory frameworks for media.* Laws that govern freedom of the press may encourage or discourage the growth of ethnic media, depending on the environment those laws create. Regulatory frameworks are dependent on media, social, and other types of government policy within a particular country; Chapter 8 deals with policy around ethnic media in more detail. As our earlier discussion in this chapter indicated, *market demand* resulting from an influx of new immigrants or from the demands of an indigenous or ethnic minority group, can provide economic opportunities for ethnic media entrepreneurs. These market forces can also contribute to changes in regulatory frameworks governing media. We discuss these ethnic media market forces more deeply in Chapters 5 and 6.

¤ For Further Discussion

Use the three-part framework described above:

1. State policies toward minorities
2. Regulatory media frameworks
3. Market demand

and apply it to a country we have discussed in this chapter to explain ethnic media development in that country. How did these three elements constrain or enable the development of ethnic media? If you know enough about the social conditions of a country we have not included here, you are welcome to apply this framework to that country as your example.

Summary

This chapter detailed the development of ethnic media for immigrant, ethnic minority, and indigenous groups in different parts of the world, and traced their evolutions over time. The development of these media in different parts of the world was contrasted, and the reasons for different rates of ethnic media development were discussed. In the next two chapters, we turn to the specific functions that ethnic media serve for different groups: in Chapter 3, we focus on immigrant groups' relationships to their media, and in Chapter 4, we look at the relationships that ethnic minority and indigenous groups have with their media.

Study Questions

1. Under section heading, "Ethnic Media in Europe in the 19th and Early 20th Centuries," we discussed how ethnic media produced outside of Bulgaria was an important contributor to the growing desire for independence from the Ottoman Empire. Other countries, including Greece and Serbia, developed similar long-distance nationalism projects for independence from the Ottoman Empire, where ethnic media produced in other countries played an important role. Can you think of a case in recent history where ethnic media, including online outlets, have been produced in a host country to impact events in the country of origin? Explain how your chosen case is similar or different to the Bulgarian case.

2. In our discussion of the history of the African-American press (see section, "The Beginnings of Ethnic Media in the United States"), Page (2006) comments that "Black press not only covered Black history as it happened, but also made it happen" (p. xii). How do you think that the ethnic media can act as an advocate for change in their communities, or in the larger society? Make a list of at least three ways that ethnic media might fill this role, and describe each of these ways in detail.

3. The section, under heading, "Ethnic Media and Politics of Loyalty: World Wars I and II" points to the difficulties of immigrants who are still perceived to feel greater loyalty to their country of origin than to their country of settlement. How do you think these assumed crises of loyalty should be handled by the government of the settlement country during times of war?

4. Radio has served a particularly crucial role in the ethnic media development of indigenous populations in Canada, Mexico, and Australia. Think of the major characteristics of radio that make this possible. Do you think that other communication technologies could potentially also serve these roles or perhaps even serve these functions more efficiently? Give support for your answer.

5. Concerns about media conglomeration, defined as a single individual or corporation owning multiple forms of media serving a particular area, is a topic of serious debate in many countries. In some parts of the world, legislative actions have been taken to prevent monopolies on the ways in which people receive information. Do you think that the same concerns apply for ethnic media conglomeration as for mainstream media, or are they different? Justify your answer. Refer to the Fairchild Group (see section "The Rise of Third Language Media") and Greek Media Group (see section "Immigrants, Their Descendents, and Their Media") as examples of ethnic media conglomeration.

Notes

[1]The first newspapers as we know them today appeared in Europe around the turn of the 17th century. An extensive discussion of Europe's early newspapers is beyond the scope of this book; for a detailed history, see Starr (2004).

[2]The Ottoman Empire spanned from 1299 to 1923, and at its height, included much of Southeastern Europe, Western Asia, and North Africa as part of its territory.

[3]The *Cherokee Phoenix* has been published intermittently since 1838 (La Course, 1979), and is now available online at: http://www.cherokeephoenix.org

[4]Languages spoken by First Nations are not considered "third language," so this term applies specifically to the languages of immigrant groups.

[5]The full text of the CRTC policy is available at: http://www.ncra.ca/CRTC/PublicNotice/1999–117.html

[6]A common way for researchers to measure media exposure is to ask people about their media connections the day before.

[7]Flinders Island is an island in the Bass Strait, located about 20 kilometers off Cape Portland, at the northeastern tip of Tasmania, Australia.

PART II

The Consumers

CHAPTER 3

Immigrants and Their Media

CHAPTER OBJECTIVES

By the end of this chapter, you will have learned more about:

- The differences between immigrants and other types of migrants.
- How migration experiences are different depending on where people have come from and where they have settled.
- The roles that ethnic media play in immigration and settlement.

Why Immigration Matters

What percentage of the world's population do you think lives outside of the country where they were born? 10%? 25%? Maybe even more? Most of you will be surprised to learn that international estimates put the number around 3% (International Organization for Migration, 2005). If almost everyone stays where they are born, why do we hear so much about immigrants, and why does where they move to and how they settle matter so much? The answer lies in who immigrates. People who are the most likely to immigrate tend to be young and/or highly skilled (Fischer, Martin, & Straubhaar, 1997). This means that those who are most likely to move are disproportionately highly trained and educated, or alternatively, are young and capable of physically challenging work, in the case of low-skilled workers. Immigration therefore becomes a high-profile issue because sending countries stand to lose valuable parts of their workforces, and the country receiving these immigrants stand to gain a great deal from their strengths (Carrington & Detragiache, 1999).

Defining Immigration

To properly understand migration and the roles that media play in the movement and settlements of different groups of people, it is necessary to identify the differences between types of migrants. A *migrant* is any person who moves from one country to live in another one. A migrant can be either a *sojourner* or an *immigrant.* A sojourner is a migrant who only intends to spend a short time in the new country. An immigrant leaves the home country intending to make a permanent move. Many sojourners end up becoming immigrants when their temporary move stretches into permanent settlement in the host country.

Why is it important to distinguish between temporary and permanent movers? We make this distinction because people relate to their new environment differently if they are planning a permanent move rather than a temporary one. Sojourners, such as students who study abroad, are not likely to feel that they really need to learn their new environment because they will be going home soon. Sojourners' media connections will also focus mainly on home country news and events, reflecting a commitment to returning home. Immigrants, on the other hand, are usually more motivated to make conscious and unconscious changes in their behaviors, media connections, commitments, and relationships. For these reasons, this chapter is primarily concerned with immigrants and their media, rather than with sojourners.

People immigrate for a variety of reasons. Researchers generally distinguish between voluntary and involuntary immigrants, although this distinction is sometimes hard to make. *Voluntary immigrants* are motivated by economic reasons: seeking a better life. However, many people who leave their home countries because there are no jobs or very few opportunities for their children would be unlikely to describe their economic motivations as "voluntary." There are other kinds of voluntary immigrants, like family members who move to join relatives who are already settled in the host country, or people who move because they have married a citizen of another country.

Involuntary immigrants are asylum seekers and refugees who are given permission to live in a new country to escape war, personal persecution (for religious reasons, for example), or other similar dangers. There is a lot of controversy regarding which groups are granted refugee status and which are not. For example, Cuban immigrants receive automatic asylum in the U.S. (and therefore refugee status) upon arriving on American soil because they are fleeing a communist regime. In contrast, immigrants from El Salvador fleeing their country's civil war in the 1980s and 1990s were not granted refugee status by U.S. courts (Coutin, 2003). The official status immigrants are granted on arrival has a profound effect on their settlement patterns. Salvadorans were forced to choose between returning to El Salvador—which for many would have been a death sentence—or having to live in the United States without legal documentation.

Refugees in other countries also face difficult odds in their quests to gain asylum, and treatment also depends in part on one's country of origin. In the European Union, fewer than 5% of those seeking asylum are actually granted permanent petitions. During the 2001 genocide in Bosnia-Herzegovina, almost

Figure 3.1 Political Cartoon Responding to New Australian Restrictions on Asylum Seekers

Source: Cartoon by Nicholson from *The Australian.* www.nicholsoncartoons.com.au

all petitioners were granted at least temporary asylum in the EU. In contrast, the EU has not extended this kind of blanket acceptance, even temporarily, to applicants suffering from similar crises, such as the Darfur region of Sudan (Reynolds, 2002). Asylum seekers in Australia have also faced increasingly restrictive policies, as the cartoon above, originally published in *The Australian,* points out in an ironic way (see Figure 3.1).

How and why people immigrate are complex questions that are beyond the scope of this book to answer.[1] What is important to consider is that the conditions that prompt immigration profoundly impact how immigrants settle in their new country, as well as what issues arise during the processes of movement and settlement that can be addressed by the ethnic media. For example, the content of ethnic media serving involuntary immigrants may be different from that of media targeting voluntary immigrants, since the pre-migration and settlement experiences of these immigrants give rise to different sets of needs. Refugees who leave their countries under threat or after periods of deprivation or abuse of their human rights suffer disproportionately from conditions like post-traumatic stress disorder and other psychological and physical concerns resulting from their ill treatment (Chong, 2002). Media serving these populations may, for example, broach issues of mental health more frequently and in more depth than ethnic media serving voluntary migrants.

Ethnic media are part of immigrants' settlement experiences, which take place in the particular context of reception immigrants face upon arrival in their new country. In the next section, we detail the most important factors constituting immigrants' context of reception and their relationship both to ethnic media and to immigrant settlement.

Context of Reception

Many factors affect who is accepted by a host society, and who is not. Four major factors affect immigrants' *context of reception*, as developed by Portes and Rumbaut (1996). The first is the *policies of the host government*, including legal definitions of (il)legal migration and status—for example, who qualifies as a refugee. As we discuss in more detail in Chapter 7, government policies vary widely. For example, Austria only extends protections of free speech and publishing privileges to ethnic media produced by groups legally recognized as ethnic minorities (Böse, Haberfellner, & Koldas, 2002), whereas these rights are more universally protected in other EU countries. In these ways, production and consumption of ethnic media can be constrained by government policies.

The second factor is the *condition of the labor market*. In strong economic periods when jobs are plentiful, immigrants filling empty positions in the labor market may be welcomed. In an economic downturn, when immigrants are perceived as competition for the few jobs, government services, or housing resources available, immigrants will face a more hostile context of reception. However, even in difficult economic times, immigrants who possess education, trade knowledge, and other occupational skills highly valued by the host country may experience a more favorable context of reception than lower-skilled immigrants. For example, a professor hired from another country for his particular expertise may not face the social resistance that immigrants who do not possess such specialized skills might.

Immigrants who have skills that are not recognized or valued in the host country may face a loss in occupational status that forces them to compete for lower-skilled jobs or to reinvent themselves in new professions. Ethnic media can be one such occupational shift. Many ethnic media entrepreneurs were not involved in media production in their country of origin, but see economic opportunities in doing so in their new country.

The third factor, *characteristics of the settlement community*, affects immigrants most on a day-to-day basis. The immigrant or family that settles with others from the same home country will have a different immigration experience from the family that settles in a mixed ethnic community. Research shows that immigrants' decisions about where to settle are usually based on economic considerations. Poorer immigrants tend to settle in urban areas with other immigrants from their home country. These areas are called *ethnic enclaves* (Waldinger & Lichter, 2002), and these are the Japantowns, Little Ethiopias, or Koreatowns that are found in the urban areas of most major cities.

Most professional migrants do not settle in these poorer neighborhoods because their work is usually located elsewhere, and they can afford to live in the pricier suburbs (Alba, Logan, Stults, Marzan, & Zhang, 1999; Alba & Nee, 2003). Many immigrants who initially settle in ethnic communities may move out to the suburbs as their economic conditions improve. Some suburbs are ethnically diverse. Other suburbs, particularly in large cities, might be middle- or upper-class communities of immigrants from a particular country (Alba et al., 1999). In these instances, moving to the suburbs might mean an economic step up without having to leave the ethnic community, as is the case for mainland Chinese and Taiwanese-origin immigrants living in San Francisco's Peninsula and South Bay suburban regions, for example.

Immigrants who live in ethnic enclaves or ethnically homogeneous suburbs can maintain their cultural customs and language more easily than can immigrants living in ethnically mixed communities. In a Thai Town, for example, business can be conducted in Thai rather than English, and an ongoing influx of new Thai immigrants to these areas can replenish the linguistic vitality of these communities (Zentella, 1997). Children in these communities often speak their parent's native language at home and in the local community. For this reason, children are more likely to speak their parents' primary language fluently when they grow up in more ethnically concentrated communities (Alba & Nee, 2003; Lieberson, 1981; Lopez, 1996).

Ethnic enclaves and ethnically concentrated suburbs are also likely to have a range of ethnic media options. These media range from small "mom-and-pop" local publications and free newsletters to media produced by international conglomerates. The presence of these media further encourages children being bilingual as many of the media are produced in the immigrants' native language (Zentella, 1997). In a larger sense, ethnic media are carriers of the home culture. When they are seen and heard in the home, on the street, and in the public spaces of an immigrant community, they reinforce ethnic and cultural identity.

Immigrant parents who move their families to mixed-ethnic suburbs usually face unintended consequences of this decision (Alba & Nee, 2003). There are likely to be lower rates of bilingualism in the second generation, because children go to school with groups of mixed peers, parents work with individuals from a variety of backgrounds, and English is the common language at school and at work. Children in mixed ethnic suburbs can still be bilingual, but not hearing their parent's language outside of the home means that parents have to go to a lot of trouble to insure bilingualism in their children. Children who grow up in mixed-ethnic suburbs are more likely to develop habits of connecting to mainstream media, and if they are not bilingual, ethnic media produced in the home language may not be accessible to them at all.

Finally, attitudes toward immigrants in *the larger society* are part of the newcomer's context of reception (Portes & Rumbaut, 1996). Host country hostility toward outsiders can affect how and where immigrants settle and what kinds of jobs and opportunities are made available to them and their children (Martin & Nakayama, 2007b). Some immigrants may face more discrimination than others based on the color of their skin or country of origin. For example, Zolberg and Woon (1999) argue that the size and visibility of the Mexican immigrant community in the United States results in more discrimination and hostility than is experienced by other groups; they also contend that Muslim immigrants in Europe face similar prejudice for the same reasons. World events can also shift societal attitudes toward particular groups of immigrants. In the wake of the September 11, 2001, attacks, many countries have responded with stricter limitations on immigration from Muslim countries than they had in place before the attacks (Cainkar, 2002; Schildkraut, 2002).

Immigration restrictions can have a big impact on the development of ethnic media. Ethnic communities that have fewer new residents needing media content in the home language and/or information about settling in the new community have to shift their focus to cover news that suits the tastes of longer-settled readers. For example, when the Johnson-Reed Act restricted annual Syrian immigration to 100 people per year in 1924, media serving this population had to adapt to these restrictions in order to survive (Naff, 1987). *The Syrian World* (published between 1928 and 1932) was the first newspaper that explicitly targeted the needs and interests of the "Syrian American," meaning the American-born children of Syrian immigrants. Published in English, the editor's stated goal was to give readers

> a broader vision of their racial heritage . . . that our Syrian-American generation will come to better understand the country of their parents and appreciate more fully their racial endowments which constitute a valuable contribution to the country of their birth [the United States]. (Naff, 1987, p. 11)

This publication was a clear departure from media targeted to the immigrant generation, as a direct result of the legal restrictions placed on immigration from Syria.

The Syrian World represents one possible outcome of immigration restrictions, but some consequences are more clearly negative. When groups face a hostile reception from the host society, immigrants may choose to settle in less ethnically diverse areas to shield themselves from prejudice (Kasinitz, Waters, Mollenkopf, & Anil, 2002). Ethnic enclave communities can be distinct from the host society in terms of income, employment, educational attainment, and other social factors. When these distinctions are maintained because the host society desires to keep a group separated, we say that that migrant or ethnic minority group faces *segregation*. When migrants choose to maintain their original culture by avoiding interaction with the host culture, we call them *separatists*. The Amish, certain Muslim sects, and Hasidic Jews, are examples of separatist groups (Martin & Nakayama, 2007b).

Table 3.1 summarizes these four factors affecting immigrants' context of reception, and the potential outcomes each factor may have on ethnic media development.

Table 3.1 Relationship Between Immigrants' Context of Reception and the Development of Their Ethnic Media

Factors Affecting Immigrants' Context of Reception	Potential Impacts on Ethnic Media
• **Government policy:** Includes definitions of (il)legal migration, recognition of minority status and attendant rights.	• Restrictions in immigration policy, media policy, and freedom of speech can constrain or enable ethnic media production.
• **Labor market conditions:** Level of competition with other groups (immigrant and native born) for jobs.	• A strong labor market combined with open immigration policy can encourage a steady flow of new immigrants who create ongoing demand for ethnic media, and opportunities for ethnic media entrepreneurs.
• **Characteristics of the community of settlement:** Living in an ethnic enclave, ethnically homogenous or mixed-ethnic suburb has consequences for linguistic and cultural retention in the second generation.	• Settling in an ethnic enclave can provide consistent access to a wide range of ethnic media outlets and contribute to bilingualism in the second generation, giving them greater access to ethnic media produced in their parents' native language.
• **The larger society:** Attitudes toward immigrants generally, and potential hostility toward specific groups of immigrants can affect how and where immigrants settle.	• Hostility toward an immigrant group can result in restrictions on media-produced in home country languages, particularly in times of war. In other contexts, hostility from the larger society may encourage immigrants to develop ethnic media outlets that provide their community's perspective on their experiences and issues.

¤ For Further Discussion

Suppose two migrants from Chile both immigrate to the United States at the same time. Eduardo comes from a rural village, has little formal education, and only speaks Spanish. Carlos has a college degree, is fluent in English, and has years of work experience as an aeronautical engineer.

Refer to Table 3.1, and describe possible differences between Eduardo and Carlos' contexts of reception.

How you would expect Eduardo and Carlos' contexts of reception to affect:

1. The communities where Eduardo and Carlos would be likely to settle;
2. How these migrants would adapt to life in the host country; and
3. The media (ethnic and/or mainstream options) with which you think Eduardo and Carlos would be most likely to connect?

Most immigrants, however, are not separatists. Most immigrants wish to adapt to their new community and country, even as they may wish to maintain cultural and ethnic ties to their home countries. *Adaptation* is the long-term process of adjusting to and feeling comfortable in the host culture (Kim, 2005). Ethnic media can serve as important tools for immigrants' adaptation to their new environments.

Ethnic Media as Resources for Immigrants

Ethnic media serve an important function in connecting the immigrant to news and events in the home country (*connective function*), while also orienting the newcomer to their new community and new country (*orientation function*) (Adoni, Caspi, & Cohen, 2006). The introduction of new communication technologies has made the connective functions of ethnic media increasingly rapid and accessible. A good balance of connective and orientation stories contributes to the creation of a *dual frame of reference* (Reese, 2001) where immigrants know the norms of both the country of origin and the host country and can use both sets of cultural rules. Ethnic media can serve as resources for immigrants by serving both connective and orientation functions.

Understanding What Is Happening in the Settlement Community

As we discussed in Chapter 1, media can be teachers of culture for immigrants by portraying the social norms and communicative rules of the settlement country, which is key for developing a dual frame of reference. For example, ethnic media may include articles on how to enroll children in school (Valdés, 1996), open a bank account, or similar explicit guidance on how to get established in the local community. Ethnic media can be resources for new immigrants in learning about available health and social services in the community (Wilkin & Ball-Rokeach, 2006). News coverage of local events, cultural festivals, and community meetings can help immigrants connect with other residents and become integrated into their new communities.

For example, *New Vision—The Independent Refugee News and Information Service* in London serves Ethiopian refugees by connecting them with local resources (Georgiou, 2003). Calling itself "The Voice for the Voiceless," New Vision serves as a message board, updated with events, information, and news that affect refugees as they establish themselves in London. There are links to jobs and other community resources that new refugees might need to access when they arrive. The Web site also promotes positive images of refugees by reporting integration success stories, such as profiling a refugee trained as a nurse, or the UK-born children of refugees performing well in English schools (Georgiou, 2003).

Some ethnic media focus almost entirely on news from the country of origin and do not produce the kinds of stories that help immigrants learn about their new community. A study of Chinese, Korean, and Spanish-language ethnic newspapers in Los Angeles found that the ratio of home country to local community news has consequences for immigrants' sense of belonging to their new community

(Lin, Song, & Ball-Rokeach, in press). When ethnic newspapers focus entirely on home country news, readers are encouraged to look homeward (*connective function*), away from their new community (*orientation function*). Residents reported higher levels of belonging to their new community when newspapers told stories about that community in addition to providing home country news. We discuss ethnic media as local media in greater detail in Chapter 9.

Kerr (2007) found a similar imbalance between connective and orientation-related content in the Polish-language media in Ireland. Ireland imposed no restrictions on workers moving from states added to the EU in 2004, including Poland. Since then, ethnic media serving these newcomers have developed as rapidly as the Polish population itself has grown. When Kerr conducted research in Ireland at the beginning of the summer in 2006, there were three Polish-owned, Polish-language newspapers being produced in Dublin alone; one weekly, the other two fortnightly. By the end of that same summer, two more Polish-language print publications had emerged (Kerr, 2007, p. 177). Kerr found that these publications have a strong focus on the home country, in that there is "an implicit assumption by the producers that many Polish workers will return home, and that they have a constant need for basic information on Ireland and information about communicating, traveling and sending money home to Poland" (p. 186). Therefore, information provided on living in Ireland tends to be focused only on the bare necessities of temporary settlement, with most content related to ways to remain fully connected to the home country.

Immigrants in Germany also find that their ethnic media do not always strike the perfect balance between their connective and orientation functions. Geiβler and Weber-Menges (2009) surveyed 2,208 Turkish, Italian, and Russo-German immigrants living in Germany and found that the majority of all three groups think that ethnic media provide insufficient coverage of topics related to living in Germany. However, the majority of all three groups believed their ethnic media served a strong connective function by helping them sustain their language and culture and helping them manage feelings of homesickness. Italian and Turkish immigrants also indicated a desire to see inserts in their own language in the German media, demonstrating a desire for some merging between mainstream and ethnic media content.

Ethnic media serve different functions for different kinds of immigrants, and some immigrants have strong connections to both ethnic and mainstream media outlets. For example, professional immigrants who are more likely to live in mixed-ethnic neighborhoods are able to access mainstream and ethnic media sources due to their bilingual proficiencies. These professionals are able to connect with both mainstream and ethnic media outlets to stay on top of what is going on in their country of origin, their country of settlement, and in their local community as well (Bendixen & Associates, 2006; Durham, 2004). On the other hand, immigrants with limited English language proficiency are more likely to connect only with ethnic media outlets. This means when local news is missing from ethnic media content, these immigrants may not be able to access other media resources that can help them learn about their new community.

Some immigrants may face not only language barriers but literacy barriers as well. Ethnic radio broadcasts can be a valuable alternative for immigrants with limited literacy to connect with the news and information they need. This potential use for radio was first recognized with the advent of radio broadcasting in the U.S.

in the early 1900s: "Many émigrés could not read or write the languages of their mother tongues . . . the advent of an explicitly oral medium [radio] might have provided hope that there would soon be broadcasts in Italian, Spanish and other languages" (Browne, 2008, p. 24). Such broadcasts may have been slow to materialize, but today they provide limited literacy immigrants with information resources they may otherwise be unable to access.

Finding Jobs

For many immigrant groups, information that informs the decision to move, where to move to, and the availability of resources like jobs and housing comes from family, friends, and other members of their communities. Many people immigrate because a friend or family member has arranged a job for them (Waldinger & Lichter, 2002). This is the reason why immigrants from a particular hometown tend to settle in the same places.

For skilled immigrants, ethnic media can be a crucial part of finding work before moving. Family and friends can inform a potential migrant of job opportunities in businesses owned by other immigrants who often advertise in the ethnic media or in online postings. Once potential migrants contact the hiring company and secure jobs and necessary visas, they would make the decision to migrate. As discussed in Chapter 1, immigrant-receiving countries have ties with the developing countries that are their largest sources of migrant workers. Connections between emigrant-sending and immigrant-receiving countries may be the result of previous colonization, as is the case of Great Britain with Jamaica, India, and Pakistan, and of France with the countries of North Africa. Sending/receiving country connections can also result from the global nature of business today, as in the case with China's migration flows to the United States (Martin & Nakayama, 2007a).

Close ties between the sending and receiving countries can prepare immigrants for life in that new place (Sassen, 1998). For example, working for a British-owned company in India can prepare a potential migrant for the corporate culture and values of British business, making a potential migration to Britain more likely. Media produced in India as well as ethnic media targeted to Indians living in Britain can be transmitted by satellite. These media are information resources for potential immigrants as they decide whether to stay or go. India, by virtue of its strong historical and cultural links, has a high *degree of international interaction* (Sassen, 1998) with Britain. Media content contributes to the degree of international interaction, because media content and images can reinforce familiarity with Britain's culture and history, making assimilating seem less difficult to potential migrants. Migration therefore becomes more likely.

Understanding Their Rights

Ethnic media can play important roles for new immigrants in developing an understanding of their rights in the host society. For example, new immigration or citizenship policies often prompt ethnic media to cover these changes in a way that informs new immigrants about how these changes will affect them. Coverage might include a step-by-step explanation of the changes or requirements and information about where to file necessary forms or to get help (Pew Project for Excellence in Journalism [PEJ], 2009a). Advertisements in ethnic media for immigration attorneys and related professional aid can be additional resources.

Proposed changes in immigration policy can also incite ethnic media to galvanize the community for protests or demonstrations. In Los Angeles in 2006, for example, disk jockeys for the three largest Spanish-language radio stations encouraged a peaceful protest of proposed U.S. immigration reform. Almost half a million listeners were mobilized, many of whom were new immigrants (Félix, González, & Ramírez, 2008). Figure 3.2 is a collection of pictures taken at that immigration rally.

Figure 3.2 The immigration rallies that took place in Los Angeles and nationwide on May 1, 2006, were advertised and participation was heavily encouraged by Spanish-language radio disk jockeys. These rallies gave immigrants and their supporters an opportunity to peaceably register their opposition to proposed legislative changes to immigration policy in the U.S. These pictures were taken at the Los Angeles rally, and the poster in the picture at bottom right aims to tie the plight of current immigration issues to the historical origins of the United States as a nation of immigrants.

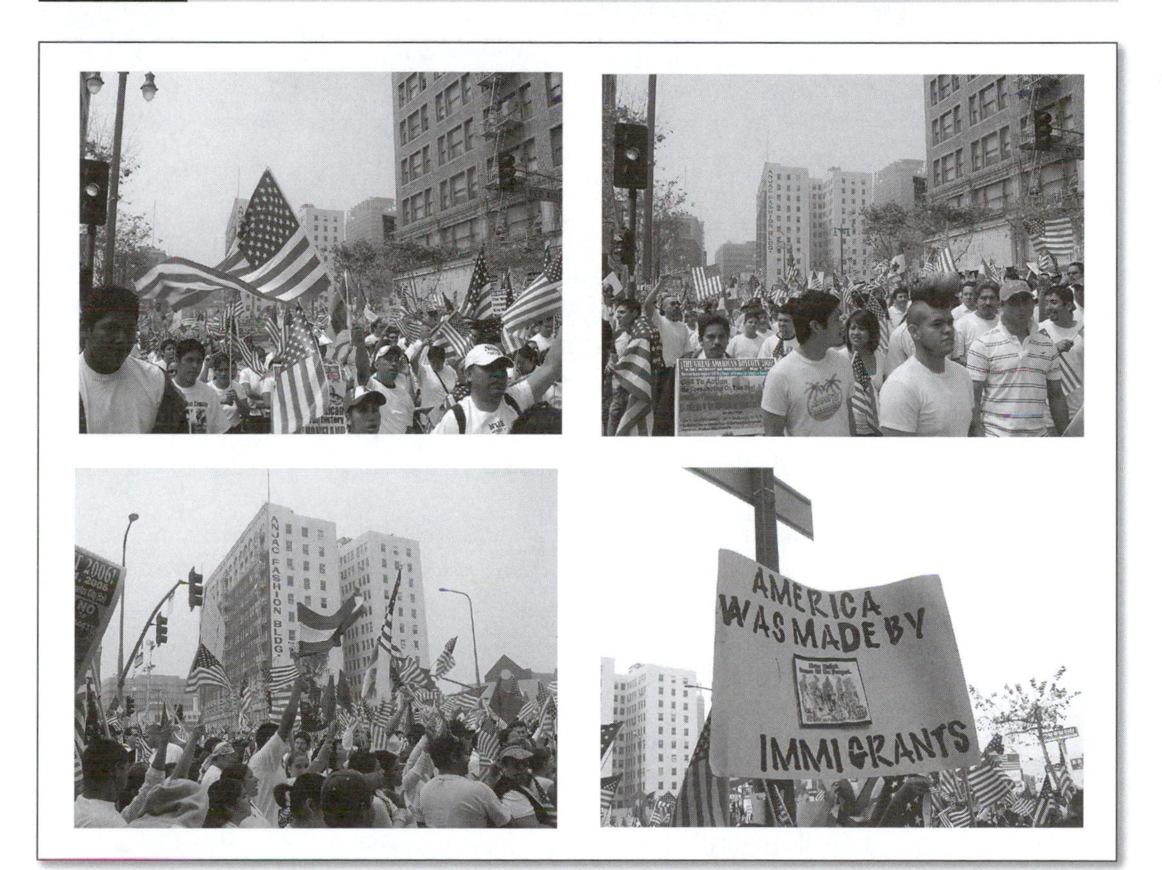

Photos: Michelle Hawks.

Ethnic media play similarly important roles in educating their communities about voting rights. During the 2008 U.S. election period, the Pew Project for Excellence in Journalism (2009) found that Latino and African-American media took more of a hands-on approach to election reporting than their mainstream counterparts. Specifically, they found that:

> In many cases the ethnic media acted as teachers, voter-advocates and even watchdogs . . . Spanish-language and African American newspapers devoted more than twice the space as English-language ones to explaining specifics on voting, such as necessary documents and when polls close. (PEJ, 2009a)

These media outlets also kept a close eye on potential irregularities at voting booths and explained what their readers should do if they were turned away from a voting booth.

As these examples illustrate and as we will discuss further in Chapter 10, there are times when ethnic media organizations may balance the values of journalistic "objectivity" and community advocacy differently from their mainstream media counterparts.

¤ For Further Discussion

The 8 o'clock news on a U.S.-based ethnic television station reports that they have confirmed that ICE (Immigration and Customs Enforcement) will be conducting a surprise raid the next day in a certain neighborhood to round up undocumented immigrants for deportation.

- Do you think that the station should have reported this story? Why or why not?
- Do you think this story differs from reporting other public interest stories, such as, for example, naming restaurants that have recently failed a health test or reporting on a particular disease that disproportionately afflicts that ethnic community? Is this news story in the public interest?
- Does this report violate the notion of "objectivity" in reporting? Why or why not?

Ethnic media can serve other advocacy roles. For example, in the wake of Hurricane Katrina in 2006, New Orleans residents began returning to a city where there was fierce competition for the few remaining apartments. Black newspapers ran a stinging series of editorials on what they called "linguistic profiling" (Bullock, 2006). An investigation conducted by the National Fair Housing Alliance had Black and White callers inquire about available apartments. They found that landlords were discriminating based on accent, renting to people who "sounded White," and telling callers who "sounded Black" that the apartment was taken. These findings were printed alongside information about renter's rights, state and national policies on racial discrimination in housing, and legal resources for people who had experienced this discrimination firsthand.

Immigrants often struggle with linguistic profiling as well. Ethnic media can be instrumental in informing newcomers of their legal right to fight linguistic profiling and other discriminatory practices. Ethnic media can also teach newcomers about their rights to freedom of speech, religious practice, assembly, and peaceable protest. For many immigrants, these rights are not protected in their countries of origin. Particularly in the case of refugees, having protections for such rights may have been their reason for seeking refuge in the first place.

Connecting to Immigrants With Similar Experiences

Ethnic media are important resources for new immigrants in their own right, but can also work to connect newcomers to other immigrants with similar experiences. Immigrants can become resources for each other by sharing information about available services and events in the new community.

Connections with other new immigrants matter for a number of reasons. Relationships with other migrants, family, and friends from the same home country affect the degree of *culture shock* new immigrants experience in their initial adaptation. Culture shock is defined as the set of short-term feelings of disorientation and discomfort caused by unfamiliar surroundings. The stress and anxiety resulting from the need to relearn "natural processes," like how to buy groceries, order a meal, or express oneself in a new language or dialect, are all examples of culture shock. Culture shock causes immigrants to question many of their own cultural habits and ways of doing things, which have to be modified or replaced to get by in their new environment (Kim, 2002; Kim, 2005). Ethnic media are much more likely to include information that can help immigrants get through their initial culture shock than mainstream media sources that do not directly target a new immigrant audience.

For new immigrants who arrive without a support system in place (e.g., family or friends living in the local community), ethnic media can be especially useful for locating other immigrants from the same home country who have similar interests. For example, ethnic media often have community calendars giving the time and location of events related to religious organizations, recreational activities, or hometown associations. Ethnic media thus can serve as links between new arrivals and local organizations and activities, putting the newcomers in touch with other members of the community.

In 1999, 3CW Radio in Melbourne became the first 24-hour Chinese-language radio station operating in Australia. In Australia, as in other parts of the Chinese diaspora, community members believe that there are "three pillars" that maintain a Chinese identity and lifestyle in a new environment: Chinese community associations, newspapers, and schools (Gao, 2006; Li, 1999). While newspapers, including *Huaxia,* which is owned by the same company as 3CW, are important elements of community life, 3CW is perceived by community members as connecting all three "pillars." According to Gao (2006), listeners see 3CW as having three primary roles in the community: supporting community businesses, coordinating social and cultural activities and events, and providing a platform for community members to share ideas, opinions, and information. In these ways, 3CW connects residents to community organizations and associations, provides them with information resources, and helps to educate the community on local and international issues that affect them. By informing newcomers about community events, issues, and organizations, 3CW provides new immigrants with ways to connect with other immigrants and become integrated into local support networks.

Keeping Up With Developments in the Home Country and Community

Ethnic media's orientation functions are generally coupled with connective functions, by providing immigrants with news from the country and community they have left behind. New communication technologies make it possible to keep up with home country events in real time. In addition, many ethnic media organizations are actually transnational organizations, with offices in the country of origin and in major immigrant-receiving countries. Immigrants can connect with the same newspapers, for example, that they received in the country of origin with an insert that covers events and news from the host community as well (Lin, Song, & Ball-Rokeach, in press).

The concept of transnationalism has become very popular in immigration research in the United States and in Europe. It was originally borrowed from research on business, where "transnational" referred to businesses that operate in more than one country. Large ethnic media corporations are often transnational. The term, however, is increasingly used to describe individual migrants' experiences of being both "here" and "there." In this context, *transnationalism* is defined as the set of connections that individuals maintain across borders between their home and host country (Levitt & Waters, 2002). These home-host country connections could be interpersonal, such as phone calls to family members, but are also made through a wider range of media connections.

The day-to-day connections maintained by most immigrants are with individuals or news in the particular region or town that they come from, rather than national news from the home country (Waldinger & Fitzgerald, 2004). Immigrants generally focus more on national-level coverage when a crisis or major event occurs in the home country. Crises bring the nation or the ethnic group to the forefront, and generally increase immigrants' dependence on ethnic media. This trend was certainly visible in the days following the September 11, 2001, attacks on the United States (Kim, Jung, Cohen, & Ball-Rokeach, 2004). As the United States declared war on Afghanistan in the days following 9/11, with Britain following soon after, Afghani residents of the United Kingdom and Germany became "active viewers" of ethnic media to follow the events in their country of origin (Mousavi, 2006). Afghani immigrants reported that they felt Western media were biased, and therefore depended primarily on ethnic media and satellite broadcasts for news they felt they could trust (Mousavi, 2006).

During the same post-9/11 period, a large-scale survey revealed that Britain's Arabic-speaking population turned to *Al-Jazeera,* a major Arabic news network, because they believed that coverage was "more credible and balanced" than CNN or the BBC (Miladi, 2006, p. 947). These studies, including a third conducted with

British Arab Muslim audiences in Wales (Harb & Bessaiso, 2006), found that times of crisis increase the strength of immigrants' connections to ethnic media—not just for trusted news, but as a reinforcement of ethnic identity. In all cases, Muslims indicated they sought out news sources that reinforced a positive image of Islam and Muslims living in Europe.

Ethnic media can serve similar functions in more routine times as well. In a Cypriot Greek community in London, Georgiou (2001a) observed people viewing the 6 p.m. news broadcast in a local Cypriot community center. She found this public and communal viewing of ethnic media fostered a sense of community. A core group of immigrants attended this nightly ritual, but the group expanded when there was a big event on the island of Cyprus. Following their viewing of the broadcast, members of the community would stay to discuss and debate the latest news events. This ritual of nightly viewing and discussion would be less remarkable if these immigrants could not watch the news broadcast at home. However, Georgiou found that more than a third of the regular nightly viewers had satellite cable and, therefore, could have watched the broadcast privately. The news became more than a daily update on Cyprus when shared and discussed with family, friends, and members of the community. This is why people would go the trouble of attending this evening ritual.

¤ For Further Discussion

Imagine that you are an Indonesian immigrant living in Sydney, Australia. A recent dispute between Indonesia and Australia over control of the waterways between the two countries has made you depend on and connect with Indonesian ethnic media more than you usually do, to follow the events as they unfold.

For the duration of this particular event, how do you think increased awareness of your nationality or ethnicity might affect:

- Relationships with friends from other ethnic groups, including the Australian majority?
- How you define your own identity–are you Indonesian, Australian, or both?
- Interactions with other Australians as you go about your daily activities?

Online Ethnic Media Resources for Immigrants

There are stark differences between immigrant groups' rates of Internet access (DeBell & Chapman, 2006) and, thus, their likelihood of connecting to online ethnic media content. For many groups, Internet access remains limited due to both financial and literacy barriers. There may also be a lack of *new media literacy*, meaning a lack of familiarity, knowledge, and/or comfort with new communication technologies like computers and the Internet (Kress, 2003; Potter, 2004). Traditional literacy, meaning reading and writing (either in the language of origin or in the language of the host country), may also be an obstacle for many immigrants who have not been formally educated in either the home or host country.

The majority of ethnic media lack an online presence. For many producers, the cost of creating and maintaining a virtual presence is prohibitively high, particularly if their audiences are not connecting to the Internet in large numbers. The Pew Project for Excellence in Journalism (2009) also indicates that many ethnic media outlets have not gone online due to difficulties estimating potential online advertising revenue, which is less straightforward than calculating advertising revenue from print formats. We discuss the influence of consumer demand on ethnic media production in more detail in Chapters 5 and 6.

For immigrant groups that do access the Internet in significant numbers, online ethnic media content can facilitate connections to both host and home country news around the clock. New evidence suggests that increasing numbers of ethnic media outlets are going online and are providing English-language content in recognition of the needs of second and third-generation connectors. For example, *Nguoi Viet*, a newspaper serving the Southern California Vietnamese-origin community, offers readers the choice between *Nguoi Viet Online* in Vietnamese and *Nguoi Viet 2* in English. Even ethnic media producers serving immigrant communities with limited new media literacy may see potential profit in providing online content for the children of immigrants. The second generation is generally more media literate than their first generation parents.

Online ethnic media that consciously target second generation audiences are emerging in many places. These often seek to appeal to *conglomerate identities* of a growing number of second-generation youths who identify, for example, with a conglomerate "Asian" identity rather than a more specific "Chinese-American" or "Korean-American" identity. *A*, a magazine that targeted second-generation Asian youth in the United States, closed in 2002, but was quickly replaced by *Hyphen* magazine, which has a strong online presence and Web-only components available for consumers at *hyphenmagazine.com*. *Africana.com* has no offline presence, but is geared to a conglomerate African identity. This site became so popular that it was bought out and incorporated into America Online's *blackvoices.aol.com* (Hsu, 2002). We examine conglomerate identities in more detail in Chapter 4.

In Austria, collaborations between radio stations targeting African communities living in that country have led to the development of a shared online presence. Over the last 10 years, Radio 1476 and Radio Africa have established Internet services that supplement their radio content and have cooperated with other ethnic broadcasters to create African television programs in Vienna as well (Herczeg, 2009). And in Ireland, the Internet facilitated the development of *Africans Magazine* as an inexpensive medium for launching a magazine, which later became a print version as well when the online version had helped the editors secure the necessary funds for printing (Ugba, 2002).

Africans Magazine's strategy may have worked in part because immigrants to Ireland appear to disproportionately access the Internet with the goal of connecting to both local and home country news. O'Donnell and Ní Leathlobhair's (2002) study of immigrants and ethnic minorities in Ireland reported that connecting with "news and newspapers from home" and with "their communities, both in Ireland and at home" was the third most popular reason for these groups to go online

(p. 12). However, Ugba (2002) points out that Ireland has one of the most expensive Internet connection rates in Europe, and that there are few well-maintained places where Irish residents may access the Internet for free, such as public libraries. These factors likely indicate that there are real barriers to online access in Ireland, even if immigrants to Ireland are more connected to the Internet than newcomers in other countries.

Finally, Web sites linked to hometown associations are a popular form of ethnic media among Latinos in the United States, even though Internet penetration is generally low in these communities (DeBell & Chapman, 2006; Livingston, Parker & Fox, 2009). Hometown associations have been a feature of immigration, particularly amongst Mexican-origin migrants, for more than 100 years (Fitzgerald, 2008). Recall earlier in this chapter when we noted that immigrants from the same hometown tend to move to the same community in the host country. As the population of immigrants from a particular hometown grows, hometown associations are started in order to develop a formal connection between the two places. These hometown associations often take on improvement and development projects in their hometown, including building and supplying hospitals and sport stadiums, resurfacing roads, and setting up electricity plants[2] (Fitzgerald, 2008). As part of this connection, many hometown associations have active Web sites, where news from the hometown (*connective function*) and the host community (*orientation function*) are regularly published along with news on fundraising for ongoing hometown projects. Many hometown association Web pages have added webcams to their sites. These cameras are usually placed in the hometown's main square, so that immigrants can watch what is going on "back home," in real time.

As the examples in this section demonstrate, online ethnic media are developing asymmetrically as resources for immigrants. In some communities, new communication technologies are valuable platforms for ethnic media to reach large audiences quickly with relatively low costs. In other communities, low media literacy rates make online ethnic media less viable and attractive options. However, this area of ethnic media development is relatively new and is still taking shape. In the coming years, clearer patterns may emerge as to the shape that online ethnic media outlets are taking.

Summary

This chapter focused on immigration to identify who moves and why and how these experiences might be different depending on their pre-immigration experiences and their context of reception in the host country. Ethnic media serves a *connective function* to the news and events of the home country. These media also serve an *orientation function* by familiarizing newcomers with resources in the local community, and explaining the laws, protections, and norms afforded by the host country. In the next chapter, we focus on the *symbolic functions* of the ethnic media in the maintenance and creation of ethnic minority identities.

Study Questions

1. Select a home and host country of your choice, and refer to Table 3.1. How would you describe the context of reception you think an immigrant from that country would encounter in the host country you have chosen? Give reasons for your answers to each of the four factors, and consider how ethnic media could potentially help that immigrant to deal with the settlement challenges you have identified that he or she may face.

2. Under section heading, "Understanding What Is Happening in the Settlement Community," a study of Korean, Chinese, and Spanish-language newspapers showed immigrants' feelings of belonging to their new community relates to ethnic media's coverage of the local area. What particular kinds of content do you think would help improve immigrants' feelings of belonging to their new community?

3. Under section heading, "Finding Jobs," the degree of international interaction between India as an emigrant-sending country and Britain as an immigrant-receiving country illustrated how ties of history, culture, and media can make a move seem more viable for potential migrants. Can you think of other ways that these media can help the migration process, or might misrepresent the challenges of moving?

4. Under section heading, "Keeping Up With Developments in the Home Country and Community," we discussed immigrants' increased dependence on ethnic media during crises in the home country. How do you think spending more time with ethnic media would affect connections to other media forms during that time? For example, do you think that immigrants would spend more, less, or the same amounts of time connecting with mainstream media, or the Internet? Provide support for your answer.

5. Using terms and ideas from this chapter, describe (using examples as necessary) how ethnic media may contribute to immigrants' ability to create a dual frame of reference, as discussed under heading, "Online Ethnic Media as Resources for Immigrants."

Notes

[1]For more comprehensive answers to these migration questions, please see Castles and Miller (2009) and Massey et al. (2005).

[2]See http://sixthsection.com for more information on a hometown association that connects immigrants living in New York with their hometown in Mexico.

CHAPTER 4

Ethnic Minorities and Their Media

CHAPTER OBJECTIVES

By the end of this chapter, you will have learned more about:

- How ethnic minority groups define themselves.
- How ethnic media and ethnic identities can reinforce each other.
- The roles ethnic media have played in social movements around the world.
- Key issues for creating ethnic media that are responsive to the changing tastes and needs of their audiences.

What Is an Ethnic Minority?

The term *ethnic minority* is only one of many ways that we might reference peoples who are part of culturally, racially, and/or ethnically distinct groups. The term "minority" can be misleading, because many urban centers no longer have a clear majority group. For example, Latinos in Los Angeles are referred to as an "ethnic minority" even though Latinos and Whites are about the same proportion of the overall population. There are cities in Northern England where Indian, Pakistani, or Bangladeshi immigrants and their descendents are the clear majority—and yet, the term "minority" remains. When the term "ethnic minority" is used in this book, we are referring to (1) *indigenous peoples*, such as Aborigines in Australia or Native Americans in the United States, (2) peoples who are *language minorities* living in their country of origin, such as the Breton in France or the Q'eqchi in Guatemala, or (3) peoples who are the *descendents of immigrants.* These may be the descendents of voluntary immigrants, of refugees, or of involuntary immigrants, such as African-Americans.

Racial Versus Ethnic Identities

The differences between ethnicity and race are complex, and many scholars have been discussing the definitions of these terms for many years. For our purposes in talking about media, ethnicity is a more useful term than race. Why? Because, as we will learn in this chapter, the development of an ethnic identity, and of media that reflect this identification, is something *that people do for themselves.* Race is often something that is assigned to a minority group by another, more dominant group. These racial assignments can differ from place to place. For example, a person who is racially labeled as Black in America might be considered *mestizo* (of mixed heritage) in Mexico (Cornell & Hartmann, 1998), or considered Moreno or Pardo in Brazil.

The distinctions between race and ethnicity also play a large part in what we know about particular groups of people, and what people call themselves. For example, little attention has been paid to ethnic media serving African-origin groups living in the U.S. because of the assumption that the needs and concerns of Black people, regardless of their backgrounds, will generally be the same as those of African-Americans (Viswanath & Lee, 2007). This would be a generalization based solely on *race:* Africans and African-Americans are both phenotypically Black, but their *ethnicities* are distinct and their needs and tastes are different.

The same is true for Caribbean-origin peoples, who often do not consider themselves African-American (Waters, 2000). These groups have long histories of producing ethnic media in English in their adopted countries. For example, Radio Tropicale, which began in 1989, was the first 24-hour radio broadcast in French/Creole, targeting Caribbean-origin groups living in the New York region (Viswanath & Lee, 2007). Peoples from the same country of origin may also have vastly different experiences settling in different countries. For example, Caribbean-origin communities living in the U.S. do not have the long histories of settlement that the Caribbean communities in Britain do. Caribbean communities have been settled in Britain since colonial times and, as such, have a wide range of ethnic media that have been established over many years. The more recent influx of African immigrants to the UK does not connect with these same media (Georgiou, 2003). Again, although peoples of Caribbean and African descent may share a racial classification, their ethnicities are clearly distinct.

Groups that are ethnically different and yet racially considered the same often face the question of what to call themselves. For example, Aboriginal newspapers in Australia were the site of a long debate over how to self-identify, and many newspaper writers involved in this debate took into consideration how ethnic minorities in other countries had chosen to self-identify. Since their skins were dark, the writers mused did this mean that Aborigines were Black, like African-Americans? Despite similarities in skin color, Aboriginal editors decided that they had more of a historical brotherhood with the "Red" Native-Americans than with African-Americans (Rose, 1996), because of their similar experiences following the arrival of Europeans in their respective countries. This illustrates that ethnic identities are developed partly through comparing oneself to others, whether the others are the majority group in a society or are other ethnic minority groups. Ethnicity is not a fixed category. Ethnicity is something that members of a minority group can—and do—define over and over again for themselves, and the ethnic media are often the loudspeaker through which these debates are conducted.

Developing Ethnic Identities

So, what does it mean to have an ethnic identity, and how does such an identity develop? For most people, an ethnic identity is developed early in life. Parents and communities are often the first teachers of ethnic identity, and ethnic media can reinforce these lessons. Ethnic identity can be conceptualized as having three main dimensions (Martin & Nakayama, 2007b). First, one needs to possess the necessary cultural knowledge associated with that identity, which might include traditions, customs, and values. This is called the *cognitive dimension* of ethnic identity formation that develops via lessons taught by older members of the ethnic group. However, it is not enough to just *know* the cultural tenets of the ethnic group; one also has to behave in accordance with group norms, which is the *behavioral dimension* of an ethnic identity. Finally, there is the *affective dimension,* which refers to feelings of belonging to a particular ethnic group, and to identifying with its history and its current concerns. Figure 4.1 shows that these three dimensions of an ethnic identity are interrelated.

These three dimensions are not only interrelated, but they can reinforce each other. For example, a child raised with a Jewish ethnic identity will learn the traditions associated with the different Jewish holidays (*cognitive dimension*), how to cook certain foods, and will also be expected to go to synagogue on certain days (*behavioral dimension*). However, if this child does not develop a feeling of belonging to a Jewish culture (*affective dimension*), she may not continue to maintain these

Figure 4.1 Three Dimensions of an Ethnic Identity, Shown as Interconnected and Mutually Reinforcing

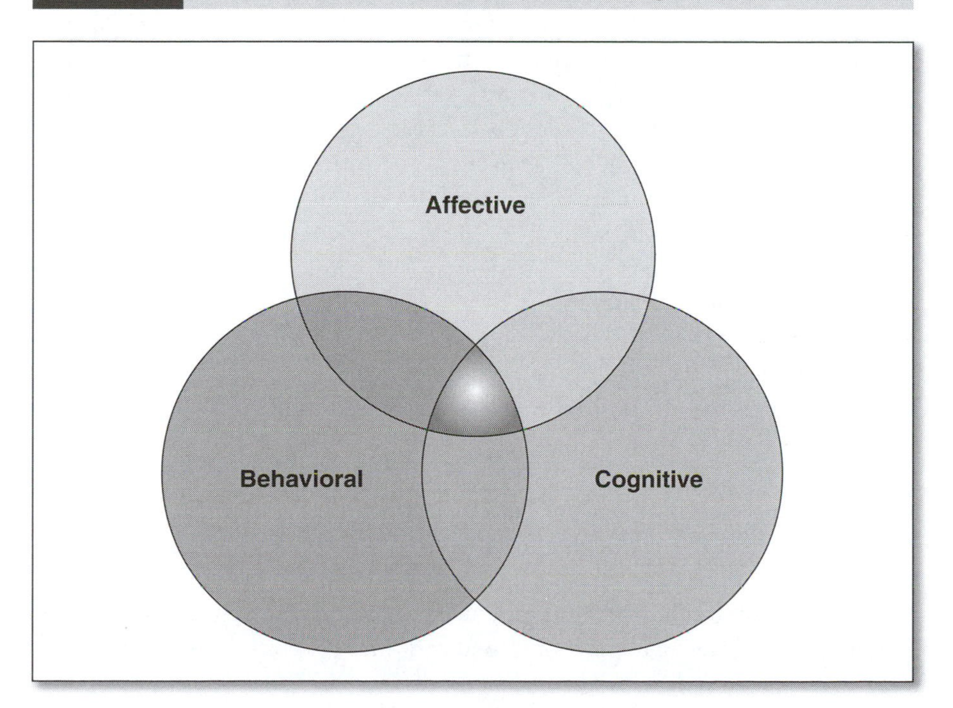

practices when she has left home and is living on her own. This is where ethnic media can be very important in the maintenance of ethnic identity. There are a large number of U.S.-based Jewish publications printed in English, Hebrew, and to a lesser degree, in Yiddish (Goren, 1987). Jewish media aimed at college students and young adults can encourage this young woman to build a personal, emotional tie to the ethnic identity she began to develop as a child. These ethnic media, aside from educating her on social issues related to Judaism, can also connect her with other young people from the same ethnic group. Ethnic media, then, can be a way for her to meet others like her, and to create an ethnic support network of her own.

It is important to remember that an ethnic identity is not an object passed from one generation to another without changing. Identity is not like a piece of heirloom jewelry. Rather, an ethnic identity is dynamic; it can, and does, change over time and situations. An ethnic identity might be born at home, but it has to be developed in adulthood in a way that is relevant and valuable to particular individuals or groups. Ethnic media can be an important platform for negotiating ethnic identity in different contexts. In the following sections, we highlight three prominent types of ethnic identity formations and the relationships between these types of identities and ethnic media.

Developing Hyphenated Identities

When someone identifies as Chinese-American or British-Pakistani, this describes a *hyphenated identity*, where two distinct parts are joined because one person lives these two cultural traditions. "Life on the hyphen" (Perez-Firmat, 1994) can be a challenging personal experience at times when the two sets of cultural rules clash. Living on the hyphen can also be difficult for an ethnic group as a whole, and for their media. For example, the Swedish-American community and their media found themselves in an uncomfortable position during the Vietnam War. The United States was deeply involved in Vietnam, and Sweden publicly criticized and opposed America by being the first country to recognize North Vietnam (Burton, 2003).

Unlike German-Americans or today's Arab-Americans, the Swedish-American community had never had to consider a clash between the two sides of their hyphenated identity. "They never had to choose between defending their homeland and distancing themselves from it before. If they distanced themselves from Sweden, were they still fully Swedish? . . . If they supported Sweden, were they real Americans?" (Burton, 2003, p. 275). Many of the ethnic presses sidestepped the issue by focusing on entertainment and social information rather than politics. The long-settled Swedish-American community accepted this softer role of their media. This meant that when Swedish newspapers provided material to the Swedish-American papers that expressed the uncensored Swedish view of the Vietnam War, readers were no longer paying full attention, because they read these newspapers primarily for light entertainment, as long as the Vietnam War remained the divisive issue for their community (Burton, 2003, p. 288).

The relationships between nations can also boost interest in ethnic media over multiple generations to reinforce a hyphenated identity. When the first English-language Syrian publication was produced in the United States in 1928 in response to the growing number of second and third generation youth who could not read Arabic, many believed this to be the beginning of the end of Syrian media (Naff, 1987). However, America's active involvement in Middle Eastern politics over the following decades revived Syrian-American media in both English and Arabic. Today, these media continue to provide information and opinions on the Middle East that are not found in the mainstream media (Viswanath & Lee, 2007).

Developing Conglomerate Identities

While many groups experience life on the hyphen (Perez-Firmat, 1994) over multiple generations, some ethnic minority youth are now identifying themselves as Asian-American or Asian-British instead of Chinese-American or British-Pakistani.[1] These *conglomerate identities* are a shift away from identifying with a particular country of origin toward acknowledging a larger shared experience with people who the mainstream often assumes are members of the same group. Writers like Wu (2002) and Dávila (2001) discuss the common experience of being mistaken for another ethnic group, such as the assumption that all Asian-Americans are of Chinese origin, or all Latinos are of Mexican-origin. Mainstream media and advertisers have also played a central role in the creation and reinforcement of conglomerate identities, which they use to define ethnic minority youths' media consumption and purchasing patterns (Dávila, 2001).

Kasinitz (2004) and others question whether the rise of conglomerate identities is a new way of self-identifying, or if minority youth are just accepting the blanket racial/ethnic categories that mainstream society and/or mainstream marketers assign to them. Either way, conglomerate identities are changing the ways that people live. Youth who identify themselves as Asian-American, for example, may not see marriages between people from different Asian countries of origin as "intermarriage" anymore (Kasinitz, 2004), contributing to a rise in the number of couples who will raise children with a conglomerate sense of ethnic identity.

Conglomerate identities also affect the types of media that ethnic minorities choose to connect with. A growing number of ethnic media outlets are covering issues central to young people by consciously trying to reflect and encourage a conglomerate sense of identity with its content. One example is the rise of *Latina* magazine, which covers issues and topics related to Latin America for women born and raised in the U.S., in a self-conscious mix of Spanish and English. Such publications are developing in other parts of the world as well. Figure 4.2 is a snapshot of a typical magazine rack in London, where a large range of magazines appealing to women's conglomerate Asian identities are available.

Conglomerate identities are sometimes encouraged in social campaigns to bring together groups suffering similar discriminations so that they can address common problems. However, ethnic media that appeal to conglomerate identities generally do not enjoy the same levels of popularity that ethnic media that target specific groups do (PEJ, 2009a). In part, this may be because ethnic identities are closely tied to particular social conditions, and the boundaries of a conglomerate identity may shift to include or exclude different groups at different times, making it difficult for producers to define the boundaries of a conglomerate ethnic media audience.

Figure 4.2 Fashion Magazines Targeting a Conglomerate Asian Audience, in London

Photo: Vikki Katz.

Developing Hybrid Identities

Even more recent than the rise of conglomerate identities, there has been increasing research interest in whether youth may be developing *hybrid identities* (Gilroy, 1993). This term implies the mixing of two identities—that of the ancestral country and of the country of settlement—coming together to create something new that is not recognizably of either culture. Examples of ethnic media that serve hybrid identities are recent and are primarily related to music production and radio broadcasting. For example, in France's North African communities, second and third generation youth have established two radio stations that broadcast in a mix of French and their ancestral African dialects. These youth have developed a new genre of music called *raï* that mixes home and host country traditions, just as these youth themselves identify themselves as a mix of two cultures (Echchaibi, 2001).

Youth of East Indian-origin in New York have made similar moves, mixing traditional Hindu sounds with American rap and hip hop lyrics to create *bhangra* music that plays in the clubs these young adults go to with their friends (Maira, 2002). The popularity of *bhangra* music in New York is being mirrored on the streets of London. These new music forms reflect youth identification with two cultures and their desire to make something that draws from both in order to create something new and different. The hybrid identities in these music forms are reinforced when ethnic minority youth go to clubs and other events to play or listen to "their own" types of music with other second generation youth like themselves.

Ethnic Media and Identity Formation

Our preceding discussion makes it clear that ethnic media develop as expressions of different types of ethnic identities, but also that ethnic identities are developed, negotiated, and reinforced by media that serve these ethnic groups. Ethnic identity development and ethnic media development can, therefore, be mutually reinforcing. Earlier, we considered three components of ethnic identity development and how ethnic media might transmit the cultural knowledge associated with an ethnic identity (*cognitive dimension*), serve as a way for individuals to express that ethnic identity (*behavioral dimension*), and encourage a sense of belonging and pride in that ethnic group identity (*affective dimension*).

For hyphenated, conglomerate, and hybrid identity formations—among the many other potential formations—the ways that ethnic media may support these three dimensions of ethnic identity may be quite different. However, it is important to remember that individuals do not consciously "choose" one type of ethnic identity, nor does identifying with a conglomerate identity (for example, Arab-American) preclude the possibility that in other contexts, that same person might identify with a hyphenated identity (e.g., Iraqi-American). Ethnic identities are negotiated on an ongoing basis, and ethnic media can be spaces where people negotiate how they identify themselves and their communities.

¤ For Further Discussion

Review our discussion of hyphenated, conglomerate, or hybrid identity formations discussed in the preceding sections.

How do you think a *bhangra* radio station in New York might support the cognitive, behavioral, and affective components of their target audience's ethnic identity, and how might this differ from the ways an Italian-Australian newspaper might fulfill these functions for their target community?

Ethnic media's role in negotiating and reinforcing ethnic identities is one of the many, often interrelated, functions that ethnic media can serve. In the following sections we take a look at some of the other key functions that ethnic media serve in ethnic minority communities.

Ethnic Media's Roles in Ethnic Minority Communities

In Chapter 3, we discussed how ethnic media develop in response to the particular needs of the immigrant communities that they serve. Just as ethnic media serving one particular immigrant community may cover issues that the ethnic media of another immigrant community do not, ethnic media serving particular ethnic minority communities are tailored to respond to the needs and concerns of their target communities. Ethnic media development has followed an uneven course across ethnic minority communities and across different countries, growing in response to ethnic communities' needs that presented themselves at particular points in time.

An Independent Voice

Ethnic media often emerge from a community feeling a need for a voice of its own. Tired of hearing their group cast in a negative light or not hearing their concerns discussed in the mainstream media, people may decide to produce their own media. Print media tend to be the first ethnic media a group produces, due to the relatively low cost of publishing content in small newspapers or pamphlets. This is true even in communities where literacy is limited. For example, African-American newspaper publishing had a limited audience around the time of the Civil War because literacy rates were very low. However, the desire to hear about African-American concerns, from African-American writers, created a practice of "pass on readership." This meant that people would read the newspapers aloud to others who could not read for themselves. The cost of buying a newspaper would be split among the people "reading" it, becoming a communal rather than a personal expense (Viswanath & Lee, 2007).

The *Freedom Journal,* published from 1827 to 1829, was one of the first African-American newspapers. The editors declared that, "We wish to plead our own cause. Too long have others spoken for us. Too long has the publick [*sic*] been deceived by misrepresentations, in things that concern us dearly" (Barrow, 1977, p. 118). And so, the pages of African-American newspapers spoke to their communities about the achievements of free Blacks in the northern parts of the United States—about Black doctors, lawyers, and businessmen. Page (2006) commented that "the Negro press gave African Americans something no other media was ready or willing to offer: visibility and a voice" (p. ix).

For many groups, the reason to create independent media produced *by* members of that group, *for* members of that group, is to represent themselves in their own words. For example, South Africa was controlled by an apartheid government from 1948 to 1994, which enforced racial segregation in all spheres of life. These rules included the media that served different populations. Radio stations to serve Black South Africans in their own languages were not created until 1962, when the government created a set of stations collectively known as Radio Bantu. Under this umbrella, Radio Sesotho, Radio Zulu, Radio Lebowa, Radio Setswana, and Radio Xhosa (in 1963) were created to serve communities speaking these five languages. Programming consisted primarily of traditional choir music—an unsurprising choice, since discussion of anything approximating politics was banned. All content was reviewed by the Bantu Programmes Control Board, which consisted of 35 White staff members who spoke the broadcast languages (Tomaselli, Tomaselli, & Muller, 1989). When news was broadcast, it was "patronizingly insular, in that content emphasized local news, almost to the exclusion of international events" (Fourie, 2007, p. 12).

In the late 1970s and early 1980s, a loophole in the apartheid government's own laws created an opening for alternative Black voices to speak to their communities. As part of their racist national plan, the apartheid government had created semi-independent "homelands" for South Africa's Black populations, allowing the upheaval and resettlement of non-Whites to less desirable land. Since these homelands were treated as semi-independent states, the laws that restricted indigenous language broadcasting were not binding there. This loophole prompted the creation of stations, including Capital Radio, Radio 702, Radio Bop, and Radio Thohoyandou, all of which located their transmitter sites in the homelands, with frequencies that could easily reach into South Africa's large cities. These stations were able to provide alternative voices and views on South African life and politics. Through the 1980s and 1990s, these stations attracted large followings as apartheid was dismantled and democracy was ushered in with the election of Nelson Mandela in 1994.

For groups that have been marginalized or stereotyped by the mainstream media, ethnic media can provide an opportunity to tell stories in one's own way. For example, since 2008, Native Public Media has implemented the biggest drive in U.S. history to increase Native-American radio station ownership. Applications for 29 new Native-American radio stations had been approved by the Federal Communication Commission by the end of 2008, which would bring the total number of Native-American radio stations to 62, up from 33 in 2007 (PEJ, 2009b). Loris Ann Taylor, executive director of Native Public Media, highlighted why this move is significant:

> It is important to make sure Native Americans . . . have controlling interests in [their media] facilities. When Natives tell their story, it is truthful and accurate and told through the voice of the Native American experience. It shows how having control of the "pen" validates your own history and identity. (Quoted in PEJ, 2009b, para. 20)

Taylor's thoughts and motivations echo those of the director of Waringarri Radio, an Aboriginal radio station broadcasting in Kunumurra, Australia:

> There's two different types of interviews that come out. You get the white journalist's interviews, and our stories. Their story is done from the top with no feeling, just the permission. Our story comes from the hearing and the soul, because what we're talking about, we know that. It is us. It is our story. It is our life . . . And this is why we have the right to go in between the lines of all these bad stories that are written or broadcast or televised about us. (Quoted in Hartley & McKee, 2000, p. 181)

These viewpoints do not mean that the mainstream media are not capable of telling stories about ethnic minority groups in sensitive and detailed ways. Rather, these two quotes highlight that the chance to tell a story about one's own people, in one's own words, is an important part of creating and maintaining an ethnic identity. Independent media, created by members of an ethnic group for that group, create spaces for developing a sense of community, sharing common events and experiences, and arguing for common causes.

Covering Content of Interest

For an ethnic community to have a voice of their own is more than a space to publish or broadcast stories. Having media outlets where births, deaths, marriages, and other life events are chronicled is an important part of creating an *imagined community* of people who feel a sense of connection and similarity with one another (Anderson, 1991). Anderson originally used the term imagined community to describe how national identity was connected to the rise of newspapers. He argued that simply imagining so many other people reading the same news that you are reading, at the same time, can encourage a feeling of identification with those people.

For an ethnic community, being able to connect with stories about the lives of people like you is an important part of creating an imagined community. That feeling is enhanced when news that affects your own ethnic group is the primary focus, rather than being relegated to the inside pages of a newspaper or to the end of a broadcast. In Chapter 2, we discussed the indigenous radio stations in the highlands of Mexico, where the poor quality of roads and weather keep indigenous communities isolated from the rest of the country. The broadcasting of *avisos* (messages) over the air gives community members living elsewhere in Mexico or in the U.S. an easy way to share news with their relatives back home. Because their news is shared through a broadcast, the whole community stays updated on the lives of community members now living far away. These *avisos* have become a way for the radio stations to reinforce a sense of imagined community, even across significant geographic separations (Cornejo, 1990; McElmurry, 2009; Ramos & Díez, 2003; Vargas, 1995).

Feeling like part of an imagined community develops the affective component of an ethnic identity, while connecting with news about other members of your ethnic group can develop the cognitive dimension of that identity. Finally, having a media forum that provides details of ethnic community events and issues can encourage participation in ways that develop the behavioral component of an ethnic identity.

Ethnic Media as a Platform for Social Equality

At different historical moments, ethnic media producers around the world have encouraged their audiences to participate in civil rights movements. In the U.S., the African-American press was an instrumental part of the movement for racial equality. Black-Americans served in segregated units in World War I and when they returned from war, they began to move north where there were more opportunities than in the still-segregated South. The Black newspapers called for fair treatment and work opportunities, as well as recognition of the efforts of Black soldiers (Simmons, 2005). The calls for equality took different paths as time progressed (La Brie, 1977). For example, the *Pittsburgh Courier* started the "Double V" campaign after Pearl Harbor was attacked in December 1941 and the United States entered World War II. The *Courier* actively campaigned for victory overseas against the Nazis (the first "V"), as well as victory in the form of social equality for Blacks at home (the second "V"). In 6 months, 200,000 members of the Black community were recruited to the cause. The Double V campaign became a national unifier in the cause for equality. Gains were made in equal access to employment, particularly for Black women. Rosie the Riveter was no longer a role reserved for Whites, as Black women were now able to join them on the assembly line (see Figures 4.3 and 4.4).

There were also gains made in commercial equality as the *Pittsburgh Courier* enjoyed a huge increase in advertising revenue from White-owned companies who started to realize the potential impact of this particular newspaper (Washburn, 2006). Although the newspaper went out of business in 1966, the Courier's "Double V" made a real contribution to the larger civil rights movement of the 1960s.

The *Courier* may not have survived, but many of the ethnic media that make a social impact are not necessarily long-lived. Another example of a short-lived success was a weekly supplement in the German newspaper *Die Tageszeitung,* published in Berlin (Rigoni, 2002). The insert, called *Persembe,* targeted the German-Turkish community

Figure 4.3 Rosie the Riveter was one of America's enduring symbols of the World War II effort. Created by J. Howard Miller for the War Production Coordinating Committee, this poster represented the efforts of real-life Rosies, women who went to work in the factories to support the war effort while men were stationed overseas.

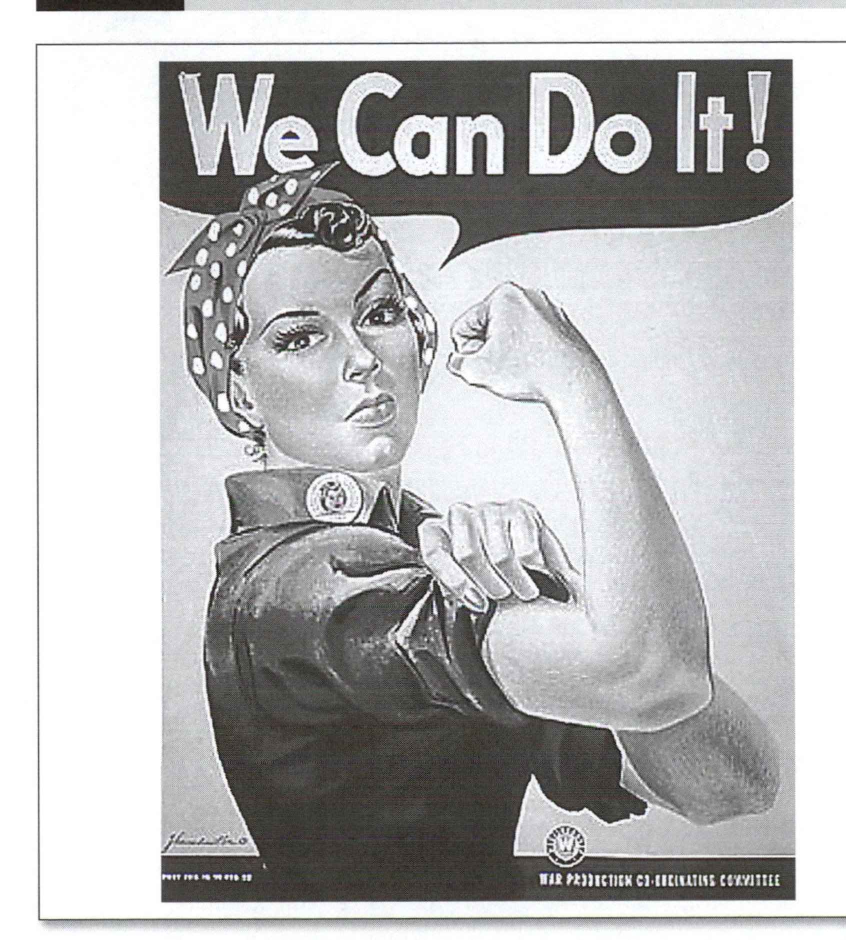

Source: Courtesy National Archives (photo no. NWDNS-179-WP-1563).

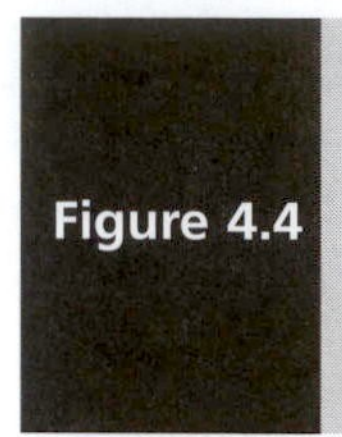

Figure 4.4 A real-life "Rosie" operating a drill on a Vengeance dive bomber in Nashville, Tennessee, in February 1943. The nationwide need for factory workers created employment opportunities for female African-Americans that had previously been closed, giving them the opportunity to work side-by-side with White women to support the war effort.

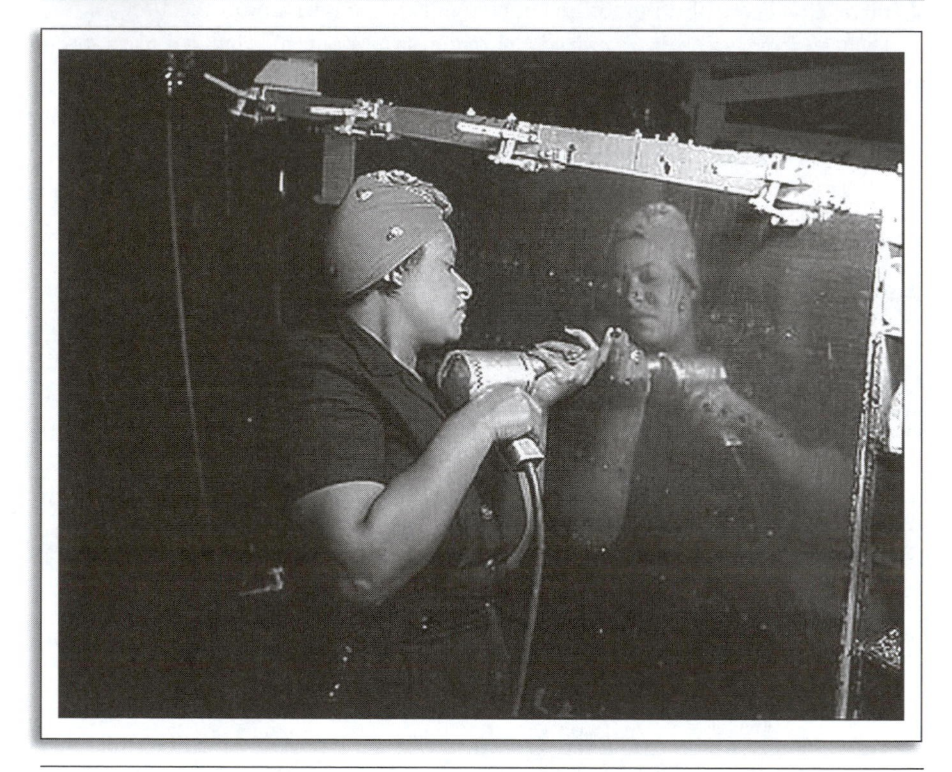

Source: Alfred T. Palmer, Library of Congress.

and was published in both languages between 2000 and 2002. For this marginalized ethnic minority, having a weekly supplement in a major German newspaper—a supplement that chronicled the events of their community and the causes that mattered most to them—was a symbolic move toward national belonging. The insert tackled questions of integration and argued for full social rights for German-born Turkish youth, including equal access to jobs, education, and other opportunities.

Persembe was not only important for the German-Turkish community. Having the supplement in a mainstream publication also meant that German nationals had a weekly reminder of the Turkish community and its needs. Even if those German readers did not actually read the insert, its presence was a dramatic increase in the Turkish-German community's visibility (Georgiou, 2003). The short-lived success of *Persembe* is a reminder of how difficult it is for new ethnic media outlets to remain viable, but that even a relatively short publication span can have a major impact (Georgiou, 2003).

Publications by Australia's Aboriginal peoples were also relatively short-lived in their early stages (Rose, 1996). However, since the mid-1900s, these publications have been a central element in the Aboriginal movement for social equality. In the 1960s and 1970s, the Aboriginal newspapers worked militantly for increased social rights for Aborigines, and displayed their anger toward the discriminatory acts of Whites in many ways. Newspapers printed detailed accounts of attacks and humiliations that fellow Aborigines had suffered at the hands of White police officers and others, as a way to generate outrage and prompt collective activity in the community (Rose, 1996).

The Native-American media have taken similar steps, with similar demands. The *Cherokee Phoenix* was the first Native-American newspaper, and began publication in 1834 in Echota, Georgia. The *Phoenix* was created to highlight and discuss the political decisions being made in the names of the tribes. These decisions would soon result in the Trail of Tears, the forced removal of hundreds of tribes to new "homelands" that President Jackson had assigned to them (Riley, 1979). From this activist beginning, Native-American newspapers, and later, radio (beginning in 1910), and television (in the early 1960s) have called for the social equality of Native-Americans. They also called for recognition of the damages suffered as a result of their displacements, such as high rates of alcoholism, poverty, and crime on the reservations (LaCourse, 1979). In more recent times, the Internet has become an important medium for promoting Native-American causes. *Indian Country Today* has an Internet presence that has the highest visitor traffic of any original-content Native-American news Web site,[2] and acts as a clearinghouse for news, events, and editorials related to Native American social and political concerns.

Moments of crisis can activate an ethnic identity and create a set of social or political demands that bring an ethnic group together. For example, the invasion of Cyprus by Turkey in 1974 contributed to the development of a Greek-American political lobby that continues to lobby on behalf of ethnically Greek Cypriots in Washington, DC. Today, the island of Cyprus is divided into ethnically Turkish and Greek halves, and there is an uneasy truce between the two sides after decades of fighting. However, events in Cyprus continue to be a major issue for ethnic Greek communities living abroad. Kopan (1987) commented that "the Greek ethnic press . . . is once again publishing news on overseas concerns, albeit to an American-born readership" (p. 174). Georgiou (2001a) also indicates that the Greek-language television and radio content in London is just as important to British-born Greeks for the same reasons. Cyprus has become an enduring political issue passed down as an ethnic concern from one generation to the next.

These examples only begin to display the range of social concerns that can become rallying cries for ethnic communities when highlighted by their ethnic media. Sometimes the seemingly unrelated difficulties of another ethnic group can prompt discussions in the ethnic media of common ground among ethnic groups. For example, it seems unlikely that the civic unrest in Los Angeles that resulted from the Rodney King trial verdict in 1992 would be an issue for the ethnic Thai community. When White policemen were acquitted of charges for beating a Black man (Rodney King)—a beating that had been caught on camera—a large swath of metropolitan Los Angeles became the scene of rioting and looting that went on for days. Sudarat (1993) documented how Thai newspaper editors used this story to discuss the social discrimination that Thais and other minority groups feel in Los

Angeles, as well as to extend sympathy to the Korean businesses in the affected area that were often targets for looting. This example demonstrates that a significant local event can reveal the connections between ethnic minority groups that are usually invisible, except in times of crisis. In these kinds of difficult times, ethnic media are often more than a source of information; they can encourage communities to rally in support of each other.

Ethnic Media as a Social Institution

Every community has its own institutions that help the community to function. For example, educational institutions like schools, political institutions like local chapters of political parties, and religious institutions like churches can serve important roles in their communities by helping people access resources that they want and need. The ethnic media can also be considered a social institution that has relationships with other important pillars of the community. For example, religious institutions have often been connected to the survival of ethnic media. Church services conducted in Dutch fostered retention of Dutch language capacity in the Dutch-American community over multiple generations. When these churches began to conduct services in English, the ethnic media suffered. Doeszema (1987) notes, "When the Dutch language disappeared in the churches, most of the Dutch language publications also disappeared" (p. 72).

However, religious institutions can maintain ethnic media and can even be their own publishers. The Greek Orthodox ethnically has been and continues to be a major publisher of ethnic media in ethnically Greek communities throughout North America and Europe. The monthly *Orthodox Observer* is published in New York in Greek and English and has one of the largest circulations of Greek ethnic media in the world; and it has now expanded its reach by making content available online.[3] Kopan (1987) argues that because religion is so intertwined with cultural and ethnic traditions and events in the Greek communities, second and third generation youth remain tied to their ethnic Greek identities and the Greek language through the church and its media.

Media tied to other social institutions can also be a way of maintaining an ethnic identity. For example, some of the most successful and longest-running Jewish-American publications are connected to social organizations. The B'nai B'rith youth movement reports that their monthly print and online newsletter has a combined readership of 20,000 nationally, and Hadassah, a women's Zionist charitable organization, reports that their monthly magazine has a national readership of about 400,000. Similar to the Dutch and Greek cases, connecting to an ethnic medium might come through membership in an ethnic organization or institution that helps to keep an ethnic identity intact.

Recreational groups can also be important community social institutions. For Japanese-Americans living in the San Francisco Bay Area, participation in local basketball leagues—many of which have online and offline community bulletin boards for their members—supports a sense of ethnic group membership through a related group membership (Kitano, 1987).

☐ For Further Discussion

Can you think of other ethnic groups where a religious or other social institution plays a primary role in how the group maintains its ethnic identity?

- Can you describe the ways that this institution might contribute to the survival of that group's ethnic media outlets?
- Does this social institution encourage retention of the minority group's language of origin?
- How does the language of publication factor into the survival of this group's ethnic media?
- Overall, do you think that maintaining distinct ethnic identities results in separation from a mainstream society? Give three points that argue in favor of ethnic identity maintenance and three that argue against it.

The family is another social institution that is closely tied to both ethnic media development and the sustaining of ethnic media over generations. In the next section, we take a closer look at the intersections of family, ethnic identity, and ethnic media.

Ethnic Media and Family Life

Within the family home, ethnic media can be a source of news and information about events in the home country and in the local community. As we discussed in Chapter 3, ethnic media can help immigrant parents adapt to the new community by connecting them with news about the country they left behind (*connective function*) and provide information that helps them find their way around the new community (*orientation function*). For second, third, and subsequent generations, ethnic media can also serve a *symbolic function* by helping these youth develop their own ties to their families' country of origin.

Language Development and Maintenance

Traditionally, researchers have worked from a "three generation" model of language proficiency: The first generation remains fluent in their home country language, and their children are likely to be bilingual as a result of speaking different languages at home and at school. When the second generation form their own families, however, they are more likely to speak the host country language with their spouses and children than their parents' language. Their third generation children are therefore unlikely to be fluent in the first language of their grandparents; and by the fourth generation, the family is considered to have experienced *language shift* (Fishman, Gertner, Lowry, & Milan, 1985; Lieberson, 1981).

However, this model may not hold true in this era of rapid globalization. Bilingualism has become increasingly important and is seen as a skill that can contribute to a wide range of careers in a global economy. Travel has become easier and less expensive, allowing for more frequent contact with family, friends, and colleagues that can reinforce usage of traditional languages. Proliferation of new communication technologies can also make connecting with media content in traditional languages easier. For ethnic minority youth who are able to communicate in their traditional languages, ethnic media can serve as a language teacher. Ethnic media, whether written (such as newspapers or Internet content) or verbal (such as television or radio), can reinforce language learning within the home and promote bilingualism. Zhang's (2008) study of Chinese-origin families in Philadelphia demonstrates that parents' tastes can increase their children's contact with media in the home country language, as "second generation children report that they have been frequently immersed" (p. 131) in their parents' preferences for Chinese-language media. All these factors may potentially contribute to a lowered likelihood of language shift in ethnic minority families.

Ethnic Media as a Cultural Teacher

Ethnic media can also serve as a teacher of culture for ethnic minority youth. Durham (2004) indicates that second generation youth connect with mainstream media and ethnic media in different ways. As teenagers and young adults, second generation youth connect with mainstream media individually, and often in private. By contrast, these youth generally connect with ethnic media with other family members, or with friends from the same ethnic group. Most often, family members will connect with television or movies together, but parents and children may perceive ethnic media content in different ways.

Differing perceptions of mainstream and ethnic media can help parents and children to discuss cultural divides and misunderstandings. Explaining ethnic media content to their children can give parents an entry point to discuss issues that are difficult to raise at other times, such as the appropriate age to start dating. Likewise, mainstream media can prompt children to discuss the realities of growing up in the host country with their parents. Durham's (2004) study of Indian-origin families living in America explored portrayals of intermarriage in ethnic media and Bollywood productions that these families viewed together. In some cases, these media portrayals of intermarriage prompted both parents and children to consider another point of view. There were also times when the daughters' attempts to broach this issue resulted in a family argument. Whether the outcome is compromise or conflict, ethnic media can prompt family discussions and cultural negotiations of values and ideas.

Viewing ethnic media as a family unit can also strengthen ties across generations and across national borders. In a study of Mexican-American teenagers in New Mexico, Mayer (2003) found that these girls watch *telenovelas* (soap operas produced in Latin America and distributed across the United States and Latin America) alongside their mothers, sisters, and grandmothers. The nightly *telenovela* episode became a separate, female-only time that promoted discussions across generations. The connections were not limited to the family members watching together in New Mexico. Because this particular *telenovela* was being aired in Mexico at the same time, these teenage girls talked with their cousins in Mexico about events on the show. This shared interest led to conversations and connection across other issues and even encouraged summer visits by the U.S.-born teens to

Mexico to spend time with extended family. In these families, ethnic media served as a cultural teacher and as a way to connect with family in both countries, which helped to reinforce the girls' ethnic identities.

The family may be where ethnic identity is first created and developed, but we have also discussed how ethnic identities are not handed down from generation to generation unchanged. Ethnic identities are negotiated and redefined in individual ways, and often change and develop over the course of a lifetime. Staying in touch with the changing tastes of ethnic minority youth is essential for ethnic media trying to remain viable across generations and across their audiences' stages of life. The next section highlights some of the major concerns that ethnic media have to address to stay current in their communities.

The Challenge for Ethnic Media to Remain Viable

Whether ethnic media are serving a language minority, indigenous group, or the descendents of immigrants, these media face considerable generational challenges. There are issues of both content and shape to consider. The content of the media, meaning what issues are covered, is going to have to be different across generations as tastes and social conditions change. The challenges of addressing content issues across generations are complicated by the fact that the line between immigrants and ethnic minorities are not always clear. In the case of the ethnic Chinese in Indonesia, the community is mixed. Chinese nationals began to migrate to Indonesia at the end of the 19th century, and have maintained their language for more than 100 years and a number of generations. However, ongoing immigration from mainland China resulted in marriages and intermingling between the Chinese who had become a language minority group over generations, and newly arrived immigrants (Hoon, 2006). This continued immigration has also replenished language stores, making it easier for Indonesian-born Chinese to maintain their language of origin.

However, between 1966 and 1998, Suharto's rule of Indonesia officially banned Chinese-language media and even the use of Chinese in public, as part of an agenda that considered minority identities incompatible with Indonesian nationalism. Many of the Chinese-language media that have flourished since this rule was abolished in 1998 are produced by journalists who worked in this sector prior to 1966. This has caused a real generational disjuncture, since the older generation is producing media content to suit their tastes and interests. Younger generations find little in these media that they can connect with (Hoon, 2006), leaving them to choose between ethnic media that do not reflect their interests and the mainstream Indonesian media that do not often recognize or feature them.

There are also issues of shape, which refers to the methods used to present content (Shahn, 1992). This includes, for example, decisions about which language to use and who to employ in an ethnic media outlet.

Local Content

Deciding what kind of content to emphasize is a key concern for ethnic media. For indigenous peoples like First Nations and Aborigines, ethnic media focus primarily on the local and national ethnic communities in Canada and Australia, respectively. For ethnic minorities who are the descendents of immigrants, the balance is a little trickier. Although news about the country of origin will continue to be important, the local community is likely to be much more so.

Connections to the local area start to take precedence for later generations as the main site of their ethnic experiences. The Croatian-American community is one example of this shift. By the 1960s, the Croatian press began to publish increasing proportions of their newspapers in English, recognizing that the second and third-generation readers could not read Croatian well. The content changed as well: "[*Zajedni ar*] maintained a . . . [focus on] Yugoslavia . . . However, news of the Croatian Fraternal Union bowling tournament [in the U.S.] would take precedence over both national and international news in many issues" (Prpi & McAdams, 1987, p. 55).

We found the same pattern among 11 ethnic communities in Los Angeles. Survey data from 2,400 respondents, shown in Figure 4.5, indicate that while home country news is more important than local neighborhood news for the immigrant generation, the preference switches by the second generation, and even more so by the third generation.

Figure 4.5 Based on data collected from 2,400 residents in 11 ethnic communities in Los Angeles, this figure illustrates the relative importance of home country and local neighborhood news by immigrant generation (indicated on the horizontal axis). Respondents ranked the relative importance of different types of news. The numbers on the vertical axis are rank order correlation coefficients reflecting the relative importance of home country and neighborhood news.

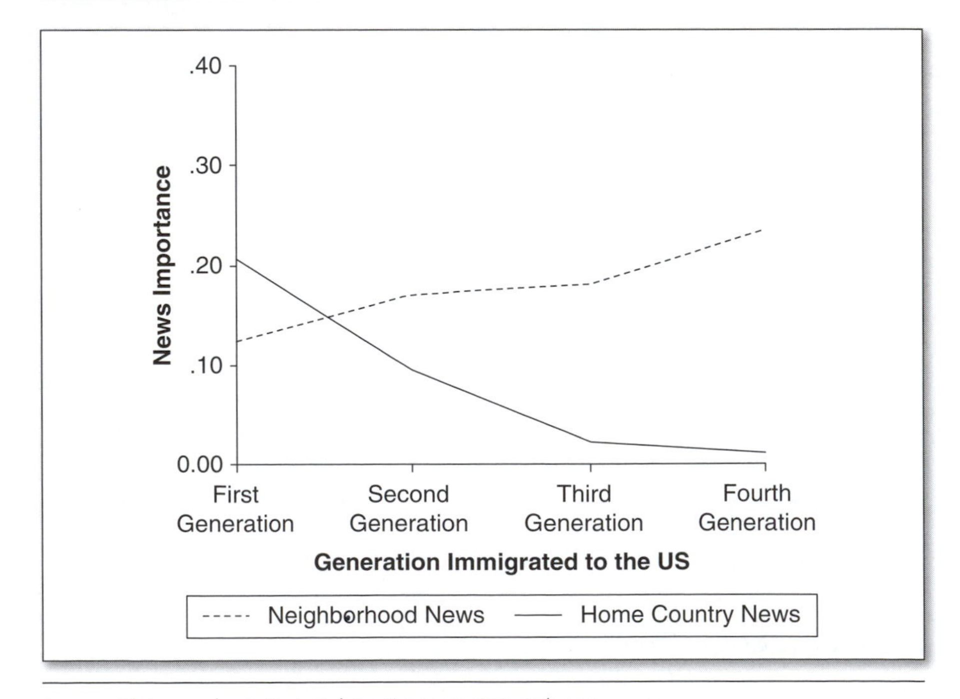

Source: Metamorphosis Project: http://www.metamorph.org

The general rule here is that coverage of the local community becomes more important as generations pass. This does not mean that later generations lose all interest in home country news. For many ethnic groups, the country of origin remains a major point of interest, as discussed earlier in the case of Syrian-Americans' focus on Middle Eastern politics (Naff, 1987), and the Greek diaspora's attention to Cyprus (Georgiou, 2001a). Striking a balance of home and host country content requires that producers really understand the audience and their needs. That understanding has to extend beyond content to issues of language use and newsroom staffing as well.

Language of the Ethnic Media

To remain viable, ethnic media have to follow the needs and tastes of their audience. Of all ethnic minorities in the United States, Japanese-Americans have the highest rate of intermarriage (consistently over 70% since 1990), which has contributed to particularly low rates of language proficiency among later generations born in the U.S. (Alba & Nee, 2003). The Japanese-American community is also one of the longest-settled and integrated in the U.S., particularly on the West Coast. Kitano (1987) indicates that the media have not reflected the changes of the community they serve, as most of the newspapers are still written primarily in Japanese rather than English, even though very few second and third generation Japanese-Americans are proficient enough to be able to read in Japanese.

This situation indicates a disjuncture between what the newspaper producers themselves think people *should* know or want to read—and the realities of the readers themselves. This disconnect has resulted in smaller circulations for these Japanese newspapers, and these outlets find themselves serving the limited number of Japanese immigrants in the United States, rather than the Japanese-American ethnic market (Kitano, 1987). This case also shows how intertwined language and culture can be. Many ethnic media outlets have gone bankrupt when they continued to produce content in a language that was no longer spoken by most of the community. And yet, many ethnic media outlets continue to resist changes like bilingual publishing.

For the Welsh, struggles for local control of their media went hand-in-hand with their battle to preserve their language. Although, at one time, Welsh was the majority language, extended British rule has made Wales a predominantly English-speaking country. Although the two languages legally have equal standing, at the time of the last census in 2001 only 21% of Welsh residents reported an ability to speak Welsh. Over the past few decades, Welsh-language media have been part of a larger social campaign to rejuvenate the traditional language, and with it, the traditional Welsh ethnic identity. The launch of the first Welsh-language television station in 1982 was the result of a bitter fight for an ethnic, and self-governed, television channel (Barlow, Mitchell, & O'Malley, 2005).

Through the 1970s, Welsh activists campaigned for a television channel in their own language, which at that time already had a radio station, *BBC Radio Cymru*. The British government promised to permit the creation of such a station in 1979, but reneged on that decision in 1980. This reversal was met with civil disobedience in Wales, including widespread refusal to pay television licenses, sit-ins at the BBC, and even the threat of a hunger strike by the movement's leadership (Allan & O'Malley, 1999). London decided to uphold their original promise, and *Sianel*

Pedwar Cymru (S4C, meaning Channel Four Wales in English) was launched on November 1, 1982. Today, there are two versions of S4C: an analog bilingual station that produces both English and Welsh content, and a digital television station that broadcasts exclusively in Welsh (Allan & O'Malley, 1999). These channels continue to act as parts of the larger social campaign to not only preserve the Welsh language but to increase its use and standing among younger generations.

Exclusivity and Authenticity

Why would language be such a touchy subject? Because maintaining traditional languages becomes symbolic and can be a way for the ethnic group to remain distinct from mainstream society. Assimilation into mainstream society is seen as a sign of success by some and as a threatening proposition by others. For groups who are invested in remaining distinct—and the media that serve them—continuing to publish in the home country language can become a statement of exclusivity: We are who we are because we have the ability to communicate in our language. One of the newspapers serving the Polish-British community in London, somewhat humorously, reflects this viewpoint in Figure 4.6.

Figure 4.6 A Polish Newspaper Slogan in London

Photo: Vikki Katz.

Keeping the language of publication exclusive is also a statement of "authenticity" in that it sets a bar for inclusion as a "real" Pole, or a "real" member of any group. Language can be used to draw a clear line between who "really" belongs and who does not.

Questions about the authenticity of an ethnic media outlet do not stop at language. For example, the *Koori Mail* started in Sydney, Australia, in 1991, and became the first commercially viable Aboriginal newspaper. Because a number of the editorial staff are not Aborigine and some of the newspaper's content comes from the Associated Press, some question if the newspaper is "really" Aboriginal or not. Whether or not an ethnic media outlet manages to stay viable may depend on how these sorts of questions of authenticity are answered and on who asks. If the goal is to be exclusively Aborigine, for example, the *Koori Mail* may make a statement by having an all-Aboriginal staff. But, if the goal is to be Aboriginal and have crossover appeal to mainstream readers as well, then the game becomes a balancing act between keeping the Aboriginal audience and having content that introduces non-Aboriginal readers to the history and concerns of Aborigines.

For Further Discussion

Reread the last paragraph with your classmates, and argue your perspective on this important issue. How many of the decision makers need to be from that ethnic group for the coverage provided to be considered "authentic"? List the pros and cons of your approach, and then compare it with the points of other groups in the class.

Summary

This chapter focuses on ethnic minorities and their media, and describes how these groups are distinct from immigrants. Ethnic media play an important part in the development of an ethnic identity and in how that identity is defined over time and in different geographic contexts. The social issues that are most important to an ethnic group are often the reason ethnic media develop, and these media work as a platform for group members to discuss important issues and to campaign for social rights. The last section of the chapter introduces some of the key dilemmas in making ethnic media viable and relevant over multiple generations. This issue is covered in more detail in the chapters that follow. In Chapter 5, we turn our attention from the groups that connect with ethnic media to focus on the individuals and organizations that produce these media.

Study Questions

1. Apply the three-part definition of ethnic identity described under section heading, "Developing Ethnic Identities," to your own ethnic identity. What would be examples of the cognitive, behavioral, and affective components of your ethnic identity?

2. Studies show that the likelihood of intermarriage increases from the immigrant generation to the second generation, and again from the second to the third generation. Do you think intermarriage poses a challenge to the viability of ethnic media? What changes, if any, do you think could keep ethnic media relevant for mixed ethnic families?

3. The section headed "Ethnic Media and Family Life" notes that children of immigrants tend to connect with mainstream media alone and with ethnic media alongside family or friends with the same ethnic background. How do you think consuming media in the presence of others might affect the meaning of that media's content? Give examples and comparisons to support your answer.

4. Which term: hybrid, hyphenated, or conglomerate identity—do you think is most useful in describing your ethnic identity development, or the identity development of people you know? Make a case, using the materials in this chapter, for the term that you choose.

5. How important do you think language is in maintaining an ethnic identity? Can you be a "real" member of an ethnic group if you do not speak the language? Is an ethnic media outlet "really" authentic if it stops publishing in the traditional language? Make your case either way, based on material covered in this chapter.

Notes

[1]In the United States, the conglomerate term "Asian" generally refers to peoples with historical roots in East Asian countries such as Japan, China, and Korea. In Britain, the term "Asian" generally refers to people from countries on the Indian subcontinent, including India, Pakistan, and Bangladesh, and peoples from East Asian countries are generally referred to by their specific national origin (i.e., Chinese, Japanese, Korean).

[2]The Pew Project for Excellence in Journalism (2009b) also reports that *Indian Country Today* in its print form is the most widely read newspaper in the Native-American community.

[3]The *Orthodox Observer* can be read online at: http://www.goarch.org/news/observer

PART III

The Producers

CHAPTER 5

Ethnic Media Audience Trends and What Lies Behind the Numbers

CHAPTER OBJECTIVES

This chapter is the first in the book that looks at ethnic media as organizations. By the end of this chapter you will be able to:

- Explain why circulations and ratings are important to ethnic media, advertisers, and researchers.
- Describe major trends in the circulation and ratings of print and electronic ethnic media, and explain major shifts.
- Discuss the politics behind the calculation of ratings for ethnic television and radio.
- Describe two different strategies that ethnic media with small audiences have employed to attract funding and sustain their operations.

Introduction

Our focus up to now has been on how ethnic communities incorporate ethnic media into their lives. Beginning with Chapter 5, we shift attention to the issues ethnic media producers confront in the day-to-day operation of their organizations.

In this chapter, we will discuss the methods used to quantify the audience of ethnic media, why having circulation numbers and ratings matters to producers, advertisers, and researchers, and why it can be difficult to get these figures. We will also discuss the politics behind the creation of measures used to capture the audience of ethnic media. Finally, we will take a look at the most recent data available on the audience of print and broadcast ethnic media in the United States, and highlight the major trends and shifts that emerge from these figures. The most recent statistics we discuss here were generated in 2008 and 2009, a period marked by a major, global financial crisis. During that same time, the proliferation and spread of new communication technologies forced media across the world to think long and hard about how to reorganize their businesses and make them sustainable.

Several pilot projects were underway in 2009, but no models offering considerable promise to large, commercial media have yet to emerge. We discuss, however, two models that have begun to deliver encouraging results to smaller, local, and community-oriented ethnic media organizations. The first model emerged in the U.S., while a successful test of the second was undertaken in Britain in 2002.

Unfortunately there are very few data available that capture the shifts in ethnic media audience preferences in countries other than the U.S. While the data we draw on are limited to one country, they arguably allow us to better understand several general tendencies that we are likely to observe in other countries, too.

Ethnic Newspapers: The Importance of Circulation Audits

Ethnic media need to know how many people they reach. This information is crucial, first of all, to media producers who want to know if they are addressing the needs of the ethnic community they seek to serve. Fluctuations in the size of the audience are used as indicators of how well they are doing their job. Journalists often look at circulation numbers (if working for a print medium) or the ratings (in the case of television, radio, and Internet-based media) to determine how well the audience has received a particular story. If a story on the job market led to a spike in newspaper sales or the ratings of a television program, then similar stories are likely to be produced again. Equally important, media management needs to have audience ratings at its disposal to attract advertising. Advertisers want to know that they are getting the most out of the money they invest in a particular medium. And that means either getting access to a broad audience or to a population with particular demographics (e.g., young African-American women) that is likely to be interested in their product. Circulation figures or ratings are trusted more by advertisers, if they have been produced by an independent organization and not the media organization itself.

The Audit Bureau of Circulations (ABC) is one such organization.[1] It is a nonprofit organization that was founded in 1914 by advertisers, advertising agencies, and publishers. Their goal was to "establish an industry watchdog to independently verify circulations" (ABC, 2009, para 2).[2] Until that time, publishers reported their own circulation numbers, and that was the only data advertisers had at their disposal when they had to decide where to place their ads. Without independent verification, there was no way for them to know whether they were actually reaching as many people as each publisher claimed. There are a number of organizations that operate under the ABC name worldwide. They calculate circulation, measure readership, and collect audience information (e.g., area of residence, breakdown by gender, and age) for the magazines, newspapers, and other publications produced by its member organizations.

Circulation refers to the number of single copies sold by a newspaper or magazine every time it is published (e.g., every day, week, or month). In North America, ABC has more than 4,000 members, including daily and weekly publications, business publications, consumer magazines, regional and national advertisers, as well as many advertising agencies. All these members pay membership dues to ABC. Publishers that are ABC members also pay fees to ABC to have their circulation numbers verified on a regular basis. Today, ABC also offers audits of the traffic its members receive on their Web sites.

¤ For Further Discussion

Access the Web site of the ABC in North America via the following link (http://www.accessabc.com/index.html). Follow the link to the *Free Reports* that are available to everyone with access to the Internet. Select two newspapers of interest to you (e.g., a Spanish-language publication and an English-language newspaper) and examine their profiles: (a) How do the two publications differ and in what ways are they similar? (b) What information in the reports do you believe is most useful for advertisers and why? (c) How can soliciting the auditing services of an independent organization like the ABC help ethnic newspapers?

Jerry Gibbons, the West Coast director of the American Association of Advertising Agencies, in an interview with the *San Francisco Chronicle*, cited the lack of circulation and ratings data generated from independent auditing organizations as one of the reasons that advertisers are hesitant about buying space and time in ethnic media (Raine, 2002). Although there has been a significant increase in the number of print media that do get audited in the U.S., most ethnic newspapers and magazines do not. According to the 2009 annual report of the Project for Excellence in Journalism (see Profile 5.1), data collected by the Latino Print Network (Profile 5.2) indicate that the number of weekly Spanish-language newspapers audited grew from 76 out of 304 (25%) in 2003 to 127 out of 417 (31%) in 2007 (the most recent year for which auditing information is available). The number of audited Spanish-language newspapers that are published on a less-than-weekly basis grew from 8 out of 322 (2.5%) in 2003 to 14 out of 377 (3.7%) in 2007. Figure 5.1 shows the changes in the number of Spanish-language print media audited in the U.S. from 2003 to 2007. Notice that the number of Hispanic dailies that are audited has remained about the same from 2004 onwards (i.e., 18 in 2004 versus 19 in 2007).

Figure 5.1 Latino Newspapers Audited, 2003–2005

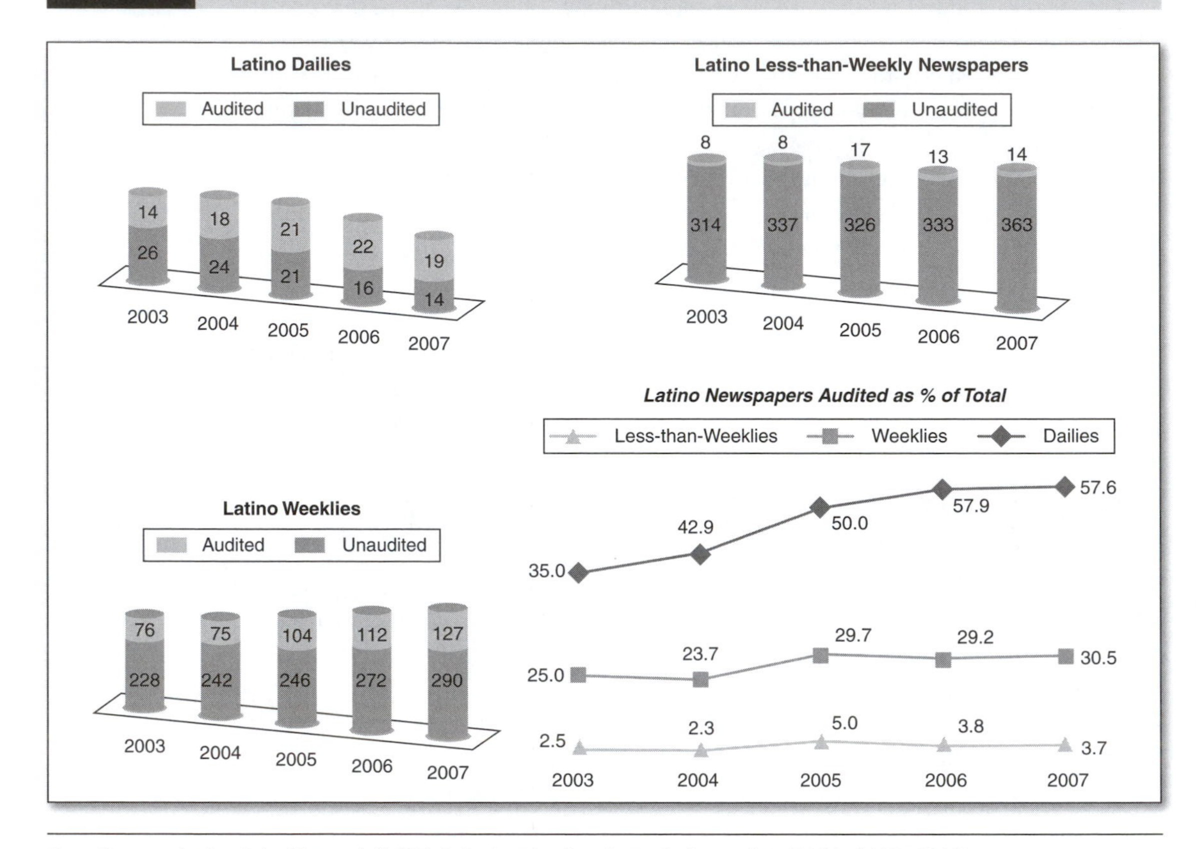

Data Sources: Latino Print Network (2005) & Project for Excellence in Journalism (2006, 2007, 2009).

Figure: Matthew Matsaganis.

These increases suggest that ethnic newspapers are becoming more aware of how important it is for them to have independently produced circulation data when they approach advertisers. The larger numbers of audited publications also indicate that more of these media organizations are maturing, growing larger, and developing into formal corporations as opposed to mom-and-pop type of businesses. Moreover, these data suggest that competition among Spanish-language publications is becoming stronger. Newspapers and magazines are hoping to get an edge over the competition by building up their credibility as businesses. In this respect, subscribing to an independent auditing service is an advantage.

Even though there has been an increase in the number of Spanish-language print media audited in the U.S., the vast majority of these media still publish self-reports of circulation or do not collect and release any circulation data at all. This is also the case for publications targeted to other ethnic groups in the U.S. and ethnic print media, in general, in the major media markets worldwide (e.g., Australia, Canada, Germany, the UK).

The Black press in the U.S., for example, has a long history dating back to 1827, when the first Black newspaper, *Freedom's Journal,* was founded in New York. However, PEJ research indicates that only three African-American publications are audited by the Audit Bureau of Circulations: *The Amsterdam News,* a daily published in New York, *The Philadelphia Tribune*, published three days a week, and *The Afro-American*, a weekly published in Baltimore and Washington, DC. When interviewed by the PEJ, De Carla Livers, the managing editor of BlackPress.org (see Profile 5.3) said that "papers have not worked to audit their circulations, so advertisers don't know exactly what they [are] getting" (PEJ, 2007a, para. 5). She indicated that BlackPress.org is devoting a lot of its efforts to push Black print media to audit their circulations in order to better leverage the advertising market (PEJ, 2007a).

Ethnic newspapers targeting audiences of Asian origin in the U.S. have had similar problems attracting advertisers. Some of these publications, though, did solicit independent audits for the first time early in 2008. Later that year, however, as the American and world economies entered a recession, many publishers of Asian ethnic newspapers and magazines abandoned those initiatives (PEJ, 2009a). They either could no longer afford to pay for the auditing services or saw the benefits of doing so diminished, as the advertising market shrunk considerably.

Ethnic print media that can only provide self-reports of circulation or that cannot provide any data at all to potential advertisers find themselves at a disadvantage compared to other ethnic and mainstream media than can supply audited circulation information. This is one of the important lessons learned from examining the limited data available on audited versus unaudited print media. To counter this disadvantage, some of the smaller, community ethnic media that cannot afford to join an auditing bureau have entered alliances or networks of ethnic media producers. These networks are able to connect with advertisers who want to get their ads placed in a wide

Profile 5.1 Project for Excellence in Journalism

The Project for Excellence in Journalism (PEJ) is a research organization located in Washington, DC that studies and evaluates the performance of the press. It relies heavily on empirical research methods and aims to help journalists and the public better understand what the American press is delivering. The PEJ was founded in 1997; initially, it was affiliated with Columbia University's School of Journalism (CSJ). In 2006, it separated from CSJ and joined the Pew Research Center in Washington, DC. The Pew Research Center administers six other projects as well, all funded by the Pew Charitable Trust.

Profile 5.2 Latino Print Network

The Latino Print Network emerged in 1996. It is an ad-buy agency[3] that represents over 350 Latinos newspapers (published in Spanish and in English) in the United States. Its parent company, Western Publication Research, has conducted media research on Latinos in the U.S. since 1978.

Profile 5.3 BlackPress.org and the Historical Black Press Foundation

BlackPress.org is a part of the Historical Black Press Foundation. The Foundation was founded in 2000, and its mission is to provide professional development for young professionals and executives who work for Black media organizations. The organization prides itself for being an essential resource for information pertaining to the Black press in the United States and a "gateway to over 450 Black newspapers and magazines" (BlackPressMagazine.com, 2007, para. 10). Apart from BlackPress.org, the Historical Black Press Foundation is also responsible for the production

(Continued)

(Continued)

of (a) *Black Press Magazine*, (b) BlackPressRadio.com (an Internet-based radio station), (c) the BlackPressWeek.com (a weekly e-mail newsletter also found at BlackPressWeek.org and BlackPressWeek.net), and (d) the *Black Press Year: Who's Who in Black Media* directory.

spectrum of ethnic newspapers, magazines, and electronic media that target either one ethnic population or a variety of ethnic communities.

These ethnic media networks essentially offer advertisers a one-stop-shop solution, while raising the profile and credibility of their members. That is to say that they provide advertisers access to a wide spectrum of media outlets and are able to deflect advertiser concerns about the circulation numbers or ratings of anyone medium. Even if they are not auditing bureaus themselves, these intermediary organizations collect at least some data from their members, which they can in turn present to advertisers. Information made available in this fashion seems more objective and credible to advertisers, compared to the figures any individual ethnic media outlet may provide on its own. New America Media is an example of such a network of ethnic media (see Profile 5.4). In 2009, it had approximately 2,500 members from across the U.S. and across all media platforms (i.e., print and electronic).

Profile 5.4 New America Media

New America Media (NAM) is one of the first and largest U.S.-based collaborations of ethnic news organizations. It was founded by the nonprofit organization Pacific News Service in 1996, and its headquarters are in California. NAM's goal is to promote the editorial visibility and economic viability of ethnic media. NAM produces and aggregates editorial content from and for the ethnic media sector and develops marketing services on behalf of corporations, foundations, and non-profits that are targeting ethnic media and ethnic communities.

¤ For Further Discussion

Consider the following scenario: You are the manager of a major automobile dealer and you want to promote three new car models in your local market. A friend of yours suggested that you might benefit from advertising in the ethnic media that are available in your area. No matter how hard you search, though, you cannot turn up audited circulation and ratings data on these media. What other information would help you determine whether your friend's suggestion is a good one and how would you go about getting it?

A second and equally important point that becomes clear in studying audited and unaudited publications is that as ethnic populations grow in size, their print media become more likely to solicit independent audits. That is because population growth offers the promise of a larger audience base. Feeling more confident about the size of their audience, ethnic print media are more likely to get independent audits, which in turn are likely to attract advertisers.

This tendency is obvious in the case of Spanish-language print media in the United States. The size of the Spanish-speaking population in the U.S. as a proportion of the total population of the country is larger than that of any other ethnic group (except English-speaking, non-Hispanic Whites). The U.S. Census (2006) projected that close to 47.8 million people would identify themselves as Hispanic in 2010 (16% of the total population). That is an increase of 113%, compared to the 1990 estimate of the number of Hispanics in the U.S., which was 22.4 million people (Guzmán, 2001). California, New York, Texas, and Florida are states in which Latino communities have been thriving for years. But a number of studies suggest that Latinos are also moving into other regions of the U.S. (Aponte & Siles, 1994; Charvat-Burke & Goudy, 1999; Gouveia & Stull, 1995; Passel & Zimmerman, 2000).

Latino populations in states in the Midwest and the South grew significantly from 1990 to 2000. In the Midwest, the Hispanic population was 81% larger in 2000 than it was in 1990; in the South, 71% larger (Guzmán & Diaz McConnell, 2002). The growing Hispanic population is also of interest to advertisers who seek to leverage a growing Latino market. As noted in Chapter 1, the buying power of Latinos in the U.S. is predicted to reach $1 trillion in 2010. That would be over $260 billion higher than it was estimated to be in 2006 (Humphreys, 2006).

Ethnic Television and Radio: Trends and Politics Behind the Ratings

Television ratings for mainstream media in the U.S. are calculated by Nielsen Media Research. Radio ratings were provided exclusively by a company called Arbitron until 2008 when Nielsen announced it would begin to provide radio ratings as well (*The New York Times,* 2008).[4] The ratings that both these firms report refer to the number of people who tuned in to watch or listen to a particular program and a particular channel. The method of calculating ratings, however, is different for television and radio.

How Television and Radio Audiences Are Quantified

In television, ratings capture the number of people who tuned into a particular show during the average minute (Nielsen Media Research, 1993). In radio, the research firm Arbitron measures the average number of people listening to a particular station for at least 5 minutes during a 15-minute period. This is called the Average Quarter-Hour Persons. When it is expressed as a percentage, it is called the Average Quarter-Hour Rating (AQH Rating). If an Arbitron report indicates, for instance, that the AQH Persons from 10 a.m. to 3 p.m. for a particular radio station (e.g., WXYZ) is 50,000, that means that an average of 50,000 people were tuned in to WXYZ during any given 15-minute period between 10 a.m. and 3 p.m., beginning with 10 a.m. to 10:15 a.m. and ending with 2:45 p.m. to 3 p.m. If the station is located in a city with a population of 2 million people, then the AQH Rating for that station from 10 a.m. to 3 p.m. would be 2.5%. Arbitron provides other measures of station and program popularity. The Time Spent Listening (TSL) measure, for instance, is an estimate of the amount of time the average listener spent with a station during a particular part of the day (Arbitron, 2007), while CUME (short for cumulative audience) captures the estimated total number of listeners who tune into a station during a specified part of the day. Some ethnic radio stations may prefer the TSL measure, as they tend to have smaller, but more loyal audiences who tune into their frequencies for longer periods of time (F. Gutiérrez, personal communication, August 22, 2009).

The Audience of Electronic Ethnic Media: Two Examples From the United States

Most ethnic television and radio stations are highly local and relatively small scale operations, scattered around the United States. This makes getting accurate ratings data on many of them at least as difficult as getting circulation information on ethnic newspapers and magazines (PEJ, 2007b). There are some exceptions, though, primarily among Latino and African-American media. For these media, data are easier to find and more reliable.

Nielsen has provided data on the African-American audience and programs targeting this audience since the early 1990s (Steadman, 2005). There are several key reasons that led to this development. The size of the African-American audience is one of them. African-Americans comprise over 12% of the total U.S. population according to the 2000 U.S. Census.[5] As a television audience, African-Americans also have distinct characteristics. Overall, African-Americans watch significantly more television than the U.S. population as a whole. On a daily basis, while American men (18 years of age or older) watch television for about 4 hours and 40 minutes a day, on average, African-American men spend 6 hours and 26 minutes a day watching television. Similarly, all women (18-plus) in the U.S. watch an average of 5 hours and 20 minutes of television per day, while African-American women watch TV for an average of 7 hours and 8 minutes a day (Steadman, 2005). Over the course of a week, this means that African-American women watch television 25 hours more per week than the average American woman (Liss, 2003).

Additionally African-Americans navigate their choices in television channels, seeking different programs than Americans from a different ethnic background. A study by Nielsen, conducted in 2005, that focused on the African-American audience found that award programs and ceremonies were rated as the number one choice in African-American households, and among African-American women and children. Police-related programs (labeled *Official Police* by Nielsen) were ranked first among African-American men (Steadman, 2005). Networks targeting African-Americans can rely on the foregoing distinct viewing patterns of this population to attract viewers, as can advertisers who want to reach out to this large and increasingly financially powerful ethnic group.

The increase in the spending power of African-Americans is another factor that pushed rating agencies, like Nielsen, towards providing data on the African-American audience. The spending power of African-Americans is expected to reach $1 trillion by 2010 (Crupi & Consoli, 2006; see also Nielsen, 2008). Three major African-American cable television networks have emerged since the 1980s and have attempted to leverage the increasing power of African-American consumers: Black Entertainment Television (BET), TV One, and the Africa Channel.[6] In 2008, all three African-American cable channels expanded their reach considerably compared to the previous year.[7]

Data on the audience of Latino broadcasters have also become more readily available since the early 1990s. Both Nielsen and Arbitron frequently publish reports about the Hispanic audience and Latino radio and television channels. Several factors have pushed rating agencies to include Hispanic audiences and broadcasters in their reports. The first key driver has been the substantial increase in the size of the Hispanic population, which made advertisers see an opportunity to enlarge their market share. The second has been the fact that Hispanics, like African-Americans, are heavy viewers of television and avid radio listeners. Arbitron data suggest that since 1998 there has been a continuous increase in both the number of listeners across all age groups and the number of available Hispanic radio stations (Arbitron, 2007).

With regard to television, the Project for Excellence in Journalism (2006) estimates that Spanish-language television news has even greater growth potential than print, as Latinos of all age groups watch more television than the average American household. Additionally, more and more Latino households are able to purchase a television (PEJ, 2006; Allied Media Corporation, 2007).[8]

Challenges in Measuring Electronic Ethnic Media Audiences

Although these trends have been compelling reasons for rating agencies to invest more effort in the careful study of the Hispanic audience and Latino broadcasters, changes in the way data are collected and reported have not come quickly. Nielsen created the National Hispanic Television Index (NHTI) in 1992 to capture the audience of Spanish-language programming. However, the sample of people Nielsen used to estimate these ratings was not incorporated in the national sample the agency used to get ratings for English-language programming on broadcast and cable networks. Having two separate sets of data resulted in many advertisers overlooking Spanish-language media. Even the software used by advertisers to create their media buying plans (budgets) typically did not include Spanish-language shows (James, 2005).

Monica Gadsby, chief executive of Tapestry, a unit of media buying giant Starcom MediaVest Group, in an interview with *The Los Angeles Times,* explained that, "The fact that the research has been segregated has been an excuse for some general market advertisers to focus only on the general market networks. . . . [b]ut it shouldn't be thought of that way any longer. Spanish-language media [are] part of the new general market" (James, 2005).

Counted along with the other major networks, in 2005 and 2006 Univisión was the 5th most popular television network in the U.S. among viewers under 50 years old, after CBS, ABC, NBC, and Fox (PEJ, 2007b). In the 18 to 34 age group—the prime age group for advertisers—the Spanish-language medium often ranked second, just behind Fox (James, 2005). In response to the changing demographics in the country, shifts in the television landscape, and the persistent pressure applied by ethnic media producers and advocates over the course of 30 years (F. Gutiérrez, personal communication, August 22, 2009), Nielsen finally announced in 2005 that Spanish and English-speaking Latino viewers would be added to the national sample and that Spanish-language channels and programs would be rated along with English-language media.

But the transition to the new system was not smooth. There were delays along the way that caused controversy. Univisión and Telemundo, the second largest Spanish-language broadcaster in the U.S. (owned by NBC parent company General Electric), attributed the delays to pressures put on Nielsen by the major English-language networks (James, 2004a; James, 2004b; Lindorff, 2000) who did not want the status quo changed and who did not want to compete with a Spanish-language network for advertising.

Various issues needed to be resolved before Nielsen's new system of reporting could go into effect. A very important one had to do with the composition of the Latino sample that was incorporated into the national sample. In the initial tests, run by Nielsen to assess the new system, Univisión's audience appeared to be lower than it was before (i.e., when two samples were used) in some of its most important markets, including Los Angeles. Univisión challenged the agency in court, charging that Nielsen's new system would cause the company irreparable harm, as lower ratings would translate into diminished revenues from advertising. Univisión argued that the new national sample included too few Spanish-speaking Latinos. Also, the media giant said that households included in the national sample were considered "Latino" only if the head of the household self-identified as Hispanic and not if anyone else in the household did. In November 2004 Univisión Communications, Inc., withdrew the lawsuit. After lengthy negotiations with Nielsen, the company's President and Chief Financial Officer, Ray Rodriguez, said in December 2005 that, "Univisión will finally be measured alongside its main competitors, the major English-language broadcast networks" (Entertainment Magazine, 2005; James, 2004b; James 2005).

Similar controversy was caused 2 years later, in 2007, when Arbitron announced that it was rolling out new methods of measuring radio station audiences. Instead of diaries, which a sample of listeners fills out relying on memory, Arbitron implemented the use of devices it called *portable people meters.* The new devices are able to capture automatically what station and program a person is listening to, as well as for how long. The company indicated these new devices would be in use across all 50 markets in the U.S. by the end of 2010 and that until then a combination of listening diaries and portable people meters would be used (PEJ, 2009).

When the first data collected via the portable people meters were released, radio stations catering to African-American and Latino communities saw substantial decreases in their ratings. For example, station WBLS, which targets a primarily African-American audience, slipped from 4th place to number 11, while Spanish-language station WCAA dropped to number 20. Prior to the introduction of the new system of collecting data, WCAA was ranked number 5 (Stelter, 2008).

Ethnic media producers, but also mainstream radio executives (e.g., Clear Channel Communications), charged that the sample used by Arbitron was too small and that it under-represented minorities. Black and Latino radio stations feared that these lower ratings would hurt their advertising revenue stream. Electronic media catering to other ethnic populations shared their concerns. In 2008, New York State Attorney General Cuomo sued Arbitron arguing that the new system Arbitron was implementing discriminated against minorities by undercounting them (Stelter, 2008). Following in the footsteps of New York, the state of New Jersey sued Arbitron later that year as well. Eventually Arbitron agreed to settle the lawsuit in January 2009. The settlement forced Arbitron to make significant improvements to its methodology and to pay $390,000 to New York and New Jersey. In addition, Arbitron agreed to pay $100,000 to the National Association of Black-Owned Broadcasters and to the Spanish Radio Association to support minority radio, and to fund an advertising campaign of at least $25,000 that would promote minority radio stations (Office of New York State Attorney General, 2009; *Los Angeles Times,* 2009; Stelter, 2009).

The struggle of ethnic media to persuade Nielsen and then Arbitron to improve their research methods suggest at least two conclusions:

- First, that ethnic media, large and small, need to continue to pressure media research firms to ensure that ethnic populations are accurately represented. Not doing so can hurt their ability to generate revenue. In the wake of the Nielsen case, it is remarkable that Arbitron deployed a new methodology that had not been widely accepted by ethnic radio producers.
- And second, that ethnic media should continue to invest in developing those organizations that can represent their interests effectively and to pursue those political coalitions that are necessary to have their voices heard. The Arbitron case indicates that ethnic media have the capacity to accomplish these goals. Rallying the support of New York State and the State of New Jersey contributed positively to the outcome.

Two Alternative Models for Sustainable Ethnic Television and Radio

The examples of Spanish-language and African-American television in the U.S. are exceptional. That is because they both have a very long history, and with respect to Latino media, in particular, they are serving a growing population. In addition, both the Latino and the Black population are becoming financially stronger, which makes them very appealing to advertisers. Nonetheless, these examples highlight the hurdles that smaller scale and more local ethnic media face in their efforts to attract major advertisers. In most cases, they need to seek alternative ways to attract advertising and to fund their operations. The model that New America Media represents (discussed earlier in this chapter) offers promise to many small and mid-size media operations.

A very different model has been tested in Britain by the Radio Authority, the regulator of radio broadcasting licenses.[9] In 2002, 15 groups were selected to participate in a program referred to as "Access Radio" (and later as "Community Radio"). These groups were chosen from a pool of nearly 200 applicants. In launching the program, the Radio Authority's goal was to create a new tier of radio services created *by* and *for* local communities. These services were not connected to the BBC and were not considered commercial ventures. They were to run not for profit but, as then British government culture secretary noted, for "social gain" (Brown, 2003, para 1).

"Social gain" was realized in several ways: For example, many stations offered training in the use of new communication technologies and radio production to community members who volunteered; others produced programming intended to help combat social exclusion of particular populations (e.g., seniors or ethnic minorities) in the areas in which they were based; still others sought to build civic engagement in diverse ethnic communities. The Radio Authority did not provide funding for these projects, but instead encouraged them to "experiment with a range of funding models" (Everitt, 2003, p. 19). Many of these community radio ventures have raised funds from the communities they serve, but they have also won grants from public sources (e.g., city council, local police), and various foundations. Among the 15 projects selected to receive a license, four were launched by ethnic community groups:

- Awaz FM was launched in Glasgow, and its goal was to improve communication between the isolated South Asian community, the city council, the police, and other public agencies.
- Radio Faza, based in Nottingham, UK, was concerned with promoting empowerment for women in the Pakistani (and predominantly Mirpuri)[10] community (and Asian women more broadly).
- Desi Radio, located in Southall (west of London), aimed to reconcile differences among the various segments of Punjabi society (e.g., Punjabis of various faiths: Sikhs, Muslims, and Hindus).[11]
- New Style Radio, launched in Birmingham, UK, aimed to empower people of Caribbean-origin and to address issues of inequality, social and economic exclusion, as well as unemployment.[12]

In an evaluation of the Radio Authority's initiative, Everitt (2003) found that "Access Radio promises to be a positive cultural and social development and should be introduced as a third tier of radio broadcasting in the United Kingdom" (p. 8). He recommended that the government create an Access Media Fund to provide partial support to Access Radio stations. In addition, he argued that Access Radio stations should be permitted to receive up to half their income from advertising sales and that doing so would not affect the viability of small scale commercial radio ventures that operated in the same areas. Similar models of community radio have been tested in other European countries (see Chapter 7 for an example from France), and also Canada and Australia.

⌑ For Further Discussion

Think about how the model of Access Radio implemented in Britain may be implemented in the area where you live. What would be the nature of the "social gains" you would seek to achieve through the creation of a community radio station?

Trends in Print Media Circulation

In the pages that follow our focus is on identifying important trends in the circulation of ethnic newspapers and the forces that drive them. Unfortunately, there are few reliable circulation data on newspapers beyond those serving Latino and African-American communities. Despite this limitation, careful analysis of the cases of Hispanic and Black print media in the U.S. can provide valuable insight that can be employed in much needed research on newspapers and periodicals serving other ethnic communities in the U.S. and elsewhere.

Latino and African-American Print Media: Two Different Stories

The most comprehensive data are those pertaining to the circulation of Hispanic newspapers in the United States. Still, only 160 of 737 (22%) Hispanic newspapers are audited by one of five major auditing services, including the Certified Audit of Circulation (CAC), which serves mostly Hispanic and African-American publications (Latino Print Network, 2005; PEJ, 2009a; Latino Print Media, 2007).[13] Over the course of more than 3 decades, Latino daily newspaper circulation has grown considerably, from under 2 million copies a year in 1970, to 17.6 million in 2005 (Latino Print Network, 2007). *La Opinión,* founded in 1926 and based in Los Angeles, has the largest circulation, with a readership of over 100,400 copies per day in Southern California. It is followed by *El Nuevo Herald,* based in Miami and distributed in South Florida, which hovers around the 77,500 mark. *El Diario* in New York, the oldest Latino newspaper still publishing, stands third with a circulation near 52,000 (PEJ, 2009a).[14] The total number of Latino newspapers published in the U.S. has been on the rise consistently from the 1970s through 2005. While there were only 8 daily Latino newspapers in 1970 and 14 in 1990, there were 34 in 2000 and 42 in 2005. Similar growth is observed for weeklies. Their numbers climbed from 74 in 1970 to 152 in 1990, to 417 in 2007. In addition, the number of newspapers published on a bi-weekly, monthly, or less frequent basis has grown from 150 in 1970 to 377 in 2007. The majority of the weekly and less-than-weekly publications tend to be smaller, local community media that cannot afford (or do not want) to become dailies. The increase in their numbers indicates that the Hispanic community press is growing. Finally, Latino magazines have also grown considerably in number. The

Latino Print Network (2007) reported that there were 513 magazines in 2006, compared to 477 in 2005 and 352 in 2000.

Many of these newspapers are found in California, Florida, New York, and Texas, where Hispanic-origin populations are larger. Data from a 2005 Latino Print Network study, however, suggest that Latino newspapers may be found in many other states, such as Colorado, Illinois, Kentucky, Michigan, Minnesota, and Oklahoma (see Figure 5.2.).

Figure 5.2 Location of Latino Newspapers in the United States (This is not a media census.)

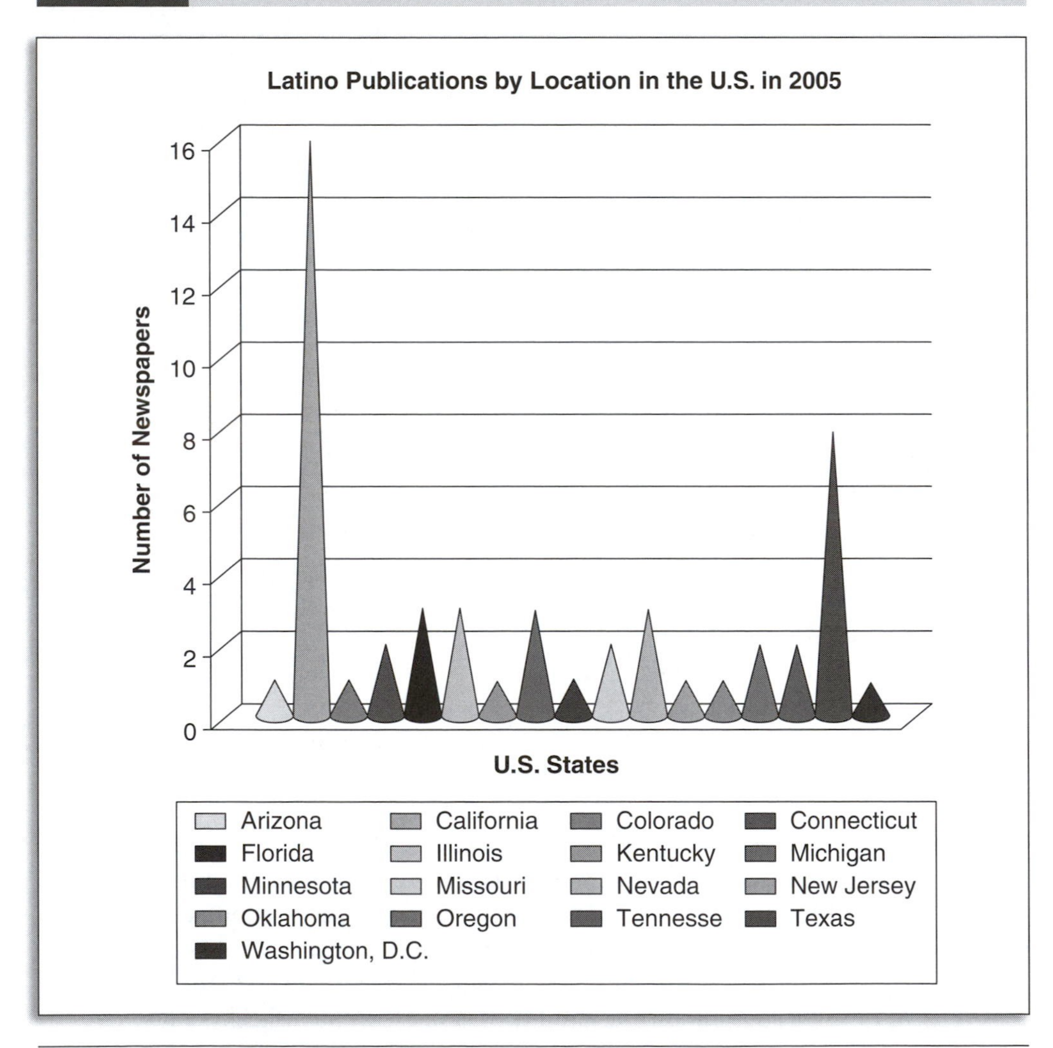

Source: Latino Print Network (2005).

Note: The figure indicates the wide variety of locations across the U.S. where Latino newspapers have been founded. These data are not the product of a census of Latino ethnic newspapers in the U.S. Some states such as New York, where a number of Latino newspapers are thriving, were not included in the Latino Print Network study that produced these data.

Research also suggests that more and more metropolitan areas in the United States are being served by Latino newspapers. In 1995, Latino print media were present in 80 major U.S. metropolitan areas. In 2006, there were Latino newspapers in 130 metropolitan areas; that is an increase of 163%. Additionally, the Latino print media, founded in major metropolitan areas in the U.S., were published more frequently in 2006. While in 1995 the vast majority of new Latino print media organizations founded in metropolitan areas were published on a "less-than-weekly" basis, in 2006 weekly publications represented 55% to 60% of newly founded media. When interviewed by the Project for Excellence in Journalism, Kirk Whisler, the president of the Latino Print Network, said that this change "shows that publishers not only believe Hispanic publications can thrive, but that the populations they serve are big enough, or media-interested enough, to warrant a more regular publishing schedule" (PEJ, 2007b).

Contrary to the image of overall growth one sees in the Latino print media landscape, the circulation of African-American publications has dwindled considerably since 2000. The average circulation of weekly newspapers in 2000 was approximately 500,000. In 2008, that number was reduced by half (Frazier, 2008; PEJ, 2009a). The three largest African-American newspapers, *The Philadelphia Tribune, The Afro-American,* and *The Amsterdam News* all saw their circulations decline in 2008, particularly later in the year when the world's economic health deteriorated dramatically; their circulations in September 2008 were down 4%, 15%, and 11%, respectively. The overall negative picture that the circulation numbers of African-American newspapers paint is attributed largely to the fact that their audiences, comprised largely by the generation of the 1960s civil rights era, are aging (PEJ, 2009a).

Decreases in Latino Print Media Numbers and Circulation

Not all news is positive for Latino print media. For the first time ever, circulation for dailies and less-than-weeklies dropped in 2006. There were also fewer daily newspapers in 2006 than there were in 2005. The number of dailies dropped from 42 to 38 and their combined circulation was 0.2% lower. The number of less-than-weeklies rose by about 1%, but the total circulation of less-than-weeklies shrunk by 1%. This is contrasted to the 9.7% increase in the number of weeklies founded in 2006 (compared to 2005) and the 2.2% increase of the weeklies' total circulation. Currently, it is hard to assess how significant these decreases really are and what they signal for the years ahead. In any case, there are several hypotheses about what is causing these decreases (or the leveling off) in numbers and circulation of Latino publications.

One hypothesis suggests that the decline in the overall circulation of Latino dailies may be related to the fact that there were fewer Latino dailies altogether in 2006 than there were before. The circulation decrease may also be attributed to the fact that more and more publications released audited circulation figures and not self-reports. Self-reports tend to be less accurate and usually inflated.

Another possible explanation may be related to the language of publication and to the changing demographics of the Latino population in the United States. In 2006, 95% of the daily Latino newspapers, 88% of the weeklies, and 28% of the less-than-weekly newspapers published in the U.S. were printed in Spanish. Of the Latino magazines, 78% were published in Spanish. At the same time, U.S. Census data indicated that while the Hispanic population in the country continued to grow, for the first time, this growth was due more to births of Hispanic-origin Americans than to immigration. This can be attributed mainly to the tighter control of the U.S.-Mexican border. In 2006, according to a study by the Pew Hispanic Center (2008), 40% of Latinos in the U.S. had been born abroad. However, based on that study and other reports, the number of the foreign-born as a percentage of the total number of Latinos in the country has been declining since 2000 (Jordan & Dougherty, 2008; Passel & Cohn, 2008; Pew Hispanic Center, 2008). U.S.-born Latinos are more likely to be fluent in English, and many are likely to feel less comfortable speaking and reading Spanish. That means that they are likely to read fewer Spanish-language newspapers and more English-language print media. Therefore it is also plausible that these changes in the demographics of U.S. Latinos have and will negatively impact Spanish-language media, albeit not Latino media in general.

These changes may explain the decline in Latino dailies that are mostly (95%) published in Spanish, but they may also explain the increase in the number and circulation of weeklies and less-than-weeklies that are more likely to be published in English. Based on the Latino Print Network's (2007) figures, over 10% of Latino weeklies and approximately 70% of Latino less-than-weeklies are published in English. The above mentioned changes in the profile of the Hispanic audience are relatively new, and only tentative conclusions about how they will influence Spanish-language newspapers can be drawn.

Another plausible explanation for the shrinkage in the number of daily Latino newspapers may be found in the changes in print media ownership. In San Jose, California, for instance, Spanish-language *Nuevo Mundo* was closed when the Knight-Ridder chain of newspapers was sold (PEJ, 2007b). Ethnic media ownership issues will be discussed in more detail in Chapter 7.

The Impact of the Larger Industry Context

Changes in circulation numbers should be considered in the larger context of what is happening in the newspaper industry. The question is whether a decline in circulation of ethnic newspapers may be attributed to more general trends affecting the newspaper business.

In the United States in 2001, "major public [newspaper industry] companies had operating profits averaging about 15% and net profits averaging about 12%" (Picard, 2004, p. 114). Seven years later though, the newspaper industry suffered its worst year on record. Just compared to 2007, the total advertising revenues of U.S. newspapers in 2008 declined 16.6% or $37.85 billion (Newspaper Association of America [NAA], 2008; Schonfeld, 2009). Nevertheless, today, the newspaper industry continues to be one of the largest in the world, rivaling in terms of profitability not only other communication industries, but also many of the manufacturing industries.

As alluded to in the earlier discussion about auditing circulation, newspapers operate in a *dual market,* which means that they compete against each other for better circulation and for more advertising. While daily circulation of American newspapers grew by 18.9% from 1950 to 1990, a jump from 53 million copies to 62.3 million, circulation tumbled about 5% from 1990 to 2000, due largely to the fact that many evening editions of morning papers ceased (NAA, 2001). Circulation continued to drop in the first decade of the new millennium.[15] In April 2009, U.S. newspaper circulations experienced a drop of 7% compared to a year earlier (Arango, 2009).

The decline in circulation of Latino newspapers from 2006 onwards is linked to this more general trend. This trend can be attributed in part to the proliferation of media available to people today (e.g., broadcast television and radio, cable, satellite programming) and particularly to the fact that more and more individuals are migrating to the Internet to get their daily news.

The case of Latino newspapers in the U.S., suggests that the number of ethnic newspapers available and the size of their circulations are likely to be affected by both (a) general industry trends (e.g., incorporation of multiple new media in people's lives) and (b) by forces that have less (or little) impact on mainstream newspapers. The latter include the growth or decline in the ethnic population's size and significant changes in an ethnic community's demographics. Second and third generation members of an ethnic community tend to be fluent in the language spoken by the majority of the people in the country their parents or grandparents settled in and may or may not be fluent in the language spoken by the immigrant generation. That means that they are likely to feel more comfortable reading newspapers in English, for example, rather than in Spanish, or Greek, Korean or Chinese. A 2005 study on Asian-Americans found that Asians who are second generation and beyond consume far more English media (i.e., newspaper, radio, and TV), than the first and "1.5 generation."[16] They also consume less Asian-language (or in-language) media than the "1.5" and first generation (Cultural Access Group & Interviewing Service of America, 2005). These findings suggest that ethnic newspapers need to be attuned to the changing needs of their readerships (see also Chapter 4). Some ethnic publications (and electronic media) in the U.S. have developed bilingual or separate English editions for younger audiences. These English-language editions do not compete directly with mainstream English-language media, as they provide cultural news and information that is not available in the latter (PEJ, 2009a). Still, to date, there is a paucity of reliable data available that would help answer the question of when and under what conditions adopting a "dual-language" strategy is most successful.

The Effects of the 2008 Economic Crisis

In addition to the general decline the newspaper industry has been experiencing in the United States and elsewhere from the turn of the century through 2009, the world economy entered a period of recession in 2008. Reports released just before the end of 2009 suggested that the newspaper industry was significantly affected by the crisis. The three major Hispanic publications, *La Opinión, El Diario/La Prensa,* and *El Nuevo Herald* saw declines in their circulations, but they were not as large as the ones experienced by mainstream U.S. newspapers (PEJ, 2009a). In response to the crisis, a number of Latino, African-American, and Asian publications discontinued their print editions and migrated to the Web. We discuss the challenges and opportunities for newspapers that are associated with the Internet in the following chapter.

The Audiences of Ethnic Television and Radio

Reliable trend data on the ratings of ethnic television channels are scarce, with the exception of major African-American and Latino broadcasting networks in the U.S. Overall, though, it appears that through 2008 and early 2009, ethnic electronic media continued to grow (PEJ, 2009a). Certain television and radio networks were able to expand their operations, while a number of smaller ethnic television and radio channels were founded in unexpected places. For example, two Spanish-language radio stations, KTBK (1210 AM) and WZUP (104.7 FM), came on the air in Seattle and La Grange, North Carolina, respectively. Both these cities had not been associated in the past with a strong presence of Latinos. In addition, one Spanish-language radio station in Atlanta, WFTD (1080 AM), changed format and language to cater to the increasingly larger Korean community (New America Media & Bendixen & Associates, 2009). These findings attest to the impact that increasing population diversity is having on the media landscape as we know it, and on the ethnic media sector more specifically.

Ethnic Television

Networks targeting African-Americans have a history of more than 25 years. Black Entertainment Television (BET) was founded in 1980 by Robert L. Johnson, a former cable industry lobbyist. Initially, BET programming aired 2 nights a week on the USA Network (a cable network). In 1983, it launched its first 24-hour schedule. Its viewership was estimated to be 7.6 million people. In 2001, BET was acquired by the media giant Viacom, which also owns the CBS network. The price tag was $3 billion. The network saw its ratings grow in the first year after the acquisition. Ad revenue figures went up as well. During the 2001–2002 television season, BET's advertising revenue increased by 17 to 18% compared to the previous year (Brady, 2002; Brady, 2003). Five years later, in 2006, the network continued to improve its position in the U.S. media market. It maintained its number one ranking among African-Americans, 18 to 34 years of age ("BET wraps up record-setting," 2007). According to Nielsen Media Research, in 2007, BET reached over 77 million households in the United States, Canada, and the Caribbean. In 2008, a 3% increase brought BET to 90.5 million homes. In 2006, BET also introduced BET

International, and in June 2007, the network announced that it would launch a 24-hour general entertainment service in Britain, targeting Blacks of Caribbean and African descent (Holmwood, 2007).

BET is not the only contender for the African-American cable media market. In 2004, the Comcast Corporation, the largest cable operator in the U.S., joined forces with the number one radio broadcasting company in the country targeting African-Americans, Radio One.[17] Together they launched TV One, which targets African-Americans who are between 24 and 54 years old. Compared to the audience of BET, which targets primarily younger African-Americans, 18 to 34 years old (Liss, 2003), TV One's audience is older. In 2006, TV One reached 28 million households in the U.S. (Crupi & Consoli, 2006). Two years later, it had more than doubled its audience (PEJ, 2009a).

In Spanish-language television, Univisión continued to dominate the ratings in 2008. While ranked fifth overall (after English-language CBS, ABC, NBC, and Fox), Univisión was the number one network in prime time many nights a week for all viewers aged 18 to 34 (regardless of language), in markets with large Hispanic populations; these included Los Angeles, Miami, Houston, Dallas, San Antonio, Phoenix, Fresno, and Bakersfield (PEJ, 2006; PEJ, 2009a).

In 2002, Univisión Communications also launched Spanish-language TeleFutura, intended to target a younger audience than sister Univisión channels. TeleFutura *counter-programs* most other Spanish-language television networks. Counter-programming is a strategy used by television stations to compete against each other. For instance, when most Spanish-language networks are airing prime-time telenovelas (Spanish-language soap operas), TeleFutura airs blockbuster movies. In the morning, TeleFutura opts for talk shows instead of daytime telenovelas, and when its competition is broadcasting news or talk shows, TeleFutura broadcasts "originally produced novelas" ("Media Properties: Telefutura Network," n.d., para 2). TeleFutura also offers programs that are popular among teens and coverage of major sporting events.

The new channel proved to be a formidable competitor for NBC/General Electric-owned Telemundo. The latter had consistently been ranked Number 2 prior to TeleFutura's entrance into the market. But, in 2005, TeleFutura had a greater share of viewers than Telemundo in all programming zones of the day, except primetime (PEJ, 2006). Nielsen data for the first quarter of 2007 indicated that, for the first time, TeleFutura also beat Telemundo's popularity during prime-time among the 18 to 34 age group (Nielsen Media Research, cited in Univision, 2007). Data from 2005 released by Univisión suggest that the Univisión network reaches 98% of Latino households in the United States, while TeleFutura reaches 86% (PEJ, 2006).

From a revenue point-of-view, Univisión saw gains every year between 2001 and 2004, climbing from a net income (revenue minus expenses) of under $60 million to $255.9 million. In 2005, however, net profits were down to $187.2 million (a decrease of 27%). While the decline is significant, it could be attributed to the sale of stocks of the company's subsidiary Entravision. Entravision is a Spanish-language media company that owns television stations, radio stations, and outdoor billboards (PEJ, 2007b). In early 2007, the forecasts for Univisión were mixed, although it was generally thought that the Spanish-language medium still had room to grow. However, Goldman Sachs—a global investments, banking, and securities firm—noted that growth is likely to be less linear than in the past and slower, as the major markets for the Latino media (e.g., Los Angeles, New York, and Miami) are becoming saturated (PEJ, 2007b).[18]

Details about television channels serving other ethnic communities are few. However, two national surveys by New America Media and Bendixen and Associates (2005, 2009) do provide some insight with regard to ethnic television's audience in the U.S. In 2009, ethnic television reached 86% of Latinos (up 10% from 2005), 58% of African-Americans (up 12% from 2005), and 57% of Asian-Americans (including Chinese, Korean, Vietnamese, Filipino, and Asian-Indian; up 30% from 2005). The data from the 2005 survey also indicated that ethnic television reached 55% of Arab-Americans (no comparable data were available in 2009). This is due, at least in part, to the significant variety of Arab television channels made available to audiences in North America via satellite (PEJ, 2006).

Ethnic Radio

Adding up primary (meaning people who favor ethnic media) and secondary users (i.e., individuals who prefer mainstream but who connect to ethnic radio as well), close to 70% of Latinos (up from 54% in 2005) and 67% of African-Americans (up from 56% in 2005) connect to ethnic radio stations on a regular basis. That is the largest percentage of primary and secondary radio connectors among the groups included in the 2009 study by New America Media and Bendixen and Associates cited earlier. According to the same study, among Asian populations, the reach of ethnic radio is lower. Among ethnic Chinese, 31% were primary and secondary users, among Koreans 27%, among Vietnamese 34%, among Filipinos 11%, and among South Asians (Indian) 19%. Although Arabs were not included in the 2009 study, data from a 2005 survey by Bendixen and Associates indicate that only 2% of Arabs connect to ethnic radio.

Today, the two most listened to radio stations in Los Angeles, America's largest radio market, are Spanish-language stations (Boyle, 2006; Wilkin, Ball-Rokeach, Matsaganis, & Cheong, 2007). This trend started in January 1993. At the time, nearly 90,000 people tuned into station KLAX-FM/97.9 La Raza every day. The largest and most popular Latino radio stations in the U.S. are KSCA-FM/Nueva 101.9 in Los Angeles, WCMQ-FM in Miami, WSKQ-FM in New York, KESS-FM in Dallas, and WOJO-FM in Chicago ("Hispanic Media Facts," 2005). Data released by Arbitron (2007) suggest that Hispanics of all ages connect to the radio and that between 2002 and 2006 the time Latinos spent on Spanish-language radio increased by 1 full hour.

Spanish-language radio stations are broken up into nine different categories, based on their content. In 2007, there were (a) 277 stations classified as Mexican regional; (b) 145 categorized as Spanish variety; (c) 134 as Spanish contemporary stations; (d) 68 as Spanish religious channels; (e) 61 as Spanish news/talk stations; (f) 49 stations classified under the Spanish adult hits rubric; (g) 49 classified under the Spanish tropical category; (h) 27 that played Spanish oldies; and (i) 25 categorized as Tejano. Mexican regional and Spanish contemporary formats were the most popular, garnering 19.7% and 13% of the Hispanic audience share. Mexican regional stations are classified as such because they tend to play various types of music coming from Mexico. The appeal of these stations, as the name suggests, is greater among audiences in the southwestern states of the U.S. (Arbitron 2007).

Apart from large scale operations, like the Latino radio stations mentioned above, there is substantial diversity in terms of the forms ethnic radio has taken. There is a mixture of ethnic radio stations on the AM/FM frequencies and multilingual radio programming that listeners get access to by tuning in to campus, community, public radio, and VHF stations.[19]

Ethnic radio and television are also not immune to the larger social, political, and economic context in which they emerge. In Chapter 6 we discuss some of the challenges they face due to the emergence of new communication modalities that rely on the Internet or satellite technology.

Summary

In Chapter 5 we shifted focus from how ethnic communities incorporate ethnic media into their daily lives to issues and concerns that ethnic media producers have to deal with in the day-to-day operation of their organizations. We discussed the significance of circulation figures and ratings for ethnic print and electronic media, respectively, and highlighted the major trends observed in the most recent data available in the U.S. In addition, we discussed the factors that impact the circulation and ratings of ethnic media in the U.S., but also in many other countries around the world. Finally, in Chapter 5, we presented two alternative models that certain ethnic media producers have implemented to sustain their operations. These are typically smaller, usually local, community-oriented organizations that cannot count on impressive circulations or ratings to build a strong advertising base, or organizations that are not interested in turning a profit. In the following chapter we will discuss the dynamics of competition among commercial ethnic media, as well as how these organizations are dealing with the challenges and opportunities inherent in new and emerging new communication technologies.

Study Questions

1. You have been hired as consultant by the owner of a Filipino weekly newspaper, located in California. The owner tells you that she and the newspaper's staff estimate circulation to be around 15,000. However, the newspaper is suffering from a lack of advertising. You have been asked to help the newspaper decide whether soliciting the auditing services of an independent organization would be beneficial or not. The staff believes that doing so might boost the newspaper's credibility among advertisers. You are supposed to give your recommendations at the next staff meeting. Preliminary research shows you that none of your three competitors is audited by an independent third party. All three, however, produce self-reports, according to which their circulations are: (a) 20,000, (b) 12,500, and (c) 16,700. What would you recommend? Why? If you need more data to make a decision, explain what kind of data you need and how having them would inform your decision.

2. The U.S. Census indicates that approximately 15.5% of the American population self-identifies as Hispanic. That is around 48 million people. These figures are encouraging for any entrepreneur considering founding a television channel targeted to Hispanics, but more information is necessary if they want their business to be successful. Make a list of the data you believe they would need in preparing a business plan for the new television channel and justify your choices. Next to every data type, identify what the best source for that information may be.

3. You have to write a report on the future of ethnic media. What trends will you take into account in writing your report? Where would you come down? Would you be positive or negative in your outlook?

Notes

[1]The four agencies that ethnic media rely on for auditing are: (a) the Audit Bureau of Circulation (ABC); (b) the Certified Audit of Circulation (CAC), which is a member of the International Federation of ABCs and serves 15% of U.S. publications (see www.ifabc.org); (c) Better Print Media (BPA), which serves 3,000 print media in 25 countries worldwide (see www.bpaww.com); and (d) the Verified Audit of Circulation (VAC), which was founded in California in 1951 (see www.verifiedaudit.com). In 2006, ABC audited Latino newspapers that had a total circulation of 5 million copies annually; CAC's members had a combined circulation of 3.5 million copies, CVC's members had 3.3 million, BPA's members had 2.7 million, and VAC had 1.9 million copies (Latino Print Network, 2007).

[2]See Audit Bureau of Circulations Web site: http://www.accessabc.com/aboutabc/index.htm.

[3]Simply, an ad-buying agency brokers agreement between advertisers and media organizations that collects a commission for its services.

[4]Nielsen has been providing radio ratings data in other countries long before 2008.

[5]According to the 2000 U.S. Census, the number of Americans who self-identified as African-American or Black was 34,658,190, while the total population was 281,421,906.

[6]All three channels provide a wide variety of programming. The Africa Channel is particularly interesting because it offers English-language programming from African countries, including television series, documentaries, soaps, business news, and cultural and history shows.

[7]BET was available to 90.5 million households, up 3% compared to 2007. TV One reached an average of 58 million homes, up 37% from 2007, while the Africa Channel was available in close to 8 million households, doubling its reach compared to the previous year (PEJ, 2009).

[8]The number of Latino homes where English is the primary language spoken and that own a television increased 12% between 2002 and 2005. In the same time frame, the number of households with a television where Spanish was the primary or only language spoken went up by 19%.

[9]The Radio Authority was absorbed in December 2003 by the British Office of Communications (OfCom).

[10]The Mirpuri district lies at the foothills of the Himalayas, in Northeastern Pakistan.

[11]Punjabis are divided; some live in India, while others are located in Pakistan.

[12]In October 2009, all four radio stations were still in operation and had a presence on the Web.

[13]Newspapers are classified as daily, weekly, or less than weekly, while magazines are categorized as glossy or newsprint. By including annual publications, catalogs, journals, newsletters, and yellow pages to this list of Hispanic print media, the total number increase significantly. For example, the total number of Latino print media in 2005 was 1,675 (Latino Print Network, 2005, p. 10).

[14]*El Diario/La Prensa* was founded in New York in 1913. It is owned by ImpreMedia, the same company that owns *La Opinión.*

[15]Between 2000 and 2005, decreasing newspaper circulations were also observed in Canada and Latin America, across the European Union, Australia, and Japan. In contrast, sales of newspapers increased in China, India, Singapore, Malaysia, Indonesia, and across the African continent (World Association of Newspapers, 2006). However, there is a paucity of data on the circulation of ethnic newspapers in most of the above mentioned countries.

[16]The term "1.5 generation" is generally used to refer to people who immigrate to a country as children or teens (see also Chapter 3).

[17]Radio One was founded in 1980, and in 2008 the company owned and/or operated 53 radio stations across 16 U.S. urban media markets (Liss, 2003; Radio One, 2008).

[18]Data on Telemundo's revenue are not available, as they are not separated out from General Electric's revenues.

[19]This is due in part to the high cost of entry into the large scale radio business. It is also the result of the political barriers that keep ethnic groups from gaining access to the radio waves. The Canadian Radio-Television and Telecommunications Commission (CRTC), for instance, has refused to grant licenses to minority Black radio stations in Toronto as well as to a national multicultural cable television network (Karim, 1998). We will return to the political and policy aspects of this discussion in Chapter 7.

CHAPTER 6

Ethnic Media Organizations and Competition

CHAPTER OBJECTIVES

By the end of this chapter you will be able to:

- Explain how the forces of newspaper competition affect ethnic newspapers.
- Discuss the social changes that impact the sustainability of print and electronic ethnic media.
- Describe how new communication technologies are shaping the ethnic media landscape.

Surviving Competition, Achieving Sustainability

In Chapter 5, we explained that ethnic media organizations care about their circulation estimates and ratings because (a) these figures tell them whether or not they are reaching their intended audience(s) and (b) because advertisers rely on those same figures to make decisions about what media they are going to spend their money on in order to attract consumers. In Chapter 6, we turn to the short or medium-term, but also the long-term strategies that ethnic media, print and electronic, employ to compete against each other. As they strive to achieve sustainability, ethnic media are confronted with several challenges, some of which larger, mainstream media face, too, and others that are unique to the ethnic media sector. The former are related to the emergence of new communication technologies and to changes in the broader socio-economic environment in which they operate; the latter are tied to the history, demographics, and policy-context in which the communities they serve develop. Here, we discuss these challenges and highlight opportunities ethnic media should take advantage of to grow, relying on examples from the United States and Britain, and to a lesser extent from other European countries.

Competing for Advertising Revenue

Earnings from sales of single copies represent only a portion of print media revenue. Advertising is the most important source of revenue for newspapers and magazines today. The income of newspapers from advertising in 2000 was, on average, approximately 2.5% higher than it was in the 1950s (Picard, 2004). From 1970 to 2000, the advertising revenue of Latino newspapers increased by over 4,000%. The increase from 1990 to 2000 was a more modest 55%, and from 2000 to 2003 only about 8% (Latino Print Network, 2005).[1] This could be the result of saturation experienced in certain markets.

A *media market* is a region in which the population can have access to the same television and radio stations, the same newspapers, and the same Internet content. When talking about print media and especially newspapers, markets tend to coincide with metropolitan areas. In a saturated market, there are limited resources to support the founding of new media. As circulation is one source of revenue for newspapers, scarce resources could mean that the potential audience is not large enough. But lack of resources could also mean that either there are not enough businesses and other organizations active in the area that would be interested in advertising their products or services, or that the businesses in the area are not generating enough income to warrant higher advertising expenditures. In Chapter 5, we noted the decrease in the number of daily Latino newspapers from 2005 through 2007, but also the decline in the overall circulation of Hispanic dailies during the same period. These changes lend support to the saturation hypothesis, at least with respect to Latino dailies.

If true for Latino print media in the United States, it is unclear if saturation is also slowing down the founding and growth of ethnic newspapers that target other ethnic groups (in the U.S. and beyond). The case of Latino print media suggests, however, that to be able to say something about the future of any ethnic media organization, it is necessary to answer at least three questions: (a) What is the market of interest? (b) What characteristics of the population within a market may affect circulation? (c) How vibrant is the market from a financial point of view?

¤ For Further Discussion

Find one ethnic newspaper in the city where you live. Then try to put together as much information as you can on the audience of this newspaper. Who is the newspaper's audience? What is the history of this particular ethnic community in your city? What are the newspaper's sources of revenue? Who advertises in it? Are there many entrepreneurs in the area who belong to the ethnic community that is the newspaper's key target? If so, how strong are their businesses? If the owner(s) and/or editor(s) of this newspaper asked you for suggestions that would help them boost their sales and increase their ad revenue, what would you recommend based on your research?

Competition Among Ethnic Print Media

Newspapers compete for larger readerships and for more advertising dollars. When the audience is small in a particular market and there are few businesses and organizations that can pay for advertising, competition between print media ensues (Carroll, 1987). The scarcer the financial resources in a market become, the fiercer the competition gets.

Circulation Elasticity of Demand

Circulation and advertising are highly interdependent. Lower circulation makes a newspaper less attractive to the advertisers, because it means that their message will reach fewer people. Therefore, the newspaper with the largest number of readers in a given market has an advantage over those lagging behind. By selling its larger audience to prospective advertisers, it is able to attract more advertising. More advertising means more money, which can later be re-invested to better the newspaper, by hiring more reporters, for instance, or publishing weekly special editions on particular topics of interest, like unemployment and the job market. Such investments are made to better the quality of the newspaper. Higher quality is likely to attract a larger audience (assuming, of course, that the price does not change significantly). A larger audience makes a newspaper even more attractive to advertisers, who will likely try to buy more space in that newspaper.

Circulation is therefore the link between the two products newspapers sell: (a) printed matter to readers and (b) space to advertisers. An increase in a newspaper's circulation should lead to higher demand from advertisers. If the relationship between demand and circulation were graphed it would take the shape of a line or a curve. This shape is called the *circulation-elasticity of demand* (Corden, 1953; Picard, 2004; Thompson, 1989). In Figure 6.1 we describe the mechanics of the dual market in which newspapers operate and explain what may make circulation-elasticity of demand "steeper" or "flatter."

Circulation Spirals

Because of the interdependence of circulation and advertising, the newspaper that has the largest number of readers, and therefore the largest income from advertising, sends its smaller competitors down a *circulation spiral* (Picard, 2004), which will eventually lead them out of business. Smaller scale operations see their circulation numbers dwindle, as they progressively also lose advertising (see Figure 6.2). The benefits of driving a competing publication out of a market are quite substantial. Research has shown that, in fact, the result—on average—is a 17% rise in circulation for the newspaper that survives (Dertouzos & Trautman, 1990).

Ethnic Newspapers and Market Dynamics

Ethnic newspapers are also subject to these market dynamics. In New York, for instance, in 2004, the daily Spanish-language *Hoy* claimed a circulation of 90,000,

Figure 6.1 Circulation-Elasticity of Demand in the Newspaper Industry

The Mechanics of the Dual Market in the Newspaper Industry

Newspapers operate in a dual market.They compete for the most readers and for the most advertising dollars.This figure explains how circulation links these two sources of revenue, based on the seminal work of W. M. Corden (1953). Figure 6.1a explains how newspapers can boost their sales of single copies. Figure 6.1b explains how newspapers increase their revenue from selling advertising space.

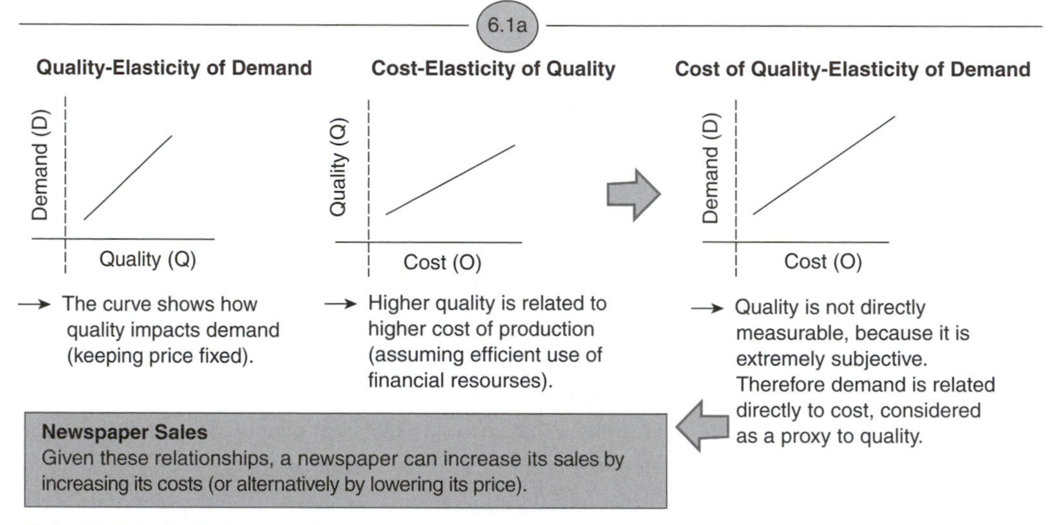

Note: Elasticity is another way of describing the shape of a curve (or line). A steeper demand curve, for instance, is less elastic than a flatter one.

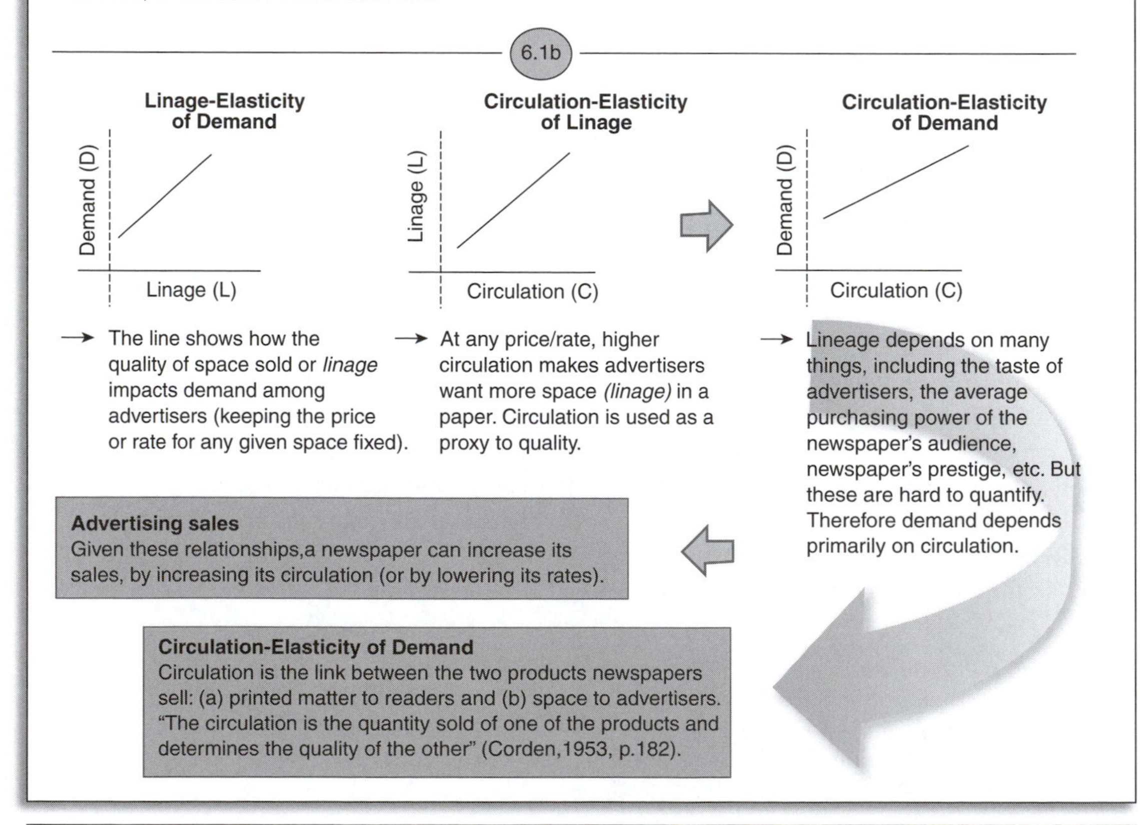

Figures: Matthew Matsaganis.

Figure 6.2 Circulation Spiral in Newspaper Competition

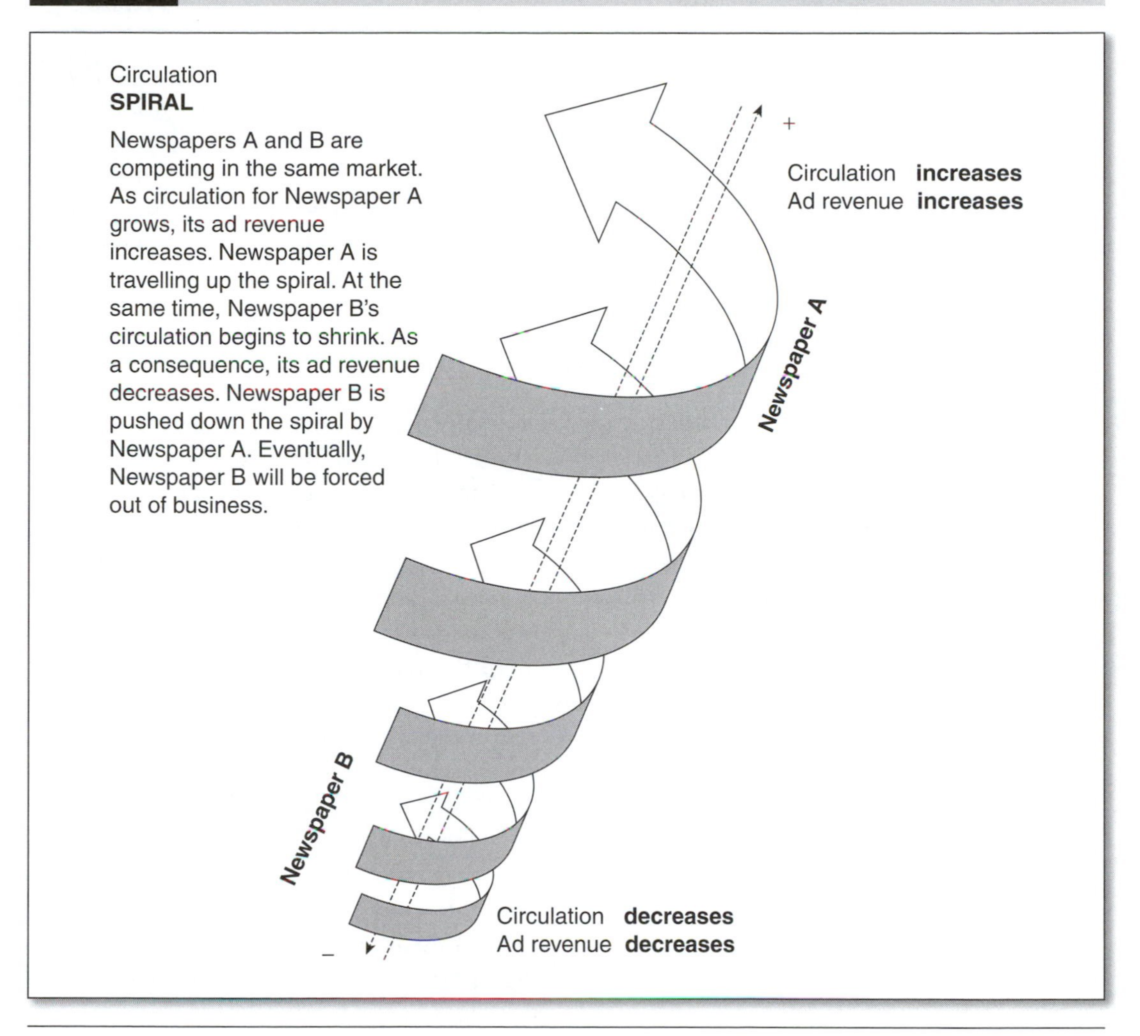

Figure: Matthew Matsaganis.

while its competitor *El Diario* reported that 50,000 people bought it every day. Based on these data, advertisers would likely see *Hoy* as more attractive and spend more money buying space in that newspaper. That would allow *Hoy* to invest in development and research, which would eventually make it more appealing to a larger audience. *El Diario,* most likely, would lose more and more of its audience.

However, on July 20, 2004, ImpreMedia, LLC—the owner of *El Diario*—published a surprising report that could have altered the balance of power between the two competitors in the New York market. The company indicated that it had commissioned a survey of New York City newsstand dealers, which showed that *El Diario,* in fact, outsold *Hoy* by 2 to 1. In a letter to the Audit Bureau of Circulation, Douglas Knight, chairman and CEO of ImpreMedia, wrote:

> We are providing this information to you to emphasize our desire to get to the bottom of this issue, to seek full disclosure as to the extent of the misrepresentation

at *Hoy*. Can we be confident that the ABC audit and the Tribune Company's internal investigation have actually discovered the full extent of the misrepresentation? (ImpreMedia, 2004)

The details of the disputed circulation numbers are not particularly important. It is, however, key to understand two things: first, the importance of having accurate circulation numbers for owners of ethnic newspapers and managers to make informed decisions and for ethnic media to better leverage the advertising market; and second, that, in the absence of reliable data, (mis)impressions alone may be enough to affect market dynamics.

"Umbrella" or Intercity Competition

Because of the dual market dynamics discussed above, newspapers that survive competition within a particular market tend to establish monopolies. But markets can be defined at various levels of geography. One newspaper, the bilingual weekly *Mexican American Sun,* for instance, is published in Los Angeles and distributed across Los Angeles County (including the city of Los Angeles, Boyle Heights, Downey, South Gate, Paramount, Rosemead, Santa Fe Springs, and Pico Rivera). Its circulation is estimated to be 16,000 (Circulation Verification Council, 2007). The size of its audience is limited, compared to a newspaper like the daily *La Opinión,* which enjoys a circulation of over 100,000 every day across the six counties of Southern California. The geographic area that *La Opinión* considers to be its market (i.e., Southern California) includes the smaller geographic area (i.e., Los Angeles County), which the *Mexican American Sun* identifies as its market. Therefore, there is competition between these two newspapers. This type of competition is referred to as "*umbrella*" or *intercity competition* (Lacy, Coulson, & Cho, 2002; Lacy & Martin, 2004; Lacy & Simon, 1993; Rosse, 1975).

In 1975, Rosse postulated that in large metropolitan areas newspapers can be divided into four layers or tiers. In the first layer there are metropolitan dailies that provide regional coverage. In the second layer we find dailies based in satellite cities around a metropolitan center. These papers cover the region just as metro dailies, yet they offer more local stories. The third layer consists of suburban dailies that tend to be very local in their coverage.[2] In the fourth layer (lowest tier), we find publications targeted to shoppers living in a particular area and weekly newspapers that are even more locally focused than the publications in the second and third layer. A fifth layer could be added to include newspapers that offer national coverage, such as *The New York Times* or *USA Today.* This fifth layer would be the national market, and it would subsume the other four (Lacy, 1987). In his study, Rosse (1975) hypothesized that competition between newspapers in different layers tends to be more vigorous than competition between newspapers that are in the same layer (i.e., *intra-city competition*). His research findings and subsequent studies by other researchers have generally supported this hypothesis.[3] Today, in most major mainstream media markets around the U.S., there is only one daily newspaper (and in some no newspaper at all). In major cities where residents have access to more than one daily newspaper, there is usually a clear differentiation in content between them. New Yorkers, for example, have access to *The New York Times, The New York Post,* and *The Daily News.* Yet, these newspapers target different segments of the population. While *The New York Times* is seen as an authoritative source for news and unbiased analysis of current events, *The New York Post* and *The Daily News* tend to be more sensationalistic in their coverage. Therefore competition among *The New York Times* and *The New York Post* or *The Daily News* is not particularly intense. Competition between higher and lower tier newspapers may be more vigorous though, because daily newspapers, for instance, have to (a) differentiate themselves from their competition and (b) serves as good substitutes for the more local newspapers. Dailies differentiate themselves by providing, for instance, extensive coverage of international news, which smaller, more local newspapers may not have the resources for. At the same time though, if dailies want to take readers away from lower-tier newspapers, they need to be able to provide the quality of local coverage that those other papers do.

In intercity competition, one strategy employed by newspapers in the top layers to push lower-layer competitors out of their niches involves publishing special editions that are customized to the particular areas smaller competitors consider to be their turf. This is often referred to as *zone printing.* Strategies similar to zone printing are implemented by larger ethnic media publishers.

ImpreMedia is the parent company of the Spanish-language dailies *La Opinión* in Los Angeles, and *El Diario–La Prensa* and *Hoy* in New York.[4] The company also owns the weeklies *La Raza* in Chicago and *El Mensajero* in San Francisco, as well as another eight Spanish-language publications (ImpreMedia, 2009; Laranaga, 2009).

In October 2005, ImpreMedia created two new publications: *La Opinión Contigo* in Los Angeles and *El Diario–Contigo* in New York. These are tabloid-size publications that are distributed for free every Sunday in communities around Los Angeles and New York, where many Hispanics live. In Chicago and San Francisco, *Contigo* is inserted as an extra section of *La Raza* and *El Mensajero. La Opinión Contigo, El Diario–Contigo, La Raza,* and *El Mensajero* form the Domingo (Sunday) Network. Much of the content in these weekly publications is the same. But there are also differences that reflect the publisher's efforts to customize *Contigo* to the particularities of the audiences in the four different cities where it is distributed. Announcing the creation of the Domingo Network, ImpreMedia (2005) explained:

> The new tabloid-sized publications will take a fresh approach by creating unique content targeting Latino women and households. They will have lively, compact articles full of tips and how-to's for the home and family. The stories will primarily be in Spanish with some articles in English and will be accompanied by colorful photos and informational graphics. While each publication will create locally tailored content, editorial themes such as fashion and cosmetics, education, health, food and recipes, home improvement, decorating and automotive will be in all [four] publications throughout the nation. (para. 3)[5]

By creating the *Domingo* network, ImpreMedia is attempting to put more pressure on other weekly newspapers and magazines, such as the weekly magazine

El Clasifica in Los Angeles (circulation 210,000) or *Extra* in Chicago (circulation 71,205) that are confined to particular geographic areas. The Domingo Network has many more resources at its disposal and, in the long run, its competitors may be forced out of business, may be bought out, or may have to re-think their marketing strategy. *Extra*, for example, in Chicago, is a bilingual publication, whereas ImpreMedia-owned *La Raza* in Chicago is published exclusively in Spanish and *Contigo* is primarily in Spanish. *Extra* may appeal to younger Latinos who may prefer English-language media, but who still want to know what is new in the Latino cultural scene.

Challenges and Opportunities for Ethnic Print Media

To survive, ethnic newspapers have to worry about more than just the dynamics of competition in the newspaper publishing industry. Ethnic newspaper owners and editors also have to be attuned to the demographic changes in the communities they target. In Chapters 4 and 5 we discussed how, for instance, language preferences among the audience may change, as the second, third, and later generations become larger in numbers than the immigrant (i.e., first) and "1.5" generations of an ethnic community. However, larger changes that impact the broader society of which ethnic communities are part of, as well as changes in the media landscape due to technological innovation, also create challenges ethnic media need to confront in order to continue to grow. We discuss three such challenges next.

The Downside of Success Hypothesis

In April 1981, a riot shook Brixton in South London, a community with a large Black population of Caribbean-origin, plagued by high unemployment, crime, poor housing conditions, and lack of public services. In the days prior to the riot, the police had launched Operation Swamp 81 in an attempt to curb street crime. During the operation, making use of the "Sus law," which allowed law enforcement agents to stop-and-search anyone who seemed suspicious of planning or carrying out a crime, police stopped and searched many young Black residents. Their actions further aggravated the local community who felt the police discriminated against Blacks. On April 10, there were rumors that the police had harassed and brutally abused one man. The news led to a confrontation between the police and a crowd, which eventually came to an end when more police arrived in the area. Over night the police force grew larger. The next day, the police continued with Operation Swamp and attempted to make arrests. The tension escalated suddenly and residents and police clashed. The unrest continued for almost 2 days. The number of injured civilians and police were in the hundreds. About 100 cars were destroyed and 156 buildings were damaged—30 burned. While the Brixton riot ended on April 12, more riots broke out throughout Britain that year, most notably in Liverpool and Manchester (John, 2006).

The larger implications of the 1981 riots for Britain are beyond the scope of our discussion. However, the events of that year did make more Afro-Caribbean-origin people turn to their ethnic newspapers. As mainstream media were seen as being uninterested in the issues and concerns of the ethnic community, ethnic newspapers offered what was missing: a public voice for Britain's oldest immigrant population. As a result, the circulation of newspapers like *The Caribbean Times* and the *Voice* (both weeklies) grew. The *Voice*, at its peak in the 1990s sold 60,000 copies every week. But since then that number has shrunk. Some media commentators argue that the decrease in circulation numbers can be attributed to the fact that the mainstream media today are more in tune with the concerns of ethnic and minority communities in the UK (BBC, 2007).

In January 2007, the BBC ran a story on its Web site under the headline, "Is time running out for ethnic media?" The impetus for the story was given by the closure of *The Caribbean Times*, one of the oldest ethnic newspapers in Britain. The author of the article comments that, "As the notion of Britain as a diverse society has gained widespread acceptance more voices from those minority communities are being heard in the national press either as stories, commentators or journalists" (BBC, 2007, para. 14).

The author argues that this shift can be attributed partially to the success of ethnic media in bringing the issues of ethnic minority groups to the attention of the mainstream media and the broader British public.

The BBC commentator may be right. However, riots like those of 1981 erupted again in 1985 and again in 2001. In 1981, the epicenter was Brixton; in 2001, it was the cities of Bradford, Oldham, and Burnley in the North of Britain. If the notion that Britain is a diverse society has indeed gained widespread acceptance over the course of 20 years, then why did riots occur and reoccur? Five years after the events of 2001, Coventry University released a report on the extent to which community cohesion had improved in the areas affected by the riots. The authors of the report found that, although progress had been made (Cantle et al., 2006), significant change would require "at least a generation" (BBC News, 2006, para. 2). Are mainstream media to blame for the limited improvements observed over the years in the relationships among Britain's ethnic communities? If they are to blame, to what extent? Have the mainstream media truly given voice to ethnic communities in the UK? It is hard to say.

It is also hard to assess the plausibility of the explanation offered by the BBC for the declining circulations of Afro-Caribbean newspapers in Britain. However, there is evidence to suggest that the argument that ethnic media do have an impact on the agenda pursued by mainstream media is valid. As noted in Chapter 1, in the U.S. context, the mainstream media were caught off guard in 2006 by the massive mobilization of Hispanic communities against the immigration laws debated in the U.S. Congress. The proposed changes to the laws, however, had been discussed and debated in the ethnic media for months before they became headline news in every major media outlet in the United States (Baum, 2006; Félix, González, & Ramírez, 2006; González, 2006; Starr, 2006; Watanabe & Beccera, 2006).

Return Migration and the Ethnic Media Audience

A second and more plausible line of thought to explain the closure of *The Caribbean Times* in the UK is rooted in the study of immigration trends. Caribbean-origin immigrants arrived in Britain after World War II seeking the jobs they could not find in their place of origin. Eighty-three percent of those who moved to the UK in the years right after the war were between the ages of 15 and 44 (OPCS, 1953–1993). In the 1980s, having worked 30 or more years, many of these immigrants retired and decided to return to the Caribbean. Others returned before they reached retirement age, hoping to make a living in the place where they grew up (Byron & Condon, 1996). Byron and Condon (1996) estimated, based on 1981 and 1991 British Census data, that approximately 9% (26,988 people) of the Caribbean-born population who lived in the UK in 1981 had moved back to their home country by 1991.

Moreover, over this period there were few new arrivals that would offset the decline in the population attributed to return migration. The decrease in the size of the population is likely to have led to the shrinkage of the potential audience of ethnic newspapers serving the Caribbean community and ultimately to the closure of *The Caribbean Times.* The negative effect of return migration was amplified, according to Michael Eboda, managing director of the Ethnic Media Group and owner of *The Caribbean News* title, by a generational shift. He argues that second and third generation Britons of Afro-Caribbean origin are much more interested in what is happening in Britain today than they are in the news from their parents' and grandparents' homelands (BBC, 2007).

The Internet Challenge

Yet another challenge to ethnic newspapers comes from the Internet. Provided they have access to the Internet, ethnic communities do not have to depend solely on the ethnic press to get news stories about their home country. Provided that they have (or can afford) Internet access, they can get the same information from the Web sites of newspapers and other media that are based in their country of origin. The changes introduced by the Internet to the array of available information sources individuals have access to may negatively impact the importance audiences place on ethnic media, including ethnic newspapers. People may think twice about spending the money for a subscription to a daily ethnic newspaper, if they know they can get the same or more detailed coverage of current events in their country of origin from Internet sites of major news organizations based, for instance, in South Korea, China, Thailand, or India. In other words, the question is whether the Internet is becoming a *substitute* for ethnic media, in general, and ethnic newspapers, in particular.

The Internet as a Substitute for Ethnic Print Media

Research has shown that people develop their own media landscape or *communication ecology,* whereby they establish connections to other people and to media for accomplishing the goals they set in the course of their everyday life (Ball-Rokeach,

1985; Wilkin, Ball-Rokeach, Matsaganis, & Cheong, 2007). For different goals, people prefer different media, yet the importance they place on each medium is relative to the importance of all other media they have access to (e.g., Flanagin & Metzger, 2001). People, for instance, will connect to different media if they are looking for entertainment and different media if they are in search of information on how to go about getting health insurance (Ball-Rokeach, 1998; Wilkin, 2005). In Tables 6.1 and 6.3, notice the differences between the media that people from five different ethnic communities in Los Angeles connect to in order to get information that would help them understand what is going on in their community and the media they choose for getting health-related information (Ball-Rokeach, Cheong, Wilkin, & Matsaganis, 2004; Wilkin, Ball-Rokeach, Matsaganis, & Cheong, 2007). Notice how the Internet is the number one choice for Hispanics in Southeast Los Angeles (mostly of Mexican-origin), for example, to get information about health, while it is their seventh option for understanding what is going on in their community. Ethnic media—newspapers, television, and radio—all rank higher than the Internet for staying on top of their community.

These data indicate that the extent to which the Internet is substituting for other media depends first of all on what people seek to accomplish by connecting to them. If their goal is to get news about their home country or to get health information, then the Internet may in fact be a good substitute for ethnic media produced in their newfound country. But when people want to find out what is going on in the local ethnic community, they tend to turn to the ethnic newspapers and other ethnic media. That means that one strategy that ethnic media can employ to successfully compete with the Internet is to invest heavily in telling the stories that really matter to the local ethnic community and to focus on telling them well. The news media that are based in the home country are not likely to cover these local stories, or at least cover them as well. Michael Eboda of the Ethnic Media Group in Britain (the group that owns *The Caribbean Times* title) and Edward Schumacher-Matos, founder of the Latino newspapers *Rumbo* in the United States, seem to agree. "Part of the response is stronger journalism, which brings people information they cannot get elsewhere," said Eboda for a BBC interview (BBC, 2007, para. 28). Edward Schumacher-Matos elaborated further in an interview for the Project for Excellence in Journalism (PEJ, 2007b):

> Hispanic newspapers, both Spanish and English, are in many ways akin to community papers—we serve a targeted ethnic community—which also aren't so affected by the Web because the content is exclusive. There aren't Web sites that offer local news for the Hispanic community, and the national sites are too generic. (para. 52)

A second strategy ethnic media could employ to compete with the abundance of available information sources online is to establish their own online presence. Multiple sources, however, suggest that ethnic media are adapting to the Internet rather slowly. Sandy Close, executive director of New America Media (see Profile 5.4 in Chapter 5), said in an interview to the Project for Excellence in Journalism that ethnic print media "are five years behind the times when it comes to the Internet"

(PEJ, 2007b, para. 50). By not developing online versions of the products they offer offline, ethnic media risk losing their audience to other media that do. Additionally, they also risk losing the opportunity to connect with the next generation of potential ethnic media consumers who are avid Internet users. The former editor of *The Caribbean Times* seems to echo these concerns. Michael Eboda acknowledged that "slow reaction to the possibilities of taking *The Caribbean Times* online meant the paper lost momentum compared with its rivals" (BBC, 2007, para. 22).

However, not going online may not impact all ethnic media to the same extent. The risk is greater if the community they serve is highly connected to the Internet. That is the case, for example, with Asian populations in the U.S., which have typically been among the most connected to the Internet. As a result, some of the larger Chinese and Korean ethnic media have tried hard and developed very sophisticated Web sites. The ethnic Chinese newspaper the *World Journal* is one of them. The *World Journal* has also added a section in English to its Web site. The content is different to that on the Chinese pages and reflects a conscious attempt to cater to the increasingly larger second- and third-generation of Asian-Americans who speak more English (PEJ, 2009a).

The situation is quite different for a lot of the Hispanic ethnic media in the United States, though. "The impact of the Web is much less marked on Spanish-language print [media] . . . because so many of our readers (first generation [immigrants]) are not online," said Edward Schumacher-Matos of *Rumbo,* published in Texas (PEJ, 2007b, para 52).[6] Therefore, it would seem that the degree to which the Internet can become a substitute for ethnic media also depends on the degree to which members of the ethnic community served by ethnic media are connected to the Internet. Notice the differences between Table 6.1 and Table 6.2. Both figures depict the importance people place on available media in order to get health-related information. Table 6.1 represents the choices of people who have access to the Internet, and Table 6.2 represents those people who do not. Hispanics in Pico Union (mostly of Central American-origin), for instance, with no Internet access depend on ethnic television the most for getting health-related information. On the other hand, Hispanics in Pico Union with Internet access include the Internet as one of their two top choices, and ethnic television is ranked as their fourth option (Ball-Rokeach, Cheong, Wilkin, & Matsaganis, 2004).

The Cannibalization Dilemma

A question lies in what the impact of going online is on the printed version of a newspaper. Does the online version become a *substitute* of the offline edition? As the Internet-based version of an ethnic newspaper becomes more popular, does the audience of the printed version dwindle? This is often referred to as the *cannibalization dilemma* of print media who wonder whether going online will benefit or hurt their offline audience base. Research is generally inconclusive. A study by Chyi and Lasorsa (2002) focusing on daily newspapers in Austin, Texas—local, regional, and national—gives a very mixed picture. The study suggests that (a) simultaneous use of the print and online editions means that print and online products complement each other to some degree. Chyi and Lasorsa also found that

Table 6.1 Top Communication Connections for Achieving **Health Goals:** Comparison of Individuals **With Access to the Internet,** Living in Five Different Geo-Ethnic Communities in Los Angeles

Ethnicity	**Hispanic**		**Hispanic**		**Hispanic**		**Armenian**		**Anglos**	**(White)**
Area	Southeast	(N = 104)	Pico Union	(N = 67)	Glendale	(N = 105)	Glendale	(N = 211)	Glendale	(N = 139)
	%	*(ranking within)*	%	*(ranking within)*	%	*(ranking within)*	%	*(ranking within)*	%	*(ranking within)*
MAINSTREAM										
Television	10	**6**	13	**5**	9	**7**	6	**5**	8	**6**
(ranking across)	**2**		**1**		**3**		**5**		**4**	
Radio	3	**10**	3	**10**	17	**3**	1	**8**	23	**3**
(ranking across)	**3**		**3**		**2**		**5**		**1**	
Newspapers	4	**8**	8	**6**	12	**6**	6	**5**	6	**7**
(ranking across)	**5**		**2**		**1**		**3**		**3**	
Books/Mags	14	**5**	8	**6**	17	**3**	7	**4**	23	**3**
(ranking across)	**3**		**4**		**2**		**5**		**1**	
(GEO) ETHNIC										
Television	16	**4**	15	**4**	1	**8**	4	**7**	0	**8**
(ranking across)	**1**		**2**		**4**		**3**		**5**	

(Continued)

(Continued)

Ethnicity	**Hispanic**		**Hispanic**		**Hispanic**		**Armenian**		**Anglos**	**(White)**
Area	Southeast	(N = 104)	Pico Union	(N = 67)	Glendale	(N = 105)	Glendale	(N = 211)	Glendale	(N = 139)
	%	*(ranking within)*	%	*(ranking within)*	%	*(ranking within)*	%	*(ranking within)*	%	*(ranking within)*
Radio	5	**7**	6	**8**	0	**9**	0	**10**	0	**8**
(ranking across)	**2**		**1**		**3**		**3**		**3**	
Newspapers	4	**8**	6	**8**	0	**9**	1	**8**	0	**8**
(ranking across)	**2**		**1**		**4**		**3**		**4**	
INTERPERSONAL										
Family & Friends	22	**3**	25	**1**	16	**5**	18	**3**	22	**5**
(ranking across)	**2**		**1**		**5**		**4**		**2**	
Health Professionals	25	**2**	21	**3**	25	**2**	42	**1**	53	**1**
(ranking across)	**3**		**5**		**3**		**2**		**1**	
INTERNET	33	**1**	24	**2**	33	**1**	26	**2**	36	**2**
(ranking across)	**2**		**4**		**2**		**3**		**1**	

Source: Ball-Rokeach, Cheong, Wilkin, & Matsaganis (2004).

Note: Percentiles = The % of the sample population that indicated a particular medium as *one* of the ways they get medical and health information. *"Ranking within"* scores reflect the relative importance of communication resources in a particular community, according to the residents. *"Ranking across"* scores reflect the relative importance of specific communication resources across the communities studied.

Table 6.2 Top Communication Connections for Achieving **Health Goals:** Comparison of Individuals **Who Do Not Have Access to the Internet,** Living in Five Different Geo-Ethnic Communities in Los Angeles

Ethnicity	**Hispanic**		**Hispanic**		**Hispanic**		**Armenian**		**Anglos**	**(White)**
Area	Southeast	(N = 334)	Pico Union	(N = 234)	Glendale	(N = 49)	Glendale	(N = 93)	Glendale	(N = 50)
	%	*(ranking within)*	%	*(ranking within)*	%	*(ranking within)*	%	*(ranking within)*	%	*(ranking within)*
MAINSTREAM										
Television	8	**5**	6	**7**	11	**4**	10	**5**	12	**4**
(ranking across)	**4**		**5**		**2**		**3**		**1**	
Radio	1	**8**	0	**9**	0	**8**	0	**8**	2	**5**
(ranking across)	**2**		**3**		**3**		**3**		**1**	
Newspapers	1	**8**	2	**8**	4	**6**	1	**7**	1	**7**
(ranking across)	**3**		**2**		**1**		**3**		**3**	
Books/Mags	14	**4**	11	**4**	15	**3**	14	**3**	24	**2**
(ranking across)	**3**		**4**		**2**		**3**		**1**	
(GEO) ETHNIC										
Television	30	**1**	33	**1**	7	**5**	27	**1**	0	**8**
(ranking across)	**2**		**1**		**4**		**3**		**5**	

(Continued)

(Continued)

Ethnicity	**Hispanic**		**Hispanic**		**Hispanic**		**Armenian**		**Anglos**	**(White)**
Area	Southeast	(N = 334)	Pico Union	(N = 234)	Glendale	(N = 49)	Glendale	(N = 93)	Glendale	(N = 50)
	%	*(ranking within)*	%	*(ranking within)*	%	*(ranking within)*	%	*(ranking within)*	%	*(ranking within)*
Radio	8	**5**	8	**6**	4	**6**	2	**6**	0	**8**
(ranking across)	**1**		**1**		**3**		**4**		**5**	
Newspapers	5	**7**	11	**4**	0	**8**	0	**8**	2	**5**
(ranking across)	**2**		**1**		**4**		**5**		**3**	
INTERPERSONAL										
Family & Friends	29	**2**	28	**2**	28	**1**	11	**4**	18	**3**
(ranking across)	**1**		**2**		**2**		**5**		**4**	
Health Professionals	22	**3**	18	**3**	26	**2**	27	**1**	52	**1**
(ranking across)	**4**		**5**		**3**		**2**		**1**	

Source: Ball-Rokeach, Cheong, Wilkin, & Matsaganis (2004).

Note: Percentiles = The % of the sample population that indicated a particular medium as *one* of the ways they get medical and health information. *"Ranking within"* scores reflect the relative importance of communication resources in a particular community, according to the residents. *"Ranking across"* scores reflect the relative importance of specific communication resources across the communities studied.

Table 6.3 Top Communication Connections for **Understanding What Is Happening in Their Community:** Comparison of Five Geo-Ethnic Communities in Los Angeles

Ethnicity	Hispanic		Hispanic		Hispanic		Armenian		Anglo	(White)
Area	Southeast	(*N* = 334)	Pico Union	(*N* = 234)	Glendale	(*N* = 49)	Glendale	(*N* = 93)	Glendale	(*N* = 50)
	%	*(ranking within)*	%	*(ranking within)*	%	*(ranking within)*	%	*(ranking within)*	%	*(ranking within)*
MAINSTREAM										
Television	19	**3**	19	**3**	31	**1**	30	**1**	26	**3**
(ranking across)	**4**		**4**		**1**		**2**		**3**	
Radio	4	**9**	4	**8**	5	**6**	2	**8**	6	**6**
(ranking across)	**3**		**3**		**2**		**5**		**1**	
Newspapers	8	**6**	7	**6**	25	**3**	12	**4**	38	**1**
(ranking across)	**4**		**5**		**2**		**3**		**1**	
Books	5	**8**	2	**9**	3	**9**	4	**7**	5	**7**
(ranking across)	**1**		**5**		**4**		**3**		**1**	
(GEO) ETHNIC										
Television	51	**1**	45	**1**	27	**2**	30	**1**	7	**5**
(ranking across)	**1**		**2**		**4**		**3**		**5**	

(Continued)

(Continued)

Ethnicity	Hispanic		Hispanic		Hispanic		Armenian		Anglo	(White)
Area	Southeast	(*N* = 334)	Pico Union	(*N* = 234)	Glendale	(*N* = 49)	Glendale	(*N* = 93)	Glendale	(*N* = 50)
	%	*(ranking within)*	%	*(ranking within)*	%	*(ranking within)*	%	*(ranking within)*	%	*(ranking within)*
Radio	17	**4**	15	**5**	5	**7**	1	**9**	0	**9**
(ranking across)	**1**		**2**		**3**		**4**		**5**	
Newspapers	16	**5**	17	**4**	4	**8**	7	**6**	2	**8**
(ranking across)	**2**		**1**		**4**		**3**		**5**	
INTERPERSONAL	27	**2**	33	**2**	25	**3**	19	**3**	32	**2**
(ranking across)	**3**		**1**		**4**		**5**		**2**	
INTERNET	7	**7**	6	**7**	14	**5**	11	**5**	13	**4**
(ranking across)	**4**		**5**		**1**		**3**		**2**	

Source: Ball-Rokeach, Cheong, Wilkin, & Matsaganis (2004).

Note: Percentiles = The % of the sample population who indicated a particular medium as *one* of the ways that they stay on top of what is happening in their community. *"Ranking within"* scores reflect the relative importance of communication resources in a particular community, according to the residents. *"Ranking across"* scores reflect the relative importance of specific communication resources across the communities studied.

(b) there is significant overlap (83%) in the readership of the online and offline versions of local daily newspapers. Additionally, the authors of the study reported that (c) "readers of a particular newspaper's online edition were more likely to read that same newspaper's print edition" (p. 103).

However insightful, Chyi and Lasorsa (2002) do not directly measure the substitution effect. As they acknowledge, the fact that online readers tend to also read the printed edition does not guarantee the absence of the cannibalization effect. One cannot rule out the possibility that people who read a newspaper online may be more interested in news, in general. These people are likely to consume more news, and that might explain why they read both the online and printed versions of the same newspaper. To say that online readers are more likely to read the print edition is not the same as saying that no reader of the offline version of a newspaper switched to the free online edition.

In a different study that included 98 daily newspapers that have online ventures, representing 22 different media conglomerates, from four different European countries (i.e., France, Germany, the Netherlands, and the United Kingdom), Geyskens, Gielens, and Dekimpe (2002) provide a detailed account of the extent to which substitution and cannibalization are at work in the newspaper industry. They found that, from a financial standpoint, established firms that already own multiple media are hurt when they add a new Internet channel. Establishing a new online channel does not seem to attract a substantial number of new audience numbers, but "instead [it] may cause *cannibalization* and/or brand damaging interchannel [i.e., print and online versions] conflict" (p. 116).

To Lead or to Follow?

Another question worth asking, of course, is whether or not timing of entry into the Internet newspaper market makes a difference. The literature suggests that to a great extent, publishers and editors rushed to get online as a defense strategy (see Hendriks, 1999). Was it the right thing to do? Geyskens et al. (2002) found that timing is indeed crucial and that companies should be fast. However, the results of their study suggest that newspaper firms should "be early followers rather than pioneers with respect to Internet channels" (pp. 114–116). Letting "innovators" experiment with different technical approaches and designs may save the "early followers" money and other resources. This may be particularly good advice for ethnic newspapers that generally have limited budgets.

Competition in Ethnic Television and Radio

Like ethnic newspapers, major commercial ethnic radio and television operations have to compete for advertising. The stronger their ratings are, the larger the advertising accounts they are likely to acquire. In Chapter 5, we discussed how TeleFutura competes against other Spanish-language television networks. When others air Spanish-language telenovelas, TeleFutura airs blockbuster movies, hoping that it will attract the younger audience it targets. This is one of the strategies, referred to as *counter-programming*, that ethnic television channels use to compete against each other on a daily and hour-to-hour basis.

However, all ethnic television and radio stations have to develop long-term competition strategies as well; plans, that is, that they hope will ensure growth over time. Creating such strategies is not easy for any media organization, ethnic or mainstream. Ethnic media, though, have additional variables to account for in their calculations. The case of *The Caribbean Times*, mentioned earlier, illustrates how changes in immigration flows, for instance, can affect the viability of an ethnic media organization. There are other considerations to be made, too. The cases of Univisión and Telemundo, discussed below, are instructive.

The larger the organization, the more important long-term planning may be, as more is on the line. Poor planning may result in tremendous financial losses, and it could cost many people their jobs. Univisión and Telemundo are the two largest competitors in the Latino media market in the United States. As of 2009, their strategies for the future appeared to differ significantly. Telemundo had begun producing more original programming targeted to second- and third-generation Latinos. This choice was driven by the study of demographics, which suggested that the percentage of U.S.-born Latinos was on the rise. Telemundo's rationale was that, over time, this population will demand more programming that is sensitive to its particular life experiences and cultural references and less content imported from other Latin American countries. Telemundo had also succeeded in securing deals that would allow it to export the original Spanish-language programming it produced to Mexico. In addition, in 2001, the company launched the bilingual cable channel Mun 2, targeting younger, bilingual, and English-only speaking Latinos (Downey, 2007; Project for Excellence in Journalism, 2009). Don Browne, president of Telemundo, explained the logic of his network's strategy like this: "We have created a business model based on relevance," he said. "Language is important, but cultural relevance is more important" (Downey, 2007).

Univisión, on the other hand, planned to continue to import significant amounts of programming from Latin America. However, it had also begun producing some original content and invested heavily in its online presence (PEJ, 2009a; Univisión, 2008). Some analysts have argued that Univisión, the largest Latino network in the U.S., was relying too heavily on its current reach and size, and that it was running the risk of losing viewers in the future (Downey, 2007).

Ethnic Television, Ethnic Radio, and the Internet

Overall, just like ethnic print media, ethnic television and radio stations are also lagging behind the mainstream media when it comes to the Internet. Larger media organizations, however, such as the Latino television networks Univisión and Telemundo in the U.S. and the African-American radio network Radio One, have invested considerably in their online ventures. Radio One, in particular, launched Interactive One in 2007. At the end of 2008, the online project included seven Web sites: TheUrbanDaily.com, BlackPlanet.com, HelloBeautiful.com, GiantMag.com, MiGente.com, NewsOne.com, and Elev8.com (PEJ, 2009a; Radio One, 2009).

Among Spanish-language Web sites, Univisión and Telemundo are two of the most popular in the country (PEJ, 2007b, 2008, 2009a). Data from 2006 and 2007 indicate that Univisión had twice as many visitors who spoke mostly Spanish or who were bilingual, compared to the Spanish-language Yahoo! Portal, Yahoo en Espanol, and 4 times as many visitors as MSN Latino (Hispanic PR Wire, 2006; PEJ, 2007b). In 2006, Univisión.com had an average of 11 million unique visitors per month. A year earlier, the average was 10 million (PEJ, 2007b).

Online-Only Ethnic Media

As Internet penetration rates continue to increase among ethnic populations, the more online ethnic media are likely to emerge. Higher levels of Internet connectedness means larger potential audiences and, of course, higher potential for attracting advertising. In 2008, research suggested that the percentage of African-Americans online had increased by 22% compared to 2000 and had reached 64% (PEJ, 2009a). Within the same time frame, the increase in the number of Latinos and Whites on the Internet was about half. These figures encouraged many African-American–oriented online ventures. The increased demand for news by African-American audiences due to the Obama candidacy in the 2008 U.S. elections gave an added boost to the number and diversity of online Black media. Here is one indicator of this: Just between 2007 and 2008, the number of African-American blogs skyrocketed from 75 to over 1,250 (Garofoli, 2008).

¤ For Further Discussion

Identify two ethnic media in the area where you live. Make a list of the types of data you would need to have at your disposal in order to identify the challenges these media face as they strive to survive and the opportunities that they should consider taking advantage of.

The 2008 Global Economic Crisis: Catalyst for Innovation or Demise?

In Britain, two newspapers, the *Eastern Eye* and *New Nation,* one catering to Afro-Caribbean communities in London and the other to South Asian communities, shut down their print editions in January 2007. Justin Onyeka, the deputy editor of *New Nation* until 2007, argued that failing to establish online presence early enough was what led to both newspapers' demise. He suggested that the parent company of both ventures, the Ethnic Media Group (EMG), should have taken into account earlier the high levels of Internet connectivity among African-Caribbeans and South Asians (Moore, 2009; see also Ofcom, 2007, 2008). These two cases underscore the need for ethnic media to monitor carefully the media habits of their audience. At the same time, the demise of EMG confirms that ethnic media are not immune to changes in the larger media landscape, society, and the economy. A report released by the Project of Excellence in Journalism in 2009 drives this point home, as it reflects on the impact of the 2008 global economic crisis on ethnic media.

According to this PEJ report, the economic crisis made an already difficult situation for most media organizations, and particularly print media, even more challenging. In many countries across the world and particularly in the U.S., the crisis had severe negative effects on two of ethnic media organizations' main sources of advertising revenue: the local real estate market and the automobile market (PEJ, 2009a). Both the real estate and the automobile industry were hit hard by the crisis (e.g., Bernanke, 2008; Vlasic & Bunkley, 2008). As advertising revenue from real estate and car dealers dried up, many ethnic media were forced to either close or, alternatively, end their offline projects and migrate to the Internet (PEJ, 2009a). The effects of the crisis were felt the most by ethnic media located in places, such as Arizona, Florida and Nevada, where the local economy suffered most (Portada Online, 2009). By choosing to migrate online, several Hispanic (e.g., *Hoy,* in New York), African-American (e.g., the *San Francisco Bay View*), and Asian (e.g., *AsianWeek,* based in Northern California) ethnic media were essentially forced to innovate. Given the changes in the broader media landscape, this might be seen as a positive side effect of the crisis. However, in late 2009, it remained unclear what the impact of migrating to the Web would be for ethnic media whose audiences are not yet highly connected to the Internet. Would it guarantee sustainability, or would it just delay their demise?

Satellite Broadcasting Networks

Digital satellite technology has also transformed the ethnic media landscape. Satellite networks allow ethnic media to reach populations living in communities and countries spread around the globe. In countries where it is hard for ethnic media to get a license to operate, satellite networks offer an alternative to ethnic communities. In France, for instance, in the mid-1990s, the minister of the interior in the center-right government of Edouard Balladur, urged the country's agency that regulates broadcasting to shut Arabic-language stations out of licensed cable networks (Hargreaves & Mahdjoub, 1997).[7] The government at the time thought that exposure to Arabic stations would discourage immigrants to France from countries of North Africa (e.g., Algeria and Morocco) from becoming incorporated into French society and would preserve tension between Arab-origin and other ethnic groups. However, it is harder to control what people receive on their television screens via a satellite than via a cable network. As a result, in 1995, the number of Arab households in France that had invested in satellite receivers was times larger than the non-Arabic French households with satellite reception (Dutheil, 1995, in Hargreaves & Mahjoub, 1997).

Since the mid-1990s, high penetration rates of satellite television have been observed in a number of countries across Europe; particularly in countries with large Arab, Kurdish, and Turkish populations, including Denmark, France, Germany, the Netherlands, and Sweden (Hargreaves, 2001; Milikowski, 2001; Roald, 2004).

The constellation of satellite-based ethnic media that serve these populations include large broadcasting companies located in Middle Eastern countries, such as Dubai (e.g., Middle-East Broadcasting Corporation), Egypt (e.g., Egyptian Satellite Channel), Bahrain (e.g., Orbit TV), and Qatar (e.g., Al-Jazeera). Most of these larger satellite channels targeting Arab populations cultivate the notion of a pan-Arab conglomerate identity, as part of a strategy they hope will deliver a broader audience base. An important consequence of employing this strategy is that local Arab communities living across European countries do not "see" themselves in the content they receive. Moreover, they are not involved in the production of the content. None of the major Arab satellite stations are based in places with significant numbers of Arab-origin immigrant communities. In this respect, says Alec Hargreaves (2001), "satellite broadcasting is tending to replicate the long-standing marginalization of minority ethnic groups as suppliers of programs on terrestrial TV" (p. 143).

To remain competitive, satellite-based ethnic media branch out, create, acquire, and distribute channels they hope will either (a) appeal to particular segments of their core audience (e.g., teens, women, sports fans, and news junkies) or (b) attract new ethnic audiences. For example, in 1998, Orbit TV had 24 television stations. It broadcast in Arabic, English, and French. It offered programming of its own, but it also distributed Egyptian and Jordanian stations, as well as channels like CNN, BBC, Star, and Disney (Forrester, 1995, in Karim, 1998). In 2009, Orbit TV distributed 75 different channels, including four stations targeted exclusively to Filipino audiences (Orbit TV, 2009).

¤ For Further Discussion

What satellite networks are available in the area where you live? Do they distribute ethnically-targeted channels? If so, identify what ethnic communities they intend to reach. Then, think about whether or not the programs on these channels would appeal to members of the ethnic communities living in your area. If possible, discuss your analysis with a family member, friend, colleague, or neighbor that you think might watch that particular channel. Did they agree with you?

Summary

This chapter focused on the dynamics of competition among ethnic media and the strategies that these media organizations employ in order to survive and grow. As they look to the future, ethnic media have to take into consideration not only changes in the technological environment, which affect all media, ethnic and mainstream, but they must also be keenly aware of the particular historical, sociodemographic, political, and economic context in which the communities they serve live. As this context changes, ethnic media need to be able to change, too. The forces of globalization shape this context, and in Chapter 7 we discuss what the effects of globalization are on the ownership and organizational structure of ethnic media.

The case study that we present below is meant to aid the understanding of some of the key concepts presented in Chapters 5 and 6. Through this case study we will also introduce some ideas, which we discuss in more detail in Chapter 7.

Study Questions

1. Review Tables 6.1 and 6.3. You are the editor of an Armenian newspaper in Glendale, California, that also publishes an online version. What do these tables tell you about your audience? Given this information, would you invest more money to further develop your Web-based edition? If yes, why and in what direction? If not, why not?

2. Review Figures 6.1 and 6.2. What is circulation-elasticity of demand and what determines it? How are the following concepts related to one another: (a) circulation-elasticity of demand, (b) dual market, (c) lineage, and (d) cost-of-quality-elasticity of demand?

3. What is the downside of success hypothesis? Do you believe it holds true? Justify your answer with examples.

4. What are the broader socio-political, economic, and technological factors that affect an ethnic media organization's effort to achieve sustainability?

5. How can ethnic media organizations take advantage of new and emerging forms of communication, including various social networking platforms and mobile communication devices, to sustain themselves over time and, perhaps, even become more competitive?

Case Study

The case study below is about the Greek-American daily newspaper *Proini* and its sister publication *The Greek American,* both published in New York City. The story of these ethnic newspapers could be the story of a number of other ethnic media organizations serving the Persian, Palestinian, Israeli, Algerian, Indian, Pakistani, Bangladeshi, Thai, Korean, Chinese, Guatemalan, and numerous other ethnic communities worldwide. It offers a glimpse into the everyday life and operation of ethnic media organizations. Reflecting back to Chapter 5, this case study illustrates why producers find it hard to attract advertising, why advertisers often feel that ethnic media do not serve their needs, and why researchers find it difficult to identify trends in media markets where ethnic media are present. The example of *Proini* also demonstrates how ethnic media organizations try to solve these problems. It also shows how they try to tailor their content to changing audience demographics, as part of a set of strategies to become more competitive and to achieve sustainability; we discussed some of these strategies in Chapters 4, 5, and 6. While some of the themes that emerge through the case study pertain to print media only (e.g., distribution), others reflect realities that all ethnic media deal with (e.g., competition with other media and attracting advertising). The examples of *Proini* and *The Greek American* also speak to questions of who owns the ethnic media and how new communication technologies and economic globalization have affected ethnic media organizations. In this respect, the case study introduces, in a grounded way, some of the ideas and themes presented in Chapter 7.

A Not So Uncommon Story From the Booming Ethnic Media Market of New York

One evening in June 2000, the editor-in-chief of *Ethnospor* returned to his office after a long meeting with the board of directors of the publishing house. *Ethnospor* is a sports publication that is published, packaged, and sold with one of Greece's leading daily newspapers, *Ethnos*. The headquarters of *Ethnos* and its parent company, Pegasus Publishing and Printing, S.A., are located just a few kilometers away from the center of Athens. The main topic of discussion between *Ethnospor*'s editor-in-chief and Pegasus' board of directors was the company's most recent acquisition, Greek American Publishing, Ltd., a company based in New York. *Ethnospor*'s top editor had been asked to take on Pegasus' new venture as managing director several months earlier, when Pegasus first entered negotiations with the Greek-American publishing firm in New York to buy the majority of that company's stocks. The company in New York owned the daily newspaper *Proini* (or Morning News, loosely translated), founded in 1977, and the weekly *The Greek American* (see Figure 6.3 for a diagram of the relationships between the organizations involved in the case study).

Until 2000, Greek American Publishing, Ltd., was owned by three Greek-American entrepreneurs. Two of them had successful, booming construction businesses. The third partner had become less involved in the operation of Greek American Publishing over the past couple of years, due to personal financial difficulties. With an investment in the millions of dollars, the Athens-based company succeeded in securing ownership of 51% of the company, while 49% remained in the hands of the original Greek American Publishing owners. Pegasus Publishing and Printing also retained control of the management of both *Proini* and *The Greek American*. The editor-in-chief of *Ethnospor* formally assumed the role of managing director of the company. He did not move to New York, however, as he kept his position at *Ethnospor* and remained involved in a series of other Pegasus ventures in Greece (see Figure 6.4 for the organizational authority structure).

The agreement reached between the Athens and New York-based partners meant that there would be changes in how decisions at both newspapers were made, but also changes in the production and content of the publications.

Figure 6.3 All the Organizations Involved in the Case Study

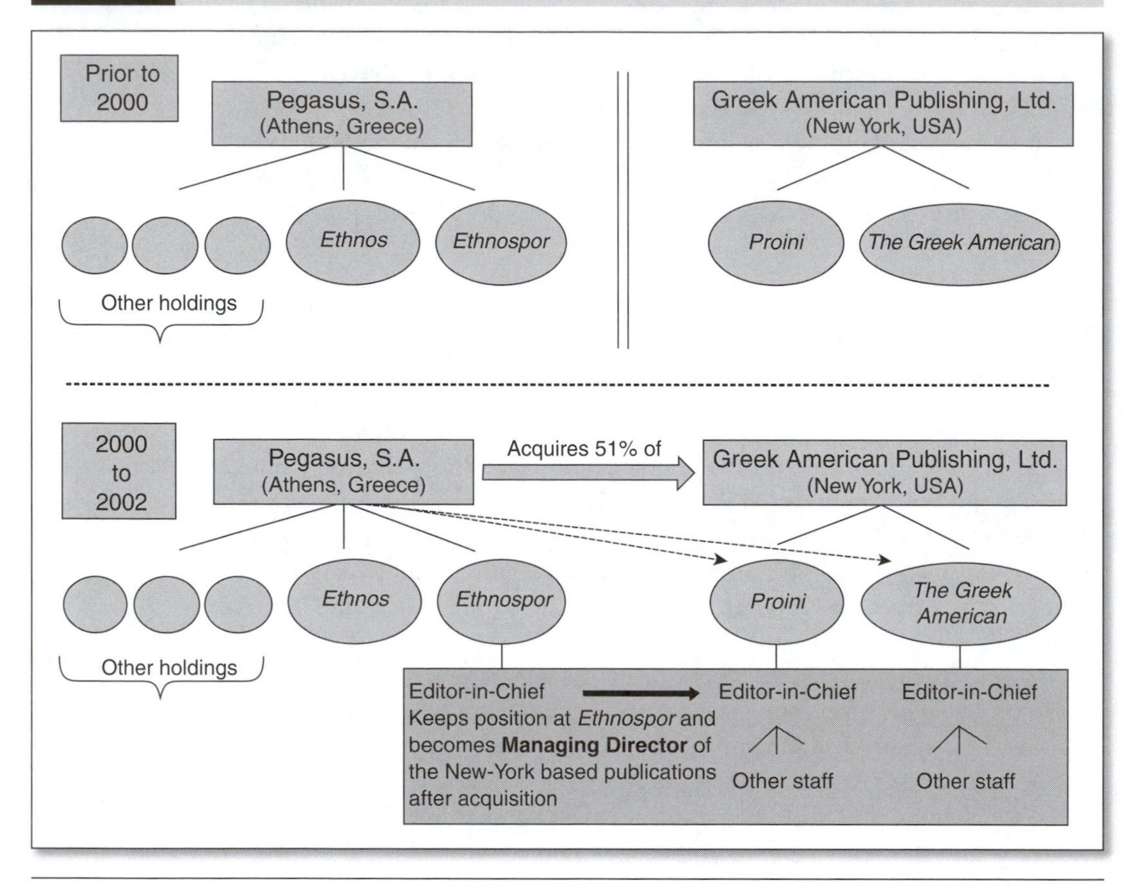

Figure: Matthew Matsaganis.

In the New York offices, there were two newsrooms. As *Proini* was a daily newspaper, its staff was larger. At least five of the reporters were Greek and Greek-American university students, undergraduates, master's degree hopefuls, and Ph.D. candidates at some of New York's finest academic institutions. Others had come to the United States as students, married, and had chosen to stay and raise their children in the Big Apple. Still others had been born in the U.S. of Greek immigrants who came to New York 20, 30, or more years ago. Most of them spoke Greek or "Greeklish" (a mélange of English and Greek) at home. As children, often reluctantly, they took Greek language classes in schools funded by the Greek Archdiocese. Business in *Proini* was conducted mostly in Greek.

The Greek American's newsroom was much smaller. Most of the staff members were second or third generation Greek-Americans. Their competency in writing and speaking Greek varied significantly. Business was conducted primarily in English. Frequently, staff writers from one publication contributed to the other, and often more senior staff, fluent in the language required for publication of a particular article, would have to edit or rewrite portions of a story they were handed.

At the time the agreement between the Athens- and New York-based companies was signed, it was decided that the editors-in-chief of both publications

Figure 6.4 Organizational Authority Structure at Greek American Publishing, Ltd., 2000–2002

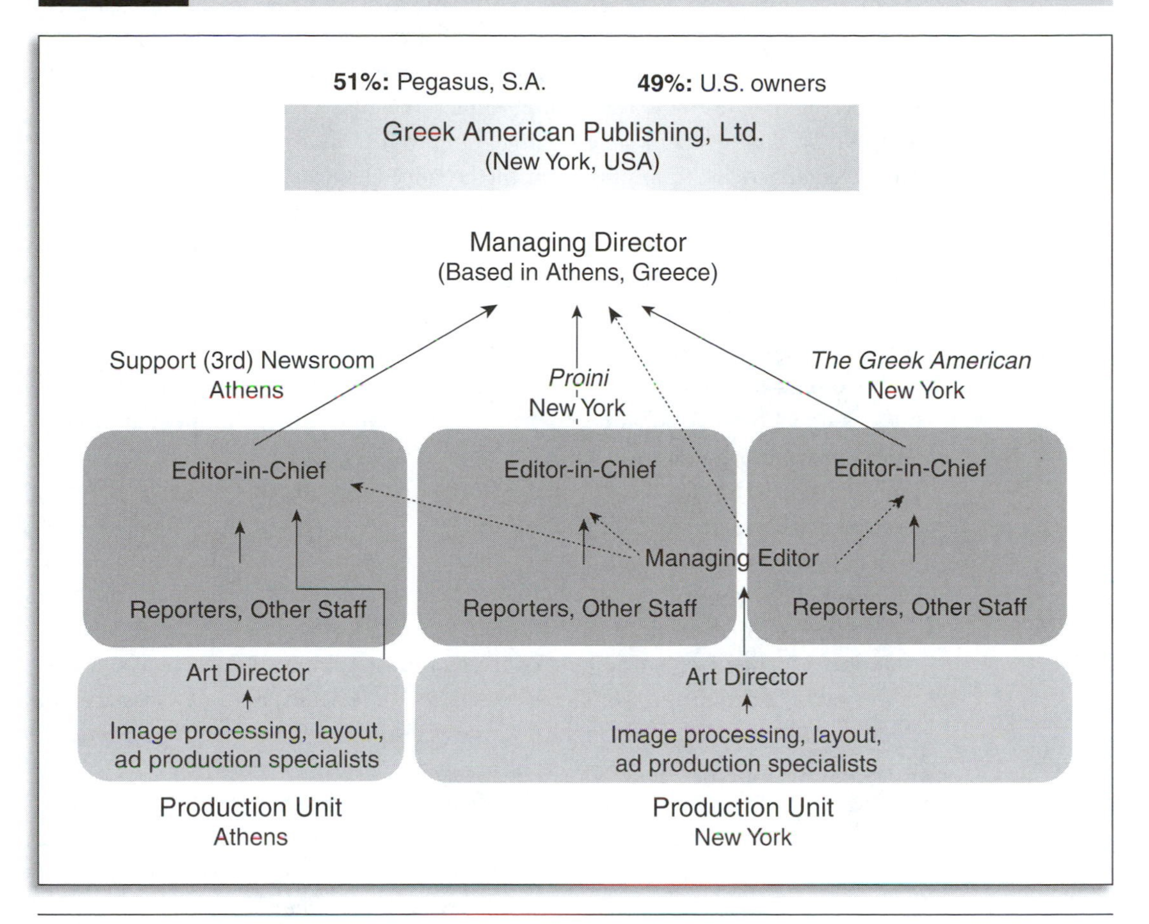

Figure: Matthew Matsaganis.

would remain in their positions. However, the new managing director wanted to make sure that decisions made about the newspapers by the management in Athens would be implemented in the New York newsrooms. To accomplish this, he recruited a young managing editor who had been working for *Ethnos* in Athens and who had recently decided to leave the company and move to the U.S. to pursue a graduate degree. In August 2000, the new recruit moved to the U.S. having agreed to assist the two editors-in-chief with the development of new storylines, with the restructuring of the newsroom, and to ensure that there would be no deviation from the production standards set by the new management.

The operation of both *Proini* and of *The Greek American* would have been nearly impossible without a third editorial team, located eight time zones away, in the headquarters of Pegasus Publishing and Printing, in Athens. This third team of reporters and editors, under its own editor-in-chief, contributed original stories, but also articles based on reports from Greek, Cypriot, and other wire services (e.g., Associated Press, Reuters, and Agence France-Presse).

Changes in the content and format of *Proini* and *The Greek American* became apparent quickly. Both papers stopped relying as heavily as they used to on wire services, such as the Athens News Agency (ANA) and the Cyprus News Agency (CNA), for stories about Greece and Cyprus, the two countries the majority of their audiences recognized as their homeland or that of their parents and grandparents. More original stories about current events and breaking news in Greece and Cyprus were produced by the editorial team in Athens. In addition, the staffs of both *Proini* and *The Greek American* were encouraged to produce more original content about the Greek-American communities in the broader New York area, New Jersey, and Connecticut. This content included: breaking news stories with a "Greek-American angle" (e.g., a Greek-American fireman risking his life to save a child), news stories on Greek-Americans involved in local and state politics (e.g., policies proposed by a Greek-American state assembly- or local council-member), coverage of pressing issues in neighborhoods where Greek-Americans lived (e.g., below-average performance of students at a local school), feature stories on the state of Greek-American businesses in New York and elsewhere, profiles of the most influential Greek-Americans in U.S. politics and business, interviews with prominent Greek-American politicians, artists, and athletes, but also stories on the events and initiatives of local, Greek-American non-profit organizations (e.g., fund drives and annual balls).

Management planned to progressively target audiences also in Boston, Cleveland, Chicago, and eventually in Los Angeles and San Francisco. All of these cities have significant numbers of first, second, and third-generation Greek-Americans. [8] Therefore, stories that concerned those communities were also found in the pages of *Proini* and *The Greek American.* Additionally, both newspapers had a correspondent in Washington, DC, who was also the correspondent of *Ethnos* in Washington and the United Nations headquarters, in New York City.

Early on, the management realized that there were very few hard and reliable data on the distribution and circulation of both newspapers, as well as the profile of the audience. These data were necessary to be able to attract more advertising from major American companies. Various tactics were employed to deal with these problems. A Greek-American, with significant experience as a political consultant in the United States and a fresh Ph.D. from Columbia University's School of International Relations, had been hired by the new management as a columnist. He was soon persuaded to put his research skills and network of contacts to work to come up with a market research scheme.

Within 2 to 3 months, the first wave of audience data from a survey and focus groups were being discussed at the weekly transcontinental staff meeting, thanks to a basic teleconferencing system. This inquiry revealed significant differences: The Greek and English-language publications were being picked up by very different audiences. Older Greek-Americans were interested mostly in *Proini,* the Greek-language paper. Younger generations were almost exclusively interested in the English-language *The Greek American,* where they could find news, but also longer feature stories on the recent trends in Greek music and culture, interviews with Greek-Americans who were prominent in American politics and the international arts and sports scenes. As a result of learning about these differences, the decision was made to unbundle *Proini* and *The Greek American* and to distribute them separately.

Getting more specific distribution and circulation numbers was a more difficult task. During the first week the new *Proini* and new *The Greek American* were published, staff members, including reporters and editors, got onboard the trucks that distributed the newspapers to newsstands across New York City. They timed the routes; they counted the number of papers dropped off. The following day they counted the unsold papers that were returned and talked to vendors about where the newspapers were placed. Placement was of particular concern, as *Proini* was not the only Greek newspaper in the city. The *National Herald* was a formidable competitor.

The informal method of measuring circulation (auditing) was not foolproof. Nonetheless, it was clear that circulation was growing. Soon after the new and improved daily *Proini* and the weekly *The Greek American* hit the newsstands, circulation reached approximately 4,500 and 5,200 respectively. The goal was set at around 10,000 for the *Proini* (daily) edition. Having circulation audited by an independent agency that specializes in circulation audits (such as the Audit Bureau of Circulations) was never discussed.

For about a year, good and important stories were published and both newspapers were getting noticed in New York, rest of the the U.S., Canada, and Greece. A year into the partnership, however, tensions between the partners developed. The Greek American Publishing, Ltd., troika started to complain that they had no control over their newspapers any more. Because they were successful entrepreneurs and newspaper publishers, they had been stakeholders in the political life of the Greek-American and Cypriot-American communities for years. They were also very involved in New York City and state politics. After the deal with Greece-based Pegasus, they increasingly felt that they had no control over the direction of their publications. Athens, for its part, grew frustrated, as the U.S. partners interfered and tried to affect the newspapers' agenda, thereby lowering the high, professional, journalistic standards they had introduced. In the meantime, other events taking place in Pegasus in Athens also created tension between the Pegasus publishers and the managing director of the enterprise. By mid-fall 2001, the future looked grim. Pegasus was not willing to continue to invest in the New York ventures if it could not maintain complete control over management and could not achieve certain profit goals within a realistic time frame. The U.S.-based partners wanted more control over editorial and management, but they no longer had enough capital to keep the newspapers afloat on their own. In a general atmosphere of discontent, key staff members in New York chose to move on. In late spring 2002, *Proini* and the *Greek American* ceased publication.

Ethnic media organizations may die, but the people who work for them often find themselves employed in new ethnic media ventures. A year after the Pegasus and Greek American Publishing collaboration ended, *Greek Press,* a new Greek-American newspaper, was founded under the direction of the former editor-in-chief of *Proini.* In the winter of 2006, another former editor of *Proini* announced that she was going to be the director of a new Greek-American radio station in New York City.

Case Analysis Questions 

- Having read the case study, identify the challenges *Proini* and *The Greek American* had to overcome, as organizations, before and after Pegasus, S.A., acquired the majority share of Greek American Publishing, Ltd., from the point of view of (a) the owners, (b) the newspapers' management, (c) the editors, reporters, and staff.

- Assume that Greek American Publishing, Ltd. is still in operation and you have been hired as a consultant to help the company achieve its goals. Based on your knowledge of Chapters 1 through 6, what would you recommend? What are some of the good decisions that the company has made from a business point-of-view and where is their room for improvement? What additional information would you request in order to provide the company with solutions best tailored to its needs?

Notes

[1]In 2006, advertising accounted for 92% of the revenue of all Latino newspapers combined (i.e., dailies, weeklies, and less-than-weeklies); newsstand sales accounted for 5% and subscriptions 3% (Latino Print Network, 2007).

[2]The distinction between satellite and suburban dailies is hard to make, as it is not always clear what the geographic limits of a city are and at what point a city or town is no longer a suburb but a different city altogether. In a study of umbrella competition, Lacy (1987) considered as satellites every city that was between 35 and 39 miles away from a metropolitan center. In San Francisco, the *San Jose Mercury News* and *The Oakland Tribune* could be considered as satellite dailies. They serve the residents of San Jose and Oakland, both satellite cities around San Francisco—the metropolitan center in the Bay area.

[3]Compaine (1980) has noted that an important consideration in inter-city competition is the cost of distribution over extended areas of coverage. He suggests that whatever benefits large metropolitan newspapers may gain by extending their coverage area may be offset by the cost of getting their newspaper to geographically distant communities. Therefore, there may be cases where competition between dailies (the first layer) and newspapers in the lower tiers is not as intense as one might expect based on the umbrella competition hypothesis.

[4]ImpreMedia stopped printing *Hoy* in 2008, but kept its online edition.

[5]In 2007, out of the 3,285,331 copies of *Contigo* that were printed every week, 1,444,494 were delivered in Los Angeles, 936,704 in New York, 274,133 in Chicago, and 630,300 in the San Francisco Bay area (ImpreMedia, 2007).

[6]A survey of 1,895 media users of various linguistic and ethnic backgrounds was conducted in the United States in 2005 by New California Media (New America Media as of 2006) and the research firm Bendixen and Associates. The study showed that Arab-Americans and Asian-Americans connect to ethnic media online the most, 76% and 68% respectively. African-Americans and Native-Americans are close at 49% and 47%, while only 23% of Latinos access ethnically-targeted Web sites. A similar study conducted by Bendixen and Associates for New America Media in 2009 indicated that ethnically-targeted Web sites increased their reach, compared to 2005, but not significantly (New America Media & Bendixen & Associates, 2009).

[7]The French agency that regulated broadcasting is the Conseil Supérieur de l' Audiovisuel (CSA).

[8]According to the 2000 U.S. Census, 1,153,295 people in the United States are of Greek heritage. Based on a 2005 U.S. Department of State report, 3 million people residing in the U.S. claim Greek descent. The majority of Greek-Americans live in the New York, New Jersey, Connecticut tri-state area, as well as Detroit, Cleveland, Chicago, and Florida.

CHAPTER 7

Globalization and the Ethnic Media Organization

CHAPTER OBJECTIVES

By the end of this chapter, you will have learned more about:

- What globalization is and why it is important for studying and understanding ethnic media.
- How globalization impacts the structure of ethnic media organizations.
- The different forms of ethnic media organizations we encounter around the world.
- The opportunities and challenges ethnic media must deal with as a result of globalization.
- Current and emerging ownership trends in the ethnic media sector.

The Structure of Ethnic Media Organizations

Changing population dynamics worldwide and the emergence of new communication technologies present both opportunities and challenges for ethnic media organizations. In this chapter we focus on ethnic media as *organizations that have a particular structure and specific goals.* As organizations, ethnic media are subjected to some of the same forces that are altering the landscape of organizations worldwide. *Organizational structure* refers to the way tasks are divided, grouped, and coordinated within an organization (Child, 1972; Robbins, 2005).To achieve their goals, ethnic media organizations rely on a series of processes that involve a number of people who are expected to perform certain *roles* (e.g., as reporters or editors), while adhering to a set of *rules* (e.g., filing a news story by a particular deadline). Gathering information, determining an agenda, and deciding how high or low on the agenda certain stories should be, and news story production and distribution, are only a few of the processes that take place in media organizations.

In recent years, processes and structures of media organizations have been changing, largely due to what we have come to call *globalization.* Technological innovation is a driver of globalization (Held, McGrew, Goldblatt, & Perraton, 1999; Scholte, 2000). It is the most obvious agent of organizational change because it most readily affects everyday organizational practices, such as meeting, discussing, and coordinating task assignments. In the pages that follow, we define globalization and examine the sources of organizational change that impact ethnic media.

What Is Globalization?

Anthony Giddens (2002), one of the prime commentators on globalization, has said that the term "has come from nowhere to be almost everywhere" and "given its popularity, we shouldn't be surprised that the meaning of [globalization] isn't always clear" (p. 7). Numerous definitions have been proposed in recent years. All of us, academics, politicians, and journalists included, use the term to describe and explain a variety of different phenomena. Generally speaking though, globalization is thought to capture an array of *processes* resulting in social, economic, and political transformation (Held et al., 1999; Monge & Matei, 2004).

Three Different Approaches to Globalization

There are three schools of thought on globalization, broadly defined: (a) the *hyperglobalists,* (b) the *skeptics,* and (c) the *transformationalists* (Held et al., 1999; Giddens, 2002; Scholte, 2000). We examine each school of thought in turn, provide a summary of the main positions held by their proponents, and discuss how each way of thinking about globalization can help us better understand ethnic media. We also identify how taking one point of view or another (e.g., a hyperglobalist's versus a skeptic's approach) may mask an important aspect of the globalization-ethnic media relationship.

I. The *hyperglobalists* argue that:

- Social relations have become thoroughly globalized.
- Globalization is "the single most important fact in contemporary history" (Scholte, 2000, p. 17).
- Many corporations have grown into global enterprises, operating therefore across state jurisdictions and outside the control of individual nation-states. The emergence of global enterprises and of many intergovernmental and international nongovernmental organizations means that individual nation-states have lost much of the power they once had to control what people and organizations do within their territories (Ohmae, 1995; see also: Castells, 2000a; Nye & Donahue, 2000).
- The world markets are far more developed today than they were in the 1960s and 1970s and they are converging into one global marketplace (Castells, 2000a; Castells, 2000b; Tehranian, 1999; Waters, 1995).

- Old hierarchies are becoming eroded and technological advancement is ushering us into an era of global civilization (Braman & Sreberny-Mohammadi, 1996; Spybey, 1996).

These positions represent five common threads that we find running through the work of hyperglobalists. Depending on their discipline (e.g., sociology, economics, or communication) and their socio-political views, some hyperglobalists see the effects of globalization as liberating and beneficial (e.g., Castells, 2000a; Castells, 2001; Negroponte, 1995), while others consider them to be devastating (e.g., see Brennan, 2003; Postman, 1992; Wallerstein, 1974).

For hyperglobalists, ethnic media might be considered important insofar as they help create global citizens. There is research that seems to lend support to such an argument. Retis (2007), for example, reports on the numerous ethnic media in Spain serving the Ecuadorans, Argentineans, and Colombians living primarily in Madrid and Barcelona. Retis' (2007) research shows that these media play an important part in the development of these ethnic communities' sense of having a unique identity. Those hyperglobalists who view globalization as beneficial might argue that these media also connect the Ecuadorans, Argentinean, and Colombian immigrants living in Spain to their home countries (e.g., by providing news from those countries of origin) and even to similar ethnic communities in other parts of the world, thereby expanding their perceptions about what the world is like. In doing so, over time, this audience's place of reference will no longer be the place they were born in; and it will not be the ethnic community or the country to which they or their parents moved. It will be both these places. Individual ethnic community members will be aware of and likely participate in what is happening both "here" and "there." It is in this sense that ethnic media can create global citizens; that is, individuals who can think and act beyond the boundaries of a single country.

Other hyperglobalists, however—those who view globalization as detrimental—might consider the mushrooming of ethnic media worldwide as an indicator of social fragmentation. In certain ethnic communities, ethnic media are focused almost exclusively on the happenings of the ethnic community. In addition, members of the ethnic community prefer to access and spend much more time with satellite and online media that bring them closer to their country of origin, instead of media produced in their country of settlement. This is certainly the case among the first (i.e., immigrant) generation of ethnic Korean and Chinese communities in the broader area of Southern California and in British Columbia, Canada (Ball-Rokeach & Lin, 2004; Lin & Song, 2006; Murray, Yu, & Ahadi, 2007; Park, 1997). This type of media connection pattern suggests that (a) these Korean and Chinese immigrant communities prefer to remain isolated from the wider society of the country of settlement, and that (b) ethnic media may indeed operate as forces of social fragmentation and not as builders of a global civil society. We turn to the second school of thought around globalization next.

II. The *skeptics* argue that:

- There is no such thing as globalization; it is merely a fad.
- The "global economy" is mythical (Zysman, cited in Scholte, 2000).

- What, in name, are "global" companies remain, in many ways, strongly attached to one country they recognize as "home" (Scholte, 2000, p. 18).
- The rifts between the economies of developed and third world countries are deepening (Hirst & Thompson, 1996).
- Arguments of global culture and a global civil society are misguided (e.g., Huntington, 1996).
- The state remains the dominant actor on the international stage.
- Any activity that takes place across nation-state borders depends largely on the acquiescence of the states involved (e.g., Krasner, 1994).

Contrary to the hyperglobalists, the skeptics argue that nation-states remain the most central actors in global politics. Therefore, while looking through the lenses of a hyperglobalist, we are promptly challenged to investigate the role of ethnic media in the lives of people and communities across borders; adopting a skeptic's perspective directs our attention to the question: How do state policies impact the development of ethnic media? The state regulates immigration flows, sets the requirements immigrants have to meet in order to be able to work, and decides who and under what conditions can own a media organization. Changes in policies that affect a person's rights to enter and live in a country, to work, and to invest in media properties may foster the creation of new ethnic media, but they can also force ethnic media to close. In Canada, immigration policies welcome young, well-educated, highly skilled, English or French-speaking, male entrepreneurs who come primarily from Korea and China (Abu-Laban & Gabriel, 2002). These new immigrants have shown a particular interest in ethnic media. In fact, as Murray, Uy, and Ahadi (2007) found, new ethnic community media founded after 2000 are "partially, if not entirely, run by immigrants with a neo-liberal sympathy under the business immigration program whose life aspiration in the new country continues to center on 'upward mobility'" (Park, 2005, p. 117). This Canadian case serves as one example of how state policies can encourage ethnic media growth.

The skeptics' perspective brings to the forefront the critical role that the state plays in the development of ethnic media through a number of different policies (we specifically discuss how the policy context in which ethnic media are founded affects their operation and development in the following chapter). By centering their attention on the role of the nation-state, however, skeptics might overlook or not adequately account for the significant impact of new communication technologies on ethnic media. The ethnic Chinese press worldwide offers a case in point. Zhang and Xiaoming (1999) note that the ethnic Chinese press in many countries around the world (primarily in North America and in Southeast Asia) has been on the decline, "due to political restrictions, financial strains, and the decline of Chinese education overseas" (p. 28). They point out that new waves of immigration from China, Taiwan, and other Chinese-speaking countries from the mid-1970s onwards may have helped slow down or reverse this trend, but that it is the Internet that holds the potential to truly boost the development of ethnic Chinese newspapers. That is, Zhang and Xiaoming (1999) argue, for two reasons: first of all, because the Internet lowers the cost of content production and distribution; and, second, because it allows publishers and journalists to avoid government censorship. This applies to ethnic Chinese media produced in the People's Republic of China and intended for Chinese audiences worldwide, but also to ethnic Chinese media produced for communities living in countries such as Malaysia and Indonesia, where government officials and non-Chinese populations view the ethnic Chinese with suspicion or hostility (Hicks & Mackie, 1994).

A third way of thinking about globalization is reflected in the research of the *tranformationalists,* who acknowledge the continued significance of nation-state power, but who also recognize that the world has changed substantially in several ways in the past few decades. We discuss their positions next.

III. The *tranformationalists* or *moderates* argue that:

- Globalization is not a new phenomenon.
- Today, we are experiencing historically unprecedented levels of global interconnectedness.
- The effects of globalization are not inevitable (Held, McGrew, Goldblatt, & Perraton, 1999).
- Globalization trends are spreading unevenly across continents and regions, classes, and age groups.
- Both convergence and divergence tendencies among cultures, ideologies, and economies are at work (Appadurai, 1996; Ball-Rokeach, Gibbs, Jung, Kim, & Qiu, 2000; Held et al., 1999; Monge & Matei, 2004).

There is evidence to suggest that hyperglobalists are right. Ethnic media are contributing to the preservation of ties among people who live thousands of miles apart, educating immigrants about their newfound country and helping them to integrate. In addition though, there is evidence that indicates ethnic media may allow ethnic communities to remain insular and disconnected from the "others" who surround them.

Moreover, data on ethnic media lend some support to the arguments of certain globalization skeptics. As discussed in the first few chapters of the book, the life of ethnic media is inextricably linked to the history of migration. The flows of migration have changed significantly over the past centuries, due largely to changes in immigration policies enacted by state governments. In most cases, more "open" immigration policies that encourage the entry of large numbers of immigrants from one country or region of the world is associated with the increase in the number of ethnic media created to serve those groups (read the Preface of the book and Chapter 8 for more on this topic). On the other hand, a significant weakening of immigration flows can undermine ethnic media production. However, as Zhang and Xiaoming (1999) argue in the case of the ethnic Chinese press mentioned earlier, there is also evidence to suggest that new communication technologies may offer ethnic media producers ways to get around restrictive state policies on immigration.

Overall, from the point of view of someone studying ethnic media, the evidence leads to the conclusion that neither the hyperglobalists' nor the skeptics' approach captures the whole picture. Determinism permeates both perspectives, prohibiting them from acknowledging the tension between continuity and discontinuity, which is inherent in globalization. In contrast, the tranformationalist approach does allow this tension. Transformationalists posit that globalization is a set of processes that are altering the social, political, and economic map of the world. But they are not changing the entire world at the same pace, nor are they doing it uniformly. There is significant variation in how globalization is experienced by countries, organizations, and people around the world (Castells, 2000a; Castells, 2001; Held et al., 1999). State policies on immigration, for instance, may differ greatly. Access to the Internet and other new technologies varies significantly from country to country, across different ethnic groups, ages, education, and income levels, and among men and women (Castells, 2000a; Norris, 2001). In addition, the ability of corporations to expand their operations and invest in global business ventures varies dramatically. The leverage of companies based in the developed economies of the world over the global marketplace is much larger than that of companies based in developing and third world countries. It is not coincidental that the biggest media companies of the world have their headquarters in the United States, Germany, France, and Australia (Arsenault & Castells, 2008; Columbia Journalism Review, 2009—see Table 7.1).

Table 7.1 Where the World's Largest Multi-Media Companies Are Based*

Company	Headquarters
Time Warner Company • ***Revenue***: $43.7 billion	*U.S.A.*
Walt Disney Company • ***Revenue***: $34.29 billion	*U.S.A.*
Bertelsmann AG • ***Revenue***: $24.21 billion	*Germany*
News Corporation • ***Revenue***: $28.66 billion	*U.S.A./Australia*
NBC Universal • As of 2004, 80% of the company is owned by General Electric and 20% owned by Vivendi • Among other holdings, NBC Universal also owns Spanish-language broadcaster Telemundo • ***Revenue***: $16.12 billion	General Electric is based in the *United States*, Vivendi in *France*. NBC Universal's headquarters are in the United States.
CBS • ***Revenue***: $14.32 billion	U.S.A.
Viacom, Inc. • ***Revenue***: $11.47 billion	U.S.A.

Data source: Arsenault & Castells (2008); Columbia Journalism Review (2009).

**Note:* Size measured by revenue, circa 2007.

A tranformationalist position on globalization is more conducive to the study of ethnic media, because it allows us to account for the general trends we are observing (e.g., continuous increase in the number of ethnic media organizations created worldwide), but also the substantial variations in the globalization trends that we are witnessing across (a) space (geography), (b) ethnicity, and (c) time.

Forces of Globalization

As a set of processes, globalization is driven by three forces: (a) technological innovation, (b) capitalism, and (c) policy (Scholte, 2000). All three impact ethnic media in one way or another.

Technological Innovation

New communication technologies impact ethnic media both from (a) the consumer's point of view and (b) from the producer's perspective.

New Communication Technologies and the Ethnic Media Consumer

In the 15th century, Gutenberg's press made it possible for ideas to travel to distant places, even if their creator could not. Today, the Internet has made it possible for media content to travel across space and time zones with the touch of a button. Technological innovation has not just facilitated communication of ideas across borders; it has also allowed people to stay in touch with friends and family members who live in distant places. Immigrants from Guatemala India, Korea, the Philippines, and Taiwan, for instance, living in Southern California, communicate with their families back in the country of origin on a regular basis via the phone, instant messaging, IP telephony, or e-mail.

As they stay connected to the people who matter to them the most "back home," they are also more likely to want to keep up with what is happening in the country they left behind. Online news portals and traditional print and broadcast ethnic media serve this purpose well. *The Indian Express* is an English-language weekly newspaper that is published in the United States and Canada. On the company's online portal, this is how the producers described their mission in 2007:

> Whether one has been here for 30 years or has recently immigrated to North America, *The Indian Express* is a brand that Indians recognize most. As more and more Indians immigrate to find opportunities in every field of economic endeavor, the need to "go home every week" has never been greater. The Express Group recognized this opportune time to serve this booming Non Resident Indian (NRI) population in North America through a weekly edition, specifically designed to meet their needs, tastes, and discerning standards they have come to expect.[1]

The links of immigrants to the country of origin are less likely to weaken today than they were decades ago, when it took letters months to cross the ocean, or when people had to wait for the rare visit by a family member or friend bearing news of "home." Continued communication between the home country and the country of settlement means that ethnic identity may be preserved for longer periods of time than once expected. Therefore, it seems plausible that ethnic media may also survive longer than they used to, as they remain significant channels of communication for the immigrant generation, but also the second, third, and later generations.

New Communication Technologies and the Ethnic Media Producer

Technological innovation also affects the way that media operate as organizations. First of all, it gives them access to an array of information sources from around the world. Ethnic media journalists can receive stories from wire services located in the country of origin; they may have access to Web sites of the most influential media in the "home country," and also be able to follow a developing story by watching live coverage offered via satellite by a television station located anywhere on the globe. Reporters working for a Lebanese newspaper in Britain for example, may be following a developing story in Beirut by watching Dubai-based MBC TV.[2] Of course the audience of the newspaper may also have access to MBC TV or other Arab-language channels, and such access may create unwanted competition for the British-based Lebanese newspaper. Technological innovation can cut both ways. It enables ethnic media journalists to do their job better and to provide their audience with more timely information, but it also introduces new challenges. The ability of the ethnic media producers to identify what their competition, *local* and *global,* is not offering and their capacity to use new communication technologies to attract audience members is critical for survival in a globalized media market.

New communication technologies have also made it easier for major media organizations around the world to establish themselves as influential players in ethnic media markets of countries worldwide, and to cut costs associated with the production and distribution of content. *Sing Tao* is a prime example of this. The organization was founded in 1938 in Hong Kong, and it opened its first international office in San Francisco in 1975. Today, the company has 22 offices globally in places like Auckland, Sydney, Paris, London, Calgary, Toronto, Vancouver, New York, Chicago, and Honolulu. New communication technologies make it possible for the *Sing Tao* family of publications and radio stations to share content produced in their local ethnic communities and in the countries these communities think of as "home" (i.e., the People's Republic of China, Hong Kong, and Taiwan). By sharing the cost of news production, they can offer more varied and better quality programming. *Sing Tao* reports that 85% of San Francisco's population that listens to Chinese radio tunes into its station.

In addition to challenging the way ethnic media organizations operate, the Internet has also created the platform for a whole new kind of ethnic media to emerge. *Hua Xia Wen Zhai* (*HXWZ*) is a weekly online-only magazine that caters to the expatriate Chinese student community that lives, primarily, in the United States, Canada, and Europe (Qiu, 2003). It was launched on April 5, 1991, in the

U.S. In *HXWZ* readers can find news stories translated from foreign news media, articles from Chinese newspapers and magazines, opinion pieces, as well as original contributions. Qiu (2003) documents the existence of similar publications in Germany, Britain, Sweden, Denmark, Holland, and Japan. As he notes, it is very hard to tell how many of these publications are published on an ongoing basis, as they are constantly changing. The appeal of this type of media operations, from their producers' point of view is obvious: Online publishing requires significantly less capital investment and therefore involves less risk.

Economic Globalization

Scholte (2000) argues globalization would not be possible if it were not for capitalism; "capitalism," he says, "is a structure of production where economic activity is oriented first and foremost to the accumulation of surplus" (p. 98). Individuals, organizations, and countries invest money or capital to make a profit (i.e., a surplus). This profit is re-invested to yield an even larger profit, and so forth. Media companies, including ethnic media organizations, do this, too. For them, larger revenue streams necessitate more advertising. And to attract advertisers, they need to continuously increase their audience base. Within the limits of a city or country, a media company can only grow so much. The size of the potential audience is finite. Theoretically it is possible for the audience of a media organization to equal in size the number of people who live in a particular geographically-defined market, whether that represents a city or an entire country. In reality, however, this is unlikely. Because it is unlikely and because corporations always need more space and resources (e.g., capital for investments and human capital) to grow, many media firms look beyond country borders and target global audiences.

The case study of the Greek newspaper *Ethnos* discussed in Chapter 5 illustrates one strategy that media corporations employ to reach audiences beyond the borders of their main market. *Ethnos* bought a majority stake in the Greek-American newspaper *Proini,* which was based in New York, in order to expand its audience base to include ethnic Greeks living in the United States. In other cases, major media institutions have opted to establish subsidiaries in countries outside their primary market. That is a strategy that the Chinese media corporation mentioned earlier, *Sing Tao,* has adopted to capture new audiences across the globe. Korean media companies based in Seoul have also employed similar strategies to grow. The cases of *The Korea Times* and the *Korea Central Daily* are illustrative. Both have created subsidiaries in major U.S. and Canadian cities where there are large Korean populations. In all four of the aforementioned cases, the content intended for the audiences based outside the parent-corporation's country has varied depending on the needs of local ethnic communities. To be able to provide this varied content, parent companies and subsidiaries have had to work together. In the case of the *Korea Central Daily, for instance,* part of the newspaper is produced in Korea and part in 11 local communities across the U.S. and Canada, where many Koreans live (e.g., Los Angeles, New York, Toronto, and Vancouver). This means that two editorial teams are working in distant locations, in different time zones, and coordinating their efforts at some level to produce the newspaper that arrives at readers' doorsteps or computer monitors. It also means that the *Korea Central Daily* can provide its audience with a significant amount of information from the home country, as well as news from the local American or Canadian community where the newspaper is distributed.

This type of organizational arrangement, made possible through technological innovation and the globalization of capital, creates the potential for ethnic media to grow and become stronger competitors in the global media market. Organizations that are larger in size and have a broader network of alliances tend to weather storms in the financial markets better (e.g., Amburgey, Kelley, & Barnett, 1993; Cyert & March, 1963; Hannan & Freeman, 1984; Salacnic & Pfeffer, 1978; Starbuck, 1965; Stinchcombe, 1965). This is likely to translate into more stable revenue streams from advertising, and thereby sustainability. In addition, a stronger organizational profile makes ethnic media organizations more appealing as employers. Aspiring Korean-American journalists and advertising or marketing professionals, for example, are more likely to seek a job with the *Korea Central Daily* than with a smaller, less established Korean newspaper serving one or more Korean communities around the U.S.

For every *Indian Express, Korean Central Daily,* and *Sing Tao* type of organization that has emerged in the global media market, however, there are hundreds of smaller ethnic media organizations founded by enterprising members of local ethnic communities. They draw employees from the community, and often a large number of their contributors—for example, writers and photographers—are volunteers. Sources of advertising are usually found within the community as well. They are often local businesses that want to promote their products to the local community and businesses that do not have the money to buy advertising space or time in other, larger media (Riggins, 1992; Georgiou, 2002b).

Regulation

Technological innovation and the free flow of capital may contribute to the growth of ethnic media, but the state controls the direction and speed of these developments through regulation, which is exercised through the implementation of an array of policies. Most media organizations become concerned when there are changes in national *media* and *trade* policies. Changes in *media* policy affect, among other things, how licenses are awarded (e.g., to run a television or radio station), and they impact the media ownership landscape. In the U.S. and Europe, for example, media policy has been moving in the direction of removing restrictions on ownership (i.e., ownership *deregulation*), at least since the early 1990s (Bagdikian, 2004; McChesney & Scott, 2004; Papathanassopoulos, 1997; Ward, 2005). In the global market, media ownership is also controlled by *trade* policies that determine how much of a company can be owned by foreign investors (OECD, 2005). Big media companies, however, have found ways to get around restrictions on foreign direct investment. Rupert Murdoch's News Corporation, for instance, owns 100% of bTV, a Bulgarian television station through its local subsidiary Balkan News Corporation (European Federation of Journalists, 2005).

Ethnic media are affected by both media and trade policy changes, but also by *immigration* and *labor* policies. The former regulates who can enter a country and for how long, and can thereby influences the size and composition of an ethnic community and, by extension, the size of the ethnic media audience. In addition, immigration and labor policy together dictate restrictions on employment for noncitizens and nonresidents. Such restrictions may discourage the founding of ethnic media and make it much more difficult for ethnic media producers to recruit personnel.

Immigration, labor, media, and trade policies can vary considerably across countries, and every policy configuration may affect the ethnic media landscape differently. In some countries, like Austria for instance, only ethnic media that are founded by ethnic minorities and formally recognized as such enjoy First Amendment-type rights (Böse, Haberfellner, & Koldas, 2002). Thereby, ethnic groups lacking official minority status are essentially discouraged from establishing formal media enterprises. Similar restrictions do not exist in states like Belgium, Britain, and the United States that better promote inclusion and integration of ethnic populations (see also Chapter 8).

In an increasingly globalized world, policy is no longer made only at the national level. Many countries are embedded in larger intergovernmental organizations, such as the European Union, the Association of Southeast Asian Nations (ASEAN), the North Atlantic Treaty Organization (NATO), and others. These intergovernmental organizations function as mechanisms through which states can better coordinate their activities. Becoming part of such institutions has become necessary largely because so much of people's and organizations' activities take place across borders (e.g., individuals cross borders to work, companies establish satellite offices or have subsidiaries in more than one country) and states are finding managing these activities more and more difficult.

In the European Union, member-states have strived to coordinate their economic, social, agricultural, media, and other policies (a process referred to as *harmonization*), so as to remove roadblocks to cooperation. Harmonization has been fairly rapid with respect to lifting state-imposed limitations on cross-country media ownership (Bruck et al., 2002). However, an important and related policy area where harmonization has been slower in coming is immigration. That is because any change in immigration policy can be regarded as a challenge to state sovereignty; the state's ability, that is, to regulate the movement of individuals in and out of its territory. Further harmonization of immigration and media policy across regions of the world, like the European Union, may encourage or discourage the development of ethnic media organizations.

Adoption of a common policy on immigration that offers a clear path to citizenship for immigrants and a common media policy that values diversity in media ownership, for example, might encourage the founding of new ethnic media in European countries. Young immigrant and ethnic communities might be encouraged by such policies to invest in building ethnic media that can help their audience members become incorporated in the host society (or country of settlement) as full citizens. Common European policies are also likely to encourage entrepreneurs to seek opportunities to expand their businesses and to serve communities with the same ethnic background that live across state boundaries (e.g., Albanian immigrants across countries of Southern Europe, Turkish-origin communities in Germany and neighboring countries). Common policies make it easier for entrepreneurs to work across borders, saving them time and money that would otherwise be spent on addressing problems created by multiple and occasionally conflicting national policy standards.

¤ For Further Discussion

Choose two different countries of interest to you. Gather as much information as you can on their media and immigration policies. Consider how in each country media and immigration policy, independent of one another and together, may affect ethnic media. Then compare the two countries. In which country would you expect to find more ethnic media? Why?

Six Types of Ethnic Media Organizations

Technological innovation, capitalism, and regulation are part of globalization and determine its impact on organizations, including ethnic media. Currently, ethnic media come in six different configurations.

Small Scale, Local Operations

Ethnic media are commonly thought of as small scale operations, and are rarely on the radar of advertisers and policymakers. A census of print ethnic media in 11 different Los Angeles County communities, conducted by the Metamorphosis Project research team in Los Angeles in 2003, revealed more than 350 small-scale publications; these included newspapers (68%), magazines (26%), tabloids (3%), and newsletters (3%) (W. -Y. Lin, personal communication, April 24, 2003). Most of these organizations are family-owned or funded by one or more entrepreneurs who rely primarily on the profits of their other private ventures to fund their media businesses. *Indonesia Media,* for example, is a bi-weekly magazine that is published by Ibrahim Irawan, Frits Hong, PhilemonTambunan, Jusni Hilwan, and Virgo Handoyo. Ibrahim Irawan admits that every 64-page edition of *Indonesia Media* is an investment he can afford to make thanks to his and his wife's successful dental practice in Glendora, California. Irawan says that their publication relies on local businesses for advertising, but that is not enough. "We seek advertising,

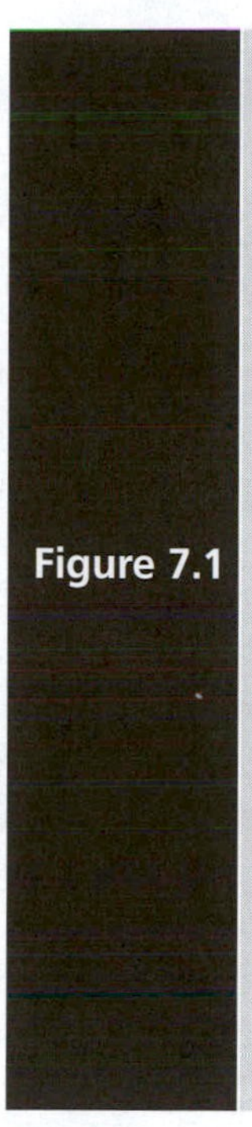

Figure 7.1 Indonesia Media (Glendora, California). According to its publisher, Ibrahim Irawan, there are 15,000 to 18,000 copies of the 64-page magazine *Indonesia Media* printed twice a month. The magazine has contributors from California, Idaho, Pennsylvania, Tennessee, and Washington DC, in the United States, as well as Toronto and Vancouver in Canada, France, Germany, the Netherlands, Australia, Singapore, and the Philippines. The magazine is distributed for free, and it can also be found online at: www.indonesiamedia.com

Source: IndonesiaMedia.com

even in Canada and the east coast, but we don't get any." Fortunately, though, "financially, we don't have a problem," he says. "I am a dentist, my wife is a dentist, so we have a little bit of money to compensate for the lack of advertising . . . So far, we are considered healthy [as a business]" (I. Irawan, personal communication, August 10, 2007).

Research suggests that this is not a pattern unique to ethnic media in Los Angeles. Amy Eddings, host of a nationally syndicated public radio show in the U.S., says that, "Eighty-six percent of English language newspapers are owned by corporations, but the ethnic press is primarily independent—started by entrepreneurs who sometimes work second jobs to finance their paper" (OnTheMedia.org, May 19, 2001). Studies indicate that this is the case beyond the U.S. as well (Georgiou, 2002b). The natural question, of course, is why do these individuals invest in ethnic media, if they are not yielding satisfactory profits?

Like Ibrahim Irawan, Pashree Super Pat relies on other ventures to fund his English-language newspaper *InterThai/Pacific Rim News,* which is based in Los Angeles. "It's almost like a donation," he says to Daniel Akst (2003) of the *Carnegie Reporter*, "[made] for the education of young people, to continue the Thai culture and tradition" (p. 6).

The *Haitian Times* is a small weekly newspaper, based in Brooklyn, New York. It is published in English and not Creole (French Patois), and it serves the approximately 500,000 Haitians that live in the city. The newspaper was founded in 1999 and is managed by Garry Pierre-Pierre, a former reporter for *The New York Times.* The cost of producing and printing 15,000 copies every week is so high that Pierre-Pierre says he cannot take out a salary for himself (Akst, 2003). As for what keeps him doing it? Pierre-Pierre notes that the *Haitian Times* aims (a) to bridge the gap between Haitians in the U.S. and Haitians in Haiti, (b) encourage young, educated, upwardly mobile Haitians to become more involved in the community, and (c) to raise readers' political consciousness.

Solvency is a constant preoccupation for small ethnic media, like the ones mentioned here. But it is a burden that many producers are willing to bear for a long time because they believe that they offer a valuable service to their communities. They are invested in keeping members of the community connected to the country of origin, helping immigrants and their children preserve their ethnic identity, while simultaneously pushing their audience to take on a more active role in the local community, in the country of settlement. These small ethnic media organizations act as communication switchboards that allow their audiences to connect to "here" and "there," effectively defying the limitations imposed on them by geography and time. It is because of this role they play in the lives of individuals, families, and communities that make these media as much a part of globalization as large multinational ethnic media enterprises are.

¤ For Further Discussion

Select two ethnic media available in your community or via the World Wide Web. Spend some time going through some of the stories each medium has featured in recent weeks. What differences and similarities do you detect in the type and tone of stories that these media cover compared to each other, but also to mainstream media available to the same audiences? What does this exercise tell you about the motivations of the publisher(s)? If these media are in your area, try to interview the producers to find out if your assessment is accurate.

Large Ethnic Media Corporations

Much of the data available on ownership trends only cover the largest media outlets (e.g., Spanish-language broadcaster Univisión in the United States), which serve the most prominent and visible ethnic populations in a particular country (e.g., Latinos in the U.S., Asian communities in Canada, Indian and Middle-Eastern immigrants in the UK). Some of these outlets are part of even larger media corporations. It is common for those larger, parent companies to have multiple media holdings that cater to the same ethnic group.

ImpreMedia, for example, owns six Spanish-language newspapers based in five different markets across the U.S. Their audiences come from a host of Latin American countries, but they all speak Spanish. In the U.S.-Hispanic case, such cross-market ownership reflects the rapidly increasing number of Spanish-speakers and the emergence of U.S.-Hispanic conglomerate identity—that is the idea that Latinos essentially share the same ethnic identity regardless of their country of origin (Dávila, 2001; PEJ, 2006; Rodriguez, 1999; see also Chapter 4). The rise of conglomerate identity allows media corporations to maximize the size of their potential audience by targeting all Spanish speakers in the U.S., not just Mexican-origin Hispanics, for example, or people with Honduran, Dominican, or Cuban origins.

Since the turn of the century, a similar pattern has been developing in Spain to where many immigrants from Latin America have moved seeking better employment opportunities. Retis (2007) has mapped the plethora of Spanish-language media that have emerged in Madrid, Spain's capital, to serve ethnic communities of Argentineans, Bolivians, Ecuadorans, Peruvians, and Venezuelans, among others. Some of these media, as the titles of the monthly newspapers *Mi Ecuador* and *Bolivia-Es* indicate, target specific communities from one country or another. Others, as is the case with many U.S. Spanish-language media, are taking advantage of the commonality in language spoken by these groups and the fact that they all come from Latin America to expand their audience base. This is the case with newspapers like the biweekly *Latinoamérica Exterior* and the monthly *El Latinoamericano,* and magazines such as *Tiempo Iberoamericano* and *Fusión Latina.* As of 2007, however, these ethnic media are generally small in size and do not have the status that publications like *La Opinión* and *El Diario* have in their respective U.S. markets.

The Multinational Media Enterprise

The story of large ethnic media corporations is predominantly an American one, and it involves mostly Spanish-language media. Language differences make it harder for similar corporations catering to Asian and South Asian ethnic communities, for example, to emerge. Due to such limitations, several organizations have taken a different route to expanding their business. They choose to target multiple ethnic communities that may live across more than one country but have the same country of origin and/or speak the same language.

The example of the Cinéyama Media Group, which is based in New York City, is instructive. The company has newspaper, magazine, and other media holdings in the U.S., Canada, and India. Of their newspapers, *The Indian Express North American Edition* is an English-language paper targeted to all Indians living across the U.S. and Canada (i.e., communities from the same country of origin). Another newspaper, *Divya Bhaskar North American Edition,* is geared towards the Gujarati Indian communities; the weekly *Amritsar Times* serves the Punjabi Indian communities;

and the bi-monthly *Telugu Times* is aimed towards Telugu-speaking Indians across the U.S. and Canadian markets (i.e., communities that speak the same language and come from the same country). Cinéyama has managed to build up its business (a) by turning the apparent weakness of ethnic and language diversity among Indian immigrants into a strength, through the creation or acquisition of multiple media titles targeting more than one particular Indian immigrant community; and (b) by appealing to similar ethnic and linguistic groups living in multiple countries (i.e., the U.S. and Canada).

Transnational or Global Ethnic Media

Thanks to technology, some ethnic media, especially electronic media (i.e., television and radio), develop into *transnational* or *global enterprises.* According to Parker (2005), transnational enterprises are organizations that:

> (a) Acquire resources from a global pool, (b) view the world as their home, (c) establish a worldwide presence in one or more businesses, (d) develop a global *business* strategy for their businesses that operate worldwide, and (e) transcend internal and external boundaries. (italics in original, p. 63)

Transnational ethnic media may have headquarters in one country, but as they set out to serve communities dispersed around the globe, the world becomes their home turf. Zee TV is one of the largest Indian (Hindi) broadcasters worldwide. The company is based in Mumbai, India, but it has offices in Canada, Hong Kong, Singapore, South Africa, the United Arab Emirates, the United Kingdom, and the U.S. All of these are countries with significant Indian-origin populations. Another satellite broadcaster, SAT-7, is an Arab-Christian broadcaster that was founded in 1995. It targets primarily Christian-Arabs in North Africa and the Middle East, but its headquarters are in the United Kingdom. Both Zee TV and SAT-7 count on ethnic communities worldwide not only as viewers, but also to provide the talent needed to staff their local offices, as well as their regional production and distribution teams. They do therefore, as Parker prescribes, acquire significant resources from a global pool.

Over time, Zee TV and SAT-7 have achieved a global presence by reaching the television and computer monitors of Indians and Christian-Arabs, respectively, worldwide. Zee TV, for instance, reaches over 500 million people worldwide in over 120 countries ("Business," 2009; Chalaby, 2002). And while the many communities they each serve may have things in common, they undoubtedly also have differences due to the particularities of the social context in which they have developed. It is very likely that tastes of Indians living in South Africa, for example, and Indians who live in Canada, with regard to television programs, are very different. Such differences are likely to be even more pronounced among the younger members of these Indian communities who grew up in South Africa and Canada watching not only Zee TV, of course, but also non-Hindi programming produced in the country of settlement. For companies like Zee TV to be successful, such differences must be carefully considered in developing a global business strategy.

In addition, for transnational organizations to function smoothly, it is important for personnel located in distant locations to be able to communicate and effectively coordinate their activities. Cultural differences often create problems. The script and images that are appropriate for an advertising campaign in one country, for example, might be inappropriate in another. Or there may be differences across countries with respect to how a boss is expected to treat an employee in the workplace.

To counter such problems, transnational organizations emphasize the building of a strong *organizational culture.* Organizational culture refers to a "system of shared meaning held by members that distinguishes [one] organization from other[s]" (Robbins, 2005, p. 485; see also Eisenberg & Riley, 2001). But organizational culture does not just distinguish one organization from others. The stronger it is, the more likely it will override clashes of meanings rooted in employees' unique, personal cultural backgrounds. Such clashes are possible even in transnational ethnic media organizations where most members share the same language and have similar ethnic backgrounds. That is because employees of these organizations view the world not only through the filters of the culture they share with their co-ethnics (Hindi in the case of Zee TV), but also through the culture of the country they live in.

Public and Non-Profit Broadcasters

Apart from commercial media operations, there are also some less visible public and non-profit broadcasters that offer "special programming" (Moss, 1991) for a variety of ethnic communities. Many of these media, especially in the United States, are affiliated with educational institutions (e.g., Fordham University's WFUV and Columbia University's WKCR). According to a 1991 study, radio station WNWK-FM, based in New York City, claimed to be the "the only multi-ethnic station in the tri-state area [i.e., New York, Connecticut, and New Jersey]" (Moss, 1991, p. 10). The station transmitted in 27 languages. Between 22.5 and 34.5 hours a week consisted of Greek and Italian programming, while several 1-hour (or shorter) segments were broadcast on a weekly basis in Arabic, Armenian, Bengali, Farsi, Macedonian, Serbian, Slovak, and Urdu. WNWK-FM also offered programming in Spanish. However, it did not treat Latinos as one group. Instead, programming was tailored to target Argentinean, Chilean, Dominican, Ecuadorian, and Peruvian groups specifically. The format of WNWK changed though when it was sold in 1998 to Heftel Broadcasting, a company that owns primarily Spanish-language radio stations (Watrous, 1998). Heftel announced that WNWK would broadcast a Tropical Spanish Hits music format (Business Wire, 1998), thus disconnecting from many former audiences.[3]

Public television channels on UHF frequencies, in North America and many European countries, also broadcast programming for particular ethnic and immigrant communities (Gaya, 2002; Ormond, 2002). WNYC and WNYE in New York City are two examples. They operate under the auspices of the City of New York (Moss, 1991). WNYC (Channel 31) carries programming targeted to the Italian ethnic communities in the city, as well as Japanese and Chinese-origin (Cantonese and Mandarin) residents.

It also carries programs for the East Indian, Greek, Polish, and Brazilian communities of New York.

Virtual Ethnic Media Organizations

There are many online media that are extensions of existing ethnic newspapers, magazines, and ethnic broadcast media. Apart from these, however, there is also a new type of ethnic media organization that has emerged, and which exists only in cyberspace. Technological innovation has lowered the barrier of entry into the media market for many ethnic communities, by reducing the costs associated with production and distribution (Karim, 1998; Karim, Smeltzer, & Loucher, 1998). This is true at least for ethnic communities or segments of ethnic communities that have Internet access and are more educated. The cases of *Hua Xia Wen Zhai (HXWZ), Lian Yi Tong Xun* (or *News of the Association),* and *Feng Hua Yuan* are illustrative; they are all online-only magazines, produced by and intended for expatriate Chinese students in the United States, Canada, Europe, and elsewhere (Qiu, 2003).

Virtual ethnic media organizations do not produce only online newspapers and magazines. Some have experimented with Web-based radio and Web-based television, in part because so far, and in most countries, there are no formal licensing requirements (Browne, 2005). In addition, Web stations allow ethnic communities to get around problems related to the incompatibility of Internet applications with certain languages (especially Asian) that require special scripts. This is less of a problem today than it was a few years ago (Karim, 1998), but nevertheless, Web radio and television may provide a more user-friendly alternative for certain ethnic populations, especially if the language spoken does not have a written form or if the literacy rates among the population are low.

¤ For Further Discussion

Consider the following scenario: You are an entrepreneur intending to start up an ethnic media corporation in your city. You need to select the ethnic group(s) you will target and justify your choice. You also need to select the organizational structure that you believe would fit your enterprise best and justify your choice. Finally, consider how the media and immigration policy context in which you have to operate would affect the range of options and choices you make in accomplishing your goals as an ethnic media entrepreneur.

Who Owns the Ethnic Media?

The number of ethnic media that are active in the American media markets continues to grow (PEJ, 2005, 2006, 2007b). According to the annual report of

The Project for Excellence in Journalism for 2005, "While some of the data are soft, and there were declines in the circulation of print publications, the general picture was robust" (p. 17).[4] During the same year, New California Media, an alliance of over 600 ethnic media organizations on the West Coast of the United States that serves as an advocate and advertising broker for its members, commissioned a study of several ethnic groups in the U.S. The study, "The Ethnic Media in America: The Giant Hidden in Plain Sight," found that 51 million Americans (24% of the adult population) are either primary or secondary consumers of ethnic media (New America Media & Bendixen & Associates, 2005, p. 11).[5]

Unfortunately, trend data for other countries are limited. The number of ethnic media in a variety of European countries is impressive, but there is no baseline to compare these data to. Baseline information is necessary to reach some conclusion with regard to what is happening in the European ethnic media sector as a whole. Globally, however, research suggests that there is growth. Bates (2005), for instance, found that the number of ethnic television channels that are distributed via satellite worldwide jumped from 378, in 2000, to about 1,000 in 2003.

Apart from making it difficult to say something about the size of the ethnic media market across countries, the fact that most of the available longitudinal data come from the United States makes it challenging to speak with certainty about ongoing and emerging trends in ethnic media ownership worldwide. Clearly, additional research is required in a variety of media markets, and this type of work might bring to light ownership arrangements that have thus far not been documented in the literature. That having been said, though, with respect to ownership, it would be a mistake to think that what happens in the ethnic media market in one country or another is completely independent of the trends in the broader, national and global, media markets, where ownership consolidation seems to be the name of the game. The data available suggest that in the ethnic media sector there are four trends: (a) ownership consolidation among ethnic media that serve similar ethnic communities, (b) acquisition of ethnic media by large multinational or transnational corporations (not necessarily media organizations) that are based in immigrant-sending states, (c) acquisition of ethnic media by "mainstream" media, and (d) a decrease in the number of owners of media who are members of a minority group (e.g., African-American in the U.S.). We discuss each of these trends in turn. Before that, however, we must note that a large (if not the largest) number of ethnic media remain small, "mom-and-pop" type of operations. As the majority of these publishing or broadcasting ventures remain "under the radar" of auditing and rating agencies though (see also Chapter 5), it is difficult to assess if family-owned ethnic media are becoming more plentiful or if this segment of the market is shrinking.

Ownership Consolidation Among Ethnic Media Serving Similar Communities

Some ethnic media organizations bolster their position in the media market by buying out other media organizations that serve similar ethnic and linguistic populations.

For example, in 2007, ImpreMedia owned the largest Spanish-language publications in the United States, including *La Opinión* in Los Angeles, *Hoy* and *El Diario* in New York, *El Mensajero* in San Francisco, and *La Raza* in Chicago. By bringing these five (and other) publications under its umbrella, ImpreMedia can successfully leverage not only the advertising market in the various cities where its publications are distributed, but also the mainstream advertising market. In doing so, ImpreMedia positions itself as a competitor of many mainstream, English-language publications in the U.S.

Ethnic Media Acquisitions by Transnational and Multi-National Enterprises

There are several examples of major media firms established in one country—especially one that has historically been an immigrant-sending state—that have expanded their operations and entered the ethnic media markets of other countries. The Korean media firm *Hankook Ilbo* is one example. *Hankook Ilbo,* based in Seoul, is the parent company of *The Korea Times,* the largest Korean media firm in the U.S. In 2000, *The Korea Times* expanded its operations by joining forces with Leonard Green & Partners, L.P., a Los Angeles-based private equity firm, to form the Asian Media Group, Inc. In turn, the newly created company bought the International Media Group, Inc., the "preeminent multi-lingual television broadcaster in the United States," according to Business Wire (2000, October 11). The estimated value of the transaction was $165 million. The International Media Group, Inc., is based in Los Angeles and operates KSCI-TV (Channel 18; licensed in Long Beach, California) and KIKU-TV (Channel 20, in Honolulu, Hawaii). This is what Chairman and CEO of *The Korea Times Los Angeles, Inc.,* Jae Min Chang said about the acquisition: "Our agreement to acquire International Media Group is the first step toward the creation of the leading Asian diversified media company in the United States serving the various Asian communities" (Business Wire, 2000, para. 2). The acquisition put Asian Media Group in a powerful position, compared to competitors, as they now had the resources to challenge other rivals, print media, and broadcasters focused on the Asian-American market. In 2009, Asian Media Group provided content in 13 Asian languages, including Chinese (Cantonese and Mandarin), Korean, Tagalog, and Vietnamese. (Figure 7.2 illustrates the ownership structure behind the Asian Media Group, Inc.)[6]

Another example, again from Korea, indicates that the web of ownership can get even more complicated. The *Korea Central Daily* is another Korean media firm that is active in the U.S. and Canada, with offices in Los Angeles, San Diego, San Francisco, Hawaii, Seattle, Dallas, Atlanta, Chicago, New York, Washington DC, as well as Toronto and Vancouver. The parent company of the *Korea Central Daily* is *Joong-Ang Ilbo,* a media firm based in Seoul. However, *Joong-Ang Ilbo* is also part of the Korean multinational enterprise Samsung (Kim, personal communication, September 20, 2009; Song, personal communication, September 21, 2009).[7] Both these cases, that of the Asian Media Group and that of the *Korea Central Daily*, illustrate that it may be difficult sometimes to decipher in whose hands certain ethnic media organizations are, regardless of their size and geographic location. These cases also suggest that larger companies are beginning to pay attention and express interest in the growing ethnic media markets.

Figure 7.2 The Ownership Web That Supports the Ethnic Korean Newspaper *The Korea Times* and the Asian Television Network KSCI-TV Channel 18

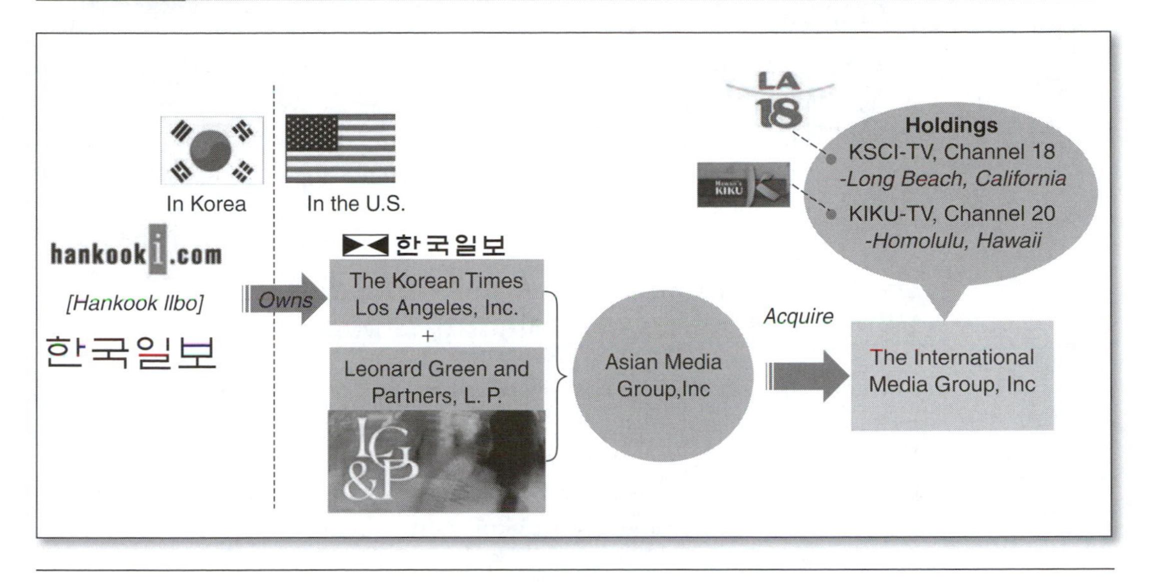

Figure: Matthew Matsaganis.

Acquisitions of Ethnic Media by Mainstream Media Organizations

As mainstream media organizations continue to look for ways to expand their markets, some explore opportunities to partner with or acquire successful ethnic media operations. In Boston, for example, *The Phoenix,* an English-language weekly publication, purchased 35% of *La Planeta,* which is the largest ethnic newspaper in the area (Pfeiffer, 2005; PEJ, 2006).

The "growth of ethnic media offers mainstream newspapers a prime opportunity to broaden their reach and enrich their coverage by partnering with the ethnic press" concluded a panel at the National Expo of Ethnic Media (Fox-Alston, 2005, para. 3). The Expo was hosted by New California Media, the Independent Press Association–New York, and Columbia University. Such collaborations between ethnic and mainstream media may offer both sides a certain degree of financial security, although some caution that "the deep pockets" mainstream media offer ethnic media operations may "come with some strings" (PEJ, 2006). To what extent do and will such kind of organizational arrangements affect the content of ethnic media and their relationship with their audiences? In his testimony at a public hearing held by U.S. Federal Communications Commission on media ownership consolidation and diversity, the co-director of New American Media, Julian Do (2006) noted:

> Although there are now many nation[al] media broadcast networks offering multilingual programming, there is a big difference when the station is actually owned by a minority operator. It would give the minority broadcast

operator a greater chance of being sustainable and also greater resources to cover issues concerning ethnic communities that are often overlooked or cannot be covered well by large mainstream media. (p. 6)

As Do (2006) suggests, acquisitions by mainstream media may cripple the ability of ethnic media producers to manage and deploy resources (i.e., staff and money) as they find fit, in order to cover the stories they know are not being told by the mainstream media. While this is a possibility, there are not enough data available to warrant generalizations.

Decrease in Number of Owners of Media Who Are Members of a Minority Group

Information on ethnic media ownership is not readily available, even for the most mature media markets of North America (i.e., the U.S. and Canada) and Europe. However, over the course of the past 15 years, a series of studies have been published in the United States focusing on the extent to which women and ethnic minorities own media (National Telecommunications & Information Administration, 2000; Turner & Cooper, 2007). These data speak more clearly to the more general question of what media ownership consolidation means for diversity and pluralism of ideas and points-of-view available in the media landscape. However, as ethnic minorities are more likely to be owners of ethnic media in the U.S. (and elsewhere), these data provide some insight with regard to (a) who owns ethnic media in the country, and (b) what significant changes, if any, have occurred in recent years in the ethnic media market.

According to a Free Press report (Turner & Cooper, 2007) on minority and female TV station ownership, minorities comprise 33% of the American population, but own only 43 full-power, commercial television stations, or 3.15% of all stations. Breaking that figure down by ethnicity indicates that Latinos own a total of 17 stations; that is 1.25% of all stations, even though they represent 14% of the entire American population. African-Americans comprise 13% of the total population and own 8 TV stations (0.59% of all stations), while Asians represent 4% of the entire U.S. population and own 13 stations (0.44% of all stations). American Indian or Alaska Natives control 5 television stations nationwide (i.e., 0.37% of the total). The majority of the rest of the television stations, 1,116 in total (81.88%), are in the hands of non-Hispanic Whites. No media are owned in the United States by Pacific Islanders or Hawaiian Natives, while there are also 203 (14.89%) stations in which no one group has a controlling interest (see Figure 7.3).

The authors of the report stress that while there has been an increase in the ownership rates of businesses in other economic sectors (i.e., transportation and health) by females and minorities, the level of ownership of broadcast TV businesses has remained the same since 1998. For some minority groups, however, the number of broadcast television stations owned has dropped precipitously. And that is even though the overall number of TV stations since 1998 has increased by 12%.

Figure 7.3 Media Ownership by Minority Populations in the United States (in 2007)

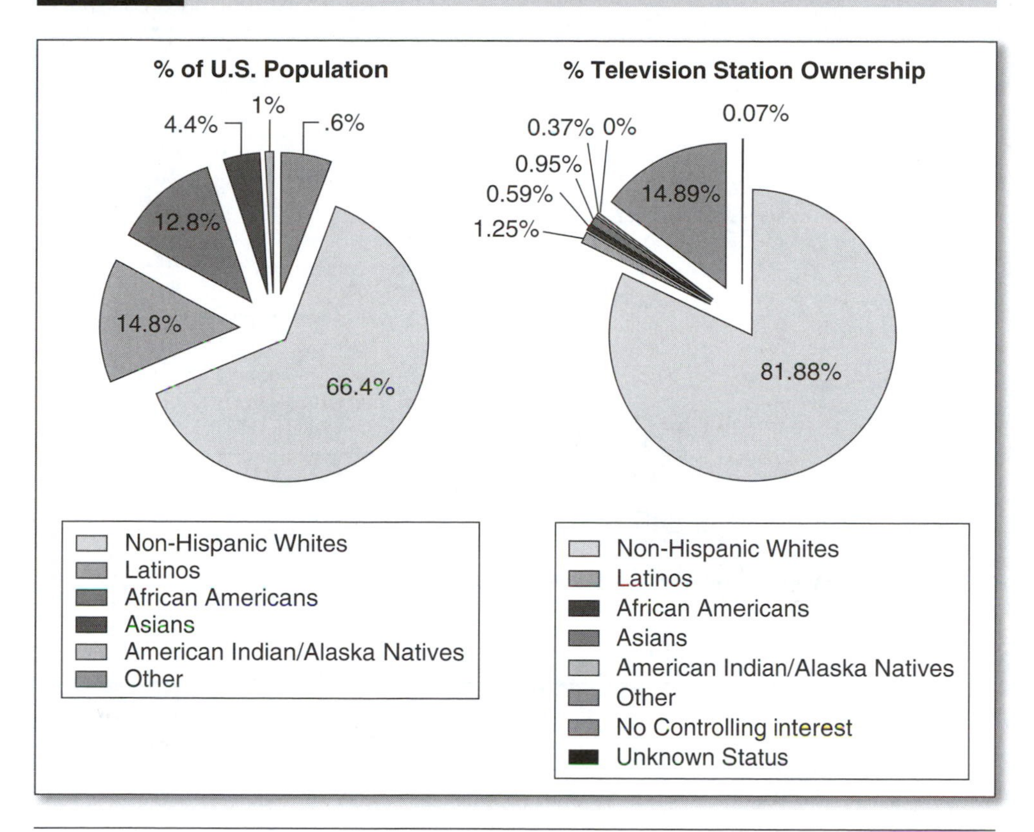

Data source: Turner & Cooper, Free Press (2007).

Note: The figures on the chart on the right reflect the percentage (%) of full-power, commercial television stations owned by all ethnic groups (as defined by the U.S. Census) in 2007.

The number of African-American-owned TV stations, in particular, plummeted by 70% between 1998 and 2006 (see Figure 7.4). This large decrease is attributed generally to policies enacted during this time period, which allowed for the sale of a majority of the minority-owned stations. These transactions, note Turner and Cooper (2007), "would not have been permitted under the pre-1996 nationwide ownership cap or under the pre-1999 ban on local duopolies" (p. 3).

The largest minority television station owner in 2006 was Granite Broadcasting, an African-American company. The company controlled 10 television stations in 1998. It controlled 9 in 2006, after selling 3 stations and acquiring 2 new ones. Another African-American owned company, Roberts Broadcasting, controlled 4 television stations in 1998. Two of those stations were still owned partially by the company in 2006 (KTFD in Boulder, Colorado, and WRBU in St. Louis, Missouri),

Figure 7.4 Trend of Media Ownership by Minority Populations in the United States (1998–2007)

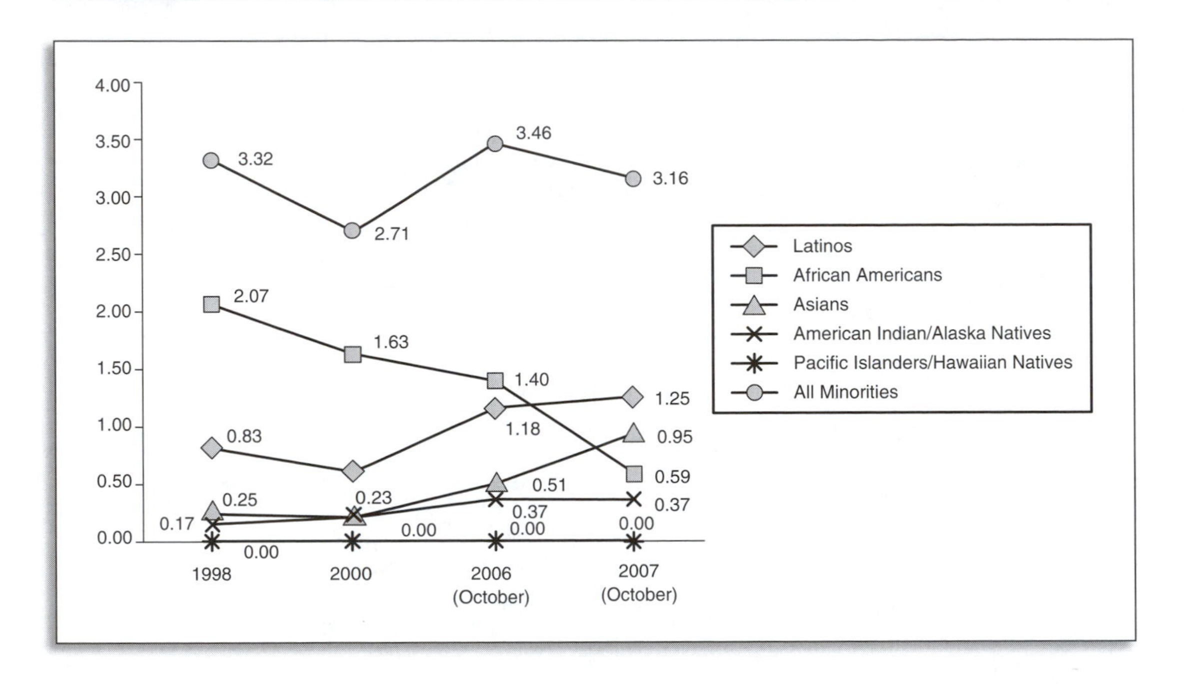

Source: Cooper & Turner (2007); U.S. National Telecommunications and Information Administration (2000).

Note: The percentage of full-power, commercial television channels that are controlled by members of minority populations in the U.S. was lower in 2007 than it was in 1998. While for most groups there has been a slight increase, the percentage of stations owned by African-Americans plunged 70% between 1998 and 2007.

but 50% of them belonged to Spanish-language giant Univisión, which also had complete control of both stations' management. In 2006, Roberts Broadcasting owned two new media properties, one in Columbia, South Carolina, and one in Jackson, Mississippi. These were "the only two African-American owned stations in the South [of the U.S.]" (Turner & Cooper, 2007, p. 20). Overall, between 1998 and 2006, 17 television stations owned by African-Americans were sold to other companies, including CBS, NBC, Sinclair, and the Tribune company, but also Univisión. In fact, 4 of the 17 stations that changed hands, passed into the hands of the Spanish-language corporation.

An interesting finding that emerges out of the 2006 and 2007 data on minority media ownership is that Latino-owned television stations in the U.S. tend to be located in markets with large Hispanic populations; Black-owned stations, on the other hand, tend not to be located in the markets with the largest African-American populations. Turner and Cooper (2007) conclude that "language, particularly Spanish, is an important factor underlying ownership" and that "due to difficulties with capital access and other institutional barriers to ownership, African-American owners may be purchasing stations where they can—in certain smaller, less lucrative Midwestern markets" (p. 33). This might mean that African-American producers may not be able to reach large communities that are located on the east and west coast of the U.S, where the advertising markets are also larger. And even if they do, thanks to technology, their content will most likely not be fine-tuned and targeted to the specific needs of those more distant populations.

The Free Press report by Turner and Cooper (2007) supports the notion that Univisión has become a force that the English-language media will have to reckon with. However, the impact Univisión will have on other Latino media, but also on African-American media is unclear. Will it act as a guarantor of media diversity or will it follow in the steps of the other four networks: ABC, CBS, NBC, and Fox? That remains to be seen.

Summary

Ethnic media are the products and creators of globalization. We started Chapter 6 by defining globalization, and discussed three key perspectives on globalization and how they relate to the study of ethnic media. Subsequently, we addressed the question of what challenges and opportunities the forces that are driving globalization create for ethnic media producers. In addition, we analyzed the six types of ethnic media organizations that can be found around the world today. We concluded our discussion on globalization and the ethnic media organization by reflecting on available data to provide some insight into current and emerging trends in ethnic media ownership. In Chapter 7 we investigated the impact of policy decisions on ethnic media organizations and how different regulatory or state policy frameworks across countries affect the development of ethnic media and the communities they serve.

Study Questions

1. How do the hyperglobalist position on globalization and that of the skeptics differ? Adopting each position in turn, what would you predict for the future of ethnic media around the world? Justify your answer and discuss what variables and information you considered in developing your answer from either perspective.

2. In Chapter 7 we discussed a variety of different organizational structures that ethnic media have adopted. Do you think that the history, country of origin, country of settlement, language spoken, and size of an ethnic community are related to the type of ethnic media organizations that serve them? Justify your answer and provide examples. Reviewing Chapters 1 through 4 may help you develop your answer.

3. In what ways has globalization affected media ownership?

4. You have just become the Chief Executive Officer (CEO) of a global media corporation that targets Chinese-origin populations, which speak either Cantonese or Mandarin. The headquarters of the company are based in Hong Kong, but you have publications serving communities in a number of countries, including Britain, the United States, and Indonesia. Discuss the unique challenges you expect to deal with in working with your staff in each of these three countries to further develop your company, and how you plan to address them.

5. In this chapter we discussed a number of different ways in which globalization affects ethnic media. Can you think of ways in which the opposite may also be true? Are there ways that ethnic media may, in fact, shape globalization? Explain your answer.

Notes

[1]*The Indian Express* was launched in the U.S. and Canada in 2000 by Eastern Media Holdings, Inc., a subsidiary of CinéMaya Media Group, under a franchise agreement with the Express Group, based in India. CinéMaya Media Group owns a variety of ethnic newspapers, radio and television stations, as well as online media, all targeted to South Asian communities. For more details, see the company's Web site: https://www.iexpressusa.com/new/aboutus.php

[2] Middle East Broadcasting Center (MBC) was founded in 1991 and began to transmit via satellite from London in September of that year.

[3]The Tropical Spanish Hits format includes mainly Caribbean Latin music (i.e., salsa, merengue, cumbia, and raggaeton).

[4]For more information on the Project for Excellence in Journalism, refer to www.journalism.org

[5]New California Media joined forces in 2006 with East Coast-based Independent Press Association to form New America Media, which in 2009 claimed to represent and serve approximately 2,000 ethnic media organizations nationwide.

[6]See the Web site of Channel KSCI 18 for more details on the various Asian communities they serve and the languages in which they offer programming: http://www.la18.tv/Landing/Default.aspx?PI=1017

[7]Similarly, General Electric is the owner of NBC in the United States, but GE is not active in the media industry only.

CHAPTER 8

Policy and Ethnic Media Development

CHAPTER OBJECTIVES

By the end of this chapter, you will have learned more about:

- Who makes policy that impacts the creation and development of ethnic media.
- How globalization affects policymaking around ethnic media.
- Models of policy through which nation-state governments support and influence ethnic media organizations and programming.
- How current trends in media policy are transforming the landscape of ethnic media.

Governance and Ethnic Media

In an era of accelerated globalization, we are seeing ethnic media emerge and grow in many countries. As organizations, they vary significantly in the number of people they employ, their ability to take advantage of technological innovations, the geographic location and socio-demographic make-up of their audiences, as well as their capacity to acquire and develop original programming. As is the case with all types of organizations—including corporations and non-governmental entities—ethnic media do not grow in a vacuum. Their operation depends on and is shaped by regulations and policies put in place by local, regional, and nation-state governments, and increasingly by international and *global governance* bodies, like the United Nations (UN) and the European Union (EU). Global governance has been defined as "systems of rule at all levels of human activity—from the family to the international organization—in which the pursuit of goals through the exercise of control has transnational repercussions" (Rosenau, 1995). The decisions made, for example, at the UN Security Council are intended to change the way countries that are members of the UN behave with respect to the treatment of ethnic minorities living within their territories.

Naturally, media policies at national and international levels impact the development of ethnic media most directly. The emergence, vitality, and sustainability of ethnic media, however, is linked to a much more complex web of policies around immigration, social integration and citizenship, language and cultural production, labor, and education, among others. In this chapter, we will profile the stakeholders involved in making policies that are relevant to ethnic media and discuss the relationships among policy areas that influence their evolution in a variety of national contexts. In doing so, we will focus primarily on immigration, social integration, and citizenship policies. In addition, we present five different models of media policy through which nation-state governments have influenced ethnic media and explore how current trends in media policy, including deregulation, are shaping this media sector.

Policymaking in a Globalizing World

Traditionally, nation-states have been considered the primary context in which policies are made and implemented. That includes policies that impact social domains most closely related to globalization; namely, the economy and the financial markets, technology, communication, cultural production (e.g., production of film and media), and immigration. As discussed in the two previous chapters, the growth of the ethnic media in many countries across the world is strongly connected to these changes that we attribute to globalization.

Despite the centrality of national governments and state institutions in policymaking, international relations scholars suggest that because of globalization, state power "is juxtaposed . . . with the expanding jurisdiction of institutions of international governance and the constraints of, as well as the obligations derived from international law" (Held, McGrew, Goldblatt, & Perraton, 1999, p. 8). Institutions of international governance include intergovernmental (e.g., UN and NATO), as well as nongovernmental and nonprofit organizations (e.g., Greenpeace, Red Cross, and Doctors without Borders) (Nye & Donahue, 2000). All of these institutions complement nation-state actors in exercising governance (Brown, Khagram, Moore, & Frumkin, 2000). Humanitarian aid, for example, could not have been delivered promptly to people in the region of Darfur in Western Sudan, when civil war broke out in 2003, if the UN did not coordinate with state governments and nongovernmental organizations (NGOs), such as Oxfam International and others.

Figure 8.1 indicates the web of actors—organizations and institutions—that are involved in policymaking. The increasing number of NGOs is both the cause and the effect of having more and more issues (e.g., environment, trade, and security) addressed by international forums, instead of nation-state governments alone. As businesses expand their operations globally, nation-states try to keep up by forming

Figure 8.1 Who Makes Policy in a Globalizing World

Global Policy-Making Actors

	Private Sector	Public Sector	Third Sector
Supra-state level	Multi-national and global firms	Inter-Governmental Organizations (IGOs)	International Non-Governmental Organizations[3]
National level	Country-based firms	Central state government[1]	Nation-state-based NGOs[2]
Sub-state level	Local firms	Local government	Local non-profits

Index

(dark gray) The most central actors in policymaking that impacts ethnic and minority media.

(light gray) Level at which most policies that affect ethnic media are made and implemented.

Notes

[1] Government actors include the legislature, the cabinet and various government departments, regulatory agencies, and the courts.

[2] State based NGOs include organizations that provide media services, lobbyists, watchdogs, and nonprofit organizations.

[3] Also referred to as INGOs.

Source: Adapted from Nye & Donahue (2000) and complemented by the work of Browne (2005).

intergovernmental institutions that can address global issues, including major financial crises such as one the world entered in 2008. As private and public sectors seek ways to coordinate activities at the global level, citizens of the world strive to organize and make their voices "heard" globally, too. They do so, at least in part, through founding and participating in NGOs. In the decade between 1990 and 2000, observers indicate that the number of NGOs worldwide increased fourfold (Brown et al., 2000). Together, all these NGOs form what is referred to as the *third sector* of organizations (i.e., non-private and non-public). As these three sectors of organizations "go global," state power is redefined, and governance is increasingly exercised through relationships across and within state borders (Bernard, 2002; Castells, 2000a; Nye & Donahue, 2000; Schneider 2004; Scholte, 2000). This is especially evident in the case of the European Union, where governance is divided between international, national, and local authorities. Figure 8.2 shows the interrelationships that emerge among policymakers that operate at multiple levels, within and beyond the confines of any one country. Policies made and enacted at each of these levels have the potential to impact ethnic media (see Figure 8.2).

Policymaking at the Global and International Level

Since the 1990s, more and more ethnic media organizations have been investing in new technologies, including satellite and Internet-based innovations, to reach audiences who live across country borders. In this process, regional, international, and global organizations have arguably become more important stakeholders in making policy that enables or constrains ethnic media operations. The emergence

Figure 8.2 Levels of Policymaking and Relationships Among Them

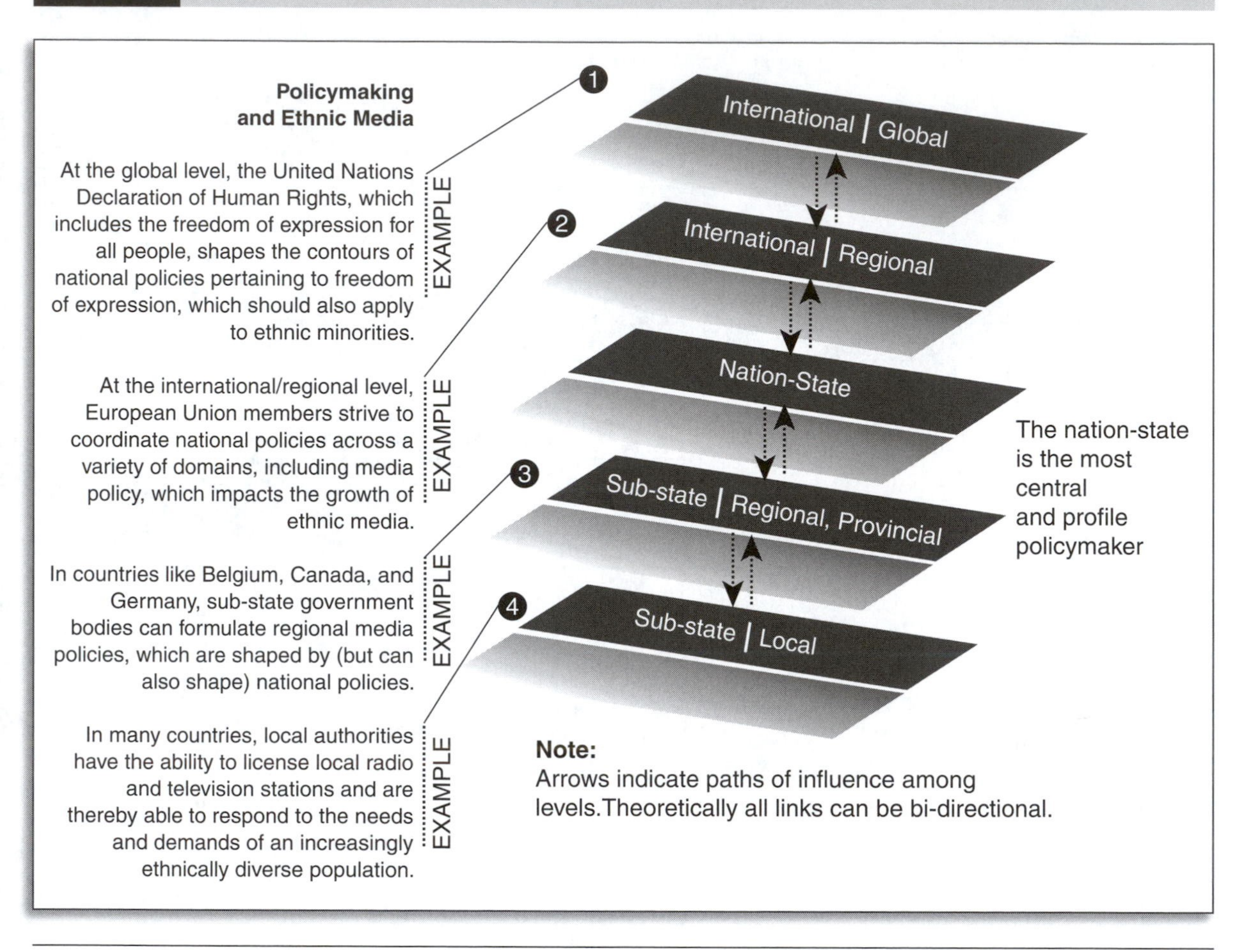

Figure: Matthew Matsaganis.

of transnational and global ethnic media organizations (see Chapter 7) also complicates the media landscape from an ownership perspective. This, too, suggests a more central role for global institutions, especially intergovernmental organizations such as the EU or the World Trade Organization (WTO). Both the EU and the WTO serve as places where issues can be debated and resolved, issues such as whether or not a firm based in one country can own a media company established in another. Furthermore, any one country may feel apprehensive about allowing certain ethnic minorities to establish their own media, to have access to media programming targeted towards them from outside state borders (e.g., via satellite), and to use their language. State governments may see ethnic media as organizations that are likely to inhibit the integration of ethnic minorities into mainstream society, thereby causing social instability (Browne, 2005).

To prevent governments from making policies that curtail ethnic minority rights, global and regional intergovernmental organizations (IGOs) can—or at least can try to—create certain "safety nets" for ethnic minorities. The example of the Council of Europe (COE) is instructive. Founded in 1949, the COE is comprised of 47 countries. Its goal is to develop "common and democratic principles based on the European Convention on Human Rights and other reference texts on the protection of individuals" ("Council of Europe in brief," n.d., para. 1). Promoting awareness and encouraging "the development of Europe's cultural identity and diversity," as well as finding solutions to problems such as "discrimination against minorities, xenophobia, [and] intolerance" are some of the COE's objectives ("Our objectives," n.d., para. 3). Decisions and resolutions made by the COE on these issues filter down through national policies and therefore protect the freedom of expression-related rights of ethnic minority populations living throughout Europe.

The COE, says media and communications scholar Myria Georgiou, has done more over the years for the development of ethnic media across the continent than any other European intergovernmental organization (personal communication, July 2009). The Council of Europe adopted a Charter for Regional and European languages in 1992. The countries that have signed and ratified the convention have agreed to forward policies that protect and promote linguistic and cultural diversity within their territories. The Council periodically monitors the progress made by the countries that have adopted the Charter and recommends improvements. Among other things, COE committees assess whether regional or minority languages are used in education and the media (COE, 2009).[1] In 2009, for example, a COE committee issued a report on the extent to which Swedish authorities had fulfilled their obligations according to the Charter.[2] While the committee acknowledged certain improvements since the last assessment in 2006, it also urged the Swedish authorities "to take concrete measures to encourage and/or facilitate the creation of a newspaper in Sami" (European Charter for Regional and Minority Languages, 2009). The Sami are indigenous people that live mostly in the northern territories of Sweden and represent one of the largest linguistic minorities in the country. This is but one example of how the COE contributes to the development of ethnic media in Europe.[3]

The example of the COE, however, represents an exception to the rule. Generally, policies instituted by IGOs can create a positive environment in which ethnic media can develop, but these international organizations do not direct country-members to support the creation of ethnic media in one way or another. This is the case with some of the most well known IGOs, including the United Nations, the International Telecommunications Union (ITU), and the United Nations Educational, Scientific, and Cultural Organization (UNESCO) (Browne, 2005).[4]

Nongovernmental organizations (NGOs) contribute to the work of intergovernmental organizations at the global level, too. They usually play the role of a watchdog organization or a supporter of ethnic minority rights. As these international and global NGOs aim to shape the agenda of IGOs, they too are rarely concerned with ethnic media specifically. We discuss a few examples of IGO and NGO involvement in policymaking that affects ethnic media next.

Intergovernmental Organizations

UNESCO is involved in policymaking that transcends national borders. Its mission is to contribute to "the building of peace, the alleviation of poverty, sustainable development and intercultural dialogue through education, the sciences, culture, communication and information" (www.unesco.org). As part of an initiative focused on cultural diversity, UNESCO has produced an interactive map of the world's languages that are in danger of or have gone extinct (see "For Further Discussion" below). While this initiative may not directly impact the growth of ethnic media in any part of the world, it holds the potential of raising awareness among policymakers (across levels and sectors) with respect to threats to a country's cultural heritage. Sensitized governments and nongovernmental organizations may, for instance, work together to create legislation that would enable the production of media in languages that are critically endangered. For example, Provençal and Breton are two of the 26 languages spoken in France that are marked by UNESCO as "unsafe" or "endangered." In this context, the audience for programming in either of these languages is likely to be too small to keep one or more radio stations, for instance, alive unless French authorities (of the central and local governments) make a conscious effort to keep the languages alive through funding the radio stations or other means. As we discuss later in this chapter, French media policies aimed towards accomplishing these goals were created but they were short-lived.

Are such policies successful? In his book on electronic media and indigenous peoples, Browne (1996) says:

> There is virtually no "hard" (scientific) evidence to indicate that the initiation of an indigenous language media service helps to restore or revive its usage [i.e., of the language] but all stations broadcasting substantial amounts of such languages certainly have that hope and expectation. (p. 169; see also Cormack, 2007)

¤ For Further Discussion

Go to UNESCO's Web site where you can find the atlas of endangered languages of the world: (http://www.unesco.org/culture/ich/index.php?pg=00206). Focus on the country you live in or the country from which your parents or grandparents are from and find out if any of the languages spoken there are endangered. Search the Internet, interview relatives or friends, and do a little research in your school's library: Is there any evidence of media produced in that language? Are those media still in operation? Are they based in the country you chose to focus on or somewhere else? If they are based somewhere else, why is that? Report back to class with your findings.

International Nongovernmental Organizations

At the global level there are several international nongovernmental organizations (INGOs) concerned with protecting the rights of ethnic minorities for self-expression (as dictated by the UN Universal Declaration of Human Rights), as well as the fair treatment of ethnic minorities by the media (see, for example, the organization known as Article 19, the South East Europe Media Organization, and the International Federation of Journalists).[5] However, in 2009, we did not find any INGOs whose mission and activities specifically addressed ethnic media. Four years earlier, Browne references the European Ethnic Broadcasting Association (EEBA) as an example of an INGO that dealt primarily with programming exchanges among ethnic minority radio producers in Europe. The EEBA also worked as a watchdog organization that put pressure on national governments to provide support to ethnic media producers. The organization was founded in 1996, but a little over 10 years later it seems to have ceased to exist.

One may wonder why there is a lack of NGOs at the global level positioned to support ethnic media around the world (e.g., as rights advocates, incubators of new ethnic media ventures and young professionals, programming producers or sponsors, and content distributors). The fact that so many of the ethnic media are small-scale and local operations may have something to do with this. Many of them may not see the benefit of working with an international organization or they may not have the funds, personnel, or time to spend building relationships with an INGO and participating in an international forum.

The evidence suggests that in Europe, at a more regional level, there is a stronger presence of INGOs that are concerned with ethnic media producers specifically. That is perhaps due to the rising awareness among EU member-states and within EU institutions that the population of the continent is becoming more and more diverse, due both to people moving across borders within the Union, but also thanks to migration flows that connect the EU to countries beyond its borders. As each European nation is forced to deal with the complexities of increased population diversity, so is the EU as a whole. In this context, the roles ethnic media play has become a more salient issue.

There are at least three pan-European INGOs that address ethnic media concerns. The Institut Panos in Paris is one of them. Founded in 1986, this organization set out to "to foster a media environment that reflects the diversity of our contemporary societies, where all communities, *including the most marginalized* (italics in original), are able to express their points of view, exert their influence and contribute to local and international public debates"[6] ("Presentation," n.d.). One of its major initiatives between 2000 and 2003 focused squarely on the issues of international migration and media (MIME). Out of MIME came the Mediam'Rad Project to study ethnic and diasporic media, particularly in France, Italy, and the Netherlands. The program's objectives were to identify ethnic media and analyze the information they produce, connect ethnic media with mainstream and community media so their stories get disseminated across a broader audience, and allow "public opinion to access renewed information and perspectives on the diversity and dynamics of the contemporary world" (Institut Panos Paris, 2007, p. 1). Mediam'Rad has produced an ethnic and diversity media directory for France and published a bilingual newsletter (in French and English), the latest of which circulated in April 2007.

The work of the Institut Panos on Mediam'Rad was complemented by the efforts of COSPE (from the Italian equivalent of Co-operation for the Development of Emerging Countries), which is based in Italy, as well as Mira Media in the Netherlands. COSPE is an INGO. It is active primarily in Europe and to a lesser extent in Latin America, Asia, and elsewhere. Mira Media is an NGO active primarily in the Netherlands.

Another interesting initiative is MIDAS (Minority Dailies Association), a European Association of Daily Newspapers in Minority and Regional Languages, which was officially established in 2001, in Palma De Mallorca, Spain. Around 2008, MIDAS had members from 29 countries, and it was expecting to expand, adding members from Wales in the UK, as well as Estonia and other Central and Eastern European countries. The Association's goals are: (a) to help and support new newspapers, (b) to promote EU and state legislation in support of minority newspapers, (c) to lobby political and financial support, and (d) to raise awareness for minority and regional languages (MIDAS, 2008).[7]

The foregoing examples suggest that the presence and work of INGOs, such as Institut Panos Paris, COSPE, and MIDAS, is important for the growth of ethnic media for at least two reasons. First, through research, international conferences, and lobbying, these INGOs help raise awareness around ethnic media among diverse European publics and policymakers at the international and national level. Second, these organizations act as support mechanisms and networks that foster the professionalization of ethnic media producers. Institut Panos Paris, COSPE, and MIDAS have at different times created opportunities for producers to come together and share their experiences and points of view; all three NGOs have also served as forums where ethnic media journalists can discuss the particular problems they encounter and explore solutions.

Policymaking at the Nation-State Level

National governments remain the most important policymakers, and definitely the most prolific. They are particularly important when we are talking about ethnic media, because policies around immigration and citizenship are primarily the responsibility of nation-states. Apart from central government officials who guide the process of policymaking in a country, there are quasi-independent regulators, such as the Federal Communications Commission in the United States and the Conseil Supérieure d' Audiovisuel in France, that formulate the rules by which anyone interested in becoming involved in the media industry has to abide. Further, within most states, there are nongovernmental and nonprofit organizations that act as watchdogs looking out for ethnic minority rights, as providers of media services, or as supporters of such services.

Public Sector Policymakers

State legislatures and government departments and ministries are perhaps the most visible policymaking actors from the public sector. In the United Kingdom, the Office of Communications (OfCom) makes most media policy. In the U.S., no cabinet-level position is dedicated to addressing media and communication issues per se, as policy is guided by the Federal Communication Commission (FCC), a quasi-independent regulatory authority. Courts are also directly involved in media policy development in the U.S. The courts play a smaller role in most of continental

Europe, as media cases do not reach the courts very often, but are more significant in countries like the United Kingdom, Australia, and the United States (Browne, 2005); that is, in countries with a strong common law or case law tradition.

Quasi-independent regulatory bodies have also been formed in many countries that are mandated to deal with media issues, particularly electronic media issues such as the electromagnetic spectrum, through which radio and television signals travel. In many countries, the press is subject to much less oversight than electronic media. The Canadian equivalent to the FCC is called the Canadian Radio-television and Telecommunications Commission (CRTC); in France, the regulator is the Conseil Supérieure d' Audiovisuel (CSA); in Australia, it is the Australian Broadcasting Authority (ABA); and in South Africa, it is known as the Independent Communications Authority of South Africa (ICASA). Most of these state agencies are mandated to detail and expand on the more general policies made by legislatures with respect to media (Browne, 2005). The FCC, for instance, has had, over the years, to address the question of whether ethnic minority populations in the U.S. (e.g., African-Americans and Latinos) have adequate capacity to overcome barriers that prevent them from entering the electronic media market and owning television and radio stations (see Chapter 7 for an assessment of these efforts).

Public broadcasters are also fairly visible national policy stakeholders, if not policymakers per se. They are most important in countries with a long public broadcasting tradition; this includes most Western European countries. Over the years, the initiatives of these public broadcasters aimed at creating new programs that address ethnic minority issues and concerns of immigrants, and the efforts they have made to enable programming for ethnic minorities created *by* ethnic minorities shape the media landscape in the countries in which they operate (see the examples of Radio MultiKulti and Funkhaus Europa in Germany discussed later in this chapter).

Nongovernmental and Nonprofit Organizations

There is a broad variety of nongovernmental and nonprofit organizations involved in policymaking around ethnic media at the national level. This includes professional associations of journalists, publishers and owners, watchdog organizations, and nonprofits, whose mission is to support ethnic minority representation in the media.

In the United States, associations of African-American and Latino journalists, publishers, and broadcasters are the most visible. The National Association of Black Owned Broadcasters (NABOB) is but one example. Founded in 1976, it is headquartered in Washington, DC; its mission is to increase the number of African-American owners of telecommunication services.

New America Media (NAM) in the U.S. (see profile in Chapter 5), Mira Media in the Netherlands, and the National Ethnic and Multicultural Broadcasters' Council (NEMBC) in Australia are examples of NGOs that perform several roles. They can be service providers for ethnic media (e.g., as content distributors), or advocates, but also incubators for the development of ethnic media professionals. The mission of Mira Media is to "achieve more diversity and 'ethnic' pluralism by promoting the participation of immigrants in radio, television and interactive media" (Mira Media, n.d., para. 1).[8] Founded as a co-operative among the major ethnic media organizations operating in the Netherlands, Mira Media sees itself as a lobbyist that tries to influence the Dutch parliament and major mainstream Dutch broadcasting organizations. Mira Media often works with like-minded organizations in other countries in Europe. The Mediam'Rad project mentioned earlier was the result of collaboration among Mira Media, COSPE in Italy, and the Institut Panos in Paris. Interestingly, Mira Media receives most of its funding from the Dutch government, whereas NAM in the United States is funded through commissions for providing advertising services, sales of its ethnic media directory, and grants from foundations.

Finally, the NEMBC in Australia and the National Ethnic Press and Media Council of Canada have missions similar to that of Mira Media and NAM. They see themselves as representatives of all ethnic media in their respective countries.[9]

Sub-State Policymaking and Ethnic Media

Depending on how a country is organized from an administrative point of view, there may be a number of sub-national level policymakers. The power of these actors varies significantly from country to country.

Local Authorities

In Canada and Australia, the provinces play a fairly central role in the formulation of policy that affects ethnic media. Most ethnic media have a fairly circumscribed geographic range; they are mostly local or regional in character and therefore there is considerable latitude for local government to impact ethnic media growth. In the Canadian provinces of British Columbia, Ontario, and Quebec, the local government budgets for the support of radio and television stations carrying programming for First Nation populations (i.e., of Native-American and Inuit backgrounds) (Browne, 2005; Murray, Yu, & Ahadi, 2007). The Australian province of Victoria has similar appropriations for the support of Aboriginal media, as does the state of Alaska in the U.S. There is little evidence, however, of state or provincial support of media operations targeting ethnic populations of non-Aboriginal descent (i.e., immigrant communities).

In Europe, the case of Belgium stands out as an example where local (sub-state) government provides considerable support for ethnic minority media). Belgium became a federal state officially in 1993. There are three regions: the Flemish Region (Flanders), the Walloon Region (Francophone Wallonia), and the Capital Region of Brussels. Each region is responsible for its own economic policy, employment and transportation policy, housing, environmental, agriculture, urban planning, and external trade policies. Years before the country became a federal state, the government also divided the country into four different linguistic communities: a French community, a Dutch (Flemish)-speaking community, a German-speaking community, and the district of Brussels. Brussels is officially bilingual. The communities continue to exist today, and they are responsible for policies around education, social aid, family policy, as well as media regulation. Given this distribution of policymaking responsibilities, immigrant and non-Dutch, French, or German-speaking ethnic populations rely on the sponsorship and support of the communities to meet their needs (Ormond, 2002).

After a period of increased xenophobia during the late 1980s in both Wallonia and Flanders (Ormond, 2002), the state government decided to address the issue of integrating immigrant populations into Belgian society head-on. The state committed considerable resources to developing a general strategy, which communities could then adapt to their areas of responsibility as they saw fit. As a result, since the early 1990s funding has been made available from the state and the communities for a variety of different programs meant to foster social inclusion. However, the approaches and criteria adopted by the Dutch and French-speaking communities for evaluating and funding these programs have been rather different.

The Dutch (Flemish) community, taking a top-down approach, decided it would recognize and fund organizations that were "inspired by the concepts of integration" (Dewaele, 1997, p. 85) This led to a

> distinction between "old" and "new" organizations: "old" organizations being those whose priorities were to "maintain the values, religion, and traditions of [immigrants'] mother country," and "new" organizations being those that "no longer have ties with the country of origin, and are basically no different from Belgian associations." (Dewaele, 1997, p. 84; see also Ormond, 2002)

New organizations were favored by the Dutch community's administration. In contrast, the French community provided funding for organizations interested in helping immigrant communities retain their language, enterprises that created and maintained ties between immigrants' "home countries" and Belgium, a variety of cultural centers, as well as intercultural theatrical and other productions (Mangot, 1997). The approach taken by the French community was much more grassroots-based. It supported initiatives that came from the people (Ormond, 2002).

The approach adopted by each community was evident in their media landscape, too. In the Flemish community, for instance, the Intercultural Center for Migrants (Intercultureel Centrum Voor Migraten) receives funds that allow it to support associations like the Federatie Marokkaanse Democratische Organisaties, which publishes *Akhbar* for the Moroccan population, and the Latijn-Amerikaanse Federatie, so it can publish *Colibri* for populations with roots in South and Central America. Both of these publications get funding as long as they print a new edition at least once a year, and provided that some of the content is in Dutch (Ormond, 2002).

Nongovernmental Organizations

Generally speaking, the number of watchdog-type NGOs at the local level has been decreasing over time. That is because many national-level public and commercial electronic media operations have pushed aside smaller locally produced media (Browne, 2005). Therefore, NGOs see no reason to invest resources at the local level. However, with respect to ethnic media, in particular, we might expect local, community-oriented associations and nonprofits to act as lobbyists and supporters of local, ethnically targeted publications and broadcasters. This is certainly the case with African-American churches in the United States, which have traditionally played an important role in mobilizing Black communities (e.g., Jenkins & Eckert, 1986; Morris, 1984).

The Broader Policy Context of Ethnic Media Development

Especially since the mid-1980s, many countries have lifted barriers to a number of cross-border activities. Within the WTO, the EU, NAFTA (the North American Free Trade Agreement), and ASEAN (the Association of South-East Asian Nations)—all four intergovernmental organizations and agreements—nation-states are working to abolish barriers to the trade of goods and services and to coordinate their activities across policy areas that include, among others, telecommunications.

The thorniest issue signatories face is the free movement of people across borders. Even at the WTO, which promotes policies that enable free trade and free markets, initiatives for an agreement on free movement of people have generally not been met with enthusiasm (Moss & Bartlett, 2002). That is because people and territory are the two most essential resources of a nation-state. If people were allowed to move in and out of a country with no constraints, that would call into question the state's authority. Moreover, the ability of people to move from one country to another with no restraints might hamper the economic development of the nation they left behind. Thus, immigration and citizenship are areas of policy where national governments exercise extreme caution, being generally unwilling to yield power to intergovernmental institutions.

Apart from policies on immigration and citizenship, nation-states also differ in policies that specify if and how immigrants can become integrated into the society of the "host" country. They include policies regarding labor, health, education, and culture. Language policies also can directly affect the welfare of ethnic media. For example, if one or more languages are recognized as official but unofficial languages are protected (e.g., by teaching them in schools), this is likely to enable ethnic media that are produced in a protected language. The constellation of these policies around immigration, citizenship, and integration create a broader context within which ethnic media emerge, flourish, or die.

State Approaches to Immigration, Citizenship, and Their Impact on Ethnic Media

A country's approach to dealing with immigration, citizenship, and the social integration of immigrants into an increasingly more diverse society depends heavily on several factors:

- its history
- its ethnic composition when it was established as a nation-state
- its geographical location
- the state's past experiences with immigration
- the prevailing political ideology at the time new policies are formulated and old ones are revised, and
- the role of the state in current world events.

Studying these factors allows us to place a country on a continuum from *open* to *closed,* with respect to its immigration and citizenship policies, as well as a continuum that varies from *assimilation-oriented* to *multiculturalism-oriented* in terms of its social integration policies. The more open a country's policies are towards immigration, the fewer restrictions it imposes on who can come into the country and the more likely it is to provide immigrants with opportunities to obtain citizenship. In addition, a country with multicultural policies is more likely to allow people to become equal members of society in their newfound "home," while embracing and fostering ethnic diversity (Husband, 1994; Kosnick, 2007; Vertovec, 2001). That country is also more likely to allow individuals to maintain those cultural traits that make them distinct, most especially, the development of stable ethnic media. On the other hand, assimilation-oriented policies encourage individuals to cut ties with their country of origin and eventually shed all those characteristics that are not ostensibly compatible with those of mainstream society (e.g., dressing differently, speaking a different language, and consuming ethnic media). Figure 8.3 illustrates how these policies come together to create the environment within which ethnic media emerge and grow, or fail to thrive.

Figure 8.3 The Broader Policy Context in Which Ethnic Media Emerge

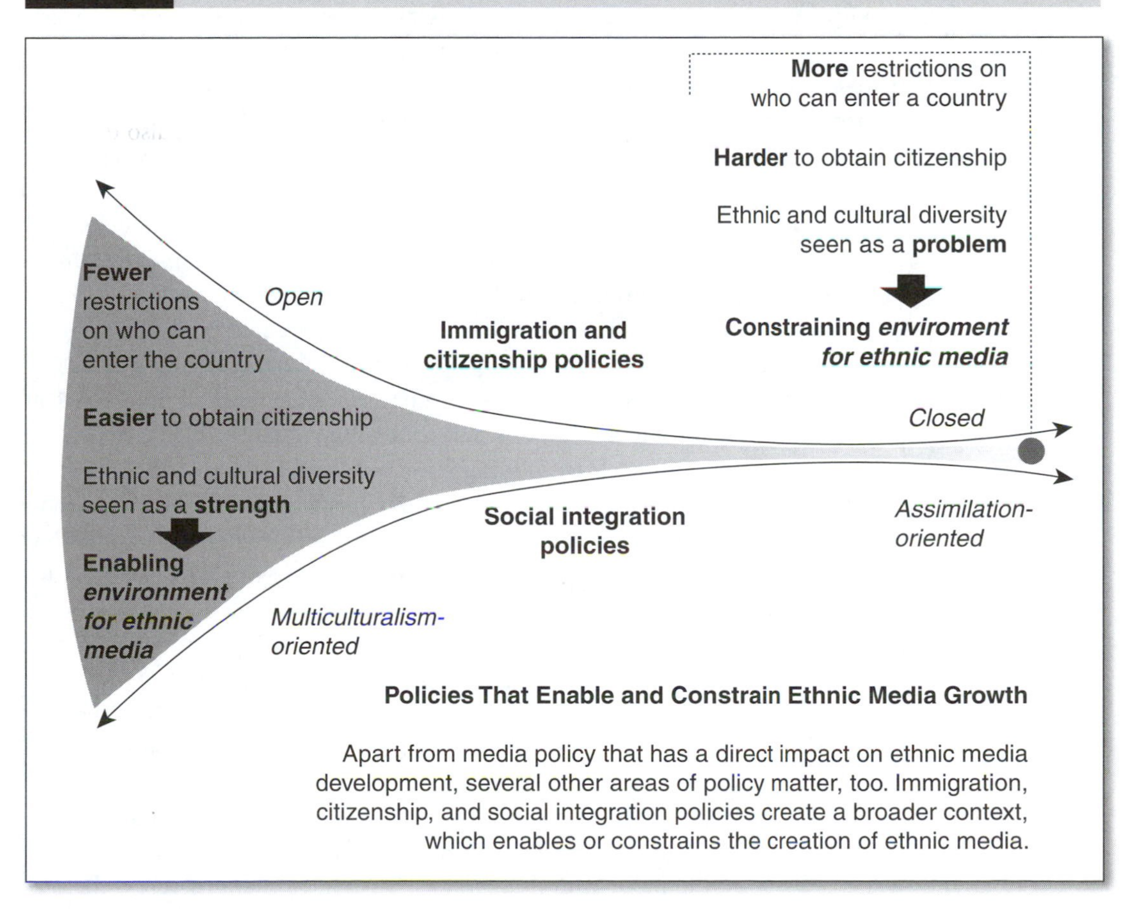

Figure: Matthew Matsaganis.

As immigration and integration policies are not the primary focus of this chapter, we will elaborate only on how the broader policy context in a limited number of exemplar countries impacts ethnic media production and consumption. Exemplars come from North America, Australia, and Europe, as that is where the most research on ethnic media and policy has been conducted. The broader analytical framework, however, can be applied in future studies of other countries.

Australia, Canada, and the United States: Multicultural at Inception

While there are important historical differences distinguishing these three countries, all three have grown through a long history of immigration. They reflect a rich, colorful mosaic of ethnicities, cultures, and languages. The U.S., Canada, and Australia have been multicultural from their inception. They have had to deal with the tensions and challenges of population diversity from very early in their history, but they have not taken the same route to address them.

Historically, U.S. policies reflect the idea that the country resembles a cultural "melting pot" (Riggins, 1992). Immigrants have been expected to *assimilate* into the mainstream, English-speaking society and eventually sever ties with the country and cultural background they came from. While the rise of Latino immigration especially has challenged this "melting pot" model of assimilation, American policies on immigration and citizenship continue to avoid endorsement of multiculturalism.

For example, in the years post-September 11, 2001, there were serious efforts to curb immigration to the U.S. (Félix, González, & Ramírez, 2008; McMahon, 2008) and to make the lives of some foreigners already in the country more difficult (Schildkraut, 2002). Because of the Middle Eastern origin of the Islamic fundamentalists that perpetrated the attacks in New York City, Pennsylvania, and Washington DC, individuals of Arab and South Asian descent were particularly affected, regardless of whether they were in the U.S. on a visa or were U.S. citizens (Cainkar, 2002).

There is little quantitative and reliable evidence with respect to the impact of post 9/11 policies around immigration and citizenship on ethnic media per se. We can speculate that a more "closed" immigration policy and "assimilation-oriented" social integration policies would have hurt ethnic media growth for three reasons: (a) the audience of ethnic media serving primarily new immigrant populations would have stopped growing or may have even decreased (e.g., because of deportations and a drop in new visas approved), (b) funding for media ventures that were not in the spirit of prevailing political ideology (i.e., anti-immigration) would be limited, and (c) audience members that felt insecure or threatened (e.g., new and especially undocumented immigrants) might have tried harder to blend into mainstream society, shedding habits, such as reading non-English newspapers, which made them stick out as different.[10]

On the other hand, some commentators suggest that certain ethnic media expanded after September 11 as a reaction against immigration policies. In 2006, we witnessed a profound mobilization of largely Hispanic immigrants across the U.S. demanding immigration policy reform. The role of ethnic media in these mobilizations was instrumental (Félix, González, & Ramírez, 2008); something that indicates ethnic media may have benefited from the otherwise negative policy context after all, because the negative context helped them solidify their role in the lives of audiences as community leaders. People looked to ethnic media for support and a sense of community (Sameer Padania, quoted in Mediam'Rad, 2006). In the case of the Arab and South Asian communities in the U.S., for instance, in the aftermath of September 11, ethnic media may have acted as apologists for the communities they served. In addition, consumers may have looked to these media for help in dealing with the backlash they experienced from the majority population.

Contrary to the situation in the U.S, both Canada and Australia, openly and, to an extent, in opposition to the United States' approach, embraced multicultural policies in the 1970s (Browne, 2005; Murray, Yu, & Ahadi, 2007). In Canada, it was the result of the work of the Royal Commission on Bilingualism and Biculturalism, a government body set up in response to the grievances of French-speaking Canadians in Quebec Province and beyond.[11] In Australia, where a "White Australia policy" guided immigration and citizenship laws since 1901, changes in immigration policy started to take place right after World War II. This was due in large part to the fact that Australia needed to strengthen its workforce (Husband, 1994). By 1975, the Australian government had passed a Racial Discrimination Act, making the implementation of any kind of race-based selection criteria illegal.

In both Canada and Australia, multiculturalism is not experienced and viewed only as ethnic population diversity, but also as the right of individuals to express their distinct, ethnic, and cultural identity. As a result, in both countries, there are media policies in place to support ethnic media programming through government subsidies and special broadcast licensing categories. In Australia, for example, in 1978, lawmakers passed an unprecedented bill, with which they founded the Special Broadcasting Service (SBS). The SBS was meant to serve the growing immigrant population, but also the country's Aboriginal communities. Indigenous media have also found support in Canada, although their development has not been unproblematic and intense lobbying on behalf of Inuit and other First Nations has been critical in getting necessary legislation passed (Meadows, 1992; Valaskakis, 1992). Regardless of the various hurdles ethnic communities have had to overcome to establish a media presence, when it comes to creating an environment in which ethnic media can emerge and grow "no other country even comes close" to Canada and Australia (Browne, 2005, p. 181).[12]

Belgium, Finland, and Sweden: Born Multicultural and Multilingual

These three European countries vary in terms of their experience with immigration. Belgium, for example, received thousands of immigrants after the end of World War II and until the early 1970s. These immigrants worked mainly in the country's mining industry (Ormond, 2002). Sweden, as well as Finland, on the other hand, were immigrant-sending countries for much of the early part of the 20th century. Many of their nationals departed the Scandinavian coasts to move to North America (Camauër, 2002; Kauranen & Tuori, 2002). The three nations also differ with respect to their experience with indigenous populations. Sami (or

Lapps) people live across the northern territories of Finland and Sweden. Belgium does not have similar populations in its territory.

Despite their differences, all three countries are similar in that they were born not only as multicultural but also *multilingual* societies. In Finland, the official languages are Finnish and Swedish; in Sweden, there is no official language. Apart from Swedish, which is the language of the majority, the state also recognizes and protects the rights of certain linguistic minorities to speak and use their languages, including Finnish, Sami, Romani, and Yiddish (Camauër, 2002; European Charter for Regional & Minority Languages, 2009). As described earlier, in Belgium there are three officially recognized linguistic communities.

The fact that all these countries have had to deal with the internal ethnic and linguistic diversity of their citizens from early on in their history has benefited them insofar as it has prepared them to address issues pertaining to immigration and social integration of immigrants into their communities.[13] In Belgium especially, familiarity with a linguistically diverse media landscape created an environment in which ethnic media have found it possible to obtain state support (see earlier discussion about Belgium). To the north, in Sweden, the combination of a relatively "open" immigration policy with multiculturalism-oriented integration provisions (Camauër, 2002) suggests a context that enables ethnic media development. Newspapers not written in Swedish, for example, may receive a state subsidy if they are directed toward "linguistic minorities living in Sweden, have their editorial office in Sweden, distribute at least 90% of the subscribed circulation in Sweden, and have a circulation of at least 2,000 copies (Statute of Annual Press Subsidies, SFS 1996: 1607)" (Camauër, 2002, p. 13).

United Kingdom and the Netherlands: Challenges in the Post-Colonial Era

As former colonial powers, the United Kingdom and the Netherlands are similar in that they have had to address the challenges faced by immigration-receiving countries for many years (Bink, 2002; Georgiou, 2001a). Britain especially has been touted as one of the European countries with the highest levels of understanding and sensitivity to multiculturalism and social integration (Blommesteijn & Entzinger, 1999; Georgiou, 2001a), while for 30 years (from 1960 to 1990) the Netherlands were known for their "open" immigration and multiculturalism-oriented policies. In the Netherlands, for example, a variety of state-subsidized programs helped immigrants from Morocco, Turkey, and elsewhere maintain their linguistic and cultural identities. From 1990 onward, however, both Britain and the Netherlands began to reassess their policies on immigration and social integration, although not for all the same reasons.

Andre Krouwel, a political scientist at Amsterdam's Free University, argues that multiculturalism in the Netherlands was supported for so many years prior to 1990 because the state hoped labor migrants would eventually go back to their home countries (Baker, 2004a & 2004b). Many did not go home. In hindsight, scholars believe that multiculturalism policies essentially divided the country into "a relatively affluent and educated Dutch 'in-group' and a mainly Muslim, under-skilled 'out-group'" (Baker, 2004a, para. 6).

Around 2004, the tension between these two groups came to a head with the murder of a controversial Dutch film director, Theodoor van Gogh, by a Moroccan-origin youth. The director was known for his anti-immigrant views. The murder of van Gogh had a tremendous backlash, as it fanned anti-immigrant sentiments across the country. From the turn of the century, but most clearly since 2004, Dutch policies have shifted towards a more assimilationism-oriented model of social integration. Krouwel explains that this means that "no longer is the model that ethnic minorities should organize themselves. . . . They should have to participate in the Dutch mainstream organizations" (Baker, 2004a, para. 1; see also d'Haenens, 2009).

Negative reactions towards immigrants have multiplied over the years in the UK, too, and British immigration policy has made access to citizenship progressively more difficult (Husband, 1994). The heated debate among British policymakers, caused in 2008 by a House of Lords report on the impact of immigration, has had on the well-being of Britons is indicative of the social climate in which more restrictive immigration policies are put in place. The report found that, "competition from immigrants has had a negative impact on the low paid and training of young U.K. workers, and has contributed to high house prices" (BBC, 2008).

These changes in immigration and integration policies in the UK and the Netherlands have affected the growth of ethnic media for and by immigrant-origin communities in rather different ways. In the Netherlands, since 2000, state, regional, and local authorities have committed more money and other resources to the production of ethnic minority programming. The budget for media and minorities policy, for example, was raised from €2.3 million in 2000 to €3.8 million in 2001. In addition, the state has made more frequencies available to municipalities so that more local, minority-oriented programming can find its way to the airwaves and audiences. These policy choices were made, among other things, to counter the growing popularity of satellite channels connecting ethnic minority audiences to home country media, which carry few to no programs about life in the Netherlands (Bink, 2002).

In quite the opposite direction, British policymakers have rolled back their support of policies that promoted the British vision of multiculturalism. Since 1996, there is no longer a policy that calls upon media to reflect the multicultural nature of the country (Georgiou, 2001a). In addition, in the 1999 annual report of the Department of Culture, Media, and Sport, there was no reference made to policy goals related to ethnic, cultural, and religious diversity (Runnymede Trust, cited in Georgiou, 2001a). Moreover, the British state, contrary to the Dutch government, offers no support to ethnic minority media.

Germany and Austria: Facing Up to the Challenges of Immigration

Since the 1960s both Germany and Austria, but especially Germany, have experienced significant inflows of migrants, particularly from Eastern and Southern Europe, as thousands left their homelands in search of better jobs in the industrialized countries of Northern Europe. However, both these countries have been relatively ethnically homogeneous for many years, and citizenship rights have traditionally been ascribed along bloodlines. Migrants arriving to work in the major manufacturing plants of Germany in the 1960s and 1970s were termed "guest workers." The assumption was (as in the case of the Netherlands) that they would come, work for a few years, and then return to their home countries. In this context, whatever media services were founded to target the migrants were intended to keep them connected to their homelands and facilitate their eventual return.

There were a few isolated efforts undertaken by regional government authorities (i.e., at the level of the *Länder*, or states) in Frankfurt and Berlin to promote anti-racism and pro-multiculturalism institutions in the late 1970s and early 1980s. Despite these efforts, Germany remained in denial until the 1990s; it refused to see that immigration was radically changing its socio-demographic map. In 2000, the federal government changed citizenship laws creating, for the first time, a path to citizenship for German-born migrants whose parents have lived in the country for 8 or more years (Raiser, 2002). These changes in perceptions and policies around immigration created more fertile ground for the development of multiculturalism-driven policies of integration and the production of ethnically-targeted media content. Although limited in geographic reach, the founding of radio programs like Radio Multikulti in Berlin and Funkhaus Europa in Cologne are indicative of the changes in policy orientation.[14]

France: Ethnic Diversity in a "Color-Blind" Society

France represents a special case on the European continent. Historically, at least since the 19th century, it has been an immigration-receiving country. Until World War II most immigrants arrived from Latin America and other European countries. After the war though, as many of its neighbors did, France started to recruit labor migrants from Southern Europe, the Maghreb countries, and other African nations. In 1991, the National Institute of Demographic Studies (INED, from the French equivalent) estimated that about 20% of the French population had at least one older family member (e.g., a parent or grandparent) who was of foreign-origin (Malonga, 2002). The French state, however, neither keeps records nor official trend data that capture changes in the ethnic makeup of the country. Contrary to what happens in the U.S., the UK, Canada, and elsewhere, the law prohibits any distinction among citizens based on ethnicity, race, religion, or gender. Individuals are only classified as citizens or non-citizens (Boucaud & Stubbs, 1994; Husband, 1994).

As France's society is becoming de facto multiethnic, the vision of a "color blind" society has been severely challenged by growing racism and interethnic tension. The lack of minority representation in the media, especially television, exacerbates the situation (Malonga, 2002). In response to the challenges of immigration, the French government (led by the conservative party) has adopted more restrictive (or "closed") immigration policies in the late 1990s. However, it has also invested more heavily in understanding the emerging dynamics of population diversity and its impact. In 1999, for instance, the Conseil Supérieure de l' Audiovisual (CSA, the regulatory authority) commissioned a study on the representation of "visible" minorities (i.e., non-White) in television. It was a significant moment because it was the first time that a state institution decided to publicly recognize and address the issue of minority representation in French broadcasting (Malonga, 2002). Since then, other organizations, such as the Institut Panos mentioned earlier in this chapter, have also become more actively engaged in research around the representation of minorities in the media, but also around the roles that ethnic, or otherwise known as *diversity media* (Mediam'Rad, 2007), play in the lives of ethnic populations. The hope is that this knowledge can help improve policies aimed at the integration of French society. These developments could encourage ethnic media growth and sustainability.

Greece, Italy, Spain: The Hard Realization of Becoming an Immigrant-Receiving Country

Up until the 1980s, these Southern European countries were thought to be immigrant-sending countries. Thousands of their citizens had left family members and friends behind in the preceding decades for North America, Northern Europe, and Australia, in search of better job opportunities. With this history, state governments and societies in all three of these countries were caught unprepared to deal with the unprecedented influx of immigrants they experienced in the 1980s, and especially post-1989 and the collapse of the Berlin Wall (Fakiolas & King, 1996; Gaya, 2002; Georgiou, 2001b). The policy vacuum in all three countries created a negative environment for immigrants. The state has been reticent in recognizing the number of immigrants in its territory and has been slow in formulating comprehensive social integration policies. For example, there was reticence in developing policies to diffuse inter-ethnic group tension, combat racism against immigrants, or to encourage the fair representation of immigrants in the media. In this context, media policy in Greece and Spain, for instance, reflects no specific provisions for the support of ethnic media ventures and programming for ethnic minorities (Gaya, 2002; Georgiou, 2001b). We next discuss how media-specific policies implemented by state authorities impact ethnic media.

Media Policy Provisions and the Ethnic Media

Since the time the first books were printed and the early newspapers and periodicals came off the presses, state authorities have tried to establish and enforce rules that impact the production and distribution of media content. Today, media policy in most countries addresses issues such as: who has the right to own media and how much of the media industry a single person or organization can control (e.g., to prevent monopolies); what content is appropriate and what is not (e.g., for the protection of minors); how media content is distributed (e.g., what satellite-transmitted programming can be disseminated in a country); as well as what financial support, if any, is provided by the state for certain media operations.

These media policies also reflect a government's willingness to address issues of population diversity and the access of ethnic minority populations to the *public sphere* (Habermas, 1989). The public sphere (or the public forum) is that "space between government and society, in which private individuals exercise formal and informal control over the state: formal control through the election of governments and informal control through the pressure of public opinion" (Curran, 1991, p. 29). Curran (1991) explains why the role of the media in general and by extension, of the ethnic media, is critical in this process:

> They distribute the information necessary for citizens to make an informed choice at election time; they facilitate the formation of public opinion by providing an independent forum of debate; and they enable the people to shape the conduct of government by articulating their views. (p. 29)

Models of Media Policies Pertaining to Ethnic Media

Reviewing media policies of a country is instructive, because it reveals the extent to which legislators recognize the diversity and whether they evaluate diversity as a positive or negative force in society. Riggins (1992; see also Cormack, 2007) suggests that when state policies support ethnic media, they do so through one of the five models presented next.

Integrationist Model

Applying this model, a country's government chooses to support the development of ethnic media, because it believes that in doing so it will encourage the integration of minorities into mainstream society (e.g., often a unilingual and ethnic majority). In providing support for ethnic media (e.g., through subsidies and preferential licensing clauses), the state presumes that ethnic audiences will be more willing to become integrated because they will see the state as benevolent (Riggins, 1992). The state government supports ethnic media because it believes that by creating an environment that allows ethnic media to grow, it will also be able to better monitor the various ethnic populations they serve and potentially prevent any movements towards independence (Browne, 2005; Guyot, 2007; Hourigan, 2007). Another reason why a state government may attempt to encourage ethnic media production is because it could see these media as valuable information dissemination conduits for reaching populations that might not yet speak the dominant language.

Elements of this model can be found in many countries, Australia being one of them (Husband, 1986). Station 5UV in Adelaide was created in 1975, and it was the first of several in a new sector of Australian broadcasting comprised of noncommercial, community-based radio stations. The founding of these stations was advocated by activists pressuring the government to grant civil rights to Aboriginals and was supported by members of the Labor Party government, which assumed power in 1972. Some of these stations also broadcast programs in non-indigenous, foreign-languages (e.g., Italian, Greek, Mandarin, and Cantonese). Right after the first community radio stations went on the air, the Australian Broadcasting Corporation (a public broadcasting service funded through license fees) created new stations targeting underserved indigenous and immigrant communities as well. Until that point in time the ABC had shown no interest in community radio. In Melbourne, another community radio channel, station 3ZZ, broadcast a variety of programs for and by some of the city's many ethnic and cultural communities (e.g., of Chinese, Greek,

Cypriot, and Italian-origin) (Browne, 2005). These community radio stations proved to be invaluable to the government in 1975, when a new nationwide health care plan was unveiled. The administration had to figure out the best way to reach approximately 15% of the population that was not fluent in English. The government contracted with several stations for airtime, but it also created two new services, which were meant to be temporary: station 3EA in Melbourne and 2EA in Sydney. The success of these stations urged the government to ask the parliament to give the two new stations permanent status. The parliament did and eventually, in 1977, both 2EA and 3EA were subsumed under the umbrella of the Special Broadcasting Service (SBS). This did not happen without a fight and long debates though. As Browne (2005) documents, parliament members posed questions, such as, "How do we know that *they* aren't saying subversive things about [God, Motherhood, the Flag] when they speak in languages that *we* [mainstream White] can't understand?" (p. 82, emphasis in original). Parliament eventually, however, supported the new service because it realized that the Australian population (and consequently the voting public) was becoming increasingly diverse. If nothing else, the new service was a useful tool to get information to thousands of non-English speakers.

Economic Model (or Shallow Multiculturalism)

Countries with policies that fit this model are superficially committed to multiculturalism. They argue for and institute policies that seemingly support multiculturalism insofar as they find it beneficial for educational and economic purposes. States with such policies find that multiculturalism can help "develop literacy and ensure that primary and secondary schools are more effective in reaching minority students" (Riggins, 1992, p. 9). In such cases, the state is not committed to multiculturalism per se, but rather to the economic advantages that a type of *shallow multiculturalism* can generate. It can help the state, for instance, attain its education goals and create a more versatile and skilled workforce. But, shallow multiculturalism means that the state is not truly committed to the long-term preservation of the culture and language of ethnic minority populations. At the end of the day, the state sees multiculturalism only as a transitional phase, prior to the assimilation of the foreign-born and indigenous populations. This model has been and is applied in many countries that have been struggling with increasing ethnic diversity, including the United Kingdom, the Netherlands, and Denmark, in Europe, and the United States and Canada in North America.

In 1992, Canadians launched Television Northern Canada (TVNC). The road to the founding of TVNC was a long one. It took 10 years of lobbying on behalf of Canada's First Nations before the federal government gave the green light for the Native Broadcast Access Program to begin in 1983. And then, 10 more years to resolve the problem of distributing programming to 94 communities living across a vast stretch of the Canadian Northern territories (i.e., 4.3 million kilometers). Implicit in the policy passed by the government was the assumption that Native media producers would be able to distribute their programs via the Canadian Broadcasting Company's (CBC) Northern Service or through CANCOM (Canadian Satellite Communications, Inc.), a northern program distributor. However, negotiations between the Native media producers and the distributors broke down "over prime time access hours and preemption of national programming" (Museum of Broadcast Communications, 2009). After persistent lobbying by First Nations organizations, the federal government finally agreed to invest $10 million towards establishing a dedicated Northern Satellite transponder (channel).

In 1991, the Canadian regulatory commission for radio, television, and telecommunications, the CRTC, approved the plan (MBC, 2009) and in 1992 TVNV was on the air. It broadcasts in 15 native languages and carries approximately 100 hours of programming per week. In 2009, TVNC continued to be the "only television network that broadcasts such a large volume of programming from indigenous sources" (MBC, 2009).[15] While this seems like a huge leap of progress in terms of state support for ethnic media (and, in this case, indigenous ethnic media), it has been argued that if the Canadian state was truly committed to multiculturalism, it would have created policies that provided fair access to distribution systems, such as satellites, early on. But that has not been the case. Television Northern Canada has relied heavily on the lobbying efforts of indigenous NGOs and on the goodwill of non-native politicians for its survival (Riggins, 1992; Valaskakis, 1992). And, since the 1990s, the federal and provincial governments of Canada have begun to cut back on the amount of money allotted to multiculturalism programs, including indigenous media projects (Murray et al., 2007; MBC, 2009; Valaskakis, 1992). Moreover, the CRTC has espoused deregulation in the media landscape. A light regulation touch with respect to licensing, ownership consolidation, and programming has had two main outcomes: an increase in the number of digital ethnic licenses launched by Canadian owners, but also the entry of many foreign language imports (Murray et al., 2007). The impact of these trends for indigenous media remains to be assessed.

Divisive Model

In this model, the state uses ethnicity to maintain or create some level of tension and rivalry among ethnic groups (Riggins, 1992). This was the case in Algeria at the time the country was a French colony. The French colonial authorities created Channel 2, a Berber language radio station, as way to foster disunity and tension between the tribes speaking Berber dialects and Arabic speakers. The station broadcast in Kabyle, which is one of these Berber dialects spoken by tribes that recognize the highlands of Kabylie, in Northeastern Algeria, as their homeland (Gellner & Micaud, 1972). In the early 1960s, Algeria became an independent state and the new government inherited the Kabyle-language radio station. Initially, the government found the channel useful in reaching a mostly illiterate population (Ihaddaden, 1992). In the post-independence years, however, and especially post-1975, Algeria committed itself to Arabization and therefore support for the Kabyle-language network deteriorated quickly (Ihaddaden, 1992). At the turn of the century, the tension between Berber populations and Arabic speakers remained significant. However, our research suggests that at least in 2005 the Kabyle-language network was still broadcasting. Its continued operation may have been aided by the fact that in 2002 President Abdelaziz Bouteflika signed a law, according to which Tamazight

(Kabyle is a dialect of Tamazight) is recognized as a national language, equal to Arabic (Assemblée Populaire Nationale, 2002).

Preemptive Model

The preemptive model manifests in two different ways. In the first case, a state government may try to establish its own ethnic media, to prevent minorities from creating organizations and programming that could promote and advocate for some level of autonomy or independence from the state (Riggins, 1992). This is what happened in France between 1970 and 2000. In the second version of the preemptive model, the state may choose to support a particular type of ethnic media that better serves its goals with respect to immigration and the integration of immigrant populations into mainstream society. This model was applied in Germany from the 1960s through the mid-1980s.

In the French case, the state tried for many years to suppress independence movements of linguistic minorities speaking Basque, Occitan, Breton, and Corse, among other less-spoken languages (Cheval, 1992). Up until the end of the 1970s, these ethnic communities were given very little attention by the media. The state monopoly of the airwaves was seen by members of these communities as "a restriction of the freedom of expression or an ideological apparatus of the state (to use a popular phrase from the time), the task of which was to perpetuate the ideas and control of the dominant class" (Cheval, 1992, p. 170). That is why around 1975 the "free radios" (or *radios libres*) were born. These were clandestine and illegal stations and were prosecuted as such by state authorities. In 1981, the Socialist party won the elections and President François Mitterand authorized the granting of licenses to local, non-profit organizations to establish radio stations. These stations were mandated to offer programming targeted to regional and local ethnic minority populations. Subsequently, many of the radios libres became legal and known as *radio locales privés* (local, private radio stations).

By the mid-1990s, these regional and local private stations were competing against regional public radio stations for a relatively small ethnic minority audience. At the time, the state government decided that private stations would no longer have to focus their programming on the regional ethnic populations and that they could become more commercial. The decision freed the central government from having to provide funding, in the form of grants, to these private stations. Relying on advertising, though, pushed the private stations to introduce programming that would be more attractive to a broader audience and thereby to more advertisers. These changes effectively left the public channels as the sole sources of programming for the local and regional populations that spoke languages other than French (Cheval, 1992). In 2003, the French regulatory council, the Conseil Supérieure de l'Audiovisuel (CSA), assessed the impact state policies had had on the radio market. It found that "insufficient space is dedicated to programs using regional languages, a situation which is against what viewers expect in their regions" (CSA, 2003, p. 25–26). In the same report, it is noted that programs in regional languages, such as Breton, dropped by over 20% in just one year. Programming in Breton in 2001 amounted to 63 hours and it was limited to about 50 hours in 2002 (Guyot, 2007).

In Germany, we find a different version of the preemptive model. In the years after World War II, Western Germany (i.e., the Federal Republic of Germany) experienced an economic boom. Labor resources in the country did not suffice and that is when the government initiated large scale "guest worker" (*Gastarbeiter*) programs and began recruiting thousands from Southern European countries (i.e., Spain, Italy, and Greece), as well as Turkey. Workers were given 2-year contracts, after which they were expected to return to their home country. The authorities soon realized that this "rotation principle" created disruptions in productivity. The principle was officially abandoned in 1964. Turks comprised the largest group among these labor immigrants. Between 1961 and 1973, over 700,000 people were recruited from Turkey (Kosnick, 2007).

Up until the mid-1980s, German policy continued to encourage labor migrants to return to their countries of origin. As part of this policy, the children and grandchildren of the first generations of labor migrants were not given German citizenship, but remained "foreigners" (*Ausländer*). Another part of this policy was to have the public broadcasting service create programs that would keep migrants in touch with developments and current events back in their home countries. These programs were meant to serve as a "bridge to home" (Kosnick, 2007) and to help guest workers better understand the political situation in Germany. When the Berlin Wall was built as a result of the confrontation between the Western Allies and the Soviet forces, labor migrants became particularly concerned and some even decided to return to their home country. In a study published by the German UNESCO commission, Hans-Wolf Rissom and his colleagues note that, "Back then, it was realized that the foreign workers, unfamiliar with the German situation, interpreted political situations differently, sometimes wrongly, and that therefore, a particular need for informational foreign-language broadcasts arose" (1977, translation from German, cited in Kosnick, 2007, p. 30). Two months after the Berlin Wall was erected, the public service broadcasting corporation of the Saarland region (southwest of Frankfurt, near the German-French border) began to air a half-hour radio program in Italian, every Saturday. It was called *Mezz'ora Italiana.* Similar programs in Greek and Spanish started in 1962, while a Turkish program aired for the first time in1964, in Cologne (Kosnick, 2007). All these efforts to create ethnic media for migrant workers served general German immigration, social integration, and labor policies, as there were no subsidies provided for founding ethnic media owned and operated by immigrant communities themselves.

Proselytism Model

In this last model, the state or a transnational organization (such as a religious organization) may explicitly attempt to promote values through the mass media and thus devise appropriate means for reaching minority audiences in their own language (Riggins, 1992). This was the case with the Catholic Church and the Mapuche Indians in Southern Chile (Colle, 1992). In 1966, Dutch Capuchin missionaries established a radio station "dedicated to the religious, cultural, and social development of the peasant population" (FREDER, translation from Spanish, cited in Colle, 1992, p. 132). The station, FREDER (acronym from the Spanish equivalent of Foundation for Rural

Development Through School Radio), was founded as a nonprofit, private foundation. As of 2006, FREDE continued to be operational. The Catholic Church as well as some evangelical Christian denominations have founded similar indigenous radio stations in Mexico, Guatemala, Brazil, Ecuador, and countries in Africa, as well as Asia (most notably in the Philippines) (Browne, 2007).

¤ For Further Discussion

Consider this scenario: You are the owner of a major Arabic-language broadcasting company based in Cairo, Egypt. You are thinking about establishing a subsidiary in a country where you are likely to find a large enough audience to keep your company viable. First, think about your options. What countries would be your top three options? Then, think about the policy context in the countries you are considering as options. In which country do you think you have the best chance to succeed? Why?

Immigrant Versus Indigenous Ethnic Communities

Many countries around the world include indigenous populations who do not identify with the ethnic majority and who speak languages other than the "official" or most commonly spoken language (or languages). This is the case in countries like the United States, Britain, Canada, Australia, Ireland, France, Spain, Nordic countries, Algeria, South Africa, the People's Republic of China, and elsewhere. At the same time, a number of these countries have large immigrant populations, new and more settled. One might assume all ethnic media, regardless of their intended audience, would be treated the same; especially in countries that recognize their linguistic minorities and indigenous populations and help them establish their own media. However, this is not always the case. In fact, frequently countries adopt a *dual approach* that awards different rights to indigenous populations and linguistic minorities, on one hand, and immigrant communities, on the other.

Both ethno-linguistic minorities and immigrant populations may in some way threaten the authority of the central state government. In Spain, for instance, two of the most readily recognizable indigenous ethnic minorities are the Catalans and the Basques. They are concentrated in the northeastern and northwestern regions of the country, respectively, and they both speak languages that are distinct from Spanish. At different times in history, both groups have challenged the unity of Spain and the authority of the central government by seeking autonomy or independence. For several reasons, state governments are skeptical about giving many immigrants a clear path to obtaining citizenship. One of these reasons is a fear that large immigrant populations may drastically alter the social demographic map of the country. Another is the fear that immigrants will overburden social and welfare services (e.g., health care services). That said, state governments feel more compelled to address the needs of particularly vocal and visible indigenous communities and find it easier to brush immigrants' demands aside. The fact that members of indigenous minorities usually have citizenship rights (and therefore can vote), as well as the fact that they are usually better prepared to mobilize and pressure the government to respond to their demands than new immigrant communities are accounts for this difference in treatment. Spain offers a case in point.

Since the fall of the Franco dictatorship in 1975, Catalonia and the Basque Country have been recognized as autonomous nations within the Spanish state. The policy of "language normalization," implemented since then, encouraged initiatives that promoted languages other than Spanish. Some of these initiatives were aimed towards the creation of Catalan-language media (Arana, Azpillaga, & Narbaiza, 2003; Corominas Piulats, 2007). While media ventures in indigenous languages other than Spanish are encouraged by the policies of the state, there is no legal framework that addresses media production for and by immigrant communities. Since the mid-1990s, the Spanish state (just as the governments of other Southern European countries) has strived to crack down on immigration. In this environment, it is hard for ethnic media serving immigrant communities to grow (Gaya, 2002).

Public Service Broadcasting and Ethnic Media

In many countries programming for indigenous and immigrant-origin ethnic communities was first carried over the airwaves of public services broadcasters. This is certainly the case for most of Western Europe and Australia (see earlier discussion about the SBS). In other countries, like the United States and Southern Europe, public television and radio played (and/or are playing) a less critical role in the development of ethnic media (Gaya, 2002; Georgiou, 2001b; Husband, 1994). State subsidies for ethnically targeted programming can be particularly important for new immigrant or small ethnic communities, which may not be able to afford the high start-up costs of broadcasting (Browne, 2005; Husband, 1994; Meadows, 1992).[16]

When ethnic media spring up from state government programs, it is necessary for NGO "watchdogs" to monitor these services for at least two reasons: first, because the state may dictate which populations get served and, in cases where ethnic community organizations are involved in production, who gets access and when to studios and equipment. In Austria, for example, only "recognized minorities, i.e., citizens with minority descent" have the same rights as Austrians to be represented in "cultural facilities," including broadcast media (Böse et al., 2002, p. 11). Recognized minorities include citizens of Slovenian and Croatian-origin, but not new immigrant groups. The second reason for NGO involvement is that the state and the public broadcasting service combine ethnic groups in meaningless categories, such as "Asian" in Britain or the U.S. (Husband, 1994). This may happen either out of ignorance or in an ill-fated attempt of management to reach a broader audience.

Public service broadcasters can be found at the state, regional, and local levels. In countries like Germany and the Netherlands, municipal, local, and community broadcasting services have offered ethnic and immigrant communities far more opportunities to generate ethnically, culturally, and linguistically targeted programming than larger regional and national public broadcasting organizations.

The existence and vitality of local and community-level broadcasting depends rather significantly on the initiative of the government at the local and regional level. In Germany, the regional governments of the *Länder* have considerable latitude in formulating their own regional media policies. Funkhaus Europa in Cologne and Radio Multikulti in Berlin emerged in regions with policies that fostered greater social inclusion of ethnic minority populations.

Public Access to the Airwaves, Open Channels, and Restricted Service Licenses

Because gaining access to television and radio frequencies and production facilities may be too costly for many ethnic communities and organizations, policymakers in certain countries have created space for "open channels" or "public access channels." They are found at the local level and accessible via cable and digital television services. Open channels provide free access to individuals and NGOs. The advantage they offer ethnic and immigrant producers, compared to many public broadcasting services, is full control over the programs they create. Reception only via cable and digital technologies, of course, limits their reach (Raiser, 2002). Open channels have enjoyed success in Germany for several years. In the city of Dortmund, the local open channel hosts two Tamil, two Iranian, and a Russian production (Raiser, 2002).

In Britain, open channels were introduced for the first time in 2001. As an alternative to open channels, ethnic communities in the UK can also apply for Restricted Service Licenses, which give them access to the airwaves for 28 days. Licensees cannot ask for a renewal and must wait for 1 year before reapplying. Far from being able to sustainably serve a community, these licenses are usually used during periods of religious holidays, like Ramadan, to convey information about events, provide entertainment, and often to run telethons and fund drives to recover the £4,500 that the licenses costs (Georgiou, 2001a). The short life of these media "can become a symbolic reconfirmation of exclusion and marginalization of minorities from the mainstream cultures of mediation" (Georgiou, 2001a, p. 20).

Deregulation and the Internet

Since the latter half of the 1980s, there has a clear tendency toward the relaxation of regulation pertaining to broadcasting and media ownership across the board (Bagdikian, 2004; Bennett, n.d.; Grisold, 2006; Humphreys, 1996; McChesney, 2003).

Researchers have found that deregulation in a host of countries has been coupled with at least partial withdrawal of state support from public broadcasting (e.g., COSPE, 2002; Georgiou, 2001b; Murray et al., 2007). Public broadcasting services have been scaled back in a number of cases, so as to allow more "space," for additional private and commercial channels to enter the landscape. This is expected, so the rationale goes, to increase competition, which will in turn lead to better media content for all.

The success of this model is at the heart of intense debates, which are beyond of the scope of our discussion in this chapter. Suffice it to say that a highly deregulated, heavily commercialized media landscape constrains the creation and threatens the sustainability of ethnic media, especially as commercial ventures need large audiences to attract sizeable advertising accounts. Only Spanish-language media in the U.S. (such as Univisión and Telemundo) have accomplished sufficient reach among a quickly growing Spanish-speaking population, so as to leverage the advertising market and compete effectively against larger "mainstream," English-language media corporations (see Figure 8.4). Smaller ethnic communities are not likely to be able to sustain their media in this type of a media environment. The case of Breton-language media in France mentioned earlier supports this argument.

Deregulation accompanied by the scaling back of public broadcasting and the removal of policy provisions meant to increase participation of ethnic minority populations in the media landscape as owners—as is the case in the U.S., Canada, and the UK—is likely to have detrimental effects on ethnic media production in the long run (e.g., see Turner & Cooper, 2007). The impact may be particularly damaging in countries with a weak or short local and community media tradition, as is the case of Britain and Italy (COSPE, 2002; Georgiou, 2001a).

The Internet may hold promise as an alternative platform that ethnic media could explore as they seek paths to sustainability. Most data, however, suggest that there are at least two reasons not to be exceptionally optimistic about this path. First of all, many ethnic media serve populations that cannot afford or lack the education necessary to access the Internet. In less developed countries it may not even be a question of cost or education, but rather the pure absence of basic infrastructure, like computers and phone cables.

Second, concentration of media ownership trends (resulting from deregulation) suggest that the technological infrastructure (i.e., the backbone) of the Internet, the points of entry to the network (e.g., portals) and the numerous Web-based media properties are also becoming concentrated in the hands of a few major media firms (Arsenault & Castells, 2008; Artz, 2007; Carveth, 2004; Chester, 2007; Compaine, 2000). In this context, it is not unthinkable that smaller ethnic media organizations may eventually find that it is more difficult for them to establish an Internet presence and, even when they do, they may have a very difficult time gaining visibility.

Looking forward, even if we disregard the question of what policies are best from the point of view of individuals, ethnic media organizations and ethnic communities, and focused instead solely on what is in the interest of state power, the evidence suggests that policymakers should make good faith efforts to support the production of ethnic media within their territory, especially at the local and regional level. That is because those are the media that can help build neighborhood

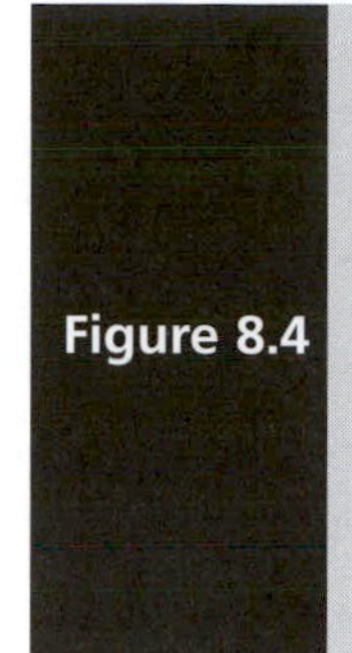

Figure 8.4 Large Spanish-language media in the United States, like Univisión, can compete effectively against major English-language mainstream media. As this ad by Univision posted in Chicago in 2008 suggests, this is because they can count on a growing audience with increasing purchasing power. A large, strong consumer base guarantees them access to the advertising market. As policies around media ownership become more relaxed, though, and big media are allowed to get even bigger, mid-size and small ethnic media are less able to compete.

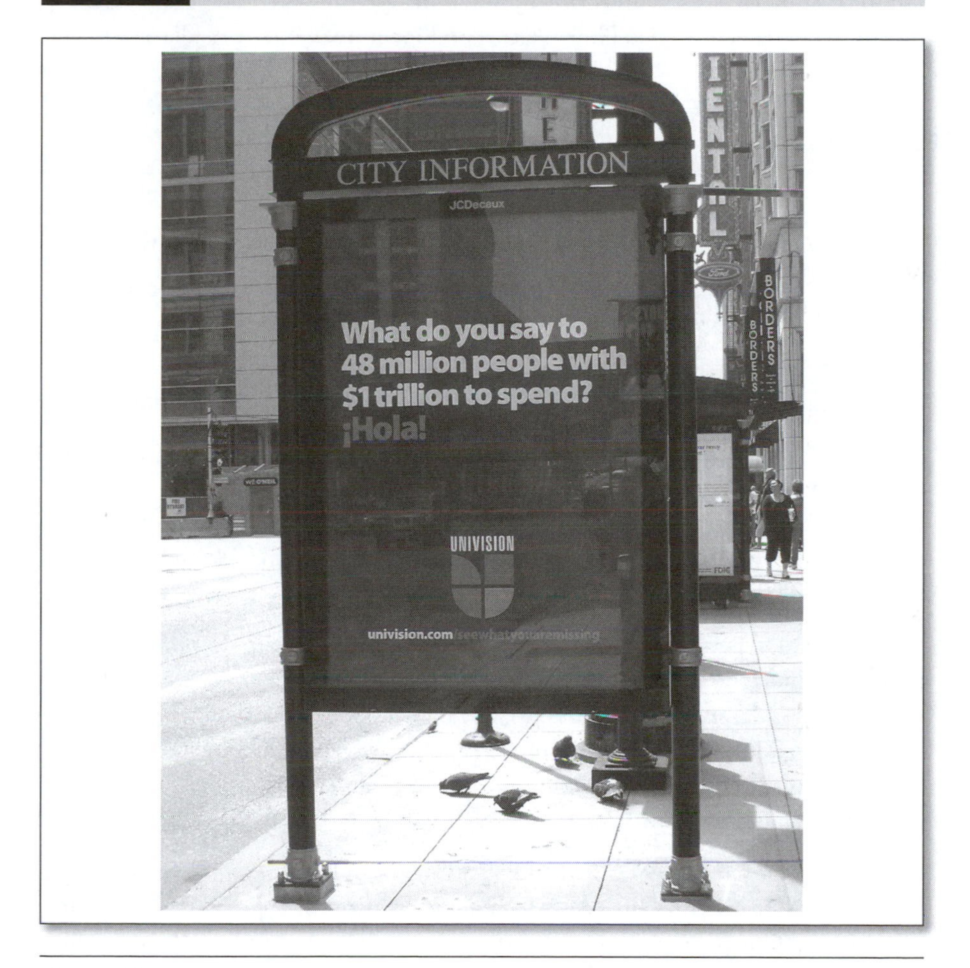

Photo: Vikki Katz.

belonging and individuals' sense that they are part of the greater "imagined community" (Ball-Rokeach, Kim, & Matei, 2001; Kim & Ball-Rokeach, 2006a). The European experience with satellite television targeting populations across multiple countries (often from a distant homeland) confirms that media that do not connect ethnic communities to their local society are unable to foster the social integration of migrants and ethnic minorities into the public sphere. We investigate these local functions of ethnic media in the following chapter.

Summary

Globalization complicates policymaking at multiple levels (from the global level to the local community), and multiple interactions across levels are possible. Immigration and integration policies, in particular, shape the contours of the context within which communication (or media) policy emerges and influences ethnic media. The nation-state remains the most central and prolific policymaker of immigration, integration, and communication policies, and therefore we discussed several models state governments have applied to support ethnic media. We close the chapter by analyzing the significance of public service broadcasting for ethnic media development and assessing the impact of deregulation and the Internet on the future of ethnic media.

Study Questions

1. Deregulation of the media industry means that the nation-state lifts an array of restrictions with respect to media ownership and licensing, as well as media content and its distribution. In principle, one might argue that deregulation is good for the growth of the ethnic media sector. Do you agree? Explain.

2. Why do intergovernmental organizations have mostly indirect and limited impact on policies that would otherwise encourage the development of ethnic media?

3. The U.S., Canada, Australia, Spain, Belgium, and Sweden all have indigenous ethnic and linguistic minority populations that have established a media presence. However, their paths to the media landscape are quite different; for some it has been easier than for others. Explain what accounts for these differences based on what you have read thus far.

4. Under the heading "Immigrant Versus Indigenous Ethnic Communities," we noted that indigenous, ethnic and linguistic communities are often treated differently than immigrant communities by state media policies. Explain why this is the case. Do you think that this dual approach to ethnic media may impact the content of media targeting indigenous communities (ethnic and linguistic) vis-à-vis that of media targeting immigrant communities? If so, how?

5. Under the heading "The Broader Policy Context of Ethnic Media Development," we talked about the ways through which a country's immigration, citizenship, and social integration policies impact ethnic media. Under the heading "Media Policy Provisions and the Ethnic Media" we discussed several models of state support towards ethnic media. In what type of context is every one of these models likely to evolve? Figure 8.3 may help you think through this question.

Notes

[1]For more information on the Council of Europe's Charter for Regional and Minority Languages, see http://www.coe.int/t/dg4/education/minlang/default_en.asp

[2]Sweden ratified the Charter in 2000.

[3]It is should be noted that the Charter clearly states that it covers regional and minority languages used within a country's territory, but that it does not cover those languages "connected with recent migratory movements" (Charter for Regional or Minority Languages, 2009, para. 7).That means that countries that have ratified the Charter are in no way obligated to promote and protect ethnic media serving new immigrant communities living in their territories.

[4]Aang Serian Drum represents one of the rare cases in which the UN has become directly involved in the development of ethnic media. Aang Serian Drum is an indigenous media center based in Arusha, Tanzania, which began in July 2002 as the Masaai Media Project. Through that project, two Masaai youth learned how to create documentary-style videos. The video they produced was sold through fair trade practices to raise money that helped establish Aang Serian Drum. After the success of the Masaai Media Project, the UN provided funding to the budding indigenous media center for the production of a series of documentaries on Tanzanian indigenous cultures, including but not limited to the Masaai (Aang Serian Drum, http://www.asdrum.org).

[5]For more details on Article 19, see Browne (2005) and www.article19.org Additional information on SEEMO can be found at www.seemo.org, and on the International Federation of Journalists at www.ifj.org

[6]See the Institut Panos Paris Web site: http://www.panosparis.org/gb/presentation.php

[7]For more information on MIDAS, see http://www.midas-press.org/welcome.htm

[8]See also Mira Media's Web site: http://www.mediamrad.nl/uk/index.htm

[9]Catherine Murray (2008) indicates that the influence of the National Ethnic Press and Media Council of Canada is fairly limited for two reasons: First, its membership is small and dominated by executives from Toronto; and second, its mission is much less activism-driven than that of similar organizations in the U.S. and elsewhere. For more information on the National Ethnic Press and Media Council of Canada, see http://www.nepmcc.ca

[10]Research indicates that in the days and months immediately following September 11, Arabs and South Asians in the U.S. were the targets of hate crimes more frequently than they had been in the past (Cainkar, 2002; see also: Howell & Shryock, 2003). In just the first week after September 11, Arabs and South Asians reported 645 hate crimes against them (Cainkar, 2002; Council on American-Islamic Relations, 2002). In addition, in late June 2002, the U.S. Department of Justice issued an internal memo to the Immigration and Naturalization Service, which was later replaced by the Department of Homeland Security, and U.S. Customs requesting that they find and search all Yemenis, including American citizens, entering the U.S. As a result, Cainkar (2002) says, "Yemeni Americans were removed from planes and boarding lines, waiting hours for security clearances."

[11]Today, French and English are both official languages of Canada. The two languages have equal status in federal courts, parliament, and all other federal institutions. This is due largely to the research and the recommendations of the Royal Commission on Bilingualism and Biculturalism, which was established in the 1960s. Among other things, the Commission found that French Canadians were underrepresented in political institutions and the country's business world. Canada officially became a bilingual country in 1969, under Prime Minister Pierre Trudeau.

[12]With the possible exception of New Zealand, according to Donald Browne (2005).

[13]That is not to say, of course, that these countries have not experienced periods during which racism and xenophobia have been particularly problematic (e.g., in Belgium in the 1980s) or during which their generally "open" immigration policy was challenged by economic downturns or a change in the prevailing political ideology (e.g., Sweden in the 1990s).

[14]Radio Multikulti was created by the Regional Broadcasting Corporation in Berlin (the SFB), and Funkhaus Europa was founded by the equivalent public broadcaster of the city of

Cologne (the WDR). Hardly any immigrant-origin individuals are part of senior management in either case (Raiser, 2002).

[15]TVNC's network is owned by 13 Aboriginal broadcast, government, and education organizations in Northern Canada. Members include: the Inuit Broadcasting Corporation (Ottawa and Iqaluit), the Inuvialuit Communications Society (Inuvik), Northern Native Broadcasting (British Columbia), Yukon (Whitehorse), the OkalaKatiget Society (Labrador), Taqramiut Nipingat Inc. (Northern Quebec), the Native Communications Society of the Western N.W.T. (Yellowknife), the Government of the Northwest Territories, Yukon College, and the National Aboriginal Communications Society. Associate members are CBC Northern Service, Kativik School Board (Quebec), Labrador Community College, Northern Native Broadcasting, Terrace, Telesat Canada, and Wawatay Native Communications Society (Sioux Lookout). Services extend to Labrador, Arctic Quebec, Nunavut (formerly the Inuit regions of the Northwest Territories), Western Northwest Territories, and Yukon.

[16]The cost of starting up print media is less prohibitive, and in many countries the press is less regulated than broadcast media. However, newspapers targeted to immigrant populations do not enjoy equal rights with "mainstream" print media in all countries. That was the case in France at least until 1994 (Boucaub & Stubbs, 1994) and Austria until 2001 (Böse, Haberfellner, & Koldas, 2002).

PART IV

Ethnic Media as Civic Communicators

CHAPTER 9

Ethnic Media as Local Media

CHAPTER OBJECTIVES

By the end of this chapter, you will have learned more about:

- How ethnic media function within a local community.
- How ethnic media can help to mobilize residents to make their communities better places to live.
- How ethnic media can be partners for improving community life and wellness.

Ethnic Media and the Communities They Serve

Until this point, we have discussed ethnic media as media produced *for* members of a particular ethnic group, usually *by* members of the same ethnic group. We can say, therefore, that ethnic media are produced with a particular community of media consumers in mind (Browne, 2005). This community could be a group of immigrants who come from the same country or be members of an ethnic minority or indigenous group. The audience for an ethnic media outlet may be spread out over a large geographic area or live within a local neighborhood. In other chapters, we have discussed the larger ethnic media outlets and organizations that serve geographically dispersed audiences, sometimes even across multiple national boundaries.

However, most ethnic media are also local media, meaning they are small, locally situated productions that serve a particular neighborhood (Viswanath & Lee, 2007). Media serving a small local area can operate relatively cheaply, since their reach is limited, and can also provide their audience with information about the immediate area that larger outlets do not know about or do not have the resources to cover. This ground-level viewpoint provides unique opportunities and challenges for what we call *geo-ethnic media*, a term that refers to the fact that these media are both ethnically and geographically specific in their focus and content (Kim, Jung, & Ball-Rokeach, 2006a; Wilkin, Ball-Rokeach, Matsaganis, & Cheong, 2007). These media engage in *geo-ethnic storytelling* when they produce culturally relevant, locally focused content for their audience that encourages residents to connect with community resources, organizations, and each other (Lin & Song, 2006).

Research on geo-ethnic media is rare, both because budget constraints limit how well these local productions are known outside of the communities they serve (Alia & Bull, 2005, p. 108) and because formal research on local-level ethnic media is not common. For these reasons, we use our research on geo-ethnic media in Los Angeles over the last decade as a case in point through much of this chapter. We also make every effort to supplement our discussions with examples from other contexts whenever possible.

Geo-Ethnic Media as Part of a Community Communication Ecology

Geo-ethnic media can take many forms: radio, television, Internet message boards, and newspapers ranging from formal publications to local "freebies" produced by residents or neighborhood businesses (Lin & Song, 2006). All of these media forms can be important to residents in their own right, but each outlet is also part of the *communication ecology* of a community.[1] A communication ecology includes all media forms available in a particular area—both ethnic and mainstream—in context of each other, and in context of the other ways residents may find out about their community, such as through interpersonal communication with their neighbors and through their connections to local organizations and institutions (Wilkin et al., 2007). Considering geo-ethnic media as part of the local communication ecology makes it possible to assess the relative importance of particular media connections in the lives of local residents (Ball-Rokeach & Wilkin, 2009; Flanagin & Metzger, 2001; Wilkin et al., 2007).

Residents' communication ecologies vary according to the different goals they may be trying to satisfy. For example, a resident's communication ecology for finding out what is going on in his or her local community may rely primarily on connections to geo-ethnic newspapers and television programming. On the other hand, the resident's communication ecology for finding health information may be primarily through interpersonal communication and online information. Different connections within a communication ecology lead residents to information resources that may reinforce each other. For example, the conversations our hypothetical resident has with friends and neighbors about a health concern may converge with information from online resources, and that convergence may make the resident more likely to visit to a local clinic. This example illustrates how an ecological approach makes it possible for researchers to consider links between residents' communication ecologies and their decisions about where to go and who to trust in their local communities.

The Metamorphosis Project at the University of Southern California has studied geo-ethnic media as part of local communication ecologies in 11 ethnic minority and immigrant communities in Los Angeles. To the best of our knowledge, the Metamorphosis Project is the only research team that has comprehensively studied the community roles of geo-ethnic media from this ecological perspective.

Figures 9.1 and 9.2 show the results of our research in five of the communities we have studied. Figure 9.1 shows the ways that Anglo, Armenian, and Latino residents of Glendale, the third largest city in Los Angeles County, find out what is going on in their communities. Notice that there are clear differences between these residents' communication ecologies, even though they share the same geographic space. The fact that these three ethnic groups have different communication ecologies has important implications for policymakers, organizations, and institutions aiming to connect with Glendale residents. Figure 9.1 shows that Latino and Armenian residents depend on television (both geo-ethnic and mainstream), in addition to their interpersonal networks and mainstream newspapers. Anglo residents depend on mainstream newspapers and interpersonal networks, as well as mainstream television and the Internet. A communication ecology means going beyond considering these communication choices as individual connections to considering how they might interact with each other.

For example, interpersonal communication ranks as one of the top ways that all Glendale residents find out what is going on in their local communities. Media

Figure 9.1 How Glendale Residents Find Out What Is Going on in Their Community

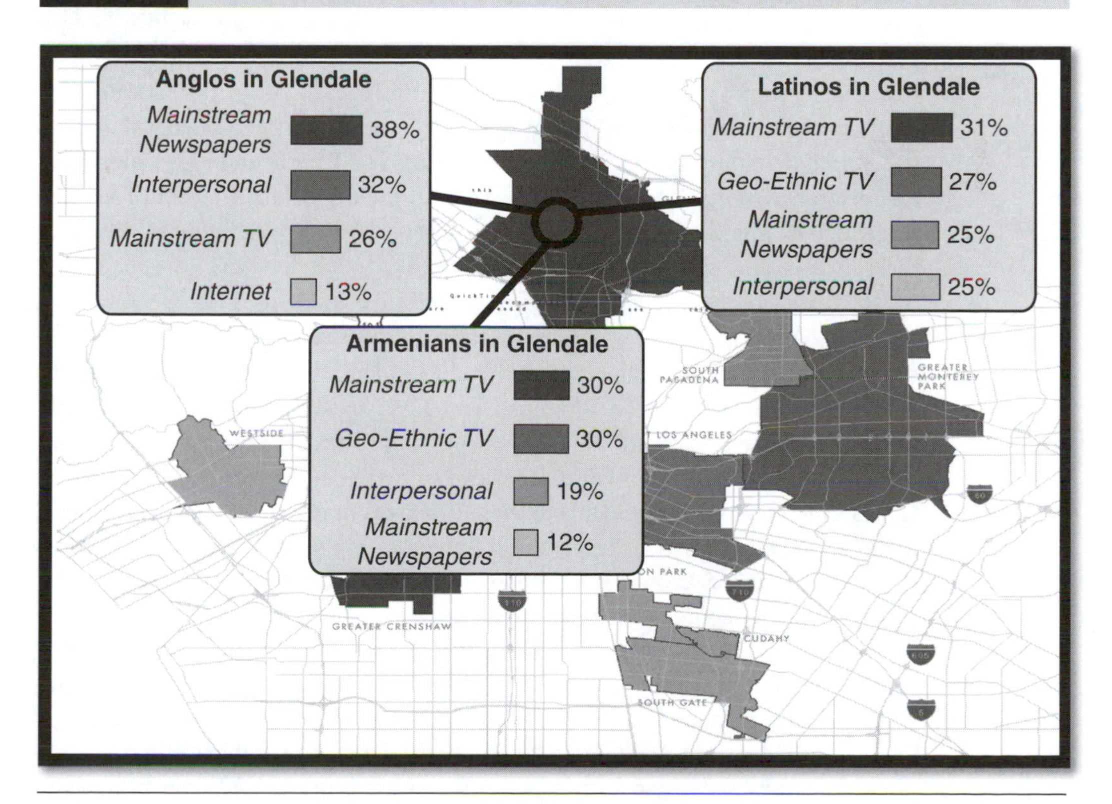

Source: Metamorphosis Project: http://www.metamorph.org

content may be able to prompt residents to have conversations about what is going on in their community. When residents hear the same message from multiple connections within their communication ecology, that message is more likely to be effective.

For Further Discussion

Take a look at Figure 9.1 and imagine yourself as the head of a political advocacy organization in Glendale that caters to one of these three ethnic groups. How could the findings in Figure 9.1 inform your outreach strategy to your target audience? Detail how your plan would incorporate these findings about your audience's communication ecology.

Figure 9.1 shows how residents who live in the same community may have different communication ecologies. By contrast, Figure 9.2 demonstrates how residents of the same ethnic origin construct different communication ecologies when they live in different geographic areas. Figure 9.2 shows how Latino residents in four predominantly Central-American and/or Mexican-origin communities report different connection patterns for finding out what is going on in their communities. Although commonly grouped together as one undifferentiated ethnic audience, these results show clear differences between Latino residents in Pico Union, East, Southeast, and South Los Angeles in terms of their communication ecologies. Even when communities are located quite close to each other, the unique geographic features of a community can result in communication ecologies that contain very different components. For example, East Los Angeles and Pico Union have a wider range of geo-ethnic media available in their areas than in Southeast Los Angeles, which had one geo-ethnic newspaper at the time we conducted research there (Matsaganis & Katz, 2004).

The different connection patterns reported by residents in these four Los Angeles communities (and by Latino residents of Glendale, as shown in Figure 9.1) depend in part on immigrant generation and residential tenure in the community and in the United States. For example, East Los Angeles' residents are primarily third and fourth generation Mexican-origin, and Glendale's Latino residents are immigrants from a range of Latin American countries and have long tenure in the U.S., averaging 38 years. Residents in these two areas report more connections with mainstream, English-language television for community information than do residents in communities where English language proficiency is likely lower.

For example, connections with mainstream, English-language media are less common in the Southeast Los Angeles cities of Southgate, Huntington Park, and Cudahy. These cities are often referred to as "gateway cities," as residents are primarily recent immigrants who have lived in the United States for 5 to 7 years on average. Despite these demographic differences, Figure 9.2 demonstrates that geo-ethnic television is consistently important, whether the community is predominantly newly arrived immigrants or third generation Americans. This finding supports the claim

Figure 9.2 How Latino Residents in Four Los Angeles Geo-Ethnic Study Areas Find Out What Is Going on in Their Communities

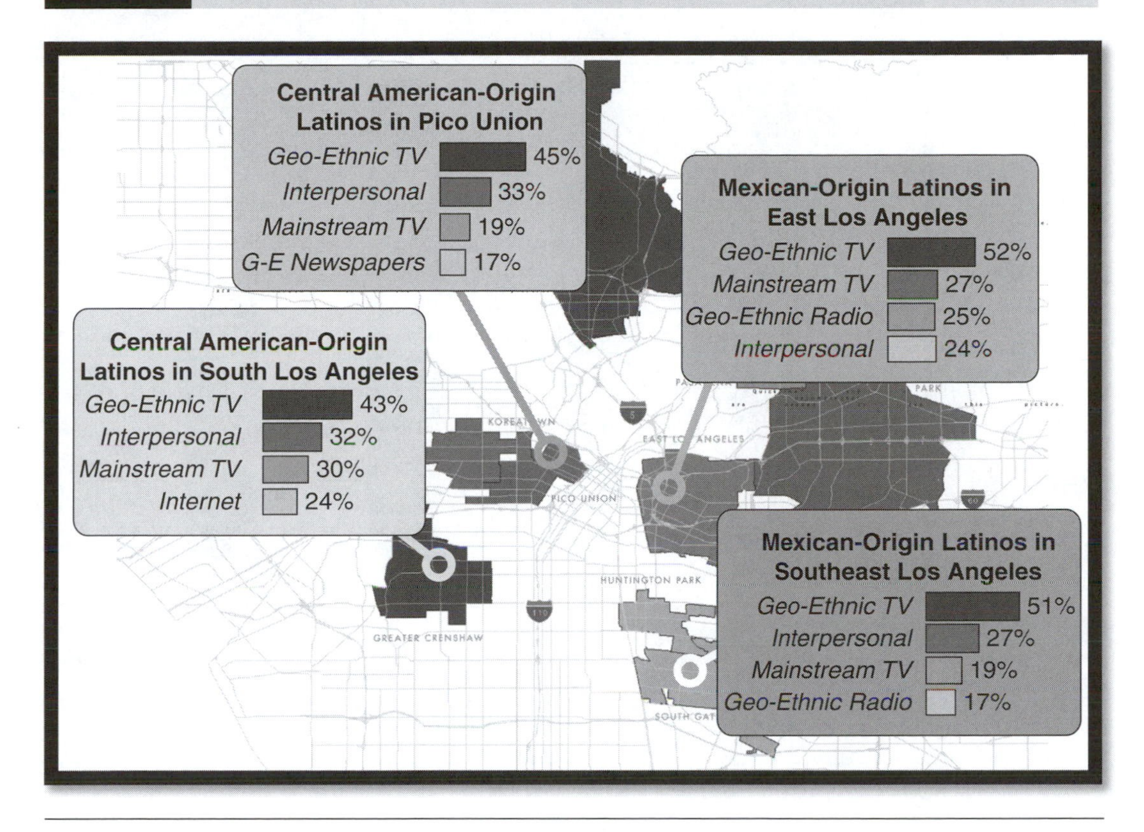

Source: Metamorphosis Project: http://www.metamorph.org

that ethnic media can remain important and viable well beyond the immigrant generation (Lin & Song, 2006; Wilkin & Ball-Rokeach, 2006).

Some may be surprised to see that within these five Latino communities, only South Los Angeles residents report that the Internet is one of their most important sources of community information (see Figure 9.3). Among low-income adults, Internet penetration remains low, and Latino residents in Pico Union and Southeast Los Angeles, the majority of whom live below the poverty line, report Internet connection rates of 22% and 24%, respectively. By contrast, 70% of Glendale's primarily middle-class Latino residents report connecting to the Internet, and among South Los Angeles' first and second generation Latino residents, Internet connection rates are 55% (Ball-Rokeach & Wilkin, 2009).

There are clear differences between ethnic minority and immigrant communities' Internet connection rates at the local community level. At the national level, Internet connection rates in immigrant and ethnic minority households in the U.S. lag behind White households; 78% of White school-age children have a computer at home, compared with 48% of Latino and 46% of African-American students (DeBell & Chapman, 2006, p. 25). DeBell and Chapman highlight income and education level as two key factors affecting Internet connection rates. These national-level findings

Figure 9.3 Internet Connection Rates in Different Latino Neighborhoods in Los Angeles

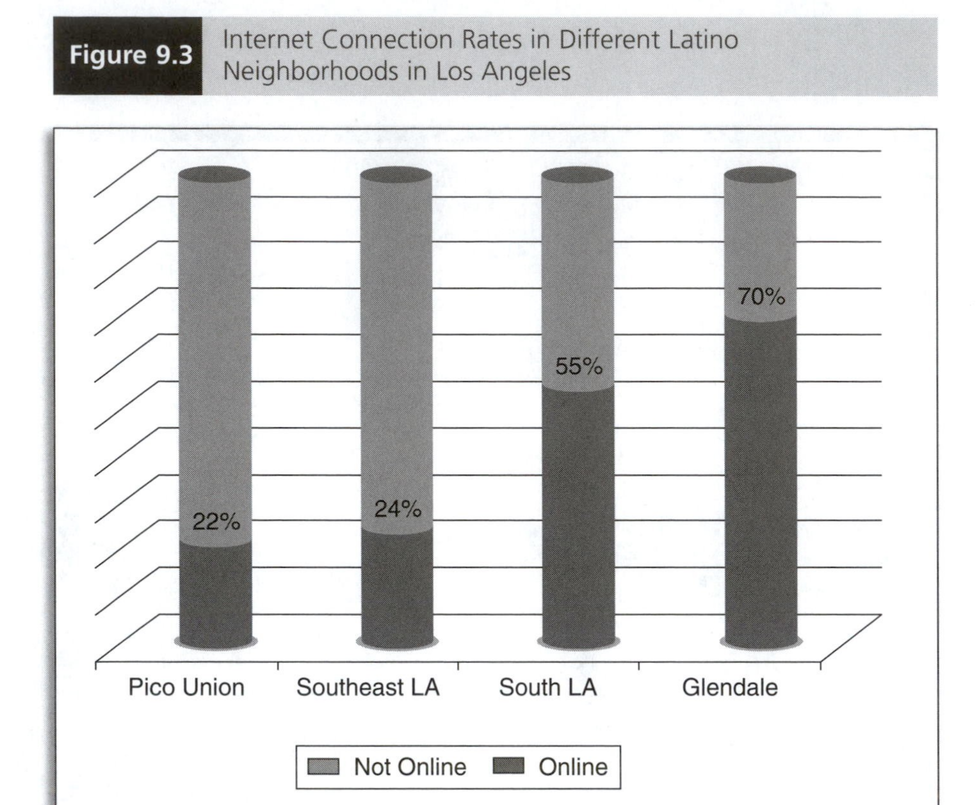

Source: Metamorphosis Project: http://www.metamorph.org

mirror our local-level findings in Los Angeles. Both suggest that the Internet may not be the most effective way for community organizations and geo-ethnic media outlets to reach out to residents in low-income communities, since the Internet is not likely to be a meaningful part of residents' communication ecologies—at least, not at this time (Ball-Rokeach & Wilkin, 2009).

Finally, Figure 9.2 again highlights the importance of interpersonal communication in all five of these Latino communities. In traditional communication research, interpersonal communication is studied separately from media connections. With an ecological approach, interpersonal and media connections are seen as potentially interwoven. Therefore, media may prompt interpersonal discussions among residents about the community, which may in turn influence how geo-ethnic media cover the community to be responsive to the needs and concerns of the residents they serve.

Ecological Approaches as a Departure From Traditional Media Measures

An ecological approach is a departure from traditional ways of understanding people's media connections. Traditionally, media connections have been measured by asking time-related questions, such as, "How much time do you spend watching television on an average day?" These sorts of questions are useful for certain types of research, but they do not help to explain what goals people may be satisfying by watching television for that period of time. That time may be purely for entertainment, but as Figures 9.1 and 9.2 clearly indicate, many residents also consider television an important source of community information. An ecological approach is a consumer-centered approach to understanding media connections, instead of being centered on the media themselves (Wilkin & Ball-Rokeach, 2006).

In essence, we all construct our own communication ecologies to achieve our everyday goals (Ball-Rokeach, Kim, & Matei, 2001). These goals may include finding a local clinic, a grocery store that stocks quality fruits and vegetables, or a safe place for children to play. An ecological approach makes it possible to differentiate between the communication ecologies people may construct for different goals. For example, residents may construct different communication ecologies for finding out what is going on in their communities than they do for connecting with health information.

¤ For Further Discussion

Think about your own communication ecologies, and compare them with your classmates. What are the connections you make when you want to:

- Find out what is going on at your university or in the city where you live?
- Find information about a health condition or illness?
- Relax and be entertained?
- Do your connections differ depending on the goal you are trying to achieve? How are your communication ecologies different from those of your classmates?

An ecological orientation is a useful tool for policymakers and community stakeholders, including the geo-ethnic media, in designing strategies to reach residents of local communities. An ecological approach considers residents as actively seeking and negotiating information about the world around them. These activities can result in the convergence of local stories from various media and interpersonal sources into messages that encourage changes in behaviors or attitudes. It is an approach grounded in the lived experiences of residents in their local communities.

The local focus of an ecological approach takes into account the communicative options residents have for finding out about their local community, and can also help researchers identify communicative options that are *not* available within a community. For example, some communities simply do not have the wide range of geo-ethnic media that other communities have. However, even in communities that have relatively rich communication ecologies, some residents may not be able to access all the options available in their neighborhoods, perhaps due to linguistic or literacy constraints. Immigrants who cannot access the English-language local media in their community have narrower communication ecologies than immigrants who are bilingual. Likewise, residents who do not have access to computers, or lack the new media literacy required to surf the Internet, will be constrained in their ability to access community resources available online. Finally, immigrants who have limited traditional literacy[2] even in their own language may not be able to access written materials like geo-ethnic newspapers without assistance.

Residents with these constraints may adopt alternative strategies to achieve their goals. One possibility would be depending more heavily on geo-ethnic radio, which does not require literacy (Browne, 2008) or connecting with local organizations to find out about community happenings. Community organizations and institutions can be important alternatives to, or partners with, geo-ethnic media.

Ethnic Media and Other Community Institutions

Residents in many communities belong to local organizations, such as soccer leagues, church groups, and political associations. These organizations can be important places for residents to come together and share community news and help to solve common problems. Community organizations often help residents to invest in and integrate into their local community through activities and events that help promote the feelings and behaviors that express *community belonging*. These organizations can also encourage a sense of *collective efficacy* (Kim & Ball-Rokeach, 2006a & 2006b; Sampson, Morenoff, & Gannon-Rowley, 2002), which refers to residents' confidence that they and their neighbors could come together to solve shared problems in the community.

Geo-ethnic media and community organizations are important links between residents and the larger local community. Community organizations provide a way for residents to come together as part of a shared community, and geo-ethnic media are well positioned to provide residents with news and information that reflect their needs and interests. The line between media producer and resident may be nonexistent in the case of geo-ethnic media, since journalists and editors are often residents of the communities they serve. This embedded position means that they can understand and cover issues of interest to their readers by knowing intimately the needs of residents and the community itself. Mainstream media and ethnic media outlets that serve more dispersed communities often do not have the local knowledge bases or staff to cover local issues as completely as geo-ethnic media can (Ball-Rokeach, Kim, & Matei, 2001; Lin & Song, 2006).

Residents may also have the opportunity to be involved in the production of geo-ethnic media in ways that would not be possible in larger and/or mainstream media outlets. Browne's (2005) study of electronic ethnic media found that residents are frequent participants in local ethnic media production. Interviews with ethnic media staffers revealed three main goals for encouraging residents' involvement in the production of electronic geo-ethnic media: First, residents who participate in media production often experience increased self-confidence and learn new paths to collective efficacy. Second, residents feel real ownership of their media when they see and hear their friends and neighbors as part of the community stories being told. Finally, these resident participants are more likely to become better informed and more skilled critics of media content in general, which arms them with skills to decode media messages more effectively (Browne, 2005, p. 120).

Browne's (2005) findings reinforce many of the ideas we have discussed in this chapter, as blurring the lines between media "producers" and "consumers" may mean more convergence between geo-ethnic media content and resident's conversations about neighborhood events and news. Convergence within residents' communication ecologies has the potential to encourage residents to mobilize around community issues of common concern and to advocate for local improvements.

In Metamorphosis Project research, we have found in some communities that residents, local media, and community organizations are better connected to each other than in other communities. In these more connected communities, geo-ethnic media are well-connected to community organizations and publicize their events and community activities, and those organizations let local media producers know when they have material for media stories that will interest and serve local residents. When geo-ethnic media outlets and community organizations enjoy this kind of mutually beneficial relationship, and both the geo-ethnic media and community organizations are well-connected to the local residents, who discuss and share local news with each other, then residents, geo-ethnic media, and community organizations are involved in "storytelling" the neighborhood. When residents, community organizations, and geo-ethnic media share news and communication resources about life in the local community, they are part of a strong *neighborhood storytelling network,* as seen in Figure 9.4.

In a strong neighborhood storytelling network, residents, geo-ethnic media, and community organizations are well-connected to each other, mutually influencing each others' understandings of what life is like in the community (Ball-Rokeach et al., 2001; Kim & Ball-Rokeach, 2006a & 2006b). Residents negotiate their sense of the community through conversations with other residents and through meaningful interactions with geo-ethnic media and community organizations. We describe this construction of community as a *process* to highlight that storytelling the local

Figure 9.4 Residents, Geo-Ethnic Media and Community Organizations as a Well-Connected Neighborhood Storytelling Network

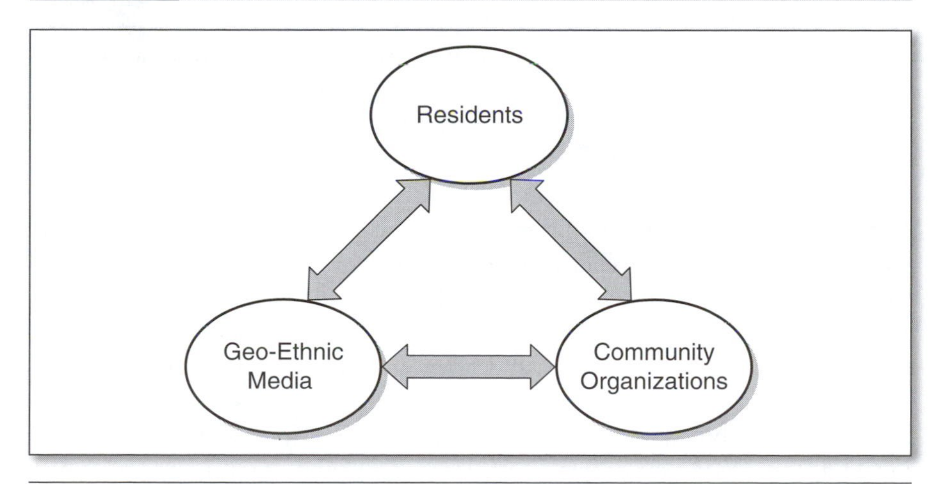

Source: Metamorphosis Project: http://www.metamorph.org

community is something that is ongoing, rather than having a fixed endpoint. And this process is *dynamic* in that all parts of the storytelling network—residents in their interpersonal networks, the geo-ethnic media, and the community organizations—are all active participants in the shared process of constructing community.

In our research in Los Angeles, we have found that the dynamic process of constructing community has important outcomes for residents. Residents in communities with strong storytelling networks report more feelings and behaviors of neighborhood belonging, higher collective efficacy, and more political participation (Ball-Rokeach, Kim, & Matei, 2001; Kim & Ball-Rokeach, 2006a & 2006b). We have also found that residents connected to a strong storytelling network find it easier to get health care when they need it (Katz, 2007; Katz, Wilkin, & Hether, 2010; Matsaganis, 2008). In sum, a strong neighborhood storytelling network facilitates residents' efforts to construct communication ecologies that can help them to achieve their goals. A strong neighborhood storytelling network can help residents achieve collective goals by encouraging them to mobilize and collectively address community challenges. In the following sections we overview research on geo-ethnic media's roles in promoting civic engagement and community health in different parts of the world. We focus on these two areas since existing research on geo-ethnic media has concentrated almost exclusively on these particular social challenges.

Geo-Ethnic Media and Civic Engagement

Residents' connections within their neighborhood storytelling networks can encourage their involvement in local activities that develop their sense of belonging to the local community, their sense of collective efficacy, and encourage their participation in political processes at local and larger levels (Kim & Ball-Rokeach, 2006b). These kinds of civic engagement activities, such as cleaning up a local park or volunteering at a school, help residents to integrate into their communities by investing their time and energy into making their neighborhoods better places for themselves and their neighbors to live. Geo-ethnic media can play crucial roles in encouraging residents' civic engagement activities, ranging from lobbying for local improvements in goods, services, and/or policies, as well as political demonstrations to support social changes in the host country or in a country of origin.

In remote areas where community organizations may be scarce or nonexistent, geo-ethnic media can help galvanize the community to achieve the most basic of life-sustaining objectives. For example, Tacanun is a remote language minority community in Mindanao, Philippines (Community Radio Impact Evaluation, 2007). In 1992, Tacanun was one of approximately 20 sites selected by the Food and Agriculture Organization (FAO) and UNICEF to fund the development of a community radio tower, providing a way for the community to broadcast its own news, prompt discussion of local issues, and lobby local governments for community improvements.

These funds brought residents representing all sectors of the community, including farmers, elderly people, youth, women, religious leaders, and health care workers, together in a community radio production and broadcasting training program. These voluntary broadcasters would meet every second Thursday to discuss relevant community issues and prepare programming to air at scheduled times (Dagron, 2001). Their discussions in these meetings and on the air included local issues such as health and nutrition, childrearing, education, religion, politics, and social events of central concern to the community.

The radio broadcasts encouraged discussions among residents and radio presenters that led to residents making formal demands to the district for improvements in local living conditions. In 1993, one year after the establishment of the radio tower, Tacanun received running water for the first time, and in 1994, electricity. In subsequent years, the community lobbied for and received financial support for local agricultural and economic development programs, like a 3,000 hectare tilapia hatchery (Dagron, 2001). Although Tacanun did not have community organizations, close ties between the geo-ethnic media and the residents still managed to produce lasting community change.

Geo-ethnic media play important connective roles by storytelling local news and events to stimulate conversation and activity among residents and within community organizations. At the same time, geo-ethnic media can report on regional, national, or international news and discuss how those issues will affect the local community. For example, the tsunami in December 2004 that devastated large swaths of Southeast Asia was heavily covered by geo-ethnic media serving communities with ties to the affected nations. That geo-ethnic media coverage helped residents find ways to donate time, money, and supplies locally that community organizations then helped transport to the hardest hit areas. Overall, Asian-American communities in California alone donate $200 million to relief efforts (Gonzaga, 2005), and although there are no formal estimates of the hours of volunteer work, the amount of money and goods that were donated speaks to the levels of community response to the disaster. Through geo-ethnic storytelling, an international event became local news and provided people with courses of local action that could strengthen ties to neighbors equally committed to helping tsunami victims in their countries of origin.

Geo-ethnic media can also be key to mobilizing the community when natural disasters strike locally. In a study of disaster preparedness in urban immigrant communities in Los Angeles (Mathew & Kelly, 2008), the authors found that the City of Los Angeles was not providing disaster preparedness information resources in accessible languages, and was therefore not prepared to provide non-English speaking communities with information they would need immediately following a disaster such as an earthquake or wildfire.

However, at local levels, Chinese, Spanish, and Vietnamese-speaking focus group participants all indicated that geo-ethnic radio is the first place they turn for information in an emergency (Mathew & Kelly, 2008, p. 7). Residents indicated that they receive information on preparing for an emergency from their geo-ethnic media connections, particularly radio and television, as well as through community organizations and the local schools. In these ways, residents' communication ecologies enable their connections to emergency preparedness information even though the city's materials may not have been made linguistically accessible to them. Mathew and Kelly (2008) concluded that the City of Los

Angeles needs to pursue meaningful partnerships with these geo-ethnic radio stations to provide their listeners with information quickly in the aftermath of a disaster, and help them to mobilize accordingly.

When geo-ethnic media engage in geo-ethnic storytelling, they can promote civic activities in the local community and help to localize international events for residents, as Southeast Asian geo-ethnic media did after the 2004 tsunami. Geo-ethnic media can also localize national-level events and policies for residents, and galvanize community action.

For example, in 2006, the U.S. Congress debated the Sensenbrenner Bill (H.R. 4437). The bill included provisions to allow local law enforcement to hand over undocumented immigrants to Immigration and Customs Enforcement (ICE), to fund the construction of a 350-mile fence along the U.S.-Mexico border, and to make it a felony to assist undocumented immigrants in the United States. While Congress was discussing the measure, Spanish-language media around the country were devoting a great deal of attention to the proposed law and how it might affect their local communities.

Geo-ethnic radio was particularly important in providing in-depth coverage of the Sensenbrenner Bill, which prompted discussion among community organizations and residents about the local impacts of the proposed national immigration policy. Many Latinos have strong connections to geo-ethnic radio. Those employed in service industries, for example, can listen to the radio throughout their commute and workday (Baum, 2006) and then discuss what they hear with their co-workers (Félix, González & Ramírez, 2008). The interplay between media connections and interpersonal conversations in these residents' communication ecologies was a very important part of prompting civic engagement in their local communities.

Eduardo Sotelo (nicknamed *el Piolín,* or Tweety Bird) and Almendárez Coello (nicknamed *El Cucuy,* or Boogeyman) are disk jockeys from competing Los Angeles radio stations who came together in an unprecedented partnership over the immigration reform issue. Both disk jockeys became part of the March 25 Coalition in 2006, so named because its goal was to organize a peaceful demonstration on that day in downtown Los Angeles. They encouraged participation by building on their well-established relationships with their listeners and by discussing their own immigration stories (Coello is from Honduras; Sotelo came to the U.S. from Mexico as an undocumented immigrant before regularizing his status). Their community-based appeals prompted resident discussions and decisions to participate in the local rallies (González, 2007). On March 25, 2006, approximately 500,000 people peacefully demonstrated against the immigration law change in Los Angeles, and on May 1, 2006, approximately 1 million took to the streets again in the largest public demonstration in the city's history (Ferre et al., 2006).

Around the country, similar demonstrations took place in at least 102 cities in April and May, drawing in a diverse group of supporters that included immigrants from all over the world, members of ethnic minority groups, and others sympathetic to the rallies' message (Ferre et al., 2006). For example, geo-ethnic media targeting Muslim-Americans encouraged their audiences throughout the U.S. to join local rallies both out of concerns related to more stringent immigration laws, but also because participation was seen as supporting the tenets of the Islamic tradition

(Muslim Public Affairs Council, 2006). The massive mobilizations were discussed as a national event, but in large part it was local partnerships between geo-ethnic media and community political organizations that engaged residents in local demonstrations advocating national change (Félix et al., 2008).

Geo-ethnic media can also be a vehicle for immigrants' local activities in support of homeland politics. For example, the Uyghur people (also commonly spelled Uighur) are a Turkic minority group who live in Eastern China. They are a distinct cultural group that is one of the oldest and most enduring in Central Asia, with a large diaspora throughout the Middle East, Europe, and North America. China's support of the U.S. war on terror since 9/11 has resulted in the Uyghur community being targeted by the Chinese government for increased surveillance, and some of their religious sites have been destroyed (Kaltman, 2007). Increasingly, the Internet has provided Uyghur emigrants (numbering approximately 500,000 worldwide [Gladney, 2005]) with online, localized platforms to protest the political position of their people within China in ways that Uyghurs still living within China are not able to do.

These online ethnic media platforms support at least 25 community-level and international organizations advocating for the independence of "Eastern Turkestan" (Gladney, 2005), and also provide message boards (Kanat, 2005) to plan local meetings and protests against Chinese government actions in the communities where Uyghur populations have settled abroad. For Uyghur communities, online geo-ethnic media are part of strong neighborhood storytelling networks, along with community members who post and discuss issues on their sites and the organizations that support independence of the homeland. That these geo-ethnic media are online encourages not only local civic activity but also an international imagined community (Anderson, 1991) between Uyghur communities living in different localities (Kanat, 2005).

Civically engaged residents participate in the sorts of political and social mobilizations profiled here and can also channel their collective efforts to address other important social concerns. Of the many social justice issues that immigrant, ethnic minority, and indigenous communities may face together, the links between geo-ethnic media and community health have received the most research attention.

Geo-Ethnic Media and Community Health

The term *community health* goes beyond focusing on individual residents' health status to also include concerns about how the community environment can affect residents' capacities to make healthy lifestyle choices. For example, a community that has safe parks and well-controlled traffic means that children and parents have places to play and exercise outside. These local opportunities for exercise, if utilized by residents, can help reduce the incidence of obesity and of chronic conditions related to obesity, such as diabetes, hypertension, and heart disease, among residents.

Community health is closely interwoven with civic engagement, since residents can mobilize to improve the safety and quality of their parks and streets, and these improvements can in turn have positive impact on community health. Whether the issue is having safe areas to exercise or helping residents learn about and access health care facilities in their area, a strong storytelling network is an important part of improving community health. Residents share health information among themselves, and community organizations can be important resources in residents' health communication ecologies.

The geo-ethnic media are also uniquely positioned to positively affect the health and well-being of local residents because they can tailor health messages to the concerns of the communities that they serve (Wilkin & Ball-Rokeach, 2006). Residents in every community—whether immigrant, ethnic minority, indigenous, or part of the mainstream of a society—face health challenges that are particular to their local environment. Some diseases are of particular concern to community residents because their ethnic community is at higher risk for those conditions. The reasons for higher risk may be genetic, or may be due to environmental factors. Whether the main health risks for an ethnic community are genetic or environmental in nature, ethnic media have the potential to positively impact the health of the communities they serve.

Ethnic media's focus on a particular ethnic group means that they can cover health-related stories on the risk factors, detection, and treatment of diseases for which their audiences are at increased risk. Residents often depend heavily on this kind of coverage. For example, Chinese and Southeast Asian-origin communities have the highest rates of Hepatitis B in Canada (Mock et al., 2007). Cheung et al.'s (2005) study of Chinese and Southeast Asian residents in Canada's Richmond, British Columbia, community found that 92% of residents felt that Hepatitis B was a concern. Fifty-six percent of respondents cited their doctor's office as a primary source of information on Hepatitis B, followed by 49% who cited the geo-ethnic media as their source of community health information. This suggests that health advocates can benefit from including geo-ethnic media in their campaigns and interventions, as residents are already connecting with these media for trusted health information.

Geo-ethnic media may not only cover more of the health content that is particularly important to local residents; researchers suggest these media are also likely to cover health issues in culturally sensitive ways. Friedman and Hoffman-Goetz (2006) found this to be the case in their analyses of cancer information conveyed in Canadian ethnic media targeting Black/Caribbean, East Indian, Jewish and First Nation communities.

By engaging in geo-ethnic storytelling, geo-ethnic media can go beyond providing information about health conditions to addressing the many other factors that can relate to poor health, particularly in low-income communities. In many cases, health disparities are closely tied to socioeconomic conditions, such as lack of health care coverage, financial resources, and a regular place for health care. Because geo-ethnic media are embedded within the local areas they serve, they can cover local health fairs and events where residents can access health care resources, such as preventative screenings. They can be the venue to announce the opening of a new clinic, a locally available health insurance program, and community organizations' health-related activities. In these ways, geo-ethnic media can address locally specific health issues—and this coverage can prompt residents' conversations about these issues and encourage them to utilize available resources.

The communication ecologies that residents construct for health information are different from those they construct for community information. In Figures 9.1 and 9.2, we assessed the ethnic and geographic differences between residents' communication ecologies for finding out what is going on in their community. Figure 9.5 presents the connections that Latino and African-American residents make to get health information in their South Los Angeles community. Interpersonal communication with friends and family is an important way that residents find out about health for both Latino and African-American residents. Health care providers are also an important resource, as is the Internet. For Latinos, geo-ethnic television is an important health resource, whereas African-American residents report frequent connections to books and magazines.

These findings support the conclusions of other studies suggesting that the combination of interpersonal communication and geo-ethnic media can have a greater impact on the health knowledge of their audiences than geo-ethnic media content

Figure 9.5 Different Communication Ecologies for Health Information Within a South Los Angeles Community

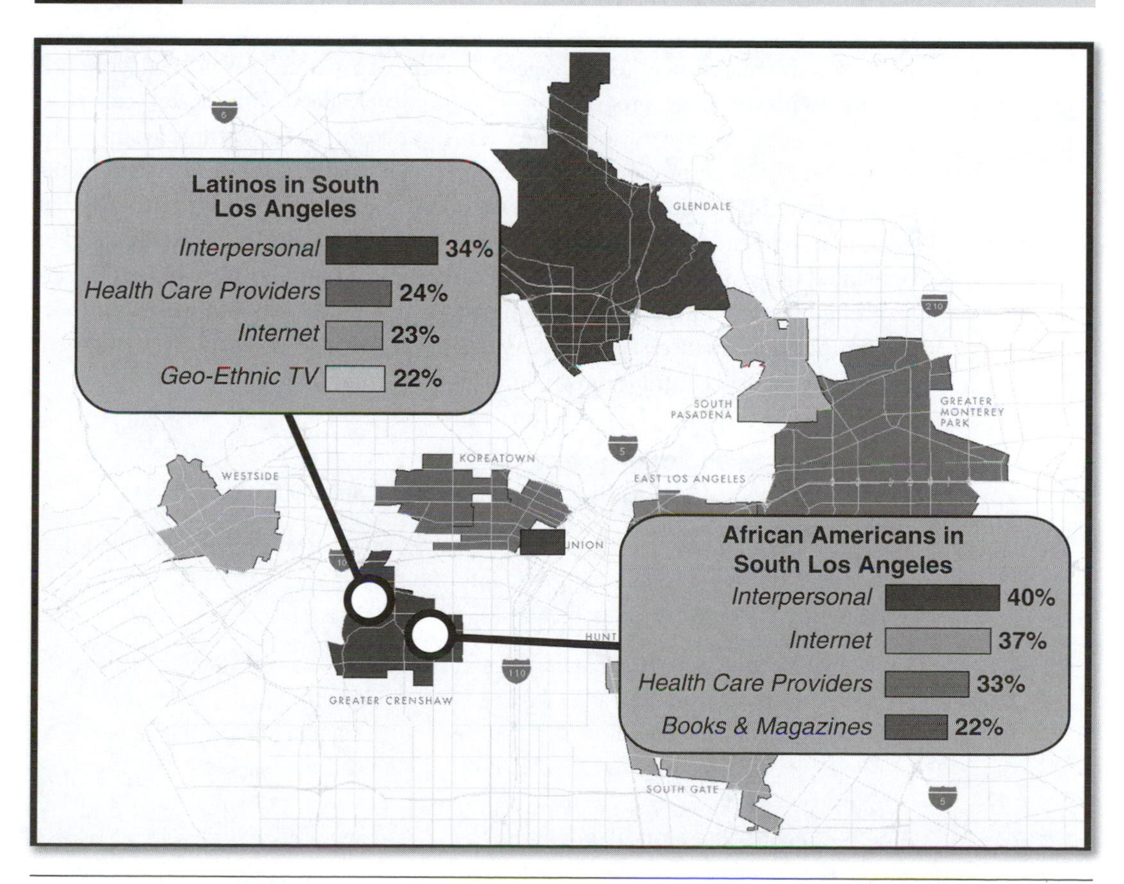

Source: Metamorphosis Project: http://www.metamorph.org

alone. When media health stories provoke residents to talk with each other about the health issue, the media story is likely to be re-constructed into shared health knowledge among residents.

For example, Vietnamese-American women have the highest rates of cervical cancer of any racial/ethnic group in the United States (Jenkins et al, 1999). An intervention project in the San Francisco Bay Area employed a media-based education campaign in local ethnic television, radio, and newspapers (Mock et al., 2007). The whole community had access to the media campaign, but only half of the community received interpersonal contact by health outreach workers as well.

Vietnamese women in both the media campaign-only group and in the media/outreach worker group were significantly more likely to have cervical cancer screenings (Pap tests) after the intervention than before. However, the effect was larger among women who had access to both geo-ethnic media coverage and interpersonal contact with health workers. This finding again highlights the potential power of convergence between media and interpersonal connections; when media messages are part of a larger communication ecology, they are more effective in changing residents' health behaviors.

Other researchers also point to geo-ethnic media messages having a stronger impact on community health when these messages converge with interpersonal connections in residents' communication ecologies. In a health intervention in a Korean-origin community, Han, Kang, Kim, Ryu, & Kin (2007) found that their most effective recruitment tool was geo-ethnic newspaper articles printed alongside endorsements of their program by community leaders with health expertise. Korean-Americans have the lowest health insurance rates of any ethnic group in the U.S. since they are disproportionately self-employed and cannot afford health insurance premiums (Kandula, Kersey, & Lurie, 2004). Lacking health insurance coverage leads to infrequent doctors' visits and higher rates of health conditions that could be prevented or managed by regular health care. For community stakeholders, understanding how geo-ethnic media content can be deployed in conjunction with other communication resources, such as community leader endorsements, can augment geo-ethnic media's contributions to improved community health.[3]

¤ For Further Discussion

The findings reported in the preceding section point to ways that convergence between geo-ethnic media and residents' interpersonal conversations can help to promote a healthier community.

- How can geo-ethnic media content help to promote conversations among residents that could lead to changes in people's health attitudes and behaviors?
- Research an ethnic community of your choosing and identify a health condition that is a central issue in that community. Describe specific ways that geo-ethnic media content could help promote residents' discussions around that particular disease.

However, the fact that geo-ethnic media have the *potential* to positively affect community health does not mean that this potential is always realized. Wilkin and González (2006) conducted a content analysis of Spanish-language television to assess the frequency and quality of health information targeted to Latinos living in Los Angeles. Los Angeles is the largest Spanish-language television market in the United States, accounting for approximately 16% of all Latino households nationwide (Nielson, 2005). The authors found that although Latinos living in Los Angeles report depending heavily on geo-ethnic television for health information, television content seldom addressed health concerns. Moreover, only 4% of health-related stories connected residents with local health resources, such as a hotline or local clinic providing particular services.

Due to the high costs of television production, a high proportion of geo-ethnic television programming is prepared for national audiences and produced primarily in Miami and New York studios (Wilkin & González, 2006). Therefore, when health information containing local contact information was broadcast, the information was almost always specific to Miami or New York, which is not as helpful to Latinos living in other parts of the country. These findings highlight some of the challenges that geo-ethnic media face in fulfilling their potential as health storytellers. The next section details these difficulties in more detail.

Geo-Ethnic Media Challenges

Although the research on geo-ethnic media is scant, this chapter demonstrates the importance of these often understudied or overlooked local productions for the health and well-being of an ethnic community. Geo-ethnic media, viewed as part of a local communication ecology, can be key players in prompting residents to improve their local conditions. For these reasons, future research would be well advised to consider these low-budget, small geo-ethnic outlets that, more often than not, are left out of research conducted within immigrant, ethnic minority, and indigenous communities.

This chapter has detailed the ways that geo-ethnic media outlets have the potential to prompt community-level mobilizations and improvements. However, there are a number of reasons why geo-ethnic stories may not be featured in these media as frequently or prominently as they might. For example, Lin and associates conducted a content analysis of Spanish, Korean and Chinese-language media available in four Los Angeles ethnic communities. They found that of all the print media available in these communities (ranging from geo-ethnic to international editions of newspapers from the country of origin), only 15% of Spanish-language stories, 13% of Korean-language stories, and 3% of Chinese-language stories, had a local, geo-ethnic focus (Lin & Song, 2006; Lin, Song & Mercado, 2004).

Lin and associates (2004) also found that the residents of communities with the least geo-ethnic news stories also ranked news about their home country as most important. Residents in the Chinese-origin community, which had the lowest level of geo-ethnic content in their local media, ranked home country news as most important, and also reported the lowest levels of belonging to their local community in Los Angeles. Korean-origin residents reported slightly higher levels of community belonging, and Central American-origin residents, who had the highest levels of geo-ethnic media content, reported the highest levels of belonging to their current community. These findings prompted Lin et al. to conclude that, "Ethnic media's democratic role in the host country may be jeopardized if they are too preoccupied with home country coverage at the expense of local news" (Lin et al., 2004).

The future challenge, therefore, is for geo-ethnic media producers to engage in geo-ethnic storytelling about the local community in order to effectively address the local needs and concerns of the residents that they serve. This may be difficult for a number of reasons, including financial constraints, small staffs, and limited professional training. The following chapter covers these and other professional challenges for ethnic media journalists.

Summary

This chapter focused on ethnic media that serve residents of geographically limited communities, and the special functions that these geo-ethnically focused local media can serve. The initial sections of the chapter discuss geo-ethnic media as part of residents' communication ecologies, and how residents' communication ecologies differ according to the goal they are trying to satisfy. The second half of the chapter surveyed the available data on civic engagement and community health campaigns that have been encouraged by geo-ethnic media outlets, working closely with community residents and community organizations within communities in different parts of the world. The following chapter turns the focus to the journalists who own, produce, and work within ethnic media outlets to explore the challenges and opportunities of working within these media.

Study Questions

1. Consider the data presented in Figures 9.1, 9.2, and 9.5. Does a goals-focused approach to understanding media connections explain more than a time-focused approach (eg., "How much time did you spend watching television yesterday")? Why or why not?

2. This chapter discussed how geo-ethnic media can work with community organizations and residents as part of a neighborhood storytelling network to improve community health and encourage civic engagement. How might geo-ethnic media contribute to local improvements that have not been the focus of extensive research, such as educational equity? Be specific in describing how geo-ethnic media's roles may be different or similar with regard to educational issues, compared with the functions these media serve for health and civic engagement activities.

3. Geo-ethnic media can encourage civic engagement for local, national, and international causes, as discussed under heading, "Geo-Ethnic Media and Civic Engagement." How do you think geo-ethnic media journalists' strategies for encouraging community mobilization might differ depending on whether the event they are covering is local, national, or international in scope?

4. The section headed "Geo-Ethnic Media and Community Health" discusses the potential of geo-ethnic media for community health interventions, as well as research that suggests these media may not always live up to this potential. What strategies could geo-ethnic media develop to better cover health issues for their communities, within their financial, personnel, and other constraints?

5. Return to the section headed "Geo-Ethnic Media Challenges" and reexamine the percentages of Spanish, Chinese, and Korean-language news content that are geo-ethnic in focus. Imagine yourself as a journalist in a geo-ethnic news organization. What challenges can you imagine you would face in producing truly geo-ethnic content?

Notes

[1]Marshall McLuhan (1964; 1994; 2005) is credited as the first scholar to coin the term "media ecology," which called for research that considered people's media connections in context of each other. Our work on "communication ecology" expands McLuhan's original formation of media ecology to include interpersonal and organizational communication as well.

[2]Within Los Angeles County, for example, approximately 1 in 10 immigrants from Central America are not able to read or write in any language (U.S. Census, 2000).

[3]In a separate study, Viswanath, Steele, and Finnegan (2006) found that membership in community organizations was related to residents' ability to recall health messages in their local (although not necessarily geo-ethnic) media, which again highlights the advantages of deploying multiple communication resources to reinforce the same health-related messages.

CHAPTER 10

Professional Challenges for Ethnic Media Journalists

CHAPTER OBJECTIVES

By the end of this chapter, you will have learned more about:

- Who the ethnic media journalists are and how their work differs from that of their colleagues in mainstream media.
- The challenges and hurdles ethnic media journalists face in doing their jobs.
- What it means to be a professional journalist and how professionalization impacts ethnic media.
- New models of collaboration between ethnic and mainstream media and why they matter.
- The role of professional journalism education in the future of ethnic media.

The Ethnic Media Journalist in the 21st Century

In the study of ethnic media, as is the case with media studies more generally, the focus is commonly on audiences, media organizations, economics, policies, or stories. We tend to spend less time talking about the storytellers—the journalists who produce the stories ethnic media publish and broadcast. These are the people we will talk more about in this chapter: Who are they? What challenges do they face? How do their working environs differ from working in mainstream media?

Ethnic media journalists are frequently viewed by mainstream media, politicians, state authorities and agencies as being less "professional." We investigate this "allegation" here. As being a professional journalist is often associated with being "objective," we investigate what being objective means especially for ethnic media journalists and how professionalization impacts the relationship that these journalists develop with the ethnic communities they cover and serve.

Subsequently we explore new modes of ethnic and mainstream media collaboration and how they impact the sustainability of ethnic media organizations. Then, we discuss the progressively more pressing issue of what the future of ethnic media looks like, particularly compared to that of the mainstream media. We conclude with a discussion of the challenges journalism schools are confronted with in light of increasing population diversity and the growth of the ethnic media sector.

In addressing these issues, we rely upon the work of other scholars, as well as the experience of the senior author who worked as an ethnic media journalist in New York City, and our joint research on ethnic media and ethnic communities particularly in Los Angeles. In addition, we draw on panel discussions with ethnic media professionals, which we convened in collaboration with New America Media (Matsaganis, Katz, Ball-Rokeach, & Do, 2007, 2008).[1]

Who Are the Ethnic Media Journalists, Editors, and Staff?

The overwhelming majority of ethnic media are relatively small organizations, few of which operate as profit-making enterprises (e.g., Riggins, 1992). As such, most ethnic media rely heavily on the work of volunteers and low-paid staff who are willing to put in long hours (Browne, 2005, p. 182) to gather information and produce stories. In the newsrooms of these organizations, we find people with a great variety of backgrounds and motivations. Some have been educated and trained as journalists and see working for an ethnically targeted medium as a stepping stone to a career in mainstream media. Others have left a career in mainstream media due to personal or family reasons, or because they felt they could help address a community need. The story of Erkan Arikan is illustrative. She became editor-in-chief of the Turkish service for an ambitious multicultural program broadcast by the German public radio station WDR. She says:

> I was the first Turkish journalist to present the television news in Germany. Then I left to work at WDR . . . In Germany there are five million people from different ethnic backgrounds and nearly three million are Turks. They need to be represented. . . . (Mediam'Rad, 2006, p. 3)

Some people manage to do both: to work for a larger, mainstream outlet and contribute to an ethnic newspaper or broadcast program. This choice may reflect a personal need for multiple venues for self-expression, or it may reflect a deep commitment to an ethnic community (Mediam'Rad, 2006). In few cases, individuals are employed as foreign correspondents by media back in a "home" country, but also offer their services to an ethnic media organization in the "host" country. This may be due to a desire to play an active and visible role in the ethnic community, both "here" and "there," or it could be a result of simply getting to know local ethnic media producers. In the local ethnic media context, such "foreign correspondents" usually serve as editorial consultants, staff writers, or special correspondents.

It is also not uncommon for ethnic media staff members to arrive in journalism after spending a number of years walking a different career path. For example, some people follow their spouses who moved from the "home" country to take a job abroad (e.g., in the diplomatic core). These people find that they can put their linguistic and cultural skills to work for the ethnic community. Others were consumers of a newspaper, magazine, or radio station that served their community and felt that they had something to contribute (e.g., as a reporter, a commentator, a producer, or a disc jockey). Such people are often willing to work as volunteers.

Among the people who make up ethnic media newsrooms, some are older immigrants who were not able, found it difficult, or were unwilling to acquire the skills and know-how to venture out to the broader job market; they feel comfortable in their community and feel that they have found the way to make a living and, perhaps, a difference in the lives of those around them. This is particularly true in areas where the community is large enough to sustain an *ethnic enclave economy* (Light, Sabagh, Bozorgmehr, Der-Martirosian, 1994; Portes, 1987; Sanders & Nee, 1987; Zhou & Logan, 1989); that is, a business sector, in which immigrants work as employees in businesses owned by co-ethnics or are entrepreneurs themselves (Bailey & Waldinger, 1991; Light et al., 1994).

Another source of human capital for ethnic media is university students in journalism or even other disciplines, who come from families with a particular ethnic background. These are often children of immigrants, but citizens who choose to take advantage of their language skills and in-depth understanding of their ethnic community to earn a living. Moreover, there are students from abroad who are working towards undergraduate and graduate degrees at local universities. As it is often the case, these students cannot work legally in the country where they are studying (or cannot work over a limited number of hours) because of their visa status. Some ethnic media owners may look the other way and offer these students a paid position, because they bring up-to-date knowledge of the "home" country that might be missing from the local community.

All of these unique backgrounds may be represented in a newsroom. This diversity can benefit ethnic media greatly, as it gives editors and program directors access to individuals who have a deep knowledge of the community's history, politics, challenges, and leadership. In addition, by employing students, ethnic media can stay in touch with the pulse of the younger generations in the community.

Journalists as Conduits to the Larger Community

Among a diverse staff, publishers and editors also have at their disposal people who can keep the newsroom open to what is happening outside the community (e.g., the debates the general population is engaged in, new trends in music and other art forms). Remaining open to the world beyond the ethnic community is important. Inwardly focused ethnic communities and media run the risk of becoming segregated and falling out of touch with larger issues debated in the cities and countries in which they live; debates, that is, that ultimately affect their lives and future. In our interviews and discussions with ethnic media producers in the United States, it appears that many ethnic media are susceptible to such *intellectual ghettoization* (Riggins, 1992). In an ethnically diverse region like Southern California, for example, it is surprising that there are very few stories about interethnic group relations in Latino, Asian, and African-American media. This is especially surprising in once ethnically homogenous areas that are in transition to a more mixed population. These are areas where intergroup tensions often occur. Issues pertaining to interethnic group relationships and conflict have been debated in California for many years and they affect everyone, irrespective of ethnic background. Ethnic media, however, tend to "glorify their own community," as Gabriel Martinez of Spanish-language newspaper *La Prensa* says. "We don't cover other communities and I am ashamed to say that. We have Anglo neighbors, African American, Korean, and we just don't; even though the laws that the city is going to implement are going to affect all of us" (Matsaganis et al., 2008).

Moreover, diversity in backgrounds frequently means diversity in skills available in the newsroom, too. Some staff members may have, for example, a formal education in journalism and know how to create rapport with community information sources and how to structure a news story. Others may have good interviewing skills or experience with digital sound and video editing. All these and other skills are necessary for developing quality programming that will appeal to a range of ethnic community members.

However, with diversity also come challenges. In bilingual newsrooms, for example, dealing with reporters with different levels of fluency in the language of the country of origin and the language spoken in the country where the media organization is based can be problematic. In assigning stories, for example, the editor may have to think about where the story is taking place, who the main sources of information will be, and how easy or difficult it will be to gain access to these sources. An interview with an older member of the community or a story about new immigrants may require fluency in the language of the country of origin; whereas, if the story involves city or other local authorities, fluency in the language of the majority population may be necessary.

Editors, regardless of whether they work for large or small media, mainstream or ethnic, also play a teaching role. In ethnic media, teaching writing skills is often one of the things editors are called upon to do, especially in newsrooms with varying levels of journalism experience. Despite certain commonalities among ethnic media production teams, however, no two ethnic media organizations are exactly the same. Each one develops a unique *organizational culture,* its own personality (Parker, 2000). Within every organization, things are done a certain way (Deal & Kennedy, 1982); goals are accomplished and problems are resolved through processes that are specific to that organization. Therefore, in some ethnic media, editors may play a more active role as teachers, whereas in others they do not.

Gloria Alvarez, editor of Eastern Group Publishing, a bilingual—Spanish and English-language—publication in Southern California, talks about the responsibility she feels towards young interns and staff members to teach them what it means to write a "balanced" story:

> Very young journalists and interns, both of them, do not understand the idea of balance because they are not challenged to listen to anyone or anything other than people who think the way they do . . . I would say it is really important that journalists are given the experience and understand that, for example, there are conservative Koreans and Hispanics, and there are liberal Koreans and Hispanics. (Matsaganis et al., 2007)

Some owners and editors will only hire individuals who meet certain professional qualifications. Of course, high standards can help organizations produce quality content. But ethnic media may also suffer negative consequences by imposing the kind of professional standards that may be more appropriate to mainstream media production. We will explore these issues in more detail, after we discuss the various challenges that ethnic media journalists face in getting their job done on a daily basis.

¤ For Further Discussion

Would you consider working full-time in an ethnic media organization? Why? Why not?

Challenges Ethnic Media Producers, Editors, and Reporters Face

Turnover among ethnic media staff is generally high, such that newsrooms are often dealing with "manpower" shortages (Murray, Yu, & Ahadi, 2007; Poon, 2007).[2] Volunteers may quit or cut back on their hours when the demands of their paying job increase. Low wages encourage some employees to seek other opportunities, even with better paying and competing ethnic media organizations. Student employees, interns, or volunteers graduate and go on to test the waters of the broader job market where their degrees translate into more money. Most owners and editors learn to live with the organizational instability caused by high turnover.

Attrition and "Poaching" From the Mainstream Media

As Paresh Solanki, executive director and producer at the BBC, explains: "Every two or three years, when a new talent emerges in the ethnic media, they are lost to the mass media. The ethnic media are often seen as stepping stones for young migrant journalists" (Mediam'Rad, 2006, p. 7). This "brain drain" or "poaching," however, is more likely to affect large-scale ethnic media organizations with the kind of visibility that allows their journalists to get noticed. It is also more likely to happen at ethnic media organizations that are part of either an ethnic media/mass media joint venture or a larger, multicultural public broadcasting service, as is the case in many European countries (we discuss these various forms of ethnic media in Chapter 6).

That it is rare for young ethnic media journalists to get approached by major mainstream media organizations and offered jobs only confirms the rule; that is, that many mainstream media organizations do not recognize the credentials of ethnic media journalists. And even though this may seem like a blessing for ethnic media who want to retain their staff, it also means that talented young journalists are less likely to choose to, at least, begin their careers in ethnic media. In the long run, talented journalists who are willing to see themselves play a role in the newsrooms and studios of ethnic media before they "move on," can only help ethnic media organizations and the communities they serve. They, for example, have a better understanding of the communities they come from and thereby can improve the way their new mass media employers cover immigrant and ethnic populations. In addition, talented young ethnic media journalists who cross over into the world of mainstream media are likely to give visibility and credibility to the media organization for which they previously worked. Ethnic media that serve as "incubators" of talent can change the perceptions of mass media executives and producers with respect to ethnic media journalists. As Ojo (2006) points out:

> Experience at the ethnic media is generally not considered to be 'real' reporting and editing experience by many managing editors at the big media outlets in Canada. To these managing editors, there is no real journalism in the ethnic media. . . . They often view journalists at the ethnic media and small-town media as 'second-citizens' in the profession. (p. 350)

Even though Ojo refers primarily to Canada, this is the reality in most countries.

Access to Sources and Resources

Ethnic media journalists may have a hard time gaining the respect of their colleagues in the mainstream and mass media, but they often have an even more difficult time getting access to news sources, especially local, state, and federal government officials. In the panel discussions we have had with ethnic media editors and reporters this has been a recurring theme. "Local government officials prefer to talk to the mainstream media reporters," says a news manager with the Southern California branch of a large Chinese-language newspaper (Matsaganis et al., 2008). "And if you want to take the initiative and call on them at a press conference, you get nothing in response. That is sad!" Kenneth Kim, a journalist who worked with the *Korea Times* newspaper in Los Angeles before taking a position with New America Media relayed this story:

> I was sharing an office at L.A. City Hall's press room with a reporter of a law publication which is a mainstream media. There was some issue we both were covering at the same time and we both had to speak with the deputy director of a city department. I called the guy first. His secretary

> answered the call. I told her who I am and asked for the official. She put me on hold. A moment later, she came back and asked me to leave a message. Immediately after I hung up the call, my office mate picked up his phone and called the same guy. He was able to speak with him right away. My office mate felt pity for me and at the end of his conversation with the official he told him that his office mate had left him a message earlier and is still waiting for a return call. After he hung up, I right away called the official for one more time. But, the official who just got off the phone with my office mate again wasn't available to take my call. I had to leave another message. . . . It is an example of a constant run around ethnic media endure as they seek information from government officials! It's also an example showing how difficult it is for ethnic media to gain access. (Matsaganis et al., 2008)

Others echoed this frustration. Eric Olander is the vice president of news and production at LA-18 KSCI TV based in Los Angeles, a station focused on Asian-American populations. He says:

> The problem we have is with politicians, with non-Asian politicians. They talk about the importance of engaging minorities, and they will never talk to us; they will never give us the time of day. We are the largest Asian station in the United States. We are the largest Asian station in Los Angeles, serving the second largest ethnic group [the first being the Latino population] and it takes a hundred and fifty phone calls to get the mayor to talk to us. (Matsaganis et al., 2007)

The problem, however, is not just at the local level. Leading up to and during the 2008 presidential election campaign in the United States, there were incidents where ethnic media journalists were shut out of press conferences and other events. In February 2007, journalists from the Chinese-language media *Sing Tao* and *The World Journal* in San Francisco were told that the Hillary Clinton fundraiser they were planning to cover was not open to "foreign press" (Chien, 2007). The next day a spokesperson for the Clinton campaign apologized saying that "this is a learning opportunity" (Chien, 2007, para. 3). He assured that the campaign would make sure that all media, including Chinese and ethnic media, were able to cover the campaign.

However, there are cases where some ethnic media find it easier than others to gain access to news sources. That is certainly the case with Latino media in places like Southern California and Miami in the United States. Large Spanish-language networks (e.g., Univisión and Telemundo) attract huge audiences in these media markets and compete directly with the mainstream, English-language media networks. In Los Angeles, in particular, the Mexican-origin mayor Antonio Villaraigosa (as well as some of his predecessors) has held press conferences both in English and Spanish. While this satisfies the large and small Spanish-language media that cater to the Hispanic populations of the region, it does marginalize media that serve other ethnic populations. Eric Olander of the Asian media network KSCI-TV in Los Angeles says:

> We complained to the mayor . . . because our reporters have to sit there twice as long while he is going through answers. If he can do it in Spanish, he should also make himself available in other languages, like Korean and Chinese. He should have staff members that can keep track of his answers and articulate [them] in those other languages. (Matsaganis et al., 2007)

The practice of holding separate press conferences, one for mainstream media and one for ethnic media (or even multiple press conferences for ethnic media targeting different groups) appears to have gained traction, at least in certain parts of the U.S. and Canada. Ethnic media journalists appear conflicted about this. Gloria Alvarez of the bilingual (i.e., Spanish and English) publications of Eastern Group Publishing explains that, "Some media were really happy [with a press conference specifically organized for ethnic media]. They said 'gee,' this is the only time we really even have access, so it is great that we can get in and begin to know" (Matsaganis et al., 2008). But, as she points out, this practice may only reify the marginalization of ethnic media, and consequently of the populations they serve. In a city as diverse as Los Angeles, she wonders, "Why do we need to be separated out?" (Matsaganis et al., 2008).

Research in Canada captures a similar tendency. In fact, after the 2004 federal election, there were a number of separate news conferences held in a variety of languages. These events, which some are calling "segregated news conferences," are "becoming more popular . . . but such strategic behavior is often kept behind closed doors" (Murray et al., 2007, p. 108).

In late 2008, a new administration led by the Democratic Party was voted into office in the United States. The country's first African-American president was elected on an agenda of sweeping change in policies and the *modus operandi* in the country's capital. He also signaled a change in the way that government officials treat ethnic media. While putting the representatives of legacy media, like *The New York Times,* on hold, he granted his first interview as president-elect to *Ebony* magazine, a publication targeted to African-American audiences across the country. He also gave his first post-inauguration interview to *Black Enterprise* magazine, his first radio interview to the Latino radio talk show host "El Pistolero"' of Radio La Que Buena 105.1 FM (a Univisión station) in Los Angeles, which was followed up by a phone interview with the immensely popular radio host "Piolin" on the Spanish-language network Radio La Nueva 101.9 FM (Rainey, 2009). In addition, his first television interview was on the Arab-language channel al-Arabiya (Macleod, 2009). The station is based in Dubai but is available to Arab-speaking audiences worldwide via satellite. Some commentators have argued that these events may just reflect the administration's efforts to find "alternatives to reach around the mainstream media and speak to loyal constituents" (Rainey, 2009, para. 4) and note that while these early overtures to the ethnic media are a step in the right direction and "long overdue," it is still too early to judge the new administration's attitude and behavior.

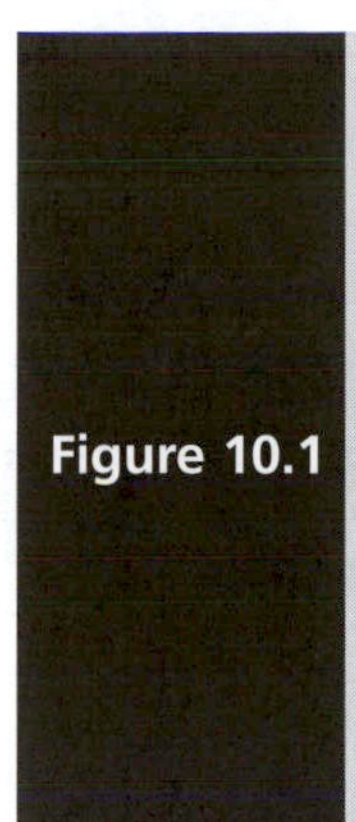

Figure 10.1 An indication that things are changing and that local, state, and federal government officials in the U.S. are becoming more responsive to ethnic media producers' calls for more access to information that might impact the lives of the increasingly larger ethnic communities they serve is shown here in an overview of ethnic media reporters and editors meeting in a press conference with Massachusetts Governor Deval Patrick in the State House in Boston, in April 2009. The media present serve many ethnic communities in the state, including Armenian, African-American, Haitian, Hispanic, Portuguese, Brazilian, Irish, Japanese, Chinese, Korean, and Indian. Among the topics discussed: in-state tuition rates for non-documented immigrants, taxes, health care, education, and translations of state brochures and manuals.

Photo: Courtesy of Frank Herron, Director, Center on Media and Society, University of Massachusetts–Boston.

¤ For Further Discussion

As a class, compile a directory of ethnic media organizations that exist in your city. Contact as many as you can and ask to interview a reporter who works there about the various challenges they have faced in getting access to local authorities. Come back to class and discuss how the experiences of the various journalists you talked to compare. Do some have a harder time than others getting information? Why is that the case?

Professionalization: Objectivity and Social Responsibility

The antidote, some argue, to the discrimination ethnic media journalists often are subjected to when they try to cover stories that demand access to certain authorities is for them to subscribe to a higher level of professionalization. But what does *professionalization* mean? It is a social process through which individuals develop common values and norms, establish a code of conduct, and agree on a set of qualifications that everyone practicing a particular occupation or trade is expected to possess (e.g., Aldridge & Evetts, 2004). Conformity with these occupation or trade-specific criteria distinguishes the professional from the amateur.

The Objectivity Standard

In journalism, one of the most enduring values since the late 19th century has been that of *objectivity.* While initially a characteristic of American journalism, over the years, objectivity has become a norm among mainstream media journalists in many democratic societies. Reacting to the sensationalist, "yellow" journalism[3] of the 1890s, many American reporters and editors clung to objectivity in an attempt to make their profession more respectable (McLeod & Hawley, 1964; Schudson, 1978). Objectivity also helped commercial newspapers gain legitimacy in the eyes of the public as watchdogs of government (Schiller, 1979). In a sense, objectivity became a proxy for social responsibility.

This link between objectivity and social responsibility has not gone unchallenged over the years. In the United States of the late 1940s, for example, there were those who argued that socially responsible journalists should not only present the facts to the public, but also help people make sense or interpret what is happening around them (e.g., see Bates, 1995; Blanchard, 1977). A significant volume of communication research from the 1970s onward has challenged the notion of objective journalism. Studies show that even the news media presumed to be objective affect not only which issues audiences pay attention to and discuss (i.e., news media have an *agenda setting* effect on the public; see Dearing & Rogers, 1996; McCombs & Reynolds, 2002; McCombs & Shaw, 1972), but also the "lenses" through which people view issues (i.e., influence the *framing* of issues; see, for example, McCombs & Bell, 1996; McCombs & Ghanem, 2001; McLeod & Detenber, 1999). What some may see as being a peaceful demonstration in the streets of a city, for example, others may view as a threat to social and political stability.

These arguments notwithstanding, objectivity has been touted as the "gold" standard of professionalism in journalism for more than a century.[4] And this is the standard that politicians and authorities, more generally speaking, as well as mainstream media institutions believe that ethnic media journalists fail to live up to. Commonly, ethnic media journalism is labeled as activist and their staff members are seen more as community advocates than journalists. Such characterizations often stem, however, from a deep-seated fear in mainstream institutions—including media—that ethnic media promote values and norms that go against mainstream culture. This is particularly true at times of crisis and uncertainty, as was the case post-September 11, 2001, in the U.S., Britain, and elsewhere. In the UK, in the aftermath of the terrorist attacks on U.S. soil, support for issues of ethnic diversity and multiculturalism declined dramatically. The negative climate was made worse by restrictive immigration laws and government policies that encouraged the assimilation of immigrants into majority society, at the expense of the preservation of their ethnic identity and communities. As media and communications scholar Myria Georgiou aptly comments, "Ethnic media are in a defensive position, and endlessly have to remind their audiences that they are not 'the enemy'" (Mediam'Rad, 2006, p. 2).

Most ethnic media journalists we have spoken to indicate that the objectivity principle guides them in their work. Most of them seek to be objective when they report on a story. But as one of the reporters we interviewed points out, objectivity has boundaries. Questions around a story's objectivity are more likely to arise when the author of the story, intentionally or inadvertently, starts to challenge common perceptions about what is in the best interest of the country he or she lives in and works. As one of the ethnic media journalists we interviewed says:

> The American newspapers are going to be objective as long as it doesn't compromise their national interests, American interests; Korean newspapers, French newspapers, Chinese papers, the same thing. For national papers, the boundary is wider because you're talking about a whole country, millions of people. But for ethnic papers, their boundary is narrow; Koreatown or Chinatown. (Matsaganis et al., 2008)

That is to say ethnic media journalists have to think about the interests of the community they serve and the country they live in simultaneously. And those interests may not always be perfectly aligned. For some, the perceived interest of Britain post-September 11 was the assimilation of all immigrant and ethnic populations into mainstream British society, presumably in order to avoid terrorist threats, for instance, from radical religious groups present among certain ethnic communities. Assimilation, though, was not in the interest of those British citizens of Arab background, for example, as well as immigrants living in the country who wished to keep their cultural heritage, customs, and language alive. In this context, staying "objective" can be a tough balancing act for ethnic media journalists and one that their colleagues in the mainstream media may not be able to comprehend.

For ethnic media journalists, the definition of social responsibility goes beyond adhering to a sense of objectivity, and the roles they are expected and choose to perform are frequently re-negotiated, debated, and prioritized in the newsroom. This is how Kenneth Kim, who worked for the *Korea Times* newspaper in Los Angeles, put it:

> We have to play multiple roles. We have to be a news and information provider, we often have to be a community leader or an activist promoting the immigrant community's interests, and we become an organizer of community events. However, not everyone appreciates our efforts. Several weeks ago,

> Governor Schwarzenegger said Hispanic immigrants can't learn English because they only read and listen to Spanish-language [media]. He blamed Spanish language media for being a culprit that prevents the immigrants from learning English. And he even suggested Hispanics [need to] subscribe more to the main stream news media, meaning English language media. Korean language media in U.S. have been facing the same criticism, too. Every time when ethnic media's effect on the immigrants' ability or chance to learn English is questioned, Korean reporters ask themselves a question [because the *Korea Times* is published only in Korean]. Are we being a hindrance blocking Korean immigrants' chance to learn English or their path to become more American? Considering all these, I think a role of ethnic media or ethnic journalists is quite unique compared to their counterparts in mainstream media. (Matsaganis et al., 2007)

Ethnic Media as Ethnic Community Advocates

Playing the role of community leaders opens ethnic media up to criticism by the mainstream media, the "majority" population and government authorities, because they are seen as taking on an activist role and abandoning their commitment to objectivity. The Korean and Spanish-language media performed a critical leadership role in organizing the 2006 rallies in the U.S. asking for immigration policy reform, at the expense of being "objective." The Internet-based channels that have been developed by the indigenous population of Chiapas, Mexico, have documented the injustices they suffered at the hands of the Mexican army, but also tell stories about the everyday life and customs of the people they serve (Browne, 2005; Castells, 2001; Knutson, 1998). Their "objectivity" may not be questioned much by people who are sympathetic to their cause, but the Mexican authorities see things quite differently. Similarly, media serving the various Greek-American communities in the United States have criticized American policy around the recognition of the Former Yugoslav Republic of Macedonia (FYROM) as the "Republic of Macedonia." They argue that American policy encourages nationalists in FYROM who harbor territorial claims in the northern Greek region also known as Macedonia. While critiquing American policy reflects the role these media see themselves playing as community leaders and as representatives of the views of the Greek-American community, their positioning could be construed as biased or even anti-American by Americans of non-Greek origin.

At other times, however, advocacy is directed within the community. In this case ethnic media may upset a portion of the ethnic community they serve. After fleeing the Castro regime, many Cuban-origin Americans and Cuban immigrants settled in Miami. Members of the older generations expressed skepticism or disapproval for the rapprochement with Cuba, which the Obama administration initiated in the spring of 2009 (Robinson, 2009). Some of the Spanish-language media in Miami, like Radio Mambi 710 AM, echoed the concerns of the "old guard" (Stolberg & Cave, 2009). However, younger generations of Cuban-American citizens and politicians viewed the shift in American policy towards Cuba more favorably

(Schmitt & Cave, 2009; Stolberg & Cave, 2009). For this younger population, the position of ethnic media like Radio Mambi might be upsetting.

Finally, some ethnic journalists see advocacy as going beyond a sense of national and community interests. Eric Olander of Los Angeles-based KSCI TV says that his staff has launched campaigns in the Asian communities they serve aimed at educating the population around issues of gender equality and domestic violence. "We do a lot," he says, "to challenge traditional Asian customs that are not consistent or compatible with American life, because in the United States it is not permissible by law or by society for a man to hit a woman" (Matsaganis et al., 2007). This type of advocacy may also trigger a negative reaction in one or another Asian-origin community.

The Professional Modus Operandi: How Formal Standards Impact Ethnic Media Content

A particular way of doing things is another characteristic that sets professionals and non-professionals apart. Often this implies that "good" stories have to be told in a particular way. Professional journalists, for instance, are supposed to know that their stories should answer the "five Ws" (Who? What? When? Where? Why?), and usually to do this in the lead paragraph of their report. Professionals should also know that one of the most common formats employed for a newspaper story is that of the "inverse pyramid"; that is when journalists begin a story by presenting the absolute basics and expand, providing more details as their story unfolds. Professionals have come to know and practice these techniques through formal education in journalism, through on-the-job experience, or both.

In her book on migrant and especially Turkish media in Germany, Kosnick (2007) draws on her experience as a journalist working for Radio MultiKulti, a station which is part of the public service broadcast organization in Berlin. The station is targeted to the many ethnic communities living in the city. It produces programming in German, but also in 18 other languages (Hurrle, n.d.). Kosnick notes that Radio MultiKulti had trouble attracting employees due to the lack of "so-called foreign [professional] journalists" in the city as well as "the standards of public service broadcasting that the station is not willing to compromise" (p. 60). Those formal standards include:

> Knowing how to write a particular kind of prose for a feature, how to conduct interviews and select appropriate statements from it, how to structure a feature and make it "interesting to the audience," and how to record one's composition during the tightly allotted half-hour production time in the studio. (p. 60)

All these and other standards that are specific to a medium (e.g., radio or newspaper, daily versus weekly newspaper) or a type of program (e.g., pure newscast versus a talk show) lead to the production of content that anyone, regardless of whether they are a journalist or just a media consumer, can identify as a "typical," "professionally" produced story. The stories, for example, in most major mainstream newspapers around the world (e.g., *The New York Times* in the United States, *The Independent* in Britain, *Le Monde* in France, *Die Zeit* in Germany, *El País* in Spain, the *Mail & Guardian* in South Africa, and *O Globo* in Brazil) have a similar structure and familiar "feel" to them, which we associate with "professional" newspaper journalism.

The editor of a Sri Lankan publication in California explains why some ethnic media journalists depart from such professional formats: "Mainstream media are the way they are; they give so little information, so little emotion. We have become what we have become, because we go the other way" (Matsaganis et al., 2008). Large mainstream media and wire services, she argues, "do not give stories in depth . . . so we have to do that" (Matsaganis et al., 2008). "This is the goal in stories [our publication] runs on the turbulent political situation in Sri Lanka, for instance, and the role of the Tamil Tigers, a militant organization in the Northeastern region of the country that demands the Tamil state become independent."

Of course many ethnic media producers try hard to comply with the standards set in their field. In fact, the larger the ethnic media operation, the more likely it is that their journalists and producers will feel the pressure to conform to professional standards of production. This tendency is evident in the programming aired on the major Spanish-language networks Univisión and Telemundo in the United States. Big, mainstream advertising agencies and corporations are likely to feel more secure advertising in ethnic media venues when they can see familiar styles of storytelling.

¤ For Further Discussion

Collect stories from ethnic media and mainstream media that were published or aired in the past month. Analyze them and determine how they differ and in what ways they are the same. Is the narrative different? Do they use images, video, or audio clips differently? Are stories formatted differently on the newspaper page, for example? Which stories seem to be more "objective"? It will be easier to detect differences and spot commonalities if you are able to find stories covered by both mainstream and ethnic media around the same time.

Professionalization and Elitism

A strong emphasis on strict professional standards may bring into newsrooms and studios of ethnic media the more educated and highly qualified journalist. However this may happen at the expense of staying grounded in the community. In a highly professionalized ethnic media organization it is easier for a sense of *elitism* to develop. Higher educated, professional staff members may not be able to relate to all segments of the ethnic community they set out to serve. They may end up overrepresenting the views and concerns of only the most visible, affluent, or largest segments of a community.

Depending on the socio-demographic profile of the audience, an elitist orientation can have a negative impact on the long-term survival of the ethnic media organization. In an ethnic community that comprises mostly of first-generation immigrants, for instance, elitism may in fact affect the media organization's bottom line. That is because as their constituency becomes too narrow, they lose broader appeal and support (Riggins, 1992). However, in large ethnic communities where the second, third, and later generations account for the majority of the population, elitism may be a conscious strategy deployed by ethnic media to increase their revenue streams. This is likely the case with magazines like *Latina,* published in the United States. *Latina* targets mostly younger, English-speaking Hispanic women (irrespective of their or their family's country of origin). These women tend to have a higher education, and are better off financially. As such, they constitute an audience that appeals to advertisers, thereby producing increased revenues. Similar media ventures targeting Asian women have developed in the United States, the United Kingdom, and elsewhere (see also Chapter 4).

When the Ethnic Community Turns Against Its Ethnic Media

Even when ethnic media are in-tune with the pulse of the communities they serve, the relationship of the journalists and producers with community members is not always harmonious. There are numerous case in which community members or whole segments of a community have turned against their media because they felt that "their" ethnic media neither represented the interests, nor reflected the values of the community. The editor of the Sri Lankan publication in California says that ethnic journalists need to be very careful, as certain issues can be very touchy in a community and people can get very emotional. "It is very easy to hurt feelings . . . [and] you can lose advertising [and] readers" (Matsaganis et al., 2008).

The producer of a weekly radio program targeted to Iranian women living in Stockholm, Sweden, talks often about the plight of women who are victims of domestic violence. Browne (2005) reports that the producer, Leila, has been the target of numerous threats, presumably because she challenges at least some community preconceptions around gender equality, as well as the role of women in the household. Leila admits that she continues to do the show because of the positive feedback she has received from a number of women, some of whom found the courage to terminate abusive relationships because of the show.

Dissatisfaction, however, can be expressed even more violently, as in the case of the *Nguoi Viet Daily,* the largest Vietnamese daily newspaper in the United States, with distribution in Australia, France, Russia, and Vietnam (Vongs, 2003). The newspaper was founded in 1978, and it is based in the heart of Orange County's Little Saigon, in Southern California. The community has a population of approximately 140,000 and represents the largest concentration of Vietnamese outside Vietnam (Vongs, 2003). In late January 2008, the newspaper ran a picture on the cover of a special insert magazine published to celebrate the new lunar year.

The photograph accompanied the main story in the magazine: a profile of Huynh Thuy Chau, a graduate student at the University of California-Davis who had recently won the prestigious Robert Haas fellowship for an art installation. Her installation included several nail salon tubs (where staff wash customers' feet) painted in the colors of the defunct republic of South Vietnam.[5] As she explained, her artwork was meant as a tribute to her mother-in-law, a refugee who put her kids through college on the paychecks she earned working at nail salons.

Neither the art installation nor the picture on the cover of the insert magazine were meant to cause an uproar. Anti-communist members of the Vietnamese community of Little Saigon found the image of the flag on salon tubs where people's dirty feet get washed insulting. Quickly, complaints started pouring into the offices of the *Nguoi Viet Daily*, forcing the newspaper's board of directors to fire its editor-in-chief and the managing editor. Community members were not appeased. Protesters demanded that the newspaper hold a public meeting, during which it would offer guarantees that a similar incident would never happen again. One of the protesters, Doan Trong, a social worker and former South Vietnamese military officer, told the *Orange County Register* (a mainstream, English-language daily newspaper in the area): "Fifty-eight thousand Americans died to protect this flag. Why did [*Nguoi Viet*] betray us? My friends sacrificed their lives during the war" (Schou, 2008). In an interview with the *OC Register*, the editor who was fired said: "I had no sense it would be controversial. But people don't think you should put the

Figure 10.2a Angry anti-communist Vietnamese-Americans protest against newspaper *Nguoi Viet Daily*, after the publication ran a controversial photograph of an art installation depicting nail salon washing tubs painted in the colors of the defunct South Vietnamese Republic's flag.

Credit: Keith May/OCWeekly.

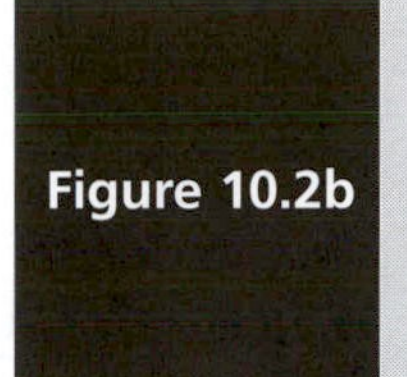

Figure 10.2b Protesters demanded that the *Nguoi Viet Daily* hold a public meeting, during which it would offer guarantees that a similar incident would never happen again. One of the protesters, Doan Truong (pictured below, center), said: "Fifty-eight thousand Americans died to protect this flag. Why did [*Nguoi Viet*] betray us?"

Credit: Steve Zylius/Orange County Register/ZUMA Press.

flag on something dirty. As soon as somebody told me that, I realized. People came up to me. My mom thought it was inappropriate; my dad did. It's not an extreme position to think it was inappropriate" (Schou, 2008).

In the weeks and months after the publication of the photograph, protesters continued to attack the *Nguoi Viet Daily* and the violence escalated. In April 2008, a protester was arrested for assaulting one of the newspaper's reporters. The protester demanded that the editors of the newspaper admit that they had ties to the Viet Cong communist party leadership (Bharath, 2008). In the meantime, newspaper staff reportedly said that they heard protesters threatening that, if the newspaper did not comply with their demands, they would dig up the grave of the founder of the *Nguoi Viet Daily,* Yen Ngoc Do. The founder of the paper had passed away 2 years earlier.

Many similar stories were shared by ethnic media journalists at a roundtable discussion that was co-hosted in April 2008 by New America Media, the California First Amendment Coalition, the Institute for Justice and Journalism (University of Southern California–Annenberg School for Communication and Journalism), the Society for Professional Journalists, the Center for Communications and Community (University of California–Los Angeles), CCNMA-Latino Journalists of California, and the Center of Ethnic and Alternative Media (California State University–Northridge).

Participants convened to discuss how ethnic media journalists can handle protests from their own communities, whether media embedded in their communities can exercise press freedom, or if fear of backlash leads them to self-censorship. Julio Moran of the Latino Journalists of California association and a former reporter with the *Los Angeles Times* proposed that ethnic media organize media literacy workshops for the community, so audience members understand how stories are written. Ruben Martinez, a faculty member at Loyola Marymount University in Los Angeles and a journalist says that "acknowledg[ing] the point of contradiction" can be important in quelling the concerns of the ethnic community (R. Martinez, personal communication, April 7, 2008). This, he says, is what Spanish-language newspaper *La Opinión* did in the U.S. when it decided to endorse an African-American, Barack Obama, as candidate for president. Steve Montiel, of the Institute for Justice and Journalism and the California First Amendment Coalition, suggested that ethnic media come together to create a foundation that would provide economic protection and legal support to an organization like the *Nguoi Viet Daily,* which faced advertisers threatening to pull their ads, as well as expenses related to legal battles with protesters (S. Montiel, personal communication, April 7, 2008).

¤ For Further Discussion

Work with your classmates to find cases in which mainstream media, in or beyond the area where you live, have come under attack by the public. Think about how those attacks were similar or different to the ones described in the preceding section against ethnic media. Given what you have learned about ethnic media thus far, do you think it is easier for mainstream media to overcome such attacks, just as hard, or more difficult? Justify your answer.

Consider the recommendations the panel co-hosted by New American Media and several other institutions and non-profit organizations based in California made for helping ethnic media address attacks like the one launched against the *Nguoi Viet Daily.* Which ones do you think might be more effective? Do you have other suggestions?

Ethnic and Mainstream Media Collaborations: Experiments, Possibilities, Challenges

In Chapter 6, we discussed ethnic media ownership trends. In certain cases, ethnic media are being bought by mainstream media. This gives major media corporations access to new audiences and entrée into new markets. Such mergers and acquisitions have been welcomed by some ethnic media organizations, journalists, and communities. They have argued that these ventures raise the profile of ethnic media, while they also guarantee increased financial stability and sustainability. Others, though, have greeted these acquisitions with skepticism, suggesting that by losing complete control over the management of their production practices, ethnic media are likely to become no different from mainstream media.

However skeptical of entering such ethnic media-mainstream media relationships, a number of ethnic media producers around the world have begun to experiment with new models of ethnic-mainstream media collaboration. The primary concern of the journalists has been to develop high-quality content, while retaining as much control as possible over it.

In France, for example, Beur FM, a radio station targeting Maghreb communities in several cities (i.e., populations with origins in Morocco, Algeria, Tunisia, and Libya), has been working with the mainstream weekly newspaper *Témoignage Chrétien* since 2001. They co-produce "15 Jours Dans Le Monde," a program that is broadcast on the station every other Saturday. Excerpts from the show are also inserted into the station's news bulletin (Mediam'Rad, 2006). Nadir Djennad, a journalist with Beur FM, explains how the collaboration has helped the radio station: "We have received several politicians, who would otherwise have been loath to appear on our station. The partnership with *Témoignage Chrétien* gives us a certain credibility. Some readers of the paper have become listeners and vice versa" (Mediam'Rad, 2006, p. 6). She also suggests, though, that the partnership is possible because Beur FM and *Témoignage Chrétien* share certain values, "such as the fight against racism and our interest in Algeria" (pp. 6–7).

A different form of collaboration has emerged in Sweden, in this case between the magazine *El Gringo* and the free Swedish daily newspaper *Metro. El Gringo* was created in 2004 by Zanyar Adami, an immigrant of Kurdish-origin, who wanted to create a newspaper for the migrants living in the country. The mass media, he says, "always talk about crime, unemployment, and negative things. I didn't feel that I was being represented, and wanted to give a positive image, to counter the one being put out there" (Mediam'Rad, 2006, p. 6). Naseem Khan (2007) explains that Adami chose to work with the free daily *Metro* because he "saw the necessity of reaching average Swedes" (p. 2). In 2007, *El Gringo* had a circulation of 1.2 million and had already won several awards including the Stora Journalistpriset and the Newcomer of the Year by the Swedish Magazines Publishers Association (both in 2005; Khan, 2007). Reflecting on *El Gringo*'s success Adami says:

> Our biggest success has been to be able to keep to our original idea. . . . We had to fight for that. Our strength is our independence; we remain in control of the content. We could have asked *Metro* for a salary, but we preferred to find the money ourselves. (Mediam'Rad, 2006, p. 6)

Brokering such agreements is not easy for ethnic media. We have already discussed the fact that ethnic media journalists are often viewed by mainstream media as being less-than-professional. In addition, as sociologist Myria Georgiou points out, mass media are nervous about entering a relationship with ethnic media because they fear that they will be "associated with specific factions" within a particular ethnic community (Mediam'Rad, 2006, p. 6), which may end up hurting their other ventures. That is at least one reason why mainstream media prefer to fully acquire an ethnic media organization they are interested in, instead of collaborating in some other way. Through a merger or acquisition, they can exert far more or even full control over the content of the ethnic media producer.

For Further Discussion

Consider the ethnic media that are based nearest the city or town in which you live. If it is a newspaper, pick up a copy. If they are electronic media, browse through their Web site or contact them directly to ask for a copy of their weekly schedule. Try to identify columns, feature series (stories organized around a theme that appear regularly), or programs that reflect a collaboration of these ethnic media with mainstream media. Now do the same by scanning through the content of mainstream media available in your area. Do you see any signs of similar ethnic-mainstream collaborations? Report your findings and identify the most interesting or innovative aspects of the collaborations you were able to find. How does each party involved in the collaboration benefit? Explain.

The Role of Professional Journalism Education in the Future of Ethnic Media

At the turn of the 21st century, we find that ethnic media emerge in a variety of organizational forms (see Chapter 6). As we discussed earlier in this chapter, organizational form is related to the degree of professionalization of ethnic media staff and the level of the ethnic community's participation in the production of media content. Different forms facilitate different relationships between ethnic media producers and their audiences. The review of the literature and the results of efforts to map ethnic media in a number of countries suggest that there is a trade-off between professionalization and participation. On one hand, high levels of professionalization are generally associated with less community participation in the production of media content, elitism, and lack of legitimacy among community members, but also increased respect from peers in the mainstream media, increased likelihood of attracting advertisers, financial stability, and sustainability. Lower levels of professionalization, on the other hand, are thought to correlate with financial instability and an uncertain future, with being marginalized by mainstream media as less-than-credible news sources, and intellectual ghettoization. However, lower levels of professionalization are also associated with higher levels of community participation in the production of media content, and high levels of legitimacy in the ethnic community. The abovementioned case of *El Gringo* in Sweden and the collaboration between Beur FM and *Témoignage Chrétien* in France represent, among other things, attempts made by ethnic media producers to reap some of the benefits of professionalization, while at the same time maintaining control over the content their audiences (i.e., their communities) care about. In both cases ethnic media producers are trying to minimize the impact of the trade-off between professionalization and community participation.

There are other ways to accomplish this balance, including two kinds of education-oriented strategies. The first targets ethnic community members who want to contribute to ethnic media production and the other targets the next generations of journalists being trained at universities and colleges around the world.

In Australia, one of the most ambitious and visible programs created to train indigenous, immigrant, and ethnic communities in journalism practices, and media production more broadly speaking, is run by the National Ethnic and Multicultural Broadcasters Council (NEMBC). The NEMBC is a nongovernmental organization whose mission is to develop policy and advocate on behalf of all ethnic broadcasters in Australia. For example, the organization launched a program in 1998, intended to provide training specifically in radio broadcasting to ethnic media staff and volunteers. Courses were offered in various formats (e.g., on site face-to-face instruction, online, and distance learning) and priority was given to regional, rural and remote areas, ethnic youth, new and emerging ethnic groups, as well as new language groups (NEMBC, 2008). In 2008, the program was still in operation. Initiatives like this one can help ethnic media organizations groom more sophisticated users of media technologies and more professional journalists, without necessarily sacrificing the active participation of community members in their operations.

In many of the cities around the world where ethnic media are springing up, university journalism departments are also seeing an increasingly diverse population of students. This diversity reflects, at least to a certain extent, the growing diversity in the larger population. Unfortunately, however, while many journalism departments are trying hard to keep up with the developments in the world of new communication technologies and the convergence of media platforms, relatively few have also acknowledged and responded to the challenges and opportunities that ethnic diversity presents. In 2004, through the EQUAL program, the European Commission's Directorate General (DG) for Employment, Social Affairs, and Equal Opportunities recommended that "an increasing number of young people for example of ethnic minority origin or with disabilities need to be aware that a career in the media is a meaningful and viable option" (EQUAL, 2004, para. 22). What the DG is recommending represents a step in the right direction, but it does not go far enough as its recommendation only reflects concern with respect to the representation of ethnic minority populations in the staff, newsrooms, and studios of mainstream media.

In European as well as many other countries worldwide, students from distinct ethnic backgrounds should realize that they may also be able to launch their careers in the newsrooms and studios of a number of ethnic media organizations. Their education can prove invaluable to ethnic media organizations who seek staff with professional training, particular language skills, and a nuanced understanding of the audience(s) they are serving. For young journalists, even if working for an ethnic media organization does not last a career, it is a way to build experience and expertise in working with a particular audience. They may be able to leverage this expertise should they decide to eventually cross over to mainstream media. The crossover to mainstream media may become easier as these media seek ways to appeal to a more and more fragmented, multiethnic audience. If developments in the media landscape at the turn of the century are any indication of what to expect in the future, the ethnic media sector will continue to grow, while new models of cooperation among ethnic media and between ethnic and mainstream media will continue to emerge and be tested. We engage in a dialogue about the future of ethnic media with academics, researchers, and professionals from various parts of the world in the next and final chapter of this book.

Summary

The ethnic media journalist was the main focus of this chapter. We talked about who the people that staff the newsrooms and studios of ethnic media are and the hurdles they encounter in doing their jobs. We also addressed the particular challenges ethnic media face as they try to balance between the calls for higher levels of professionalization, on one hand, and increased community participation in the production of media content, on the other. In addition, we discussed emerging models of ethnic media and mainstream media collaborations, as well as the role that professional journalism education can play in the future of ethnic media.

Study Questions

1. In the section under heading, "Who Are the Ethnic Media Journalists, Editors, and Staff?", we talked about the diverse backgrounds from which the journalists and other staff of ethnic media come and how organizational culture influences ethnic media operations. How do you think the culture of a large-scale mainstream media organization might differ from that of an ethnic media organization? If you were an ethnic media journalist crossing over to a job in the mainstream media, what do you think the biggest adjustment would be from an organizational culture point of view?

2. One of the challenges ethnic media face is relatively high staff turnover. What can an ethnic media organization do to limit turnover?

3. Imagine you are the incoming mayor of the city where you currently live. You know for a fact that there are at least 20 ethnic media organizations based in your city covering a number of communities with distinct ethnic origins. During your campaign, you promised fair access to the mayor and city authorities for all media, ethnic and mainstream. What problems do you anticipate in keeping your promise and how do you plan to overcome them?

4. You are the incoming editor-in-chief of the *Nguoi Viet Daily.* After many months of heated debates, protests, and attacks on your newspaper's offices and staff, tempers in the community have finally settled. The newspaper's board of directors has instructed you to develop a plan that will help the organization avoid similar problems in the future. What are your recommendations to the board?

5. Under heading, "When the Ethnic Community Turns Against Its Ethnic Media," we discussed the collaboration between *El Gringo,* an ethnic newspaper oriented towards immigrants living in Sweden, and the free daily newspaper *Metro.*

How is *El Gringo* similar to Berlin-based Radio MultiKulti, which we talked about under heading, "Challenges Ethnic Media Producers, Editors, and Reporters Face"? How are they different?

Notes

[1]See Chapter 5 for a profile and more details on New America Media.

[2]Murray, Yu, and Ahadi (2007) report on a study by Poon (2007) on editorial policy, in which the editor-in-chief of the World Journal of British Columbia is quoted as saying that his paper has a difficult time getting local news on the front page, because of staff shortages.

[3]In the 1880s and 1890s, American entrepreneurs Joseph Pulitzer and William Randolph Hearst launched newspapers that relied on sensational headlines, shocking narrative, colorful layouts, and illustrations, as well as a wide variety of stories that went beyond politics; among those, crime stories figured prominently (Campbell, 2001). The newspapers owned by both Pulitzer and Hearst also took on popular causes. With the fervor of an activist, Pulitzer, for example, criticized the inhumane conditions many immigrant laborers had to suffer working in the sweatshops of New York's garment district (Örnebring, & Jönsson, 2004). Campbell (2001) indicates that relentless self-promotion and self-congratulation made rival newspapers loath what they referred to as the "yellow" newspapers like the *New York World* and the *Journal*—so much so that in New York two newspapers, the *Sun* and the *Press,* joined a campaign launched in 1897 by conservative groups to ban the *World* and the *Journal* from reading rooms, social clubs, and libraries (Campbell, 2005). The *New York Sun* indicated that their intent was to stamp out "the licentiousness, the vulgarity, and the criminal spirit [that has been] exhibited by those shameless papers with an effrontery almost without example in the history of journalism" (*New York Sun,* cited in Campbell, 2005, p. 6).

[4]This is especially true in Western democracies, although objectivity has been espoused as a journalistic value by professionals elsewhere, too, including countries of the Middle East, Asia, and Africa (Deuze, 2005; Hafez, 2004; Josephi, 2007).

[5]The forces of Communist North Vietnam took over Saigon in 1975, effectively ending the Vietnam War. That is when many Vietnamese fled the country. Many arrived in the United States. Based on the American Community Survey of 2006, there are approximately 1,600,000 Vietnamese-Americans (see also Grigsby Bates, 2006).

PART V

The Future of Ethnic Media

CHAPTER 11

Conclusion

What Does the Future Hold for Ethnic Media?

CHAPTER OBJECTIVES

By the end of this final chapter, you will have learned more about:

- How ethnic media researchers and professionals view the future of ethnic media in different parts of the world.
- The challenges facing ethnic media producers and consumers in a globalizing world.
- Some of the critical gaps in the research on ethnic media that can be addressed in future work.

How the Experts See the Future of Ethnic Media

Through the course of this book, we have examined ethnic media from consumption and production perspectives. We have given context to the past and present formations of ethnic media in different parts of the world, and examined what social, political, historical, and economic factors have resulted in uneven growth of ethnic media in different places and for different groups. In this chapter, we turn to the question of the future of the ethnic media. Although no one has a crystal ball, throughout this chapter you will find quotes from leading ethnic media producers and researchers who offered their perspective on this question: "In just a few sentences, how do you see the future of ethnic media?" We hope their answers prompt your thoughts and discussions about this important issue.

In their responses, you will encounter some of the key issues, challenges, and opportunities for the future of ethnic media, namely: the emergence of new technologies and concerns about online ethnic media production; changes in ethnic media consumers' needs and tastes; and changes in the realities of ethnic media production. We follow these discussions by highlighting some of the gaps in knowledge and research that we had to contend with in writing this book, in the hope that these areas will become the topics of new investigations by researchers and practitioners alike.

Ethnic Media and Emerging Technologies: Opportunity or Risk?

At various points in this volume, we have broached the subject of the impact of new communication technologies, particularly the Internet, on the ethnic media. At this point, there is still much we do not know about how Internet-based options will affect ethnic media production and consumption in different places. We do know, however, that it is unlikely that these new technologies will radically change or replace the ethnic media landscape as we now know it. Historically, when a new communication technology is introduced to society, the assumption is that the new medium will change everything about the ways that people communicate. And yet, history demonstrates that new technologies tend to be incorporated into people's communication ecologies, rather than totally reordering them.

In Chapter 9, we discussed communication ecologies as the set of communicative options—including a wide range of new and old mediated communication technologies, as well as interpersonal and organizational links—that people can connect with to achieve different kinds of goals (Wilkin, Ball-Rokeach, Matsaganis, & Cheong, 2007). We

John Downing

Director, Global Media Center, Southern Illinois University, Carbondale (U.S.)

So long as global labor migration continues, at the harsh end in fields, mines, and factories, [and] at the high-paid end in hi-tech, minority-ethnic media will continue to be an important dimension of our cultural system. So long as wars, pogroms and state land-grabs continue to uproot populations, the same is true. The same applies for so long as majority media maintain their typical disinterest in, and/or hostility to, the lives and aspirations of minority-ethnic publics. So long as business can be done between expatriate communities and their homelands, the same also applies. If air transport continues to keep ongoing links live with countries of origin, the assimilation process over generations will be made less absolute. And with entry costs to media communication slashed by Internet availability, all in all the future of widely diffused minority-ethnic media looks assured.

may connect with certain options within our communication ecologies for one goal, and different options for another. For example, in Chapter 9 we contrasted the connections people make to find information about health care, with ways that they find out what is going on in their community. These findings make it clear that our connections within our communication ecologies are not only flexible, in that we can activate different connections depending on what we need, but that we also often make multiple connections for one goal. For example, a first response to waking up with a scratchy throat might be talking to Mom or a roommate about the symptoms, followed by an online search for information on that symptom, rereading an article about the latest flu that was in an ethnically targeted newspaper yesterday, and a telephone call to make a doctor's appointment. All of those connections—to family or friends, to online resources, to ethnic media, a telephone call, and to a health care professional—together comprise our response to the goal of understanding the best way to resolve our health complaint.

Our connections within our own communication ecologies, therefore, can be combined in various ways, which also highlights that we design our communicative options to fit our goals—we do not develop needs simply because new technologies become available. In their study of the Internet's place in people's communication ecologies, Flanagin and Metzger (2001) conclude that: "It appears that technologies meet needs, and not that needs meet technologies . . . [but], as the media used to address individual needs change, so too do people's perceptions of those needs" (p. 174). This means that the Internet allows us to fulfill needs we were filling in other ways before—connecting with health information, community news, or staying in touch with friends and family—but our *perception* is that the Internet is allowing us to do things we could not do before.

The reality, however, is that although ethnic media producers have to make important decisions about whether to provide online content as a supplement to their existing production, or evaluate the feasibility of creating an independent online ethnic media outlet, the Internet does not portend the death or decline of more traditional forms of ethnic media. Rather, the challenge lies in understanding the potential of online ethnic media content to contribute to and complement the ethnic media forms that are already fundamental to the communication ecologies of immigrant, ethnic and language minority, and indigenous populations worldwide. Jon Funabiki echoes this position in

Jon Funabiki

Director, Renaissance Journalism Project, San Francisco State University (U.S.)

Overall, the future of the ethnic news media in the U.S. will be strong; however, the effects will not be uniform, but will vary from community to community and medium to medium. All of the major trends that are buffeting the mainstream news media (the collapse of the advertising model, the explosion in competing social media, etc.) will also hit the ethnic media too. My research shows that many leaders in the ethnic media are concerned because they have not yet adapted to today's new technologies. But we cannot forget that many ethnic communities are exploding in growth, and that the power of culture is very strong. Consumers are choosing media that resonate more closely with their interests and passions. Ethnic news media often are more than information sources–they can become community institutions that help stimulate a sense of cohesiveness and identity. At the same time, people in the community are adopting/adapting new identity patterns. Ethnic media will change as communities change.

his view of the future of ethnic media in his discussion of the goals for which communities connect with ethnic media.

Developing online ethnic media content has both production and consumption dimensions, as a number of the quotations in this chapter suggest. On the production side, our research and discussions throughout this book indicate that ethnic media outlets have often been slower to adapt to changes in technology than the mainstream media. This may be happening for a number of reasons, including the costs associated with creating and maintaining online content, a lack of new media literacy necessary to operate an online outlet, and a general resistance to or fear of change. The attendant risk of delayed adoption is the possibility of falling behind other media, which could potentially make ethnic media less competitive than other media outlets that have been quicker to adapt to new technologies.

The other reason many ethnic media outlets do not have an online presence may be that the producers feel they are serving a community that does not connect with the Internet. If producers do not feel that the payoff will override the costs, there is no incentive to explore online alternatives. For communities that do not have easy access to online resources, traditional ethnic media are still the critical resources for information and news. In large part, this may be due to the digital divide issues that persist for low-income groups in many developed nations. Primary dependence on traditional ethnic media forms is likely even more acute in places we had difficulty covering in this book, including rural regions of Africa, Latin America, the Indian subcontinent, and parts of Asia, where underdeveloped communication infrastructures may limit or even preclude Internet access entirely.

Kira Kosnick
Author of *Migrant media: Turkish broadcasting and multicultural politics in Berlin*

University of Frankfurt (Germany)

I see several trends that are bound to have (and are already having) a tremendous effect upon ethnic media production: the increasing commercialization of media production and dissemination, the challenge to state sovereignty posed by cross-border media, and the growth of Internet access and "we-media" offer new opportunities for ethnic minority engagement, but also dangers in terms of ethnically stratified digital divides, creating an urgent need to rethink our understanding of public spheres.

However, in many places, the Internet and emerging technologies are potentially enormous opportunities for ethnic media outlets that are well positioned to incorporate them in addition to media produced in traditional formats, as we discussed in Chapter 6. If their audiences are going online, Internet-based ethnic media content can reach people across large distances with very little additional economic cost. The interactive nature of the Internet can facilitate quick feedback loops between producers and consumers. It can also allow consumers to connect with each other through message boards and other interactive formats in ways that may attract new consumers, particularly youth.

Latino and Asian media in the U.S. have begun to make these generational shifts. According to the Pew Project for Excellence in Journalism (2009a), some of the largest Latino media outlets have begun the move online, recognizing that the growing proportion of Latinos who are young, American-born, educated, and bilingual, are also the segments most likely to be online. Impremedia, a Spanish-language newspaper conglomerate, created a Web portal in 2008 that includes content from all its publications, including *El Diario/La Prensa* (based in New York), *La Opinión* (Los Angeles), and the *Rumbo* newspaper chain (Texas). The portal is more than a new venue for content published in their newspapers. Web connectors can access news content interactively, and can also network with other connectors through blogs, videos, and photo galleries (Hawkes, 2008; PEJ, 2009a).

While the move online reflects a generational shift among Latinos, Asian communities have been connected to the Internet at higher rates than any other ethnic group in the U.S. for some time (U.S. Current Population Survey, 2007; PEJ, 2009a). As such, Asian media have increasingly found the Internet an attractive option for their ethnic media content. In recent years, many ethnic media Web sites, including *Sing Tao Daily* (Chinese), *World Journal* (Chinese), and *Nguoi Viet* (Vietnamese) have added substantial English-language content, "reflective of the potential marketers see in second-generation Asians" (PEJ, 2009a).

Don Browne
Author of *Ethnic minorities, electronic media and the public sphere*

University of Minnesota, Minneapolis (U.S.)

I regard the future of ethnic media with cautious optimism. The Internet, iPod, etc., have added to the already available media, and ethnic minority radio and TV services for the most part are holding their own and even growing in number. But the overall plenitude of media outlets in the industrialized world means that ethnic media will have to work harder to publicize their presence and to identify and involve themselves with their audiences.

Being online can also boost the visibility of an ethnic media outlet and, in turn, increase its potential to attract advertising revenues. Sandy Close sees such promise in the future of ethnic media.

Sandy Close

Director, New America Media (U.S.)

New America Media's new multilingual poll on media usage underscores that whereas most mainstream news organizations are losing audience, ethnic media continue to grow their audience. This is their unique and enduring strength—they know intimately the communities they serve; they're embedded in those communities. Absent ethnic news organizations, so many people in so many regions of this country would feel isolated and invisible in our media-drenched culture.

So what will the sector's future be? The biggest challenge is how ethnic media—especially print media—can build or expand their Web presence and convert their remarkable penetration of ethnic minority and immigrant communities into mobile audiences. They are in a key position to help expand their communities' access to the digital public square, but that depends in great part on how agile they are in embracing digital media technology. They know that moving onto the Internet will keep them relevant across generational lines.

As mainstream media look for niche audiences to survive, ethnic media are itching to grow—to connect communities to one another—to expand their communities' lens. And they know they can only do that if they go online.

Paulo Rogério Nunes

Executive Director, Instituto Mídia Étnica (Salvador, Brasil)

I think ethnic media will grow in the future, especially because new digital tools are giving disadvantaged groups ways to share their vision and fight for their rights. For example, in Brasil, the African-Brasilian communities that have no voice in mainstream media are trying to maintain their identity and religion through Internet-based newspaper, radio, videos and new media. I believe that, with the help of technology, ethnic media will grow faster than we imagine.

The relatively low start-up cost of online ethnic media also suggests the potential for new business models of ethnic media production. In Chapter 3, we discussed the development of *Africans Magazine,* which serves African immigrants living in Ireland. Due to limited funds, the magazine started in an online format, but when they had developed a substantial following they created a print version of the magazine as well.

Online content provided a gateway to producing complimentary traditional media in the case of *Africans Magazine.* We may be seeing online content providing similarly cheap opportunities for ethnic media creation in other communities facing prohibitively high start-up costs for traditional media production. As Paulo Rogério Nunes points out, the nature of the Internet as an interactive forum may provide outlets for traditionally disadvantaged groups to create a sense of imagined community across geographic spaces (a concept we discussed in Chapter 4).

The interactive nature of the Internet also provides potential opportunities for collaborations among community members. For some communities, including the Aboriginal communities in Australia that John Hartley references, online ethnic media projects can facilitate co-creation of media content by members of the community, for members of the community, in ways that fit easily with traditional practices of shared meaning-making.

Overall, it is clear that the Internet has real potential to provide entry points into ethnic media production for entrepreneurs who see untapped, but online audiences. How the Internet and new communication technologies become sites of ethnic media production in different parts of the world is a story that is only starting to be written, but certainly a rich area for future research.

John Hartley

Author of *The Indigenous public sphere: The reporting and reception of Aboriginal issues in the Australian media* (with A. McKee)

Queensland University of Technology (Australia)

Ethnic media, both multicultural and Indigenous, are strongly established in Australia, and evolving creatively to meet the challenge of new platforms. This is where person-to-person networking, consumer co-creation, and user-led innovation have their strongest roots; and here too is where the most innovative programming, community relations, and participatory production have been trialed. Ethnic media are where diversity, change, learning, and adaptation are most intense. In other words they are the evolutionary cutting edge of "the media," never mind "ethnic."

The Future of Ethnic Media: The Consumers

Demographic indicators all point to ethnic media remaining important and viable in the future, as declining birthrates in Western countries continue to encourage immigration to satisfy demand for workers. As we discussed in Chapters 3 and 9, ethnic media provide new immigrants with content that connects them to their country of origin, but also with content that orients them to their new communities in ways that can encourage settlement. As Min Zhou points out, continued immigration provides an ongoing need for the services that ethnic media provide to immigrants.

> **Min Zhou**
> **Author of *Contemporary Chinese America: Immigration, ethnicity and community transformation***
>
> **University of California, Los Angeles (U.S.)**
>
> Ethnic media constitute an indispensable part of immigrant community life in the United States. It facilitates rather than inhibits immigrants' adaptation to their new homeland. Since we are a nation of immigrants, ethnic media will be there with us for a long time and will be woven into the fabric of multicultural America.

In Europe, Japan, Canada, Australia, and to a lesser extent, the United States, low birthrates among the native born are sharply contrasted by high birthrates among immigrants, leading to a rise in the overall percentage of these countries that identify themselves as immigrants and ethnic minorities. As these percentages rise—for example, the Pew Hispanic Center forecasts that the number of U.S. Latinos will triple to 29% of the overall U.S. population by 2050 (Passel & Cohn, 2008)—larger potential audiences provide opportunities for ethnic media that can tap into the changing tastes and needs of ethnic minority, language minority, and indigenous populations.

There was a time when researchers viewed the success of ethnic media as "directly proportional to [their] willingness to disappear" (Elias & Caspi, 2007, p. 179; Janowitz, 1967) as their audiences assimilated into the mainstream. However, policies of multiculturalism, as we discussed in Chapter 8, have reduced many countries' emphasis on traditional models of assimilation. Throughout this book, we have discussed how ethnic media can be central to maintaining distinct and multi-dimensional ethnic identities across multiple generations. Many of the quotations from practitioners and researchers in this chapter reference the cross-generational challenges and opportunities with which ethnic media are confronted, including the views from the U.S. and the Netherlands presented on the next page.

These viewpoints emphasize that ethnic media can, and do, remain viable over multiple generations, and that ethnic media may be an important part of people's communication ecologies alongside their mainstream media connections. The rise in bilingual media outlets is a shift in this direction; according to PEJ (2009a) sources, the number of bilingual newspapers serving Latino populations has doubled since 2000. For Asian-American audiences, English has become the common language that binds groups with different languages

Edward Schumacher-Matos

Founder, *Rumbo* Newspapers/ Meximerica Media (U.S.)

The ethnic media will always have a future because of the targeted service they provide. This is especially true of ethnic media in the language of first-generation immigrants. In the United States, much of the ethnic media, in addition to providing entertainment and a welcomed relief by being in an immigrant's mother tongue, also provide useful information in how to maneuver and succeed in this new country. In today's multicultural, segmented world, even later generation ethnic group members will seek out targeted niche publications in the language of the host country as a supplement to their mainstream media consumption. One of the keys to success for ethnic media is production quality, and in the United States and many other countries, ethnic media today have a production quality almost equal to, or equal to, the mainstream. This is in part due to technology and the great drop in relative costs of production in all media.

Susan Bink

Researcher at Mira Media (Utrecht, Netherlands)

Ethnic media are still very valuable in the Netherlands, especially for first generation immigrants who have difficulties understanding the Dutch language. They need guidance in their native language and media they can identify with. Also, youngsters like to connect with their country of origin by using ethnic media.

Unfortunately, ethnic media often have financial and organizational difficulties. Distribution is also a problem. Ethnic media will benefit from supporting structures like New America Media [in the U.S.] that can provide them with training in journalistic, marketing, research and organizational skills. This way, there will definitely be a future for ethnic media in the Netherlands.

of origin (PEJ, 2009a). Therefore, English-language ethnic media have been and continue to be an important part of a conglomerate Asian-American identity.

For younger generations, however, media content in an accessible language is only one dimension of the changing tastes and needs of consumers, as we discussed in Chapter 4. Beyond the language of production, ethnic media content that primarily targets their parents' tastes may not be as responsive to later generations' needs and experiences. This opens up significant opportunities for ethnic media entrepreneurs to create media products that better serve the younger generation. One of the factors that such productions must take into account is how globalization (as we explored in Chapter 7) continues to fundamentally affect how individuals and societies relate to one another. Today's ethnic minority youth are coming of age in a time when links between "here" and "there" are easier to maintain because technology and ease of travel make it possible to do so. Moreover, globalization and an increased awareness of the interconnectedness of our world have increased the benefits of bilingualism, multi-national, and multi-dimensional identities. Young people who can broker connections between places and peoples by putting these skills to professional or social uses may also develop tastes for media outlets that reflect their multi-dimensional lives and identities, as noted by Myria Georgiou.

As we discussed in Chapters 4 and 7, interest in development of hybrid, hyphenated, and conglomerate identities among ethnic minority youth both encourages and is encouraged by the development of ethnic media that reflect these identifications. These shifts in identification can provide opportunities for ethnic media entrepreneurs to develop ethnic media productions in new forms and with new kinds of content that reflect the needs and tastes of youth growing up in an increasingly globalized world.

These new identity formations also create potential for collaborations between distinct ethnic minority groups who share similar experiences growing up in a particular place. For example, Ugba (2002) describes his involvement as a researcher-practitioner in the creation of *Metro Eireann* in 2000, which is a monthly newspaper with an inclusive focus on the activities of ethnic minorities and immigrants in Ireland. Ugba and his associates were motivated to cover the issues of Ireland's rapidly increasing ethnic minority and immigrant populations, "to provide a forum for cross-cultural exchanges and for persons from minority ethnic groups, who by and large were denied quality access to the mainstream media, to air their view" (p. 21). The popularity of *Metro Eireann* may indicate potential for ethnic media that address a broader spectrum of conglomerate identities than those we explored in Chapter 4. In Chapter 10, we discussed *El Gringo* in Sweden as another example of this phenomenon.

Myria Georgiou
Author of *Diaspora, identity and the media: Diasporic transnationalism and mediated spatialities*

London School of Economics and Political Science (UK)

Ethnic media are here and they are here to stay... but not necessarily as we know them. Since the early days of the ethnic press, these media have faced many challenges: financial strains, marginalization, and intense competition have been among the most important. These challenges have intensified in time, making any predictions for the future of ethnic media as we know them quite difficult. In addition and in time, ethnic media have come across a new challenge, which is probably more difficult to overcome than any financial or social constraint: the generational change and the consequent shifts in ethnic identities. As younger generations replace the first migrants, community links and connections with a country of origin cannot be taken for granted anymore. Ethnic media that do indeed have a future are those that can reflect on and represent the growing diversity among their audiences.

Additionally, in Augie Fleras' comments regarding the situation in Canada, we see potential for growth in ethnic media that can traverse multiple types of "in-between"

Augie Fleras
Author of "Ethnic and Aboriginal media in Canada" in *Media-Migration-Integration: European and North American perspectives* (R. Geißler, & H. Pöttker, Eds.)

University of Waterloo (Canada)

The future of ethnic media in Canada is promising. The reasons are not hard to fathom: Ethnic media constitute a form of social capital for immigrants and racialized

(Continued)

(Continued)

minorities. They provide both a bridging (connecting with others) and bonding (constructing communities) function by securing a link between the "here" and the "there" by way of the "in-between." To be sure, conventional notions of ethnic media as print or broadcast will be challenged by cheaper and more accessible online formats for content and delivery. Nevertheless, ethnic media in one form or another will remain in the vanguard of a multicultural Canada whose integrative logic is based on the principle of treating people the same (equally) as a matter of course, but also treating them differently (as equals) when the situation arises.

to help ethnic minority and immigrant communities to be seen both equally and as equals, much as *Metro Eireann* was created to do in Ireland.

For ethnic media producers to traverse these kinds of boundaries and serve a multi-dimensional role for not only their target audiences, but for the larger society as well, is not a new phenomenon. Our discussions throughout this book demonstrate that ethnic media producers have long served as important negotiators of information resources for their communities. In the following section, we outline some of the ways that ethnic media production may shift to accommodate new trends in consumption and changing social conditions.

The Future of Ethnic Media: The Producers

Catherine Murray
Author of *Cultural diversity and ethnic media in British Columbia* (with S. Yu & D. Ahadi)

Simon Fraser University (Canada)

I would think the future will depend on (a) immigration and (b) new social contours of second and third-generation ethno-cultural groups. In Canada, as I have argued elsewhere, it will also depend on (a) loosening some regulatory restrictions at the broadcast level and (b) directing public policy on government ad spending to third-language media. In essence, my argument is that we would really like to see the Latino "problem" here in Canada: aggregation of sufficient resources to really grow. In terms of public journalism, there is a case to be made for far more collaboration on intercultural journalism standards.

One of the major questions about the future of ethnic media is the changing relationship between ethnic and mainstream media outlets. As ethnic media grow in size and prominence, they are also becoming increasingly professionalized and sophisticated, as Chapters 5, 6, and 10 documented. However, with the exception of the largest ethnic media, issues of independent auditing, clear reports of circulation, revenues, and so on, make it difficult for ethnic media to compete with mainstream media for advertising dollars. Catherine Murray discusses her desire to see Canada develop the equivalent of the Latino "problem" that exists in the United States, where Spanish-language media are buoyed by having a common language shared by immigrants from almost every country in Latin America, and a multi-generational Latino ethnic minority that continues to grow in size and prominence. After years of delay by America's major broadcasters, the Nielsen Company began rating the largest Spanish-language television stations in 2005. The reason the major broadcasters resisted this move was that when advertisers and sponsors had an impartial platform on which to compare English and Spanish-language broadcasters, it would inevitably result in diverting more advertising monies to the Spanish-language networks. We discuss this move in more detail in Chapter 6.

The Spanish-language media in the U.S. remain an unusually powerful exception, rather than the rule. As we have noted throughout this volume, the majority of ethnic media are still small, local publications aimed at relatively small audiences. Even larger conglomerates in different parts of the world are likely to serve a more limited language group. For example, since Asian groups "comprise a variety of small and fractured markets," in that they do not share a common language (PEJ, 2009c), any media serving one of these groups will be limited to audiences who understand the language of their publications or broadcasts. This creates challenges to easy growth opportunities, as audiences with multiple national origins cannot be served simultaneously with the same ethnic media product—unless that media product is in a common language like English (PEJ, 2009c).

Issues of professionalism within ethnic media—including the development of best practices and industry standards—are crucial to being able to compete with mainstream media for audience time and attention. However, we do not mean to imply that the future of ethnic media lies in their ability to match and/or beat mainstream media at their own game. Rather, we see important ways in which ethnic and mainstream media producers can collaborate with each other, to the benefit of producers and consumers alike.

¤ For Further Discussion

Knowing what you know now about ethnic media, take another look at the ethnic media operating in your area or community. What would you forecast for their future? In making your forecast, also detail what environmental, technological, or other changes helped you reach your conclusions.

For example, ethnic media producers' commitment to and consistent focus on home country issues can afford them opportunities to gather stories that mainstream media simply cannot. Channel One TV, the Iranian-language television station based in Los Angeles, provides a striking example. In June 2009, when tens of thousands of Iranians took to the streets to protest what they considered to be Mahmoud Ahmedinejad's stealing of their national election, mainstream media crews were almost entirely shut out of Iran. The leadership of Channel One TV had not only anticipated this crackdown on media access, but for almost a year before the election, they had been in Tehran and other large cities distributing pens that were much more than writing utensils (Dobuzinskis, 2009). These pens had digital video and voice recording capacities so that citizens involved in the marches could easily record what was going on around them and upload image and voice recordings to Channel One TV over the Internet when they got home from rallies. These pens were so ubiquitous that despite government awareness of their existence, the sheer number of people using them dissuaded officials from confiscating them or punishing people who used them. These images and voice recordings became not only Channel One TV's lifeline for coverage of events inside Iran, but were the major source of information for mainstream media outlets around the world as well. One could easily imagine other major political events where such ingenuity on the part of ethnic media producers could provide not just ethnic minority, but mainstream audiences, with perspectives that would otherwise go unexpressed.

These sorts of collaborations between ethnic and mainstream media outlets, where each brings their strengths to the table to provide richer coverage of domestic and international issues can help to bridge understandings between majority and ethnic minority audiences. In Chapter 2, we discussed the development of the Aboriginal Peoples' Television Network in Canada and the National Indigenous Radio Service in Australia as examples of ethnic media created with dual purposes: (1) to serve the indigenous communities in their respective countries, and (2) to help explain their communities to majority culture audiences. Such policy development and initial public funding on the part of the Canadian and Australian governments have been the exception rather than the rule, as we discussed in Chapters 2 and 8. In countries where such support is not likely to be forthcoming, private sector partnerships between mainstream and ethnic media may be a more feasible alternative.

Partnerships of this kind are undermined when officials do not grant equal access to mainstream and ethnic media. Ethnic media journalists in our panel discussions and elsewhere have described how they are often denied access to the hallways of power, be it limitations on their admittance to political and other types of press conferences, or being barred from the kind of access to key decision makers that mainstream media enjoy. These restrictions challenge ethnic media's capacities to be taken seriously as credible and professional news outlets. That government officials either actively avoid engaging ethnic media or simply dismiss them can have serious impacts on the actual and perceived quality of ethnic media production.

The consequences can be even more serious for the communities ethnic media serve. For example, in 2008, there was a major recall of spinach in the U.S. when salmonella contamination was traced back to a number of spinach processing plants. The recall was widely broadcast through mainstream media outlets. However, according to New America Media, ethnic media outlets were not contacted with press releases and information to share with their audiences. These kinds of oversights can place minority communities at significant risk. When newsmakers overlook the ethnic media as outlets for disseminating such important information, they may also be undermining ethnic media producers' efforts to earn and maintain the trust of their audience. As Frank Herron indicates, this audience trust is central to ethnic media's continued viability.

Frank Herron

Director, Center on Media & Society, University of Massachusetts, Boston (U.S.)

As is true in many news-media sectors, this is the best and worst of times. I think the positives far outweigh the negatives. The need and demand for high-quality news is keen among many ethnic groups. The audiences are distinctive. The points of view are distinctive. The sources are distinctive. All point toward robust growth for most populations. These ethnic media outlets are in a position to flourish as "trusted community voices," a term that I've heard Census officials use. Maintaining that trust is key. That's where developing a strong journalistic tradition of truth-telling comes in, I think. Best-practice journalism is vital.

Another element of community trust is suggested in Caspi and Elias's (under review) differentiation of media produced *by* members of an ethnic community, and media produced *for* members of an ethnic community by members of the majority group or members of another ethnic minority. One of their key distinctions is that media produced by members of a group is motivated by an investment in the community itself, whereas they see media produced for a community by an outsider as motivated primarily by profit. As such, they see "media-by" as maintaining greater community trust than "media-for." As Nelly Elias points out, the distinction between "media-by" and "media-for" has been quite striking in the Israeli case.

In this book, we define ethnic media as media produced *for* immigrant, indigenous, ethnic minority, or language minority groups, usually *by* members of the same group. Exploring when the distinction between "media-by" and "media-for" really matters, and under what conditions, is a fruitful direction for future research on ethnic media. In the concluding section, we identify several more gaps in the research that warrant future attention from ethnic media researchers and journalists.

Nelly Elias

Ben-Gurion University of the Negev (Israel)

Regarding the future of the ethnic media in Israel, I would say that the main cause of the almost complete disappearance of the Russian-language print media over the last decade is the structure of media ownership. Most of the Russian-language newspapers established in Israel since the onset of the mass immigration from the former Soviet Union were in hands of the Israeli-born entrepreneurs whose only agenda was profit. As such, these newspapers failed to address unique interests and express authentic voices of the Russian immigrant community, and hence, lost most of their readership. This said, we are witnessing a new beginning of the Russian-language media in Israel, flourishing on the Web, since with the assistance of the new technology immigrants can more easily make their voices heard.

Gaps in the Research: What Do We Still Need to Know to Understand Ethnic Media?

There are a host of reasons why the ethnic media cases we examine in this volume leave out large portions of the world. Some of these reasons are historical; a country like the United States, which has consciously defined itself as a nation of immigrants since its inception, has had a greater interest in the media behaviors of immigrants over a longer period of time than, say, Spain, which only become an immigrant-receiving nation in the last 15 years or so. The deep asymmetries in the available research, however, go beyond historical explanations. When we were able to find evidence of ethnic media in regions like Southeast Asia, it was generally a fleeting reference rather than a full examination. There may be research that we could not access for linguistic reasons, but another reason might be that government or other reports are not in the published literature online or offline. Perhaps the increased visibility of ethnic media will lead to more and more accessible literatures.

In particular, there is a great need for more research on ethnic media in Africa, Latin America, parts of Asia, and the Indian subcontinent. Most of what we know about these populations is limited to our knowledge of their immigrants to other parts of the world. For example, we were able to access research on Latin-Americans in the U.S. and Spain, and Africans living in Europe and the U.S.—but found almost no research on ethnic media in these immigrants' countries of origin.

We also know a great deal more about ethnic media serving immigrants than we do about media for linguistic minorities and indigenous populations. With Canada, Australia, the United States, and a handful of European countries as the notable exceptions, we found almost no research on media serving indigenous populations in other parts of the world. The same holds true for language minority groups still residing in their countries of origin. We could find little or no research, for example, on media serving minority language groups in Africa or on the Indian subcontinent. It is quite likely that immigrant media have generally received more attention because newcomers and their descendents are more visible to researchers by virtue of their novelty. Moreover, the global movements of peoples across borders are more frequently addressed in media, politics, and policy than the movements of people within the boundaries of their countries of origin. The media histories of language minorities and indigenous populations remain largely unwritten, and more research on these communities would greatly contribute to our understandings of the roles that these media play in the lives of their audiences and in society generally.

Issues related to methodology also provide potential new avenues for research. Researchers working at the intersections of media and society in fields including communication, media studies, journalism studies, ethnic studies, anthropology, and sociology often do not take ethnic media into account in their research on diverse communities. We hope that this book will underscore the importance of integrating ethnic media into research that has traditionally focused on mainstream media. As we highlighted in the Preface of this volume, the growth of ethnic media has been a veritable explosion. At a time when media institutions of all kinds are facing serious economic and social challenges, we continue to see growth in ethnic media sectors. The relative invisibility of these media in research belies their tremendous importance to communities around the world.

Although we may not be able to predict precisely what the future holds, ethnic media are here to stay and are playing important social, cultural, and political roles that remain relatively invisible to social researchers, journalists, and policymakers. Our hope is that this book will contribute to increase the visibility and recognition of these media's importance to the communities they serve, and beyond. James Ho, president of Mainstream Broadcasting Corporation and the *Chinese Canadian Times,* commented: "No longer are ethnic media serving the minorities; as minority populations grow, ethnic media are now serving majorities." As our definitions of "majority" and "minority" are challenged and minorities become majorities in many parts of the world, the media that serve these populations become increasingly important not only to the groups they serve, but to the diversity and vitality of the social fabric of our societies.

References

About ABC: An introduction/our history. (n.d.). In *Audit Bureau of Circulations.* Retrieved from http://www.accessabc.com/aboutabc/introduction.htm

Abu-Laban, Y., & Gabriel, C. (2002). *Selling diversity: Immigration, multiculturalism, employment equity, and globalization.* Peterborough, Ontario, CA: Broadview Press.

Adoni, H., Caspi, D., & Cohen, A. (2006). *Media, minorities and hybrid identities.* Creskill, NJ: Hampton Press.

Akst, D. (2003, Spring). New Americans fresh off the presses. *Carnegie Reporter, 2*(2). Retrieved September 15, 2006, from http://www.carnegie.org/reporter/06/americans/index.html

Alba, R., Logan, J., Stults, B., Marzan, G., & Zhang, W. (1999). Immigrant groups in the suburbs: A reexamination of suburbanization and spatial assimilation. *American Sociological Review, 64,* 446–460.

Alba, R., & Nee, V. (2003). *Remaking the American mainstream: Assimilation and contemporary immigration.* Cambridge, MA: Harvard University Press.

Aldridge, M., & Evetts, J. (2004). Rethinking the concept of professionalism: The case of journalism. *British Journal of Sociology, 54*(4), 547–564.

Alexander, A., Owers, J., & Carveth, R. (Eds.). (1998). *Media economics: Theory and practice.* Mahwah, NJ: Lawrence Erlbaum.

Alia, V., & Bull, S. (2005). *Media and ethnic minorities.* Edinburgh: University of Edinburgh Press.

Allan, S., & O'Malley, T. (1999). The media in Wales. In D. Dunkerley & A. Thompson (Eds.), *Wales today* (pp. 127–148). Cardiff: University of Wales Press.

Allen, J. (2009, June). *Ethnic media reaching record numbers in U.S.* Retrieved June 9, 2009, from http://news.newamericamedia.org/news/view_article.html?article_id=8bb0c256d866e8e99e74fc734d5cef67

Allied Media Corporation. (2007). *Hispanic American market: Hispanic television.* Retrieved May 23, 2007, from http://www.allied-media.com/Hispanic%20Market/hispanic%20tv.html

Amburgey, T. L., Kelley, D., & Barnett, W. P. (1993). Resetting the clock: The dynamics of organizational change and failure. *Administrative Science Quarterly, 38*(1), 51–74.

Anderson, B. (1991). *Imagined communities: Reflections on the origins and spread of nationalism.* New York: Verso.

Aponte, R., & Siles, M. E. (1994). *Latinos in the heartland: The browning of the Midwest* (JSRI Research Report No. 5). East Lansing, MI: Michigan State University, The Julian Samora Research Institute.

Appadurai, A. (1996). *Modernity at large.* Minneapolis: University of Minnesota Press.

Arana, E., Azpillaga, P., & Narbaiza, B. (2003). Local television stations, Basque and minority language normalization. *Mercator Media Forum, 7,* 86–98.

Arango, T. (2009, April 27). Fall in newspaper sales to pass 7%. *The New York Times.* Retrieved September 1, 2009, from http://www.nytimes.com/2009/04/28/business/media/28paper.html

Arbitron. (2007). *Hispanic radio today: How America listens to radio (2007 edition).* Retrieved March 1, 2008, from www.arbitron.com/downloads/hispanicradiotoday07.pdf

Arsenault, A., & Castells, M. (2008). The structure and dynamics of global multi-media business networks. *International Journal of Communication, 2,* 707–748.

Artz, L. (2007). The corporate model from national to transnational. In L. Artz & Y. Kamalipour (Eds.), *The media globe: Trends in international mass media* (pp. 141–162). Plymouth, UK: Rowman & Littlefield.

Assemblée Populaire Nationale [National Popular Assembly of Algeria]. (2002, April). *Loi n° 02–03 du 27 Moharram 1423 correspondant au 10 Avril 2002 portant révision constitutionnelle.* Retrieved April1, 2009 from http://www.apn-dz.org/apn/french/constitution 96/loi02_03.htm

Axelrod, L. (2006). *A dialogue on diversity and ethnic media in Vancouver.* Summary report prepared for the Department of Canadian Heritage & Simon Frasier University Department of Communication, Vancouver, BC.

Bagdikian, B. H. (2004). *The new media monopoly.* Boston: Beacon Press.

Bailey, T., & Waldinger, R. (1991). Primary, secondary, and enclave labor markets: A training systems approach. *American Sociological Review, 56,* 432–445.

Baker, M. (2004a, November 23). *Netherlands: Dutch immigration (Part 1)—The death of multiculturalism.* Retrieved February 8, 2009, from Radio Free Europe Radio Liberty Web site: http://www.rferl.org/content/article/1056019.html

Baker, M. (2004b, November 24). *Netherlands: Dutch immigration (Part 2)—Paying the price of political correctness.* Retrieved February 8, 2009, from Radio Free Europe Radio Liberty Web site: http://www.rferl.org/content/article/1056042.html

Ball-Rokeach, S. J. (1985). The origins of individual media-system dependency. *Communication Research, 12*(4), 485–510.

Ball-Rokeach, S. J. (1998). A theory of media power and a theory of media use: Different stories, questions, and ways of thinking. *Mass Communication & Society, 1,* 5–40.

Ball-Rokeach, S. J., Cheong, P. H., Wilkin, H. A., & Matsaganis, M. D. (2004, May). *A map to the multiethnic communication landscape of Los Angeles immigrant communities, old and new.* Paper presented at the annual conference of the International Communication Association, New Orleans.

Ball-Rokeach, S. J., Gibbs, J., Jung, J. -Y., Kim, Y. -C., & Qju, J. L. (2000). *The globalization of everyday life: Visions and reality of social justice in the Internet age* [White paper). Los Angeles: Metamorphosis Project, Annenberg School for Communication, University of Southern California.

Ball-Rokeach, S. J., Kim, Y. -C., & Matei, S. (2001). Storytelling neighborhood: Paths to belonging in diverse urban environments. *Communication Research, 28*(4), 392–428.

Ball-Rokeach, S. J., & Lin, W. -Y. (2004, December). *Positioning ethnic Chinese television and the Internet in the lives of Chinese immigrant populations: A case study* (Research Report to ETTV). Los Angeles: Metamorphosis Project, University of Southern California.

Ball-Rokeach, S. J., & Wilkin, H. A. (2009). Ethnic differences in information-seeking behavior: Methodological and applied issues. *Communication Research Reports 26*(1), 22–29.

Banks, J. A. (1991). Teaching assistants and cultural diversity. In R. D. Abbott, J. D. Nyquist, D. H. Wulff, & J. Sprague (Eds.) *Preparing the professoriate of tomorrow to teach: Selected readings in TA training* (pp. 65–72). Dubuque, IA: Kendall/Hunt.

Barlow, D. M., Mitchell, P., & O'Malley, T. (2005). *The media in Wales: Voices of a small nation.* Cardiff: University of Wales Press.

Barrow Jr., L. C. (1977). "Our own cause": *Freedom's Journal* and the beginnings of the Black press. *Journalism History 41*(4), 118–122.

Bates, J. (2005). EU broadcasting: Regional populations creating demand, via satellite. *Satellite Today.* Retrieved July 4, 2006, from http://www.viasatellite.com/broadcasting/tv/EU-Broadcasting-Regional-Populations-Creating-Demand_259.html http://www.telecomweb.com/cgi/pub/via/via09010503.html

Bates, S. (1995). *Realigning journalism with democracy: The Hutchins Commission, its times, and Ours.* Washington, DC: The Annenberg Washington Program in Communications Policy Studies of Northwestern University.

Baum, D. (2006, October 23). Arriba! A Latino radio scold gets out the vote. *The New Yorker.* Retrieved January 16, 2007, from http://www.newyorker.com/fact/content/articles/061023fa_fact

BBC News. (2006, May 25). *Race riot town "remains divided."* Retrieved May 27, 2008, from http://news.bbc.co.uk/2/hi/uk_news/england/manchester/5014764.stm

BBC News. (2007). *Time running out for the ethnic media?* Retrieved May 11, 2007, from http://www.bbc.co.uk/london/content/articles/2007/01/05/ethnic_media_features.html

BBC News. (2008, April 1). *Immigration "small benefit" to UK.* Retrieved May 29, 2008, from http://news.bbc.co.uk/1/hi/uk_politics/7322825.stm

Bendixen & Associates. (2006). *Ethnic media in America: The giant hidden in plain sight.* Miami, FL: Author.

Bennett, W. L. (n.d.). *The twilight of mass media news: Market deregulation, digital convergence, and the future of public information.* Retrieved March 25, 2007, from http://www.lsu.edu/reillycenter/twilightofmassmedianews.pdf

Bergquist, J. M. (1987). The German-American press. In S. M. Miller (Ed.), *The ethnic press in the United States: A historical analysis and handbook* (pp. 131–159). New York: Greenwood Press.

Bernanke, B. (2008, May 5). *Mortgage delinquencies and foreclosures.* Presentation at Columbia's Business School 32nd annual dinner, New York. Retrieved August 1, 2009, from http://www.federalreserve.gov/newsevents/speech/Bernanke20080505a.htm

Bernard, N. (2002). *Multilevel governance in the European Union.* New York: Kluwer Law International.

Bharath, D. (2009, September 6). Little Saigon protester denies assaulting newspaper reporter. *Orange County Register.* Retrieved September 15, 2009, from http://www.ocregister.com/articles/viet-newspaper-doan-2012121-nguoi-protesters

Bink, S. (2002). *Mapping minorities and their media: The national context—the Netherlands.* [European Media Technology and Everyday Life Network.] Retrieved November 6, 2007, from http://www.lse.ac.uk/collections/EMTEL/Minorities/reports.html

BlackPressMagazine.com. (2007). Black press all star awards. *BlackPressMagazine.com.* Retrieved September 15, 2009, from http://www.blackpress.org/homepage.htm

Blanchard, M. (1977). *The Hutchins Commission, the press and the responsibility concept.* Lexington, KY: Association for Education in Journalism.

Blommesteijn, M., & Entzinger, H. (1999). Appendix: Report of the field studies carried out in France, Italy, the Netherlands, Norway, Portugal and the United Kingdom. In H. Entzinger (Ed.), *Political and social participation of immigrants through consultative bodies* (pp. 41–64). Strasbourg, France: Council of Europe.

Böse, M., Haberfellner, R., & Koldas, A. (2002). *Mapping minorities and their media: the national context—Austria.* [European Media Technology and Everyday Life Network.] Retrieved November 6, 2007, from http://www.lse.ac.uk/collections/EMTEL/Minorities/reports.html

Boucaud, P., & Stubbs, P. (1994). Access to the media and the challenge to cultural racism in France. In C. Husband (Ed.), *A richer vision: The development of ethnic minority media in Western democracies* (pp. 85–105). Paris: UNESCO/John Libbey.

Boyle, M. (2006). *Univisión's one-two L.A. summer punch: Radioandrecords.com.* Retrieved on October 29, 2006, from http://www.radioandrecords.com/radiomonitor/news/business/top_news/article_display.jsp?vnu_content_id=1003255409

Brady, S. (2002, June 10). BET seeks more ways to work with Viacom family. *Cable World.* Retrieved October 2, 2006, from http://findarticles.com/p/articles/mi_m0DIZ/is_2002_June_10/ai_88680142

Brady, S. (2003, July 28). Cable networks deliver for Viacom. *Cable World.* Retrieved October 2, 2006, from http://findarticles.com/p/articles/mi_m0DIZ/is_30_15/ai_105892074

Braman, S., & Sreberny-Mohammadi, A. (Eds.). (1996). *Globalization, communication, and transnational civil society.* Cresskill, NJ: Hampton Press.

Brennan, T. (2003). *Globalization and its terrors: Daily life in the West.* New York: Routledge.

Brown, L. D., Khagram, S., Moore, M. H., & Frumkin, P. (2000). Globalization, NGOs, and multi-sectoral relations. In J. S. Nye & J. D.Donahue (Eds.), *Governance in a globalizing world* (pp. 271–296). Washington, DC: Brookings Institution Press.

Brown, M. (2003, March 19). Voice squad. *The Guardian.* Retrieved September 1, 2008, from http://www.guardian.co.uk/society/2003/mar/19/radio.broadcasting

Browne, D. R. (1996). *Electronic media and indigenous peoples: A voice of their own?* Ames, IA: Iowa State University Press.

Browne, D. R. (2005). *Ethnic minorities, electronic media, and the public sphere: A comparative approach.* Cresskill, NJ: Hampton Press.

Browne, D. R. (2007). Speaking up: A brief history of minority languages and the electronic media worldwide. In M. Cormack & N. Hourigan (Eds.), *Minority language media: Concepts, critiques, and case studies* (pp. 107–132). Buffalo, NY: Multilingual Matters.

Browne, D. (2008). Speaking in our own tongues: Linguistic minority radio in the United States. In M. C. Keith (Ed.), *Radio cultures: The sound medium in American life* (pp. 23–46). New York: Peter Lang Publishing.

Bruck, P. A., Dörr, D., Favre, J., Gramstad, S., Monaco, R., & Peruško Čulek, Z. (2002, December). *Media diversity in Europe* [Report prepared by the Advisory Panel on Media Diversity, Council of Europe]. Retrieved April 2, 2007, from http://archiv2.medienhilfe.ch/topics/Diversity/CoE_MediaDiversity.pdf

Bullock, L. (2006, August 20). *Testers posing as Katrina survivors encounter "linguistic profiling."* [National Newspaper Publishers Association News Report & National Fair Housing Alliance.] Available online at: http://www.berkeleydailyplanet.com/issue/2006-08-22/article/24914?headline=Testers-Posing-as-Katrina-Survivors-Encounter-Linguistic-Profiling

Burton, E. (2003). *The Swedish-American press and the Vietnam War.* Dissertation published by the Department of History, University of Göteburg, Sweden.

Business. (2009). Retrieved November 3, 2009, from Zee Television Web site: http://www.zeetelevision.com/html/Business.asp

Business Wire. (1998, May 26). *Heftel Broadcasting announces the acquisition of KJQY-FM and KKLQ-FM in San Diego and the launch of WNWK-FM in New York.* Retrieved June 2, 2009, from http://www.thefreelibrary.com/_/print/PrintArticle.aspx?id=20632631

Business Wire. (2000, October 11). *The Korea Times Los Angeles and Leonard Green & Partners announce the formation of AsianMedia Group, Inc.* Retrieved June 9, 2008, from http://www.allbusiness.com/banking-finance/financial-markets-investing-securities/6572137-1.html

Byron, M., & Condon, S. (1996). A comparative study of Caribbean return migration from Britain and France: Towards a context-dependent explanation. *Transactions of the Institute of British Geographers, 21*(1), 91–104.

Cainkar, L. (2002). No longer invisible: Arab and Muslim exclusion after September 11. *Middle East Report, 224,* 22–29.

Cainkar, L. (2004). Post 9/11 domestic policies affecting U.S. Arabs and Muslims: a brief review. *Comparative Studies of South Asia, Africa, and the Middle East, 24* (1), 247–251.

Camauër, L. (2002). *Mapping minorities and their media: The national context—Leonor.* [European Media Technology and Everyday Life Network.] Retrieved November 6, 2007, from http://www.lse.ac.uk/collections/EMTEL/Minorities/reports.html

Campbell, W. J. (2001). *Yellow journalism: Puncturing the myths, defining the legacies.*Westport, CT: Praeger.

Campbell, W. J. (2005). *The Spanish-American war: American wars and the media in primary documents.* New York: Greenwood Press.

Cantle, T., Kaur, D., Athar, M., Dallison, C., Wiggans, A., & Harris, J. (2006, March). *Challenging local communities to change Oldham.* Coventry, UK: Institute of Community Cohesion, Coventry University.

Carrington, W. J., & Detragiache, E. (1999, June). How extensive is the brain drain? *Finance & Development 36*(2). Retrieved April 22, 2007, from http://www.imf.org/external/pubs/ft/fandd/1999/06/carringt.htm

Carroll, G. R. (1987). *Publish or perish: The organizational ecology of newspaper industries.* Greenwich, CT: JAI Press.

Carveth, R. (2004). The economics of online media. In A. Alexander, J. Owers, & R. Carveth (Eds.), *Media Economics: Theory and Practice* (pp. 265–282). Mahwah, NJ: Lawrence Erlbaum.

Caspi, D., & Elias, D. (under review). Don't patronize me: Media-by and media-for minorities. *Journal of Ethnic and Racial Studies.*

Castañeda, C. (2004). *Teaching and learning in diverse classrooms: Faculty reflections on their experiences and pedagogical practices of teaching diverse populations.* New York: Routledge.

Castells, M. (1996a, 2000a). *The rise of the network society. The Information Age: Econnomy, Society and Culture* (Vol. 1). Oxford, UK: Blackwell Publishers.

Castells, M. (1996b, 2000b). *End of millennium. The Information Age: Economy, Society and Culture* (Vol. 3). Oxford, UK: Blackwell Publishers.

Castells, M. (2001). *The Internet galaxy.* Oxford, UK: Oxford University Press.

Castells, M. (2003). *Internet galaxy: Reflections on the Internet, business, and society.* Oxford, UK: Oxford University Press.

Castells-Talens, A. (2004). *The negotiation of Indigenist radio policy in Mexico.* Unpublished dissertation, University of Florida, Gainesville.

Castles, S., & Miller, M. J. (1993). *The age of migration: International population movements in the modern world.* New York: Guilford.

Castles, S., & Miller, M. J. (2009). *The age of migration: International population movements in the modern world* (4th ed.). London: The Guilford Press.

Censer, J. R. (1994). *The French press in the age of Enlightenment.* London: Routledge.

Chalaby, J. K. (2002). Transnational television in Europe. The role of pan-European channels. *European Journal of Communication, 17*(2), 183–203.

Chaliand, G., & Rageau, J.-P. (1995). *The penguin atlas of diasporas.* New York: Viking Penguin.

Charter for Regional or Minority Languages. (2009). Retrieved July 3, 2009, from the Council of Europe Web site: http://www.coe.int/t/dg4/education/minlang/aboutcharter/default_en.asp

Charvat-Burke, S., & Goudy, W. J. (1999). *Immigration and community in Iowa: How many have come and what is the impact?* Paper presented at annual meeting of the American Sociological Association, Chicago.

Cheong, P. H, Wilkin, H. A., & Ball-Rokeach, S. J. (2004). Diagnosing the communication infrastructure in order to reach target audiences: A study of Hispanic communities in Los Angeles. In P. Whitten & D. Cook (Eds.), *Understanding health communication technologies* (pp. 101–110). San Francisco: Jossey-Bass.

Cherubini, M., & Nova, N. (2004). To live or to master the city: The citizen dilemma. Some reflections on urban spaces fruition and on the possibility of change one's attitude. *Imago Urbis, Universitas de Quilmes, Buenos Aires, Argentina, 2.* Retrieved August 12, 2006, from http://www.i-cherubini.it/mauro/publications/Cherubini_Live_or_Master_21apr04.pdf

Chester, J. (2007). *Digital destiny: New media and the future of democracy.* New York: New Press.

Cheung, J., Lee, T. K, The, C. Z., Wang, C. Y., Kwan, W. C., & Yoshida, E. M. (2005). Cross-sectional study of hepatitis B awareness among Chinese and Southeast Asian Canadians in the Vancouver-Richmond community. *Canadian Journal of Gastroenterology 19*(44), 245–249.

Cheval, J. -J. (1992). Local radio and regional languages in Southwestern France. In S. H. Riggins (Ed.), *Ethnic minority media: An international perspective* (pp. 165–195). Thousand Oaks, CA: Sage.

Chien, E. (2007, February). Chinese media denied access to Clinton fundraiser. *New American Media.* Retrieved February 3, 2009, from http://news.ncmonline.com/news/view_article.html?article_id=6e28ab2ec53b123327d9f38aa3100c30

Child, J. (1972). Organization structure and strategies of control: A replication of the Aston study. *The Academy of Management Journal, 17*(2), 163–177.

Chism, N. V. N., Cano J., & Pruitt, A. S. (1989). Teaching in a diverse environment: Knowledge and skills needed by TAs. In J. D. Nyquist, R. D. Abbott, & D. H. Wulff (Eds.), *Teaching assistant training in the 1990s* (pp. 23–35). San Francisco: Jossey-Bass.

Chong, N. (2002). The Latino patient: A cultural guide for health care providers. Yarmouth, ME: Intercultural Press.

Chyi, H. I., & Lasorsa, D. L. (2002). An explorative study on the market relation between online and print newspapers. *The Journal of Media Economics, 15*(2), 91–106.

Circulation Verification Council (2007). *Circulation audit for* Mexican American Sun. Available from http://www.cvcaudit.com/media/index.aspx

Clyne, M. (2001). Can the shift from immigrant languages be reversed in Australia? In J. Fishman, (Ed.), *Can threatened languages be saved? Reversing language shift, revisited: A 21st century perspective* (pp. 364–390). Buffalo, NY: Multilingual Matters.

Clyne, M., & Kipp, S. (1999). *Pluricentric languages in an immigrant context.* Berlin: Mouton de Gruyter.

Cohen, R. (1997). *Global diasporas: An introduction.* London: UCL Press; Seattle: University of Washington Press.

Colle, R. (1992). A radio for the Mapuches of Chile: From popular education to political awareness. In S. H. Riggins (Ed.), *Ethnic minority media: An international perspective* (pp. 127–148). Thousand Oaks, CA: Sage.

Columbia Journalism Review. (2009). *Who owns what? CJR's guide to what the major media companies own.* Retrieved May 1, 2009, from http://www.cjr.org/resources/?c=cbs

Community Radio Impact Evaluation. (2007). *Community radio social impact assessment: Removing barriers, increasing effectiveness.* Retrieved February 18, 2009, from http://www.comminit.com/en/node/268152/376

Compaine, B. M. (2000). The online information industry. In B. M. Compaine & D. Gomery, *Who owns the media?* (pp. 437–480). Mahwah, NJ: Lawrence Erlbaum.

Compaine, B. M., & Gomery, D. (2000). *Who owns the media?* Mahwah, NJ: Lawrence Erlbaum.

Conseil Supérieur de l' Audiovisuel. (2003). *Bilan de la société nationale de programme France 3: Anée 2002.* Paris: CSA.

Conzen, K. N., Gerber, D., Morawska, E., Pozzetta, G., & Vecoli, R. (1992). The invention of ethnicity: A perspective from the USA. *Journal of American Ethnic History, 12*(1), 3–41.

Co-operation for the Development of Emerging Countries [COSPE]. (2002). *Mapping minorities and their media: The national context—Italy.* [European Media Technology and

Everyday Life Network.] Retrieved November 6, 2007, from http://www.lse.ac.uk/collections/EMTEL/Minorities/reports.html

Corden, W. M. (1953). The maximization of profit by a newspaper. *Review of Economic Studies, 20,* 181–190.

Cormack, M. (2007). The media and language maintenance. In M. Cormack & N. Hourigan (Eds.), *Minority language media: Concepts, critiques, and case studies* (pp. 52–68). Bristol, UK: Multilingual Matters.

Cornejo, I. (1990). *La Voz de la Mixteca y la comunidad receptora de la Mixteca Oaxaqueña.* Unpublished thesis, Universidad Iberoamericana, Mexico City.

Cornell, S., & Hartmann, D. (1998). *Ethnicity and race: Making identities in a changing world.* Thousand Oaks, CA: Pine Forge Press.

Corominas Piulats, M. (2007). Media policy and language policy In Catalonia. In M. Cormack & N. Hourigan (Eds.), *Minority language media: Concepts, critiques, and case studies* (pp. 168–187). Clevedon, UK: Multilingual Matters.

Council of Europe in brief. (n.d.). Retrieved May 7, 2009, from the Council of Europe Web site: http://www.coe.int/aboutcoe/index.asp?page=quiSommesNous&sp=visitCoe

Council on American-Islamic Relations. (2002, April). *The status of Muslim civil rights in the United States: stereotypes and civil liberties.* Washington, DC: Author.

Coutin, S. (2003). *Legalizing moves: Salvadoran immigrants' struggle for U.S. residency.* Ann Arbor, MI: University of Michigan Press.

Crawford, J. (1999). *Bilingual education: History, politics, theory and practice.* Los Angeles: Bilingual Education Services.

Crupi, A., & Consoli, J. (2006, April 10). Post-UPN, ethnic GRPs are in play. *Mediaweek.* Retrieved March 1, 2007, from http://www.mediaweek.com/mw/search/article_display.jsp?vnu_content_id=1002314236

Cultural Access Group & Interviewing Service of America (2005). *Asian American market report, 2005: The comprehensive resource for marketing to Asian Americans.*

Curran, J. (1991). Rethinking media as public sphere. In P. Dahlgre & C. Sparks (Eds.), *Communication and citizenship,* pp. 27–57. London: Routledge.

Cyert, R. M., & March, J. G. (1963). *A behavioral theory of the firm.* Englewood Cliffs, NJ: Prentice-Hall.

Dagron, A. G. (2001). *Making waves: Stories of participatory communication for social change.* Retrieved February 18, 2009, from the Communication Initiative Network Web site: http://www.comminit.com/en/node/1643.

Davies, J. (1994). *Broadcasting and the BBC in Wales.* Cardiff, UK: University of Wales Press.

Dávila, A. (2001). *Latinos, Inc.: The making and marketing of a people.* Berkeley: University of California Press.

Deal T. E., & Kennedy, A. A. (1982). *Corporate cultures: The rites and rituals of corporate life.* New York: Penguin Books.

Dearing, J. W., & Rogers, E. M. (1996). *Agenda-setting.* Thousand Oaks, CA: Sage.

DeBell, M., & Chapman, C. (2006). *Computer and Internet use by students in 2003* (NCES 2006–065). Washington, DC: National Center for Education Statistics, U.S. Department of Education.

Dertouzos, J. N., & Trautman, W. B. (1990). Economic effects of media concentration: Estimates from a model on the newspaper firm. *The Journal of Industrial Economics, 39*(1), 1–14.

Deuze, M. (2005). What is journalism? Professional identity and ideology of journalists reconsidered. *Journalism, 6*(4), 442–464.

Dewaele, A. (1997). *Beyond the noncommittal: The Flemish ethnic-cultural minorities policy: A state of things.* Brussels, Belgium: Ministry of Flanders, Interdepartmental Commission for Ethnic-Cultural Minorities.

D'Haenens, L. (2009). Whither cultural diversity on the Dutch TV screen? In R. Geißler & H. Pöttker (Eds.), *Media-migration-integration: European and North American perspectives* (pp. 97–116). New Brunswick, NJ: Transaction Publishers.

Do, J. (2006, October). *Federal Communications Commission public hearing in Los Angeles on media ownership.* Retrieved April 30, 2007, from http://www.benton.org/index.php?q=node/3380

Dobuzinskis, A. (2009, June 18). "Twitter revolution" in Iran aided by old media—TV, radio. *Reuters.* Retrieved July 18, 2009, from http://blogs.reuters.com/mediafile/2009/06/19/twitter-revolution-in-iran-aided-by-old-media-tv-radio

Doeszema, L. M. (1987). The Dutch press. In S. M. Miller (Ed.), *The ethnic press in the United States: A historical analysis and handbook* (pp. 71–83). New York: Greenwood Press.

Downey, K. (2007, March 5). The new world of Hispanic TV. *Broadcasting & Cable.* Retrieved September 8, 2008, from http://www.broadcastingcable.com/article/107969-The_New_World_of_Hispanic_TV.php

Durham, M. (2004). Constructing the "new ethnicities": Media, sexuality, and diaspora identity in the lives of South Asian immigrant girls. *Critical Studies in Media Communication 21*(2), 140–161.

Dutheil, G. (1995, October 29–30). Plus d'un million de foyers reçoivent la television par satellite. *Le Monde.*

Echchaibi, N. (2001). We are French too, but different: Radio, music, and the articulation of difference among young North Africans in France. *Gazette 63*(4), 295–310.

Ehle, J. (1988). *Trail of Tears: The rise and fall of the Cherokee Nation.* New York: Doubleday.

Eisenberg, E. M., & Riley, P. (2001). Organizational culture. In F. M. Jablin & L. L. Putnam (Eds.), *The new handbook of organizational communication: Advances in theory, research, and methods* (pp. 291–322). Thousand Oaks, CA: Sage.

Elias, N., & Caspi, D. (2007). From *Pravda* to *Vesty:* The Russian media renaissance in Israel. In A. Epstein & V. Khanin (Eds.), *Every seventh Israeli: Patterns of social and cultural integration of the Russian-speaking immigrants* (pp. 175–198). Israel: Bar-Ilan University Press.

Entertainment Magazine. (2005, March 23). *Nielsen to implement recommendations of Independent Task Force on Television Measurement.* Retrieved September 3, 2008, from http://emol.org/emclub/?q=neilsen

EQUAL. (2004, October 19). *Reflecting the colours of the world: Media, diversity, and discrimination* [Policy brief]. Retrieved April 10, 2009, from http://ec.europa.eu/employment_social/equal/policy-briefs/etg1-reflecting-color-world_en.cfm

European Charter for Regional & Minority Languages. (2009). *Application of the Charter in Sweden: 3rd monitoring cycle.* Retrieved August 3, 2009, from http://www.coe.int/t/dg4/education/minlang/Report/EvaluationReports/SwedenECRML3_en.pdf

European Federation of Journalists. (2005). *Media power in Europe: The big picture of ownership.* Brussels, Belgium.

Everitt, A. (2003). *New voices: An evaluation of 15 Access Radio projects.* London: Radio Authority.

Fairchild, D. (1999). Deterritorializing radio: Deregulation and the continuing triumph of the corporatist perspective in the USA. *Media, Culture & Society, 21,* 549–561.

Faist, T. (2000). Transnationalization in international migration: Implications for the study of citizenship and culture. *Ethnic and Racial Studies, 23*(2), 189–222.

Fakiolas, R., & King, R. (1996). Migration, return, immigration: A review and evaluation of Greece's post-war experience of international migration. *International Journal of Population Geography, 2,* 171–190.

Félix, A., González, C., & Ramírez, R. (2006). *Today we march, tomorrow we . . . naturalize? The role of political protests and ethnic media in the path to citizenship.* Unpublished manuscript, University of Southern California, Los Angeles.

Félix, A., González, C., & Ramírez, R. (2008). Political protest, ethnic media and Latino naturalization. *American Behavioral Scientist 52*(4), 618–634.

Ferre, I., Garlikov, L., Oppenheim, K., Spoerry, S., Keck, K., & Whitbeck, H. (2006. May 1). Thousands March for Immigrant Rights. *CNN.* Retrieved November 7, 2006, from http://www.cnn.com/2006/US/05/01/immigrant.day/index/html

Fischer, P., Martin, R., & Straubhaar, T. (1997). Should I stay or should I go? In T. Hammar, G. Brochmann, K. Tamas, & T. Faist (Eds.), *International migration, immobility and development* (pp. 49–90). Oxford/New York: Berg Publishers.

Fishman, J., Gertner, M., Lowy, E., & Milan, W. (1985). Language maintenance and ethnicity. In *The rise and fall of the ethnic revival* (pp. 57–76). Berlin: Mouton Publishers.

Fitzgerald, D. (2008). *A nation of emigrants: How Mexico manages its migration.* Berkeley: University of California Press.

Flanagin, A., & Metzger, M. (2001). Internet use in the contemporary media environment. *Human Communication Research (27)*1, 153–181.

Forrester, C. (1995, August 24–30). Orbit pioneers space-age television. *The European, 29.*

Fourie, P. J. (2007). *Media studies volume 1: Media history, media and society* (2nd ed.). Cape Town, South Africa: Juta Press.

Fox-Alston, J. (2005). *Six ways to partner, learn from the ethnic press.* Retrieved June 1, 2006 from the Newspaper Association of America Web site: http://www.naa.org/DiversityPages/Fusion-Website/Six-Ways-to-Partner-Learn-from-the-Ethnic-Press.aspx

Franchon, C., & Vargaftig, M. (Eds.) (1995). *European television: Immigrants and ethnic minorities.* London: John Libbey Publishing.

Frazier, M. (2008, April 7). *The catch-22 of buying black media. Advertising Age.* Available from http://adage.com

Friedman, D. B., & Hoffman-Goetz, L. (2006). Assessment of cultural sensitivity of cancer information in ethnic print media. *Journal of Health Communication, 11,* 425–447.

Gale, M. A. (1993). A brief history of writing in Aboriginal languages. *Aboriginal Child at School 1993,* 1–11.

Gao, J. (2006). Radio-activated business and power: A case study of 3CW Melbourne Chinese Radio. In W. Sun (Ed.), *Media and the Chinese Diaspora: Community, communications and commerce* (pp. 150–177). London: Routledge.

Garofoli, J. (2008, May 31). Black bloggers fight to make voices heard. *San Francisco Chronicle.* Retrieved April 29, 2008, from http://www.sfgate.com/cgi-bin/article.cgi?f=/c/a/2008/05/31/MN1T110MF0.DTL&type=printable

Gaya, B. (2002). *Mapping minorities and their media: The national context—Spain.* [European Media Technology and Everyday Life Network.] Retrieved November 6, 2007, from http://www.lse.ac.uk/collections/EMTEL/Minorities/reports.html

Geiβler, R., & Weber-Menges, S. (2009). Media reception and ideas on media integration among Turkish, Italian and Russo-German migrants in Germany. In R. Geiβler & H. Pöttker (Eds.), *Media-migration-integration: European and North American perspectives* (pp. 27–43). New Brunswick, NJ: Transaction Publishers.

Gellner, E., & Micaud, C. (Eds). (1972). *Arabs and Berbers.* London: Duckworth.

Georgiou, M. (2001a). Crossing the boundaries of the ethnic home: Media consumption and ethnic identity construction in the public sphere: The case of the Cypriot Community Centre in North London. *Gazette 63*(4), 311–329.

Georgiou, M. (2001b). *Diaspora, identity, and the media: Diasporic transnationalism and mediated spatialities.* Cresskill, NJ: Hampton Press.

Georgiou, M. (2002a). *Mapping minorities and their media: The national context—Greece.* [European Media Technology and Everyday Life Network.] Retrieved November 6, 2007, from http://www.lse.ac.uk/collections/EMTEL/Minorities/reports.html

Georgiou, M. (2002b). *Mapping minorities and their media: The national context—The UK.* [European Media,Technology and Everyday Life Network.] Retrieved October 17, 2006, from http://www.lse.ac.uk/collections/EMTEL/Minorities/reports.html

Georgiou, M. (2003). *Mapping diasporic media across the E/U: Addressing cultural exclusion.* [European Media Technology and Everyday Life Network.] Retrieved October 1, 2007, from http://www.lse.ac.uk/collections/EMTEL/reports/georgiou_2003_emtel.pdf

Georgiou, M. (2006). *Diaspora, identity, and the media: Diasporic transnationalism and mediated spatialities.* Cresskill, NJ: Hampton Press.

Gerd, H. (2003). *Radio goes to war: The cultural politics of propaganda during World War II.* Berkeley: University of California Press.

Geyskens, I., Gielens, K., & Dekimpe, M. G. (2002). The market valuation of Internet channel additions. *Journal of Marketing, 66*(2), 102–119.

Giddens, A. (2002). *Runaway world: How globalization is reshaping our lives.* Routledge.

Gilroy, P. (1993). *The Black Atlantic: Modernity and double consiciousness.* Boston: Harvard University Press.

Gladney, D. C. (2005, June). *Cyber-separatism and the Uyghur ethnic nationalism in China.* Presentation to the Center for Strategic and International Studies, Washington, DC.

Glenny, M. (1999). *The Balkans, nationalism, war and the great powers, 1804–1999.* New York: Viking Press.

Gonzaga, S. (2005, March 3). From disaster came unity: Pan-Asian communities felt affected by tsunami, donated $200,000. *Long Beach Press Telegram.* Retrieved February 23, 2009, from http://news.newamericamedia.org/news/view_article.html?article_id=be066b7158ff38d22dbd0a4b86374894

González, C. (2006). *The sleeping giant awakens: Political mobilization via Spanish-language radio.* Unpublished manuscript, University of Southern California, Los Angeles.

González, C. (2007). *The sleeping giant awakens: Latino political mobilization via communication networks.* Paper presented at the National Communication Association Conference, Chicago.

Gordon, M. M. (1964). *Assimilation in American life: The role of race, religion, and national origins.* Oxford, UK: Oxford University Press.

Goren, A. A. (1987). The Jewish press. In S. M. Miller (Ed.), *The ethnic press in the United States: A historical analysis and handbook* (pp. 203–228). New York: Greenwood Press.

Gouveia, L., & Stull, D. D. (1995). Dances with cows: beefpacking's impact on Garden City, Kansas and Lexington, Nebraska. In D. D. Stull, M. J. Broadway, & D. C. Griffith (Eds.), *Any way you cut it: meat processing and small-town America.* Lawrence, KS: University Press of Kansas.

Grescoe, T. (1994/95, Winter). Hot type. *Vancouver,* pp. 81–84, 114–118.

Grigsby Bates, K. (2006, August 23). Yen Ngoc Do, Vietnamese news pioneer. *National Public Radio.* Retrieved May 8, 2008, from http://www.npr.org/templates/story/story.php?storyId=5696535

Grisold, A. (2006). Does one deregulation fit all? The Austrian broadcasting vector after the European "liberalization" effort. *The Journal of Arts, Management, Law, & Society, 25*(4), 277–292.

Guglielmo, T. (2003). *White on arrival: Italians, race, color and power in Chicago, 1890–1945.* Oxford, UK: Oxford University Press.

Gutiérrez, F. (1977, Summer). Spanish-language media in America: Background, resources and history. *Journalism History.*

Guyot, J. (2007). Minority language media and the public sphere. In M. Cormack & N. Hourigan (Eds.), *Minority language media: Concepts, critiques, and case studies.* (pp. 34–51). Clevedon, UK: Multilingual Matters.

Guyot, J. (2002). An intercultural challenge for French regional television. In N. Jankowski (Ed.), *Community media in the Information Age.* Cresskill, NJ: Hampton Press.

Guzmán, B. (2001, May). *The Hispanic population: Census 2000 brief.* Available from United States Census Bureau Web site: http://www.census.gov

Guzmán, B., & Diaz McConnell, E. (2002). The Hispanic population: 1990–2000 growth and change. *Population Research and Policy Review, 21*(1-2), 109–128.

Habermas, J. (1989). *The structural transformation of the public sphere.* Cambridge, MA: MIT Press.

Hafez, K. (2004). Journalism ethics revisited: A comparison of ethics codes in Europe, North Africa, the Middle East, and Muslim Asia. *Political Communication, 19,* 225–250.

Han, H. -R., Kang, J., Kim, K. B., Ryu, J. P., & Kin, M. T. (2007). Barriers and strategies for recruiting Korean Americans for community-partnered health promotion research. *Journal of Immigrant and Minority Health 9*(2), 137–146.

Hannan, M. T., & Freeman, J. T. (1984). Structural inertia and organizational change. *American Sociological Review, 49,* 149–164.

Harb, Z., & Bessaiso, E. (2006). British Arab Muslim audiences and television after September 11. *Journal of Ethnic and Migration Studies 32*(6), 1063–1076.

Hargreaves, A. G. (2001). Diasporing audiences and satellite television: Case studies in France and Germany. In K. Ross & P. Playdon (Eds.), *Black marks: Minority ethnic audiences and media* (pp. 139–156). Aldershot, UK: Ashgate.

Hargreaves, A. G., & Mahjdoub, D. (1997). Satellite television viewing among ethnic minorities in France. *European Journal of Communication, 12*(4), 459–477.

Hartley, J., & McKee, A. (2000). *The indigenous public sphere: The reporting and reception of Aboriginal issues in the Australian media.* Oxford, UK: Oxford University Press.

Hawkes, R. (2008, April 15). New online community impre.com_launches for U.S. Hispanic market. *Social Media Portal Online.* Retrieved October 1, 2009, from http://www.socialmediaportal.com/News/2008/04/New-online-community-impre-com-launches-for-US-Hispanic-market.aspx

Heatta, O. M. (1984). *NRK's Samisk Sendinger, 1946–1984.* Unpublished thesis, University of Tromsø, Norway.

Herczeg, P. (2009). Migrants and ethnic minorities in Austria: Assimilation, integration and the media. In R. Geiβler & H. Pöttker (Eds.), *Media-migration-integration: European and North American perspectives* (pp. 71–97). New Brunswick, NJ: Transaction Publishers.

Held, D., McGrew, A., Goldblatt, D., & Perraton, J. (1999). *Global transformations.* Stanford, CA: Stanford University Press.

Hendriks, P. (1999). *Newspapers: A lost cause? Strategic management of newspaper firms in the United States and the Netherlands.* Boston: Kluwer Academic Publishers.

Hicks, G., & Mackie, J. A. (1994, July). Overseas Chinese: A question of identity. *Far Eastern Economic Review, 157,* 46–51.

Hirst, P., & Thompson, G. (1996). *Globalization in question: The international economy and the possibilities of governance.* Cambridge: Polity Press.

Hispanic PR Wire. (2006, September 18). *Univision.com named #1 most visited Spanish-language Web site.* Retrieved May 6, 2007, from http://www.hispanicprwire.com/news.php?1 =in&id=7037&cha=7

Hofstede, G. (1984). *Culture's consequences: International differences in work-related values.* Thousand Oaks, CA: Sage.

Hofstede, G. (2001). *Culture's consequences* (2nd ed.). Thousand Oaks, CA: Sage.

Holmwood, L. (2007, June 20). Black TV network heads for U.K. *Guardian Unlimited.* Retrieved June 23, 2007, from http://media.guardian.co.uk/broadcast/story/0,,2106667,00.html

Hoon, C.Y. (2006). "A hundred flowers bloom": The re-emergence of the Chinese press in post-Suharto Indonesia. In W. Sun (Ed.), *Media and the Chinese diaspora: Community, communications and commerce* (pp. 91–118). New York: Routledge.

Hourigan, N. (2007). The role of networks in minority language television campaigns. In M. Cormack & N. Hourigan (Eds.), *Minority language media: Concepts, critiques, and case studies* (pp. 69–87). Clevedon, UK: Multilingual Matters.

Howell, S., & Shryock, A. (2003). Cracking down on diaspora: Arab Detroit and America's "War on Terror." *Anthropological Quarterly, 76*(3), 443–462.

Howley, K. (2005). *Community media: People, places, and communication technologies.* Cambridge, UK: Cambridge University Press.

Hsu, H. (2002, Fall). Ethnic media grows up: Will increasing mainstream attention alter the ethnic media landscape? *Colorlines Magazine: Race, Action, Culture,* p. 2.

Humphreys, J. M. (2006). The multicultural economy. *Georgia Business and Economic Conditions, 66*(3), 1–15. Retrieved March 8, 2008, from http://www.terry.uga.edu/selig/publications/gbec.html

Humphreys, P. J. (1996). *Mass media and media policy in Western Europe.* (European Policy Research Unit Series, Vol. 2.) Manchester, UK: Manchester University Press.

Huntington, S. P. (1996). *The class of civilizations and the remaking of world order.* New York: Simon & Schuster.

Hurrle, J. (n.d.). *Radio MultiKulti, Berlin: Public broadcasting in 18 languages.* Retrieved March 1, 2009, from http://www.interculturemap.org/upload/att/200612140653270.Radio%20Multikulti%20CASE%20STUDY%20%20FINAL_INFO.pdf

Husband, C. (1986). Mass media, communication policy and ethnic minorities: An appraisal of current theory and practice. In *Mass media and the minorities* (pp. 1–38). RUSHSAP series of occasional monographs and papers, 17, National Library of Australia.

Husband, C. (Ed.). (1994). *A richer vision: The development of ethnic minority media in Western democracies.* Paris: UNESCO/John Libbey.

Hussein, A. (1994). Market forces and the marginalization of Black film and video production in the United Kingdom. In C. Husband (Ed.), *A richer vision: The development of ethnic minority media in Western democracies.* Paris and London: UNESCO/John Libbey.

Ihaddaden, Z. (1992). The postcolonial policy of Algerian broadcasting in Kabyle. In S. H. Riggins (Ed.), *Ethnic minority media: An international perspective* (pp. 243–255). Thousand Oaks, CA: Sage.

ImpreMedia. (2004). *Survey shows* El Diario/La Prensa *outsells* Hoy *2 to 1 on New York City newsstands* [Press release]. Retrieved November 30, 2006, from http://www.impremedia.com/press/pr07-20-04.html

ImpreMedia. (2005). *ImpreMedia launches the Domingo Network* [Press release]. Retrieved December 3, 2006, from http://www.impremedia.com/press/pr06-27-05_Domingo.html

ImpreMedia. (2007). *ImpreMedia network reaches over 9 million U.S. Hispanics in print and online in a month* [Press release]. Retrieved January 11, 2010, from http://www.impremedia.com/press/pr01-02-07_impremedianetwork.html

ImpreMedia. (2009). *ImpreMedia Publications.* Retrieved October 1, 2009, from http://www.impre.com/home.php

Institut Panos Paris. (2007). *Mediam'Rad: Ethnic and diversity media in Europe.* Retrieved April 2, 2008, from http://www.panosparis.org/gb/doc/Brochure_mediamrad_EN.pdf

International Organization for Migration (2005). *World migration 2005.* Geneva: Author.

Ipsos Reid. (2007a). *Canadian Chinese media monitor (Greater Toronto area).* Retrieved March 20, 2008, from http://www.fairchildtv.com/english/ppt/ipsos_reid_tor.pdf

Ipsos Reid. (2007b). *Canadian Chinese media monitor (Greater Vancouver area).* Retrieved March 20, 2008, from http://www.fairchildtv.com/english/ppt/ipsos_reid_2007_van.pdf

James, M. (2004a, June 10). Univisión sues Nielsen over ratings system. *The Los Angeles Times,* C2. Retrieved on May 10, 2007, from www.latimes.com

James, M. (2004b, November 30). Univisión drops suit. *The Los Angeles Times,* C2. Retrieved on May 10, 2007, from www.latimes.com

James, M. (2005, December 20). Nielsen bows to Latino viewers. *The Los Angeles Times,* C1. Retrieved May 10, 2007, from www.latimes.com

Jankowski, N. W., & Prehn, O. (2002). *Community media in the information age: Perspective and prospects.* Cresskill, NJ: Hampton Press.

Janowitz, M. (1967). *The community press in an urban setting.* Chicago: Chicago University Press.

Jayasuriya, L., Walker, D., & Gothard, J. (Eds.). (2003). *Legacies of White Australia.* Crawley: University of Western Australia Press.

Jenkins, C. N., McPhee, S. J., Bird, J. A., Pham, G. Q., Nguyen, B. H., Nguyen T., et al. (1999). Effect of a media-led education campaign on breast and cervical cancer screening among Vietnamese-American women. *Preventative Medicine 28*(4), 395–406.

Jenkins, T. G., & Eckert, C. M. (1986). Channeling Black insurgency: Elite patronage and professional social movement organizations in the development of the Black movement. *American Sociological Review, 51*(6), 812–829.

John, C. (2006, April 5). The legacy of the Brixton riots. *BBC News.* Retrieved April 10, 2007, from http://news.bbc.co.uk/1/hi/uk/4854556.stm

Jordan, M., & Dougherty, C. (2008, September). Immigration slows in face of economic downturn. *Wall Street Journal.* Retrieved on October 20, 2008 from http://online.wsj.com/article/SB122213015990965589.html?mod=googlenews_wsj

Josephi, B. (2007). Internationalizing the journalistic professional model: Imperatives and impediments. *Global Media and Communication, 3*(3), 300–306.

Kaltman, B. (2007). *Under the heel of the dragon: Islam, racism, crime, and the Uighur in China.* Athens, OH: Ohio University Press.

Kanat, K. (2005). Ethnic media and politics: The case of the use of the Internet by Uyghur diaspora. *First Monday 10*(7). Retrieved February 5, 2008, from: http://firstmonday.org

Kandula, N. R., Kersey, M., & Lurie, N. (2004). Assuring the health of immigrants: What the leading health indicators tell us. *Annual Review of Public Health, 25,* 357–376.

Kaniss, P. (1991). *Making local news.* Chicago: University of Chicago Press.

Kaplan, R. D. (1993). *Balkan ghosts.* New York: St. Martin's Press.

Karim, K. H. (1998, June). *From ethnic media to global media: Transnational communication networks among diasporic communities.* Retrieved November 2, 2006, from International Comparative Research Group, Strategic Research and Analysis, Canadian Heritage: http://www.transcomm.ox.ac.uk/working%20papers/karim.pdf

Karim, K. (2007). Media and diaspora. In E. Devereux (Ed.), *Media studies: Key issues and debates* (pp. 361–379). Thousand Oaks, CA: Sage.

Karim, K. H., Smeltzer, S., & Loucher, Y. (1998, March). *On-line access and participation in Canadian society.* Paper presented to the Knowledge-Based Economy and Society Pilot Project, Hull, Quebec, Canada.

Kasinitz, P. (2004). Race, assimilation, and "second generations," past and present. In G. Frederickson & N. Foner (Eds.), *Not just Black and White: Historical and contemporary perspectives on immigration, race, and ethnicity in the United States* (pp. 278–300). New York: Russell Sage Foundation.

Kasinitz, P., Waters, M., Mollenkopf, J., & Anil, M. (2002). Transnationalism and the children of immigrants in contemporary New York. In P. Levitt & M. Waters (Eds.), *The changing face of home: The transnational lives of the second generation* (pp. 96–122). New York: Russell Sage Foundation.

Katz, V. S. (2007). *From conversation to conversion: Children's efforts to translate their immigrant families' social networks into community connections.* Unpublished dissertation, University of Southern California, Los Angeles.

Katz, V. S., Wilkin, H. A., & Hether, H. J. (2010, June). *Does family communication affect healthy lifestyle choices?: An exploration of family talk among Latinos and African Americans.* Paper presented at the International Communication Association Annual Conference, Singapore.

Kauranen, R., & Tuori, S. (2002). *Mapping minorities and their media: The national context—Finland* [European Media Technology and Everyday Life Network]. Retrieved November 6, 2007, from http://www.lse.ac.uk/collections/EMTEL/Minorities/reports.html

Kerr, A. (2007). Transnational flows: Media use by Poles in Ireland. In J. Horgan, B. O'Connor & H. Sheehan (Eds.), *Mapping Irish media: Critical explorations* (pp. 173–186). Dublin: University College Dublin Press.

Khan, N. (2007). *ERICarts: National approaches and practices in the European Union in relation to Intercultural Dialogue* [Gringo: Case study]. Retrieved March 2, 2009, from www.interculturaldialogue.eu/web/files/44/en/Khan-CS03.doc

Kim, M. S. (2002). Models of acculturative communication competence: Who bears the burden of adaptation? In M. S. Kim (Ed.), *Non-western perspectives on human communication* (pp. 141–154). Thousand Oaks, CA: Sage.

Kim, Y. -C., & Ball-Rokeach, S. J. (2006a). Civic engagement from a communication infrastructure perspective. *Communication Theory, 16,* 173–197.

Kim, Y. -C., & Ball-Rokeach, S. J. (2006b). Neighborhood storytelling resources and civic engagement: A multilevel approach. *Human Communication Research 32*(4), 411–439.

Kim, Y. -C., Jung, J. Y., & Ball-Rokeach, S. J. (2006). "Geo-ethnicity" and neighborhood engagement: A communication infrastructure perspective. *Political Communication, 23,* 421–441.

Kim, Y. C., Jung, J. Y., Cohen, E., & Ball-Rokeach, S. J. (2004). Internet connectedness before and after September 11, 2001. *New Media & Society 6*(5), 611–631.

Kim, Y. Y. (2005). Adapting to a new culture: An integrative communication theory. In W. B. Gudykunst (Ed.), *Theorizing about intercultural communication* (pp. 375–400). Thousand Oaks, CA: Sage.

King, R., Fielding, A., & Black, R. (1997). The international migration turnaround in Southern Europe. In R. King & R. Black (Eds.), *Southern Europe and the new migrations* (pp. 1–25). Brighton, UK: Sussex University Press.

Kitano, H. (1987). The Japanese-American press. In S. M. Miller (Ed.), *The ethnic press in the United States: A historical analysis and handbook* (pp. 193–202). New York: Greenwood Press.

Knutson, J. W. (1998). Rebellion in Chiapas: Insurrection by Internet and public relations. *Media, Culture, and Society, 20*(3), 507–518.

Kopan, A. (1987). The Greek press. In S. M. Miller (Ed.), *The ethnic press in the United States: A historical analysis and handbook* (pp. 161–176). New York: Greenwood Press.

Kosnick, K. (2007). *Migrant media: Turkish broadcasting and multicultural politics in Berlin.* Bloomington, IN: Indiana University Press.

Krasner, S. D. (1994). International political economy: Abiding discord. *Review of International Political Economy, 1*(1), 13–19.

Kress, G. (2003). *Literacy in the new media age.* London: Routledge.

La Brie, H. (1977). Black newspapers: The roots are 150 years deep. *Journalism History 41*(4), 111–114.

La Course, R. (1979). Native American journalism: An overview. *Journalism History 6*(2), 34–38.

Lacy, S. (1987). *The impact of intercity competition on daily newspaper content.* Paper presented at the annual meeting for Education in Journalism and Mass Communication, San Antonio, Texas.

Lacy, S., Coulson, D. C., & Cho, H. (2002). Competition for readers among U.S. metropolitan daily, nonmetropolitan daily, and weekly newspapers. *Journal of Media Economics, 15* (1), 21–40.

Lacy, S., & Martin, H. (2004). Competition, circulation, and advertising. *Newspaper Research Journal, 25*(1), 18–39.

Lacy, S., & Simon, T. F. (1993). *The economics and regulation of United States newspapers.* Norwood, NJ: Ablex Publishing.

Ladrón de Guevara, M., Còller, X., & Romaní, D. (1995). *The image of Barcelona '92 in the International Press.* [Barcelona: Centre d' Estudis Olímpics UAB.] Retrieved March 14, 2004, from http://olympicstudies.uab.es/pdf/wp105_eng.pdf

Lai, H. M. (1987). The Chinese-American press. In S. M. Miller (Ed.). *The ethnic press in the United States: A historical analysis and handbook* (pp. 27–43). New York: Greenwood Press.

Laranaga, L. (2009, July 30). *ImpreMedia.* Retrieved August 30, 2009, from http://navigator.cision.com/ImpreMedia.aspx.

Latino Print Network. (2005). *The strengths of Hispanic-owned publications study.* Retrieved November 26, 2007, from http://www.latinoprintnetwork.com/assets/HOPS.pdf

Latino Print Network. (2007). *State of Hispanic print.* Retrieved November 26, 2007, from http://www.latinoprintnetwork.com/assets/StateofHispanicPrint.pdf

Levitt, P., & Waters, M. (2002). (Eds.). *The changing face of home: The transnational lives of the second generation.* New York: Russell Sage Foundation.

Li, M. (1999). "We need two worlds": Chinese immigrant associations in a Western society. Amsterdam: University of Amsterdam Press.

Lieberson, S. (1981). *Language diversity and language contact.* Stanford, CA: Stanford University Press.

Lieberson, S. (1985). Unhyphenated Whites in the United States. *Ethnic and Racial Studies, 8*(1), 159–180.

Light, I., Sabagh, G., Bozorgmehr, M., & Der-Martirosian, C. (1994). Beyond the ethnic enclave economy. *Social Problems, 41*(1), 65–80.

Lin, W. -Y., & Song, H. (2006). Geo-ethnic storytelling: An examination of ethnic media content in contemporary immigrant communities. *Journalism, Theory, Practice 7*, 362–388.

Lin, W. Y., Song, H., & Ball-Rokeach, S. (in press). Localizing the global: Exploring the transnational ties that bind in new immigrant communities. *Journal of Communication.*

Lin, W. -Y., Song, H., & Mercado, A. (2004). *Storytelling into community building: The role of geo-ethnic media in building communities.* Paper presented at the annual conference of the International Communication Association, New Orleans.

Lindorff, D. (2000, January). *Nielsen and Univisión at odds over Hispanic household count.* Retrieved August 30, 2007, from http://www.medialifemagazine.com/news2000/jan00/news20126.html

Liss, D. (2003, September 16). A new TV choice for African-Americans. *Business Week.* Retrieved December 1, 2006, from http://www.businessweek.com/bwdaily/dnflash/sep2003/nf20030916_3069.htm?chan=search

Livingston, G., Parker, K. & Fox, S. (2009). Latinos online, 2006-2008: Narrowing the Gap. Pew Hispanic Center report. Retrieved on January 3, 2010 from http://pewhispanic.org/reports/report.php?ReportID=119

Livingstone, S. (2002). *Young people and new media.* London: Sage.

Lopez, D. (1996). Language: Diversity and assimilation. In R. Waldinger & M. Bozorgmehr (Eds.), *Ethnic Los Angeles* (pp. 139–159). New York: Russell Sage Foundation.

Los Angeles Times (2009, January 8). Radio ratings firm Arbitron settles New York bias suit. Retrieved August 23, 2009, from http://articles.latimes.com/2009/jan/08/business/fi-arbitron8

MacLeod, S. (2009, January 28). How al-Arabiya got the Obama interview. *Time.* Retrieved February 15, 2009, from http://www.time.com/time/world/article/0,8599,1874379,00.html?imw=Y

Maira, S. (2002). *Desis in the house: Indian American youth culture in New York City.* Philadelphia, PA: Temple University Press.

Malonga, M. -F. (2002). *Ethnic minorities: Which place and which image on French television? Televisual representation of people of extra European origin.* [European Media Technology and Everyday Life Network.] Retrieved July 21, 2006, from http://www.lse.ac.uk/collections/EMTEL/Minorities/case_studies.html

Mangot, M. -T. (1997). Insertion sociale et expression culturelle: La politique de la Communauté française. In P. Blaise, R. Lewin, & M. –T. Coenen (Eds.), *La Belgique et ses immigrés* (pp. 190–201). Brussels: De Boeck.

Marchesani, L. S., & Adams, M. (1992). Dynamics of diversity in the teaching-learning process: A faculty development model for analysis and action. In M. Adams (Ed.), *Promoting diversity in college classrooms: Innovative responses for the curriculum, faculty, and institutions* (pp. 9–18). San Francisco: Jossey-Bass.

Mardakis, A., Parsanoglou, D., & Pavlou, M. (Eds.). (2001). *Immigrants in Greece.* Athens: Ellinika Grammata Publications.

Marienstras, R. (1989). On the notion of diaspora. In G. Chaliand (Ed.), *Minority peoples in the age of nation-states* (pp. 119–125). London: Pluto.

Martin, J. N., & Nakayama, T. K. (2007a). *Experiencing intercultural communication.* New York: McGraw-Hill.

Martin, J. N., & Nakayama, T. K. (2007b). *Intercultural communication in contexts* (4th ed.). New York: McGraw-Hill.

Massey, D., Arango, J., Hugo, G., Kouaouci, A., Pelligrino, A., & Taylor, J. E. (2005). *Worlds in motion: Understanding international migration at the end of the millennium.* Oxford, UK: Oxford University Press.

Mathew, A. B., & Kelly, K. (2008). *Disaster preparedness in urban immigrant communities: Lessons learned from recent catastrophic events and their relevance to Latino and Asian communities in Southern California.* Los Angeles: Tomás Rivera Policy Institute and Asian Pacific American Legal Center.

Matsaganis, M. D. (2008). *Rediscovering the communication engine of neighborhood effects: How the interaction of residents and community institutions impacts health literacy and how it can be leveraged to improve health care access.* Unpublished dissertation, University of Southern California, Los Angeles.

Matsaganis, M. D., & Katz, V. S. (2004). *Piecing the puzzle together: A communication infrastructure perspective on the South Gate recall election.* Presentation given at the National Communication Association Annual Convention, Chicago.

Matsaganis, M. D., Katz, V. S., Ball-Rokeach, S. J., & Do, J. (Conveners). (2007, August 10). *Panel discussion on ethnic media, No. 1* (Transcript #1). Los Angeles.

Matsaganis, M. D., Katz, V. S., Ball-Rokeach, S. J., & Do, J. (Conveners). (2008, May 2). *Panel discussion on ethnic media, No. 2* (Transcript #2). Los Angeles.

Mayer, V. (2003). Living telenovelas/telenovelizing life: Mexican-American girls' identities and transnational telenovelas. *Journal of Communication, (53)*3, 479–495.

McChesney, R. W. (2003). The new global media. In D. Held & A. McGrew (Eds.), *The global transformations reader: An introduction to the globalization debate* (2nd ed.), pp. 260–268. Cambridge, UK: Polity.

McChesney, R. W., & Scott, B. (2004). *Our unfree press: 100 years of radical media criticism.* New York: The New Press.

McCombs, M. E., & Bell, T. (1996). The agenda-setting role of mass communication. In M. Salwen & D. Stacks (Eds.), *An integrated approach to communication theory and research* (pp. 93–110). Mahwah, NJ: Lawrence Erlbaum.

McCombs, M. E., & Ghanem, S. (2001). The convergence of agenda setting and framing. In S. D. Reese, O. Gandy, & A. Grant (Eds.), *Framing in the new media landscape.* Mahwah, NJ: Lawrence Erlbaum.

McCombs, M. E., & Reynolds, A. (2002). News influence on our pictures of the world. In J. Bryant & D. Zillman (Eds.), *Media effects: Advances in theory and research* (pp. 1–19). Mahwah, NJ: Lawrence Erlbaum.

McCombs, M., & Shaw, D. (1972). The agenda-setting function of mass media. *Public Opinion Quarterly, 36,* 176–185.

McElmurry, S. (2009, March 20). *Indigenous community radio in Mexico.* Retrieved June 16, 2009, from http://americas.irc-online.org/am/5977

McLeod, D., & Detenber, B. (1999). Framing effects of television news coverage of social protest. *Journal of Communication, 49*(3), 3–23.

McLeod, J. M., & Hawley, S. E., Jr. (1964). Professionalization among newsmen. *Journalism Quarterly, 41,* 529–538.

McLuhan, M. (1964). *Understanding media: The extensions of man.* New York: Mentor Books.

McLuhan, M. (1994). *Understanding media: The extensions of man* (2nd ed.). Boston: MIT Press.

McLuhan, M. (S. McLuhan & D. Staines, Eds.). (2005). *Understanding me: Lectures and interviews.* Boston, MA: MIT Press.

McMahon, R. (2008). Alden on U.S. immigration clampdown post-9/11. *Council on Foreign Relations.* Retrieved February 2, 2008, from http://www.cfr.org/publication/17259/alden_on_us_immigration_clampdown_post911.html

Meadows, M. (1992). Broadcasting in Aboriginal Australia: One mob, one voice, one land. In S. H. Riggins (Ed.), *Ethnic minority media: An international perspective* (pp. 82–101). Thousand Oaks, CA: Sage.

Media Awareness Network. (2007). *Ethnic media in Canada.* Retrieved July 16, 2007, from http://www.media-awareness.ca/english/issues/stereotyping/ethnics_and_minorities/minorities_ethnicmedia.cfm

Mediam'Rad. (2006, June). *Institut Panos Paris.* Retrieved March 2, 2008, from http://www.panosparis.org/fichierProdGB/fichierProd1514.pdf

Mediam'Rad. (2007, April). *Focus Europe.* Retrieved April 10, 2007, from http://www.panosparis.org/gb/migra_mediamrad.php

MIDAS. (2008). *MIDAS: European Association of Daily Newspapers in Minority and Regional Languages.* Retrieved June 2, 2008, from http://www.midas-press.org/welcome.htm

Miladi, N. (2006). Satellite TV news and the Arab Diaspora in Britain: Comparing Al-Jazeera, the BBC and CNN. *Journal of Ethnic and Migration Studies, 32*(6), 947–960.

Milikowski, M. (2001). Learning about Turkishness by satellite: Private satisfactions and public benefits. In K. Ross & P. Playdon (Eds.), *Black marks: Minority ethnic audiences and media* (pp. 125–138). Aldershot: Ashgate.

Mira Media. (2006). Retrieved June 1, 2007, from http://www.mediamrad.nl/uk/index.htm

Mira Media. (n.d.). Retrieved April 9, 2008, from http://www.miramedia.nl/uk/index.htm

Mock, J., McPhee, S. J., Nguyen, T., Wong, C., Doan, H., Lai, K.Q., et al. (2007). Effective lay health worker outreach and media-based education for promoting cervical cancer screening among Vietnamese American women. *American Journal of Public Health 97*(9), 1693–1700.

Monge, P. M., & Matei, S. A. (2004). The role of the global telecommunications network in bridging economic and political divides, 1989 to 1999. *Journal of Communication, 54*(3), 511–531.

Moore, O. (2009, January 26). Stop the press: The future of "Black" newspapers is online. *Overground Online.* Retrieved September 22, 2009, from http://www.overgroundonline.com/?inner=article&article_id=778

Morawska, E. (2001). Immigrants, transnationalism, and ethnicization: A comparison of this great wave and the last. In G. Gerstle & J. Mollenkopf (Eds.), *E Pluribus Unum? Contemporary and historical perspectives on immigrant political incorporation* (pp. 175–212). New York: Russell Sage Foundation.

Morris, A. (1984). *The origins of the civil rights movement.* New York: Free Press.

Moss, D., & Bartlett, N. (2002, September). The World Trade Organization. *Harvard Business School* [Case study 9-703-015], 1–28.

Moss, M. (1991). The structure of media in New York City. In J. H. Mollenkopf & M. Castells (Eds.), *Dual City: Restructuring New York.* New York: Russell Sage Foundation.

Mousavi, S. (2006). Transnational Afghani audiences after September 11. *Journal of Ethnic and Migration Studies 32*(6), 1041–1061.

Murphy, S. (1974). *Other voices: Black, Chicano and American Indian press.* Dayton, OH: Pflaum/Standard.

Murphy, J. E., & Murphy, S. M. (1981). *Let my people know: American Indian Journalism, 1828–1978.* Norman, OK: University of Oklahoma Press.

Murray, C. (2008, April). Media infrastructure for multicultural diversity. *Policy Options,* 29(4) 63–66.

Murray, C., Yu, S., & Ahadi, D. (2007, October). *Cultural diversity and ethnic media in BC.* A report to the Canadian Heritage Western Regional Office (Study No. 45193670). Vancouver: Simon Frasier University.

Museum of Broadcast Communication [MBC]. (2009). *Television Northern Canada.* Retrieved February 18, 2009, from http://www.museum.tv/archives/etv/T/htmlT/televisionno/televisionno.htm

Muslim Public Affairs Council. (2006, May 1). *Muslim Americans march for immigration reform nationwide.* Retrieved February 9, 2009, from http://www.mpac.org/article.php?id=190

Naff, A. (1987). The Arabic language press. In S. M. Miller (Ed.), *The ethnic press in the United States: A historical analysis and handbook* (pp. 1–13). New York: Greenwood Press.

National Ethnic & Multicultural Broadcasters' Council. (2008). *Training.* Available at http://www.nembc.org.au/services/training/training.html

National Telecommunication & Information Administration. (2000, December). *Changes, challenges, and charting new courses: Minority commercial broadcast ownership in the United States.* Washington, DC: U.S. Department of Commerce, Minority Telecommunications Development Program. Retrieved April 2, 2006, from http://search.ntia.doc.gov/pdf/mtdpreportv2.pdf

Negroponte, N. (1995). *Being digital.* New York: Knopf.

New America Media. (2009). *New America directory: Your bridge to America's ethnic media and communities.* Retrieved September 1, 2009, from http://news.newamericamedia.org/news/view_custom.html?custom_page_id=263

New America Media & Bendixen & Associates. (2005, June). *Ethnic media in America: The giant hidden in plain sight.* Retrieved June 7, 2007, from http://news.newamericamedia.org/news/view_article.html?article_id=0443821787ac0210cbecebe8b1f576a3

New America Media & Bendixen & Associates. (2009, June). *Executive summary of a national study on the penetration of ethnic media in America.* Retrieved July 30, 2009, from http://media.namx.org/polls/2009/06/Penetration_of_Ethnic_Media_ExecutiRRve_Summary.pdf

New York Times. (2008, November 18). Nielsen to issue U.S. radio ratings. Retrieved March 9, 2009 from http://www.nytimes.com/2008/11/18/business/media/18nielsen.html?_r=3&ref=media&pagewanted=print

Newspaper Association of America. (2001). *Facts about newspapers.* Retrieved June 7, 2007, from http://www.naa.org/info/facts01

Newspaper Association of America. (2005). *Six ways to partner, learn from the ethnic press.* Retrieved June 1, 2006, from http://www.naa.org/Resources/Publications/Fusion%20Magazine/FUSION-Magazine-2005-Summer/Diversity-Fusion-Six-Ways-to-

Partner-Learn-from-the-Ethnic-Press/Diversity-Fusion-Six-Ways-to-Partner-Learn-from-the-Ethnic-Press.aspx

Newspaper Association of America. (2008). *Advertising expenditures.* Retrieved September 2, 2009, from http://www.naa.org/TrendsandNumbers/Advertising-Expenditures.aspx

Nielsen. (2008). *2008 Report to the community USA.* Retrieved August 5, 2009, from http://en-us.nielsen.com/etc/content/nielsen_dotcom/en_us/home/about/diversity.mbc.33212.RelatedLinks.81852.MediaPath.pdf

Nielsen Media Research. (1993). *What TV ratings really mean, how they are obtained, why they are needed.* New York: Nielsen Media Research.

Nielsen Media Research. (2005). *Nielsen Media Research Hispanic local market universe estimates.* New York: Nielsen Media Research.

Norris, P. (2001). *Digital divide? Civic engagement, information poverty, and the Internet worldwide.* Cambridge, UK: Cambridge University Press.

Nova, N. (2004). *Locative media: A literature review* [CRAFT Research Report_2.] Retrieved August 12, 2006, from École Polytechnique Fédérale de Lausanne: http://craftwww.epfl.ch/research/publications/CRAFT_report2.pdf

Nye, J. S., & Donahue, J. D. (Eds.) (2000). *Governance in a globalizing world.* Washington, DC: Brookings Institution Press.

O'Donnell, S., & Ní Leathlobhair, E. (2002). *Diversity Ireland—Feasibility study report.* Retrieved July 17, 2009, from http://www.lse.ac.uk/collections/EMTEL/Minorities/reports.html

Office of Communications. (2007, June 21). *Communication market special report: Ethnic minority groups and communications services.* Retrieved August 10, 2009, from http://www.ofcom.org.uk/research/cm/ethnic_minority

Office of Communications. (2008, September 15). *Ethnic minority groups continue to lead the way on digital device take-up and use.* Retrieved August 10, 2009, from http://www.ofcom.org.uk/media/news/2008/09/nr_20080915

Office of New York State Attorney General. (2009). *Attorney General Cuomo secures landmark agreement with Arbitron to cure defects in radio ratings system that threatened to drive minority broadcasters out of business.* Retrieved August 1, 2009, from http://www.oag.state.ny.us/media_center/2009/jan/jan7a_09.html

Office of Population Censuses and Surveys. (1953–1993). *Census of Great Britain, 1951–1991.* London: Her Majesty's Stationery Office.

Ohmae, K. (1995). *The end of the nation state.* New York: Free Press.

Ojo, T. (2006). Ethnic print media in the multicultural nation of Canada. A case study of the black newspaper in Montreal. *Journalism, 7*(3), 343–361.

O'Leary, C. A. (2002). The Kurds of Iraq: Recent history, future prospects. *Middle East Review of International Affairs, 6*(4). Retrieved November 11, 2006, from http://meria.idc.ac.il/journal/2002/issue4/jv6n4a5.html

Orbit TV. (2009). Available at: http://www.orbit.net/home.aspx

Organisation for Economic Co-operation & Development. (2005, May). *Regulatory environment for foreign direct investment: Preliminary inventory for selected African countries.* Report presented at the OECD/NEPAD Investment Policy Roundtable on Investment for African Development: Making It Happen, Entebbe, Uganda. Retrieved May 4, 2007, from http://www.oecd.org/dataoecd/25/6/34783838.pdf

Ormond, M. (2002). *Mapping minorities and their media: The national context—Belgium.* [European Media Technology and Everyday Life Network.] Retrieved November 6, 2007, from http://www.lse.ac.uk/collections/EMTEL/Minorities/reports.html

Örnebring, H., & Jönsson, A. M. (2004). Tabloid journalism and the public sphere: A historical perspective on tabloid journalism. *Journalism Studies, 5*(3), 283–295.

Orsi, R. (1992). The religious boundaries of an in between people: Street feste and the problem of the dark-skinned other in Italian Harlem, 1920–1992. *American Quarterly, 44*(3).

Our objectives. (n.d.). Retrieved May 7, 2009, from the Council of Europe Web site: http://www.coe.int/aboutCoe/index.asp?page=nosObjectifs&l=en

Page, C. (2006). Foreword. In P. Washburn, *The African American newspaper: Voice of freedom* (p. ix). Chicago: Northwestern University Press.

Panos Institute–Paris. (2006). *Ethnic media in Europe.* Retrieved April 1, 2007, from http://www.panosparis.org/gb/migra_mediamrad.php

Papathanassopoulos, S. (1997). The politics and the effects of deregulation of Greek television. *European Journal of Communication, 12*(3), 351–368.

Park, K. (1997). *The Korean American dream: Immigrants and small business in New York City.* Ithaca, NY: Cornell University Press.

Park, L. S. H. (2005). *Consuming citizenship: Children of Asian immigrant entrepreneurs.* Stanford, CA: Stanford University Press.

Park, R. E. (1922). *The immigrant press and its control.* New York: Harper & Brothers Publishers.

Parker, B. (2000). *Introduction to globalization and business.* Thousand Oaks, CA: Sage.

Parker, B. (2005). *Introduction to globalization and business* (2nd ed.). Thousand Oaks, CA: Sage.

Passel, J. S., & Cohn, D. (2008, February 11). *U.S. population projections: 2005–2050.* Retrieved January 12, 2009, from Pew Hispanic Center Web site: http://pewhispanic.org/reports/report.php?ReportID=85

Passel, J. S., & Cohn D. (2008, October 2). *Trends in unauthorized immigration: Undocumented inflow now trails legal inflow.* Retrieved April 3, 2009, from Pew Hispanic Center Web site: http://pewhispanic.org/files/reports/94.pdf

Passel, J. S., & Zimmerman, W. (2000). *Are immigrants leaving California?* Paper presented at the annual meetings of the Population Association of America, Los Angeles.

Perez-Firmat, G. (1994). *Life on the hyphen.* Austin, TX: University of Texas Press.

Pew Hispanic Center. (2008, January 23). *Statistical portrait of Hispanics in the United States, 2006.* Retrieved April 3, 2009, from the Pew Hispanic Center Web site: http://pewhispanic.org/factsheets/factsheet.php?FactsheetID=35

Pew Project for Excellence in Journalism. (2005). *The state of the news media, 2005: An annual report on American journalism.* Retrieved September 27, 2006, from http://www.stateofthemedia.org/2005/

Pew Project for Excellence in Journalism. (2006). *The state of the news media, 2006: An annual report on American journalism.* Retrieved on September 24, 2006, from http://www.journalism.org/node/465

Pew Project for Excellence in Journalism. (2007a). *The state of the news media, 2007: The Black press.* Retrieved April 10, 2007, from http://www.stateofthemedia.org/2007/narrative_ethnicalternative_blackpress.asp?cat=8&media=10

Pew Project for Excellence in Journalism. (2007b). *The state of the news media, 2007: Intro.* Retrieved April 10, 2007, from http://www.stateofthenewsmedia.org/2007/narrative_ethnicalternative_intro.asp?cat=1&media=10

Pew Project for Excellence in Journalism. (2008). *The state of the news media, 2008: An annual report on American journalism.* Retrieved May 1, 2008 from http://www.stateofthemedia.org/2008/narrative_ethnicalternative_intro.php?cat=0&media=11

Pew Project for Excellence in Journalism. (2009a). *The state of the news media: An annual report on American journalism.* Retrieved October 1, 2009, from http://www.stateofthemedia.org/2009/narrative_overview_intro.php?media=1

Pew Project for Excellence in Journalism. (2009b). *Overview: Native and Arab American media.* Retrieved October 1, 2009, from http://www.stateofthemedia.org/2009/narrative_ethnic_nativeandarabamerican.php

Pew Project for Excellence in Journalism. (2009c). *Overview: Asian American media.* Retrieved October 1, 2009 from http://www.stateofthemedia.org/2009/narrative_ethnic_asian american.php?media=11&cat=5

Pfeiffer, S. (2005, September 1). Phoenix buys into El Planeta. *The Boston Globe.* Retrieved April 8, 2007, from http://www.boston.com/business/articles/2005/09/01/phoenix_buys_into_el_planeta/

Picard, R. G. (2004). The economics of the daily newspaper industry. In A. Alexander, J. Owers, R. Carveth, C. A. Hollified, & A. Greco, (Eds.), *Media economics: Theory and practice* (pp. 109–125). Mahwah, NJ: Lawrence Erlbaum.

Popkin, D. (1989). *News and politics in the age of revolution: Jean Luzac's Gazette de Leyde.* Ithaca, NY: Cornell University Press.

Portada Online. (2008, September 11). *8 things you need to know about the state of Latino print.* Retrieved September 10, 2009, from http://www.portada-online.com/article.aspx?aid=4595

Portes, A. (1987). The social origins of the Cuban enclave economy in Miami. *Sociological Perspectives, 30*(4), 340–372.

Portes, A., & Rumbaut, R. (1996). *Immigrant America: A portrait.* Berkeley: University of California Press.

Postman, N. (1992). *Technopolis: The surrender of culture to technology.* New York: Vintage.

Potter, J. (2004). *Theory of media literacy: A cognitive approach.* Thousand Oaks, CA: Sage.

Presentation. (n.d.). Retrieved July 3, 2008, from the Institut Panos Paris Web site: http://www.panosparis.org/gb/presentation.php

Prosser, M. H. (1978). *The cultural dialogue: An introduction to intercultural communication.* Boston: Houghton Mifflin.

Prpi, G. J., & McAdams, M. C. (1987). The Croatian press. In S. M. Miller (Ed.), *The ethnic press in the United States: A historical analysis and handbook* (pp. 45–58). New York: Greenwood Press.

Qiu, H. (2003). Communication among knowledge diasporas: Online magazines of expatriate Chinese students. In K. H. Karim (Ed.), *The media of diaspora* (pp.148–161). New York: Routledge.

Radio One. (2008). *About us.* Retrieved September 1, 2009, from http://www.radio-one.com/about

Radio One. (2009). *Fact sheet.* Retrieved August 20, 2009, from http://www.radio-one.com/properties/fact_sheet.asp?ID=9

Raine, G. (2002, April 24). Ethnic media fail to draw advertisers. *San Francisco Chronicle.* Retrieved October 5, 2006, from http://sfgate.com/cgi-bin/article.cgi?file=/chronicle/archive/2002/04/24/BU224859.DTL&type=business

Rainey, J. (2009, February 22). President Obama and the role of the ethnic press. *Los Angeles Times.* Retrieved February 27, 2009, http://articles.latimes.com/2009/feb/22/nation/na-onthemedia22

Raiser, U. (2002). *Mapping minorities and their media: The national context—Germany.* [European Media Technology and Everyday Life Network.] Retrieved October 8, 2007, from http://www.lse.ac.uk/collections/EMTEL/Minorities/reports.html

Ramos, J. M., & Díez, A. (2003). Blending old and new technologies: Mexico's indigeneous radio service messages. In B. Girard (Ed.), *The one to watch: Radio, ICTs and interactivity* (pp. 1–5). Rome: Food & Agriculture Organization of the United Nations.

Reese, L. (2001). Morality and identity in Mexican immigrant parents' visions of the future. *Journal of Ethnic and Migration Studies (27)*3, 455–472.

Retis, J. (2007, July). *Mass media and Latin American diaspora in Europe: The rise and consolidation of the new Latino media in Spain.* Paper presented at the International Association for Media and Communication Research, Paris, France.

Reynolds, P. (2002, June 18). "Fortress Europe" raises the drawbridge: Fears over immigration may fuel racial tension. *BBC News Online: World Edition.* Retrieved November 7, 2007, from http://news.bbc.co.uk/2/hi/europe/2042779.stm

Rheingold, H. (2002). *Smart mobs: The next social revolution.* Cambridge, MA: Basic Books.

Riggins, S. H. (1992). The media imperative: Ethnic minority survival in the age of mass communication. In S. H. Riggins (Ed.), *Ethnic minority media: An international perspective* (pp. 1–22). Thousand Oaks, CA: Sage.

Rigoni, I. (2002). *Turkish and Kurdish media production in Europe: An overview.* [European Media Technology and Everyday Life Network.] Retrieved September 16, 2008, from http://www.lse.ac.uk/collections/EMTEL/Minorities/case_studies.html

Riley, S. G. (1979). The Indian's own prejudice, as mirrored in the first Native American newspaper. *Journalism History* 6(2), 44–47.

Roald, A. -S. (2004). Arab satellite broadcasting—the immigrants' extended ear to their homelands. In J. Malik (Ed.), *Muslims in Europe: From the margin to the centre* (pp. 207–226). Münster, Germany: Lit Verlag.

Robbins, S. P. (2005). *Organizational behavior* (11th ed.). Upper Saddle River, NJ: Pearson Education.

Robinson, D. (2009, April). US lawmakers hear opposing views on Obama approach to Cuba. *Voice of America.* Available at http://www1.voanews.com/english/news/

Rodis, R. (2004, December 30). Tsunami shouldn't make us forget other victims of recent calamities. *Philippine News.* Retrieved October 5, 2006, from http://news.newamericamedia.org/news/view_article.html?article_id=5263b5fd7567aacccfde97f8a6a02ae4

Rodriguez, A. (1999). *Making Latino news: Race, language, class.* Thousand Oaks, CA: Sage.

Rokeach, M. D. (1973). *The nature of human values.* New York: Free Press.

Rose, M. (1996). *For the record: 160 years of Aboriginal print journalism.* St. Leonards, NSW, Australia: Allen & Unwin.

Rosenau, J. N. (1995). Governance in the twenty-first century. *Global Governance, 1*(1), 13–43.

Rosse, J. N. (1975). *Economic limits of press responsibility.* Paper presented to a conference at the Center for the Study of Communications Policy, Duke University, Durham, NC.

Safran, W. (1991). Diasporas in modern societies: Myths of homeland and return. *Diaspora: A Journal of Transnational Studies, 1*(1), 83–99.

Salacnic, G. R., & Pfeffer, J. (1978). A social information approach to job attitudes and task design. *Administrative Science Quarterly, 23,* 224–253.

Sampson, R., Morenoff, J., & Gannon-Rowley, T. (2002). Assessing neighborhood effects: Social processes and new directions in research. *Annual Review of Sociology, 27,* 443–477.

Sanders, J. M., & Nee, V. (1987). *American Sociological Review, 52*(6), 745–773.

Sassen, S. (1998). *Globalization and its discontents.* New York: The New Press.

Schildkraut, D. J. (2002). The more things change . . . American identity and mass and elite responses to 9/11. *Political Psychology, 23*(3), 511–535.

Schiller, D. (1979). An historical approach to objectivity and professionalism in American news reporting. *Journal of Communication, 29*(4), 46–57.

Schmitt, E., & Cave, D. (2009, April 4). Obama to loosen restrictions on policy with Cuba. *The New York Times.* Retrieved April 5, 2009, from http://www.nytimes.com/2009/04/05/world/americas/05cuba.html?scp=3&sq=cuba%20miami%20obama&st=cse

Schneider, V. (2004). State theory, governance, and the logic of regulation and administrative control. In A. Warntjen & A.Wonka (Eds.), *Governance in Europe* (pp. 25–41). Baden-Baden, Germany: Nomos Verlagsgesellschaft.

Scholte, J. A. (2000). *Globalization: A critical introduction.* New York: Palgrave.

Schonfeld, E., (2009, March 29). The wounded U.S. newspaper industry lost $7.5 billion in advertising revenues last year. *Tech Crunch.* Retrieved September 1, 2009, from http://www.techcrunch.com/2009/03/29/the-wounded-us-newspaper-industry-lost-75-billion-in-advertising-revenues-last-year

Schou, N. (2008, February 27). Little Saigon's Nguoi Viet Daily News earns anti-Commie wrath. *Orange County Register.* Retrieved April 20, 2008, from http://www.ocweekly.com/2008-02-28/news/these-colorsdon-t-wash-feet/

Schudson, M. (1978). *Discovering the news: a social history of American newspapers.* New York: Basic Books.

Schwartz, S. (1992). Universals in the content and structure of values: Theoretical advances and empirical tests in 20 countries. *Advances in Experimental Psychology, 25,* 1–62.

Selig Center for Economic Growth. (2006). *The multicultural economy 2006.* University of Georgia, Athens: J. M. Humphreys.

Shahn, B. (1992). *The shape of content.* Cambridge, MA: Harvard University Press.

Simmons, C. (2005). *The African American press: A history of news coverage during national crises, with special reference to four Black newspapers, 1827–1965.* Jefferson, NC: McFarland & Company.

Soga, K. (2008). *Life behind barbed wire: The World War II internment memoirs of a Hawaii Issei.* Honolulu: University of Hawaii Press.

Spybey, T. (1996). *Globalization and world society.* Cambridge, MA: Polity Press.

Staino, K. V. (1980). Ethnicity as process. *Ethnicity, 7,* 27–33.

Starbuck, H. W. (1965). Organization and development. In J. G. March (Ed.), *Handbook of organizations* (pp. 451–493). New York: Rand McNally.

Starr, A. (2006, May 2). The Spanish-language DJs behind the new wave of Latino activism. *Slate Magazine,* Retrieved May 30, 2007, http://www.slate.com/id/2141008/

Starr, P. (2004). *The creation of the media: Political origins of modern communications.* New York: Basic Books.

Statistics Canada. (2006). Canada's National Statistics Agency. Retrieved August 27, 2006, from http://www.statcan.ca/english/concepts/definitions/ethnicity.htm

Steadman, J. (2005). *TV audience special study: African-American audience.* New York: Nielsen Media Research. Retrieved June 2, 2007, from www.everyonecounts.tv/public/documents/AfricanAmericanTVA.pdf

Stelter, B. (2009, January 7). Arbitron settles suit alleging bias in radio ratings system. *The New York Times.* Retrieved August 23, 2009, from http://www.nytimes.com/2009/01/08/nyregion/08arbitron.html

Stelter, B. (2008, October 6). Cuomo to sue ratings company, claiming minorities are under-represented. *The New York Times.* Retrieved September 29, 2009, from http://www.nytimes.com/2008/10/07/nyregion/07arbitron.html

Stinchcombe, A. L. (1965). Social structures and organizations. In J. G. March (Ed.), *Handbook of organizations* (pp. 142–193). New York: Rand McNally.

Stolberg, S. G., & Cave, D. (2009, April 13). Obama opens door to Cuba, but only a crack. *The New York Times.* Retrieved April 14, 2009, from http://www.nytimes.com/2009/04/14/world/americas/14cuba.html?_r=2&scp=2&sq=Cuba&st=cse

Sudarat, D. (1993). *The craft of ethnic newspaper-making: A study of the negotiation of culture in the Thai-language newspapers of Los Angeles.* Unpublished doctoral dissertation, University of Iowa, Iowa City.

Tehranian, M. (1999). *Global communication and world politics: Domination, development, and discourse.* Boulder, CO: Lynn Rienner.

Thomas, B., & Waldinger, R. (1991). Primary, secondary, and enclave labor markets: A training systems approach. *American Sociological Review, 56,* 432–445.

Thomas, W. I., & Znaniecki, F. (1918–1920). *The Polish peasant in Europe and America.* Boston: R. G. Badger.

Thompson, R. S. (1989). Circulation versus advertiser appeal in the newspaper industry: An empirical investigation. *Journal of Industrial Economics, 37*(3), 259–271.

Tomaselli, R., Tomaselli, K., & Muller, J. (1989). *Currents of power: State broadcasting in South Africa.* Belleville, South Africa: Athropos.

Torpey, J. (1999). *The invention of the passport: Surveillance, citizenship and the state.* Cambridge, UK: Cambridge University Press.

Tsagarousianou, R. (2002). Ethnic community media, community identity and citizenship in contemporary Britain. In N. Jankowski (Ed.), *Community media in the information age: Perspectives and prospects* (pp. 209–230). Creskill, NJ: Hampton Press.

Turner, J. (1982). Towards a cognitive redefinition of the social group. In H. Tajfel (Ed.), *Social identity and intergroup relations* (pp. 27–60). Oxford, UK: Cambridge University Press.

Turner, S. D., & Cooper, M. (2007, October). Out of the picture 2007: Minority and female TV station ownership in the United States. *Free Press.* Retrieved July 20, 2008, from http://www.freepress.net/files/otp2007.pdf

Ugba, A. (2002). *Mapping minorities and their media: The national context—Ireland.* [European Media Technolongy and Everyday Life Network.] Retrieved November 6, 2007, from http://www.lse.ac.uk/collections/EMTEL/Minorities/reports.html

UNESCO. (1996, June). *Universal declaration on linguistic rights: World conference on linguistic rights.* Retrieved March 7, 2009, from www.unesco.org/cpp/uk/declarations/linguistic.pdf

Univisión. (2008, March 14). *Disney-ABC International Television Latin America and Univisión sign unprecedented strategic production agreement.* Retrieved September 1, 2009, from http://www.univision.net/corp/en/pr/Miami_14052007–1.html

U.S. Census Bureau. (2000). Data retrieved January 10, 2009, from http://www.census.gov

U.S. Census Bureau. (2006). *Hispanics in the United States.* Retrieved August 3, 2009, from http://www.census.gov/population/www/socdemo/hispanic/files/Internet_Hispanic_in_US_2006.pdf

U.S. Census Current Population Survey. (2007). *Households using the Internet in and outside the home, by selected characteristics: Total urban, rural, principal city.* Retrieved October 1, 2009, from http://www.ntia.doc.gov/reports/2008/Table_HouseholdInternet2007.pdf

Valaskakis, G. (1992). Communication, culture, and technology: Satellites and northern native broadcasting in Canada. In S. H. Riggins (Ed.), *Ethnic minority media: An international perspective* (pp. 63–81). Thousand Oaks, CA: Sage.

Valdés, G. (1996). *Con respeto: Bridging the distances between culturally diverse families and schools.* New York: Teacher's College Press.

Van Hear, N. (1998). *New diasporas: The mass exodus, dispersal, and regrouping of migrant communities.* Seattle: University of Washington Press.

Van Vliet, R. (2003). *Elie Luzac (1721–1796).* Retrieved April 10, 2008, from http://www.uitgeverijastraea.nl/Lemma%20Luzac%20Thoemmes%202003.pdf

Vargas, L. (1995). *Social uses and participatory practices: The use of participatory radio by ethnic minorities in Mexico.* Boulder, CO: Westview Press.

Vertovec, S. (2001). *Transnational challenges to the "new" multiculturalism* [Transnational communities working paper series]. Retrieved March 2, 2009, from http://www.transcomm.ox.ac.uk/working%20papers/WPTC-2K-06%20Vertovec.pdf

Viswanath, K., & Lee, K. K. (2007). Ethnic media. In M. Waters & R. Ueda (Eds.), *The new Americans: A guide to immigration since 1965* (pp. 202–213). Cambridge, MA: Harvard University Press.

Viswanath, K., Steele, W. R., & Finnegan Jr., J. R. (2006). Social capital and health: Civic engagement, community size, and recall of health messages. *American Journal of Public Health 96*(8), 1456–1461.

Vlasic, B., & Bunkley, N. (2008, October 1). Hazardous conditions for the auto industry. *The New York Times.* Retrieved September 5, 2009, from http://www.nytimes.com/2008/10/02/business/02sales.html?partner=rssnyt&emc=rss

Vongs, P. (2003, May 2). Nguoi Viet: Building the Vietnamese community from the ground up. *New California Media.* Retrieved May 10, 2008, from http://news.newamericamedia.org/news/view_article.html?article_id=0bb7319a0012031e16bc3b15dbf35a05

Waldinger, R., & Fitzgerald, D. (2004). Transnationalism in question. *American Journal of Sociology, 109*(5), 1177–1195.

Waldinger, R., & Lichter, M. (2002). *How the other half works.* Berkeley: University of California Press.

Wallerstein, I. (1974). *The modern wold system.* New York: Academic Press.

Washburn, P. (2006). *The African American newspaper: Voice of freedom.* Chicago: Northwestern University Press.

Ward, D. (2005, January). *Media concentration and pluralism: Regulation, realities, and the Council of Europe's standards in the television sector.* Report presented to the European Commission for Democracy Through Law, Trieste, Italy.

Watanabe, T., & Becerra, B. (2006, March 28). The immigration debate: How DJs put 500,000 marchers in motion. *Los Angeles Times,* p. A1.

Waters, M. (1995). *Globalization.* New York: Routledge.

Waters, M. (2000). *Black identities: West Indian immigrant dreams and American realities.* Cambridge, MA: Harvard University Press.

Waters, M. C., & Ueda, R. (Eds.) (2006). *The new Americans: A handbook to immigration since 1965.* Cambridge, MA: Harvard University Press.

Watrous, P. (1998, January 17). A new Spanish radio station in New York. *The New York Times,* p. B19.

Wilkin, H. A. (2005). Diagnosing communication connections: reaching underserved communities through existing communication ecologies. Unpublished doctoral dissertation, University of Southern California, Los Angeles.

Wilkin, H. A., & Ball-Rokeach, S. J. (2006). Reaching at-risk groups: The importance of health storytelling in Los Angeles Latino media. *Journalism 7*(3), 299–320.

Wilkin, H. A., Ball-Rokeach, S. J., Matsaganis, M. D., & Cheong, P. H. (2007). Comparing the communication ecologies of geo-ethnic communities: How people stay on top of their community. *Electronic Journal of Communication, 17*(1–2).

Wilkin, H. A., & Gonzalez, C. (2006). *Are Spanish language television shows connecting Los Angeles Latino residents' to their health storytelling networks?* Paper presented at the annual conference of the International Communication Association, Dresden, Germany.

Wilson, C. C., Gutierrez, F., & Chao, L. M. (2003). *Racism, sexism, and the media: The rise of class communication in multicultural America.* Thousand Oaks, CA: Sage.

World Association of Newspapers. (2006). *World press trends: Newspaper circulation, advertising increases.* Retrieved October 13, 2006, from http://www.wan-press.org/article11185.html?var_recherche=circulation

Wu, F. (2002). *Yellow: Race in America beyond Black and White.* New York: Basic Books.

Zentella, A. (1997). *Growing up bilingual.* Oxford, UK: Blackwell Publishing.

Zhang, D. (2008). *Between two generations: Language maintenance and acculturations among Chinese immigrant families.* El Paso, TX: LFB Scholarly Publishing.

Zhang, K., & Xiaoming, H. (1999). The Internet and ethnic press: A study of electronic Chinese publications. *The Information Society, 15*(1), 21–30.

Zhao, X. (2002). *Remaking Chinese America: Immigration, family, and community, 1940–1965.* New Brunswick, NJ: Rutgers University Press.

Zhou, M. (2009). *Contemporary Chinese America: Immigration, ethnicity, and community transformation.* Philadelphia: Temple University Press.

Zhou, M., & Logan, J. R. (1989). Returns on human capital in ethnic enclaves: New York's Chinatown. *American Sociological Review, 54*(5), 809–820.

Zolberg, A., & Woon, L. L. (1999). Why Islam is like Spanish: Cultural incorporation in Europe and the United States. *Politics and Society, 27*(1), 5–38.

Zotova, K. (1995). Political power and periodicals. *The Serials Librarian, 26*(2), 87–94.

Author Index

Abu-Laban, Y., 150
Adams, M., 20
Adoni, H., 58
Ahadi, D., 39, 149, 150, 182, 187, 194, 200, 231, 234, 249
Akst, D., 5, 159, 160
Alba, R., 10, 11, 19, 55, 87
Aldridge, M., 236
Alexander, A., 15
Alia, V., 9, 37, 38, 43, 208
Allan, S., 87, 88
Allen, J., 3
Amburgey, T. L., 156
Anderson, B., 13, 32, 78, 219
Anil, M., 56
Aponte, R., 99
Appadurai, A., 151
Arana, E., 198
Arango, J., 68
Arango, T., 109
Arsenault, A., 152, 200
Artz, L., 200
Athar, M., 125
Axelrod, L., 38
Azpillaga, P., 198

Bagdikian, B. H., 156, 199
Bailey, T., 229
Baker, M., 188, 189
Ball-Rokeach, S. J., 11, 12, 15, 58, 59, 64, 112, 126, 127, 128, 130, 132, 134, 149, 151, 201, 208, 211, 212, 213, 214, 215, 216, 220, 228, 230, 231, 232, 233, 234, 237, 238, 239, 240, 241, 254
Banks, J. A., 20
Barlow, D. M., 87
Barnett, W. P., 156
Barrow, L. C., Jr., 31, 76
Bartlett, N., 184
Bates, J., 165
Bates, S., 236
Baum, D., 16, 125, 218
Becerra, B., 16, 125
Bell, T., 236
Bennett, W. L., 199
Bergquist, J. M., 35, 36
Bernanke, B., 138
Bernard, N., 175
Bessaiso, E., 65
Bharath, D., 243
Bink, S., 188, 189
Black, R., 29
Blanchard, M., 236
Blommesteijn, M., 188
Böse, M., 54, 157, 198, 204
Boucaud, P., 190, 204
Boyle, M., 112
Bozorgmehr, M., 229
Brady, S., 110
Braman, S., 149
Brennan, T., 149
Brown, L. D., 174, 175
Brown, M., 104
Browne, D. R., 12, 28, 30, 31, 35, 60, 164, 176, 177, 178, 181, 182, 183, 187, 192, 193, 197, 198, 203, 207, 214, 215, 228, 238, 241, 257
Bruck, P. A., 157
Bull, S., 10, 37, 38, 43, 208
Bullock, L., 62
Bunkley, N., 138
Burton, E., 72
Byron, M., 126

Cainkar, L., 56, 186, 203
Camauër, L., 187, 188
Campbell, W. J., 249
Cano, J., 20
Cantle, T., 125
Carrington, W. J., 51
Carroll, G. R., 119

Carveth, R., 15, 200
Caspi, D., 56, 58, 259
Castañeda, C., 20
Castells, M., 18, 148, 149, 152, 175, 200, 238
Castells-Talens, A., 40
Castles, S., 68
Cave, D., 238, 239
Censer, J. R., 25, 27
Chaliand, G., 10
Chao, L. M., 25, 31, 34
Chapman, C., 65, 67, 211
Charvat-Burke, S., 99
Cheong, P. H., 11, 112, 127, 128, 130, 132, 134, 208, 254
Cherubini, M., 10
Chester, J., 200
Cheung, J., 220
Cheval, J. J., 195
Chien, E., 233
Child, J., 147
Chism, N. V. N., 20
Cho, H., 122
Chong, N., 54
Chyi, H. I., 128, 135
Clyne, M., 44
Cohen, A., 58
Cohen, E., 64
Cohen, R., 9, 10
Cohn, D., 108, 259
Colle, R., 196
Còller, X., 14
Compaine, B. M., 146, 200
Condon, S., 126
Consoli, J., 101, 111
Conzen, K. N., 14
Cooper, M., 168, 169, 170, 171
Corden, W. M., 119, 120
Cormack, M., 178, 192
Cornejo, I., 41, 78
Cornell, S., 70
Corominas Piulats, M., 198
Coulson, D. C., 122
Coutin, S., 52
Crawford, J., 35
Crupi, A., 101, 111
Curran, J., 192
Cyert, R. M., 156

Dagron, A. G., 217
Dallison, C., 125
Davies, J., 28, 29
Dávila, A., 73, 161
Deal, T. E., 230
Dearing, J. W., 15, 236
DeBell, M., 65, 67, 211
Dekimpe, M. G., 135
Der-Martirosian, C., 229
Dertouzos, J. N., 119
Detenber, B., 236
Detragiache, E., 51
Deuze, M., 249
Dewaele, A., 183
D'Haenens, L., 189
Diaz McConnell, E., 99
Díez, A., 40, 41, 78
Do, J., 167, 168, 228, 230, 231, 232, 233, 234, 237, 238, 239, 240, 241
Doan, H., 220, 222
Dobuzinskis, A., 263
Doeszema, L. M., 82
Donahue, J. D., 148, 174, 175
Dörr, D., 157
Downey, K., 136
Durham, M., 59, 84
Dutheil, G., 138

Echchaibi, N., 30, 74
Eckert, C. M., 183
Ehle, J., 32
Eisenberg, E. M., 163
Elias, D., 56
Elias, N., 259
Entzinger, H., 188
Everitt, A., 104
Evetts, J., 236

Faist, T., 9
Fakiolas, R., 191
Favre, J., 157
Félix, A., 16, 61, 125, 186, 218
Ferre, I., 218
Fielding, A., 29
Finnegan, J. R., Jr., 225
Fischer, P., 51, 83
Fitzgerald, D., 40, 64, 67
Flanagin, A., 127, 208, 255
Fleras, A., 261
Fourie, P. J., 76
Fox, S., 67
Fox-Alston, J., 167
Franchon, C., 45
Frazier, M., 107
Freeman, J. T., 156
Friedman, D. B., 220
Frumkin, P., 174, 175

Gabriel, C., 150
Gale, M. A., 42
Gannon-Rowley, T., 214
Gao, J., 63
Garlikov, L., 218
Garofoli, J., 137
Gaya, B., 163, 191, 198
GeiBler, R., 59
Gellner, E., 195
Georgiou, M., 9, 58, 65, 70, 80, 81, 87, 156, 188, 189, 191, 198, 199, 200, 261
Gerber, D., 14
Gerd, H., 35
Geyskens, I., 135
Ghanem, S., 236
Gibbs, J., 151
Giddens, A., 148
Gielens, K., 135
Gilroy, P., 74
Gladney, D. C., 219
Glenny, M., 28
Goldblatt, D., 148, 151, 152, 174
Gonzaga, S., 217
González, C., 17, 61, 125, 186, 218, 223
Gordon, M. M., 18
Goren, A. A., 36, 72
Gothard, J., 44
Goudy, W. J., 99
Gouveia, L., 99
Gramstad, S., 157
Grescoe, T., 39
Grigsby Bates, K., 249
Grisold, A., 199
Guglielmo, T., 14
Gutiérrez, F., 25, 31, 34
Guyot, J., 30, 192, 195
Guzmán, B., 99

Haberfellner, R., 54, 157, 198, 204
Habermas, J., 191
Hafez, K., 249
Han, H. R., 222
Hannan, M. T., 156
Harb, Z., 65
Hargreaves, A. G., 17, 138, 139
Harris, J., 125
Hartley, J., 43, 77, 258
Hartmann, D., 70
Hawkes, R., 257
Hawley, S. E., Jr., 236
Heatta, O. M., 28
Held, D., 148, 151, 152, 174
Hendriks, P., 135
Herczeg, P., 66
Hether, H. J., 216
Hicks, G., 151
Hirst, P., 150
Hoffman-Goetz, L., 220
Hofstede, G., 12
Holmwood, L., 111
Hoon, C. Y., 85
Hourigan, N., 192
Howell, S., 203
Howley, K., 10
Hsu, H., 66
Hugo, G., 68
Humphreys, J. M., 99
Humphreys, P. J., 199
Huntington, S. P., 150
Husband, C., 185, 187, 189, 190, 192, 198
Hussein, A., 29

Ihaddaden, Z., 195

James, M., 101, 102
Jankowski, N. W., 10
Janowitz, M., 259
Jayasuriya, L., 44
Jenkins, T. G., 183
John, C., 125
Jönsson, A. M., 249
Josephi, B., 249
Jung, J. Y., 13, 64, 151

Kaltman, B., 219
Kanat, K., 219
Kandula, N. R., 222
Kang, J., 222
Kaniss, P., 10
Kaplan, R. D., 28
Karim, K. H., 5, 30, 115, 139, 164
Kasinitz, P., 56, 73
Katz, V. S., 210, 216, 228, 230, 231, 232, 233, 234, 237, 238, 239, 240, 241
Kaur, D., 125
Kauranen, R., 187
Keck, K., 218
Kelley, D., 156
Kelly, K., xiv, 217
Kennedy, A. A., 230
Kerr, A., 59
Kersey, M., 222
Khagram, S., 174, 175
Khan, N., 245
Kim, K. B., 222
Kim, M. S., 63

Kim, Y. C., 12, 64, 151, 201, 208, 213, 214, 215, 216
Kim, Y. Y., 58
Kin, M. T., 222
King, R., 29, 191
Kipp, S., 44
Kitano, H., 36, 82, 87
Knutson, J. W., 238
Koldas, A., 54, 157, 198, 204
Kopan, A., 81, 82
Kosnick, K., 185, 196, 239, 256
Kouaouci, A., 68
Krasner, S. D., 150
Kress, G., 65
Kwan, W. C., 220

La Brie, H., 31, 32, 78
La Course, R., 32, 47, 81
Lacy, S., 122
Ladrón de Guevara, M., 14
Lai, H. M., 34, 35
Lai, K. Q., 220, 222
Laranaga, L., 123
Lasorsa, D. L., 128, 135
Lee, K. K., 35, 37, 70, 73, 76, 207
Lee, T. K., 220
Levitt, P., 64
Li, M., 63
Lichter, M., 54, 60
Lieberson, S., 13, 55, 83
Light, I., 229
Lin, W. Y., 59, 64, 149, 208, 211, 214, 223, 224
Lindorff, D., 102
Liss, D., 100, 111, 115
Livingston, G., 67
Logan, J., 55
Logan, J. R., 229
Lopez, D., 55
Loucher, Y., 164
Lurie, N., 222

Mackie, J. A., 151
MacLeod, S., xv, 234
Mahjdoub, D., 16, 138
Maira, S., 74
Malonga, M. F., 9, 190
Mangot, M. T., 183
March, J. G., 156
Marchesani, L. S., 20
Mardakis, A., 29
Marienstras, R., 10
Martin, H., 122
Martin, J. N., 56, 60, 71
Martin, R., 51, 83
Marzan, G., 55
Massey, D., 68
Matei, S., 201, 213, 214, 215, 216
Matei, S. A., 148, 151
Mathew, A. B., xiv, 217
Matsaganis, M. D., 11, 112, 127, 128, 130, 132, 134, 208, 210, 216, 228, 230, 231, 232, 233, 234, 237, 238, 239, 240, 241, 254
Mayer, V., 84
McAdams, M. C., 86
McChesney, R. W., 156, 199
McCombs, M. E., 15, 236
McElmurry, S., 41, 78
McGrew, A., 148, 151, 152, 174
McKee, A., 43, 77
McLeod, D., 236
McLeod, J. M., 236
McLuhan, M., 225
McMahon, R., 186
McPhee, S. J., 220, 222
Meadows, M., 187, 198
Mercado, A., 223, 224
Metzger, M., 127, 208, 255
Micaud, C., 195
Miladi, N., 64
Milikowski, M., 138
Miller, M. J., 68
Mitchell, P., 87
Mock, J., 220, 222
Mollenkopf, J., 56
Monaco, R., 157
Monge, P. M., 148, 151
Moore, M. H., 174, 175
Moore, O., 137
Morawska, E., 14, 20, 35
Morenoff, J., 214
Morris, A., 183
Moss, D., 184
Moss, M., 163
Mousavi, S., 64
Muller, J., 76
Murphy, J. E., 32
Murphy, S., 31
Murphy, S. M., 32
Murray, C., 39, 149, 150, 182, 187, 194, 200, 203, 231, 234, 249, 262

Naff, A., 56, 73, 87
Nakayama, T. K., 56, 60, 71
Narbaiza, B., 198

Nee, V., 10, 11, 19, 55, 87, 229
Negroponte, N., 149
Nguyen, T., 220, 222
Ní Leathlobhair, E., 66
Norris, P., 152
Nova, N., 10
Nye, J. S., 148, 174, 175

O'Donnell, S., 66
Ohmae, K., 48
Ojo, T., 232
Oju, J. L., 151
O'Leary, C. A., 13
O'Malley, T., 87, 88
Oppenheim, K., 218
Ormond, M., 29, 30, 163, 182, 183, 187
Örnebring, H., 249
Orsi, R., 14
Owers, J., 15

Page, C., 32
Papathanassopoulos, S., 156
Park, K., 149
Park, L. S. H., 150
Park, R. E., 35
Parker, B., 12, 162, 230
Parker, K., 67
Parsanoglou, D., 29
Passel, J. S., 99, 108, 259
Pavlou, M., 29
Pelligrino, A., 68
Perez-Firmat, G., 72, 73
Perraton, J., 148, 151, 152, 174
Perusko Culek, Z., 157
Pfeffer, J., 156
Pfeiffer, S., 167
Picard, R. G., 108, 118, 119
Popkin, D., 27
Portes, A., 54, 55, 229
Postman, N., 149
Potter, J., 65
Pozzetta, G., 14
Prehn, O., 10
Prosser, M. H., 12
Prpi, G. J., 86
Pruitt, A. S., 20

Qiu, H., 154, 155, 164

Rageau, J. P., 10
Raine, G., 95
Rainey, J., xv, 234
Raiser, U., 5, 30, 190, 199, 204
Ramírez, R., 16, 61, 125, 186, 218
Ramos, J. M., 40, 41, 78
Reese, L., 58
Retis, J., 149, 161
Reynolds, A., 16, 236
Reynolds, P., 53
Rheingold, H., 10
Riggins, S. H., 9, 12, 45, 156, 186, 192, 193, 194, 195, 196, 228, 230, 241
Rigoni, I., 79
Riley, P., 163
Riley, S. G., 81
Roald, A. S., 138
Robbins, S. P., 147, 163
Robinson, D., 238
Rodis, R., 21
Rodriquez, A., 34, 161
Rogers, E. M., 16, 236
Rokeach, M. D., 12
Romaní, D., 14
Rose, M., 25, 42, 70, 80, 81
Rosse, J. N., 122
Rumbaut, R., 54, 55
Ryu, J. P., 222

Sabagh, G., 229
Safran, W., 10
Salacnic, G. R., 156
Sampson, R., 214
Sanders, J. M., 229
Sassen, S., 60
Schildkraut, D. J., 56, 186
Schiller, D., 236
Schmitt, E., 239
Schneider, V., 175
Scholte, J. A., 148, 149, 150, 153, 155, 175
Schonfeld, E., 108
Schou, N., 242, 243
Schudson, M., 236
Schwartz, S., 12
Scott, B., 156
Shahn, B., 85
Shaw, D., 236
Shryock A., 203
Siles, M. E., 99
Simmons, C., 78
Simon, T. F., 122
Smeltzer, S., 164
Soga, K., 36
Song, H., 59, 64, 149, 208, 211, 214, 223, 224
Spoerry, S., 218
Spybey, T., 149

Sreberny-Mohammadi, A., 149
Staino, K. V., 14
Starbuck, H. W., 156
Starr, A., 16, 125
Starr, P., 25, 27, 35, 47
Steadman, J., 100
Steele, W. R., 225
Stelter, B., 102, 103
Stinchcombe, A. L., 156
Stolberg, S. G., 238, 239
Straubhaar, T., 51, 83
Stubbs, P., 190, 204
Stull, D. D., 99
Stults, B., 55
Sudarat, D., 81

Taylor, J. E., 68
Tehranian, M., 148
The, C. Z., 220
Thomas, W. I., 19
Thompson, G., 150
Thompson, R. S., 119
Tomaselli, K., 76
Tomaselli, R., 76
Torpey, J., 27
Trautman, W. B., 119
Tuori, S., 187
Turner, J., 13
Turner, S. D., 168, 169, 170, 171

Ueda, R., 9
Ugba, A., 66, 67, 261

Valaskakis, G., 9, 38, 187, 194
Valdés, G., 58
Van Hear, N., 9
Van Vliet, R., 27
Vargaftig, M., 45
Vargas, L., 41, 78
Vecoli, R., 14
Vertovec, S., 185
Viswanath, K., 35, 37, 70, 73, 76, 207, 225
Vlasic, B., 138
Vongs, P., 241

Waldinger, R., 54, 60, 64, 229
Walker, D., 44
Wallerstein, I., 149
Wang, C. Y., 220
Ward, D., 156
Washburn, P., 79
Watanabe, T., 17, 125
Waters, M., 56, 64, 70, 148
Waters, M. C., 9
Watrous, P., 163
Weber-Menges, S., 59
Whitbeck, H., 218
Wiggans, A., 125
Wilkin, H. A., 11, 58, 112, 127, 128, 130, 132, 134, 208, 211, 212, 213, 216, 220, 223, 254
Wilson, C. C., 25, 31, 34
Wong, C., 220, 222
Woon, L. L., 56
Wu, F., 73

Xiaoming, H., 150, 151

Yoshida, E. M., 220
Yu, S., 39, 149, 150, 182, 187, 194, 200, 231, 234, 249

Zentella, A., 55
Zhang, D., 84
Zhang, K., 150, 151
Zhang, W., 55
Zhao, X., 35, 36
Zhou, M., 37, 229, 259
Zimmerman, W., 99
Znaniecki, F., 19
Zolberg, A., 56
Zotova, K., 28

Subject Index

Aboriginal or Flinders Island Chronicle, The (Australia), 42, 47n7
Aboriginal People's Television Network (APTN) (Canada), 38, 264
Aboriginals (Australia):
  ethnic media development, 26, 42–43
  ethnic media policy, 182, 187, 192–193
  online media, 258
Access Radio (Great Britain), 103–105
Adaptation, 58
Advertising revenue, 118–124, 146n1
Affective identity formation, 71–72, 75
Africa, 29, 76
  See also African-language media, *Africans Magazine*
Africa Channel, 101, 114n7
African-Americans:
  audience trends, 96–98, 100–101, 103, 107, 110–111, 112
  ethnic media development, 31–32
  ethnic media ownership, 168–171
  magazines, 234
  newspapers, 31–32, 76, 78–79, 96–97, 107
  online media, 136, 137, 138
  print media circulation, 96–98, 107
  radio, 102–103, 111, 112, 136
  television, 100–101, 110–111, 112
African-language media, 7
African media:
  Mail & Guardian, 240
Africans Magazine (Ireland), 66–67, 258
Afro-American, The (Baltimore/Washington, D.C.), 96–97, 107
Agenda setting effect, 236
Akhbar, 183
Al-Jazeera (Qatar), 64–65, 139
American Association of Advertising Agencies, 95
Amritsar Times, 161–162
Amsterdam News, The (New York), 96–97, 107
Antenna Satellite (Greece), 5
Arab-Americans, television, 112, 234, 263–264
Arabic-language media, 64–65, 138
  See also Akhbar, Al-Jazeera
Arbitron, 99–100, 101, 102–103
Article 19, 178–179
Asian-Americans:
  audience trends, 109, 112
  ethnic media ownership, 168, 169 (figure)
  magazines, 154–155, 164
  newspapers, 109, 128
  online media, 138
  print media circulation, 109
  radio, 112
  spending power, 20
  television, 112
  See also specific nationality
Asian Media Group, Inc., 166, 167 (figure)
AsianWeek (California), 138
Assimilation, 88, 185, 186
Association of Southeast Asian Nations (ASEAN), 157, 184
Audience trends:
  African-Americans, 96–98, 100–101, 103, 107, 110–111, 112
  Asian-Americans, 109, 112
  economic crisis (2008), 109–110
  ethnic media future, 259–262
  Hispanic-Americans, 95, 96 (figure), 97, 99, 101–102, 103, 105–108, 109, 110, 111–113
  industry context, 108–109
  magazines, 105–106, 108
  newspapers, 94–99, 105–110, 115n15
  print circulation audits, 94–99, 114n1
  print circulation trends, 105–110
  radio, 99–105, 110, 112–113, 115n19
  radio audience, 110, 112–113
  radio ratings, 99–100, 101, 102–103
  study questions, 95, 98, 105, 113–114

television, 99–105, 110–112
television audience, 110–112
television ratings, 99, 100–102
Audit Bureau of Circulation (ABC), 94–95, 96–97, 121–122
Australia:
ethnic media, 4
ethnic media development, 42–45
Huaxia, 63
immigration, 43–45, 53 (figure), 63–64, 187
interactive-visual media, 43
Koori Mail, 42–43, 89
newspapers, 42–43, 44, 45, 63, 80–81, 89
radio, 43, 44–45, 63–64, 77, 192–193
TA NEA, 44, 45
television, 43, 44–45
3CW Radio, 63–64
3XY Radio, 44–45
Waringarri Radio, 77
See also Aboriginals (Australia)
Australian Abo Call (Australia), 42
Australian Broadcasting Authority (ABA), 181
Australian Broadcasting Corporation, 192
Austria:
immigration, 66, 189–190
radio, 66
Awaz FM (Glasgow), 104

Balkan News Corporation, 156
BBC Radio Cymru (Wales), 87
Behavioral identity formation, 71–72, 75
Belgium, 29
ethnicity, 12
ethnic media policy, 182–183
immigration, 187–188
Bertelsmann AG, 152 (table)
Bilingualism, 83–84, 109, 230
Bink, Susan, 260
Black Enterprise, 234
Black Entertainment Television (BET), 101, 110–111, 114n7
BlackPress.org, 97–98
Bolivia-Es (Spain), 161
Brazil:
newspapers, 240
O Globo, 240
British Broadcasting Corporation (BBC), 28, 30
Beur FM (France), 245, 246
Bulgaria, 28

California:
El Clasifica, 123–124
El Mensajero, 123
Golden Hills News, The, 34
Indonesia Media, 158, 159 (figure)
InterThai/Pacific Rim News, 159
Mexican American Sun, 122
magazines, 123–124, 158, 159 (figure)
newspapers, 5, 21, 34, 36, 66, 105, 108, 110, 122, 123, 138, 155–156, 159, 166, 232–233, 237–238, 241–243, 257
Nguoi Viet 2, 66
Nguoi Viet Dailey, 66, 241–243, 257
Nuevo Mundo, 108
Oriental, The, 34
Philippine News, 21
radio, 20, 112
San Francisco Bay View, 138
television, 166, 167 (figure), 233, 234, 239, 263–264
Canada:
Cultural Diversity and Ethnic Media in British Columbia (Murray), 262
Cultural Diversity and Ethnic Media in British Columbia Project (Vancouver), 16
ethnic media, 4
ethnic media development, 37–40
ethnic minority media, 9, 24n7
Fairchild Radio, 39
Fairchild TV, 39–40
immigration, 150, 187
newspapers, 38–39
radio, 4, 37–38, 39
television, 38, 39–40, 193–194
Television Northern Canada (TVNC) 193–194, 204n15
third language media, 26, 37–38, 47n4
See also First Nations (Canada)
Canadian Radio-television and Telecommunications Commission (CRTC), 38, 181, 194
Cannibalization dilemma, 128, 135
Capital Radio (South Africa), 77
Caribbean-Americans, radio, 70
Caribbean News, The (Great Britain), 126
Caribbean Times, The (Great Britain), 125, 126, 127, 128
Catholic Church, 196–197
CBS, 152 (table), 170
Certified Audit of Circulation (CAC), 105
Channel One TV (Los Angeles), 263–264
Channel 31 (Australia), 44
Cherokee Phoenix, 32, 47n3, 81
Chicago media:
Extra, 123–124
La Raza, 123, 124
WOJO-FM, 112

Chile, radio, 196–197
China, 150–151, 219
China Daily News (New York), 36
China Weekly (San Francisco), 36
Chinese-Americans:
  ethnic media development, 34–35, 36–37
  newspapers, 34–35, 36–37, 257
  online media, 154–155
Chinese American Weekly (New York), 36
Chinese-language media:
  newspapers, 3–4, 34–35, 36–37, 85
  radio, 63–64
  television, 39–40
Chinese Pacific Weekly, 36
Chinese Times (San Francisco), 36
CHIN Radio (Toronto, Canada), 4
Cinéyama Media Group, 161–162
Circulation audits, 94–99, 114n1
Circulation-elasticity of demand, 119, 120 (figure)
Circulation spiral, 119, 121 (figure)
Civic engagement, 216–219
Clear Channel Communications, 103
Close, Sandy, 257
Closed immigration policy, 185, 186
Coello, Almendárez, 218
Cognitive identity formation, 71–72, 75
Colibri, 183
Collective efficacy, 214
Comcast Corporation, 111
Communication ecology, 126–127, 208–214, 225n1, 254–255
Community belonging, 214
Community health:
  geo-ethnic media, 219–223, 225n3
  resources for, 129–130 (table), 131–132 (table), 255
Community media, 10
  See also Geo-ethnic media; Professional journalism
Community Radio (Great Britain), 103–105
Conglomerate ethnic identity, 73, 74 (figure), 90n1
Connective media function, 59, 67, 83
Conseil Supéieure d' Audiovisuel (CSA) (France), 181, 190–191, 195
Contemporary Chinese America (Zhou), 259
Context of reception, 54–58
Cooperation for the Development of Emerging Countries (COSPE) (Italy), 17, 179–180
Council of Europe (COE), 176–177
Counter-programming, 135–136
Croatian-Americans, 86–87
Cuban-Americans, 238–239
Cultural Diversity and Ethnic Media in British Columbia (Murray), 262
Cultural Diversity and Ethnic Media in British Columbia Project (Vancouver), 15
Culture, 12
Culture shock, 63

Daily News, The, 122–123
Deregulation policy, 156, 199–201
Desi Radio (London), 104
Determinism, 151–152
Diaspora, Identity and the Media (Georgiou), 261
Diasporic media, 9–10, 24n9
Diasporic Minorities and Their Media Project (London), 4
Die Tageszeitung (Germany), 79–80
Die Zeit (Germany), 240
Diversity media, 190–191
Divisive policy model, 194–195
Divya Bhaskar North American Edition, 161–162
Domingo Network, 123–124
Downing, John, 254
Dual market operation, 109

Eastern Eye (Great Britain), 137
Eastern Group Publishing, 230–231, 234
Ebony, 234
Economic crisis (2008):
  audience trends, 109–110
  ethnic media competition, 137–138
Economic policy model, 193–194
Egyptian Satellite Channel, 139
El Clamor Público, 34
El Clasifica (Los Angeles), 123–124
El Diario-Contigo (New York), 123, 124
El Diario (New York), 34, 105, 110, 115n14, 119, 121–122, 123, 257
El Gringo (Sweden), 245, 246
Elias, Nelly, 265
El Latino-americano, 161
El Mensajero (San Francisco), 123
El Misisipí (New Orleans), 32–34
El Nuevo Herald (Miami), 105, 110
El País (Spain), 240
Employment:
  immigrant resources, 60
  professional journalism, 228–229

Entravision, 111–112
"Ethnic and Aboriginal Media in Canada" (Fleras), 261–262
Ethnic enclave, 54–55, 56
Ethnic enclave economy, 229
Ethnic identity:
affective identity formation, 71–72, 75
behavioral identity formation, 71–72, 75
cognitive identity formation, 71–72, 75
conglomerate identity, 73, 74 (figure), 90n1
defined, 12–14, 70–71
development of, 71–75
ethnic media impact, 75
hybrid identity, 74–75
hyphenated identity, 72–73
study questions, 75, 90
versus racial identity, 70–71
Ethnicity, 12, 14
Ethnic media:
application, 6–8 (figure)
community mobilization role, 16–19, 17–18
culture, 12
defined, 5, 6 (figure), 8–11
discussion questions, 8, 14, 20
ethnic identity, 12–14
ethnicity, 12, 14
geo-ethnicity, 11–12
globalization impact, 18, 19
market competition, 17–18
media contrast, 8–11
race, 15
roles of, 15–18
social change indicator, 17
societal transformations, 19–21
versus mainstream media, 10–11, 15, 21
Ethnic media competition:
advertising revenue, 118–124, 146n1
case study, 140–146
community connections, 133–134 (table)
community health resources, 129–130 (table), 131–132 (table), 255
economic crisis (2008), 137–138
media market, 118
newspaper challenges, 124–126
newspaper competition, 119–135, 140–146
online broadcasting media, 136–137
online-only media, 137
online print media, 126–128, 129–130 (table), 134 (table), 135
radio, 135–137
satellite television, 138–139
study questions, 118, 137, 139, 140
sustainability, 117
television, 135–137, 138–139
Ethnic media development:
Australia, 42–45
Canada, 37–40
Europe, 27–31
immigration, 26–27, 29–30, 35, 37, 43–45
indigenous media, 26, 32, 33 (figure), 37–38, 40–43
market impact, 46
Mexico, 40–41
migration trends, 26–27
newspapers, 27–28, 29, 31–37, 38–39, 40, 42–43, 44, 45, 47n1
policy impact, 45
radio, 28, 30–31, 37–38, 39–41, 43, 44–45
regulatory impact, 45–46
study questions, 33, 38, 46–47
television, 28, 30–31, 38, 39–40, 43, 44
United States, 31–37
Ethnic media future:
audience trends, 259–262
online media, 254–258
producers, 262–265
professional journalism, 246–248
research agenda, 265–266
study questions, 263
Ethnic Media Group (EMG), 126, 127, 137–138
Ethnic media organizations:
globalization, 148–158
large corporations, 160–161
multi-media company headquarters, 152 (table)
multinational enterprise, 161–162
online organizations, 164
organizational culture, 163
organizational structure, 147–148
public service broadcasting, 163–164
small scale operations, 158–160
study questions, 158, 160, 164, 171–172
transnational enterprise, 162–163
Ethnic media ownership, 164–171
mainstream media acquisitions, 167–168
minority ownership, 168–171
newspapers, 166, 167
ownership consolidation, 165–166

television, 166–171
transnational acquisitions, 166, 167 (figure)
Ethnic media policy:
broad context, 185 (figure)
deregulation, 156, 199–201
divisive model, 194–195
economic model, 193–194
ethnic media development, 45–46
ethnic media impact, 184–191
global governance, 173–174
globalization impact, 156–158, 174–183
global level, 175–180
global policymakers, 175 (figure)
harmonization, 157
immigration policy, 157–158, 184–191, 197–198
indigenous populations, 182, 187–188, 197–198
integrationist model, 192–193
intergovernmental organizations (IGOs), 176–178
international level, 175–180
international nongovernmental organizations (INGOs), 174–175, 178–180
labor policy, 157–158
local policymaking, 182–183
nation-state level, 174–175, 180–182, 184–191
nongovernmental organizations (NGOs), 181–182, 183
nonprofit organizations, 181–182
online media, 200–201
open channels, 199
policymaking levels, 176 (figure)
policy models, 192–197
policy provisions, 191–197
preemptive model, 195–196
proselytism model, 196–197
public access channels, 199
public sector policymakers, 180–181
public service broadcasting, 198–199
regulation, 45–46, 156–158
Restricted Service Licenses, 199
shallow multiculturalism, 193–194
study questions, 178, 197, 202
third sector organizations, 175
trade policy, 156
Ethnic Media Project (Boston), 16, 17
Ethnic Minorities, Electronic Media and the Public Sphere (Browne), 257
Ethnic minority community:
cultural information, 84–85
defined, 69
ethnic media role, 75–85
ethnic media viability, 85–89
family life, 83–85
imagined community, 78
independent voice, 76–77
language development/maintenance, 83–84, 87–89
local information, 85–87
social equality, 78–82
social institutions, 82–83
study questions, 83, 89
Ethnic minority media, 9
Ethnos (Greece), 141, 155
Europe:
broadcast media development, 30–31
ethnic media development, 27–31
immigration, 29–30
19th-20th century media, 28
post-war media, 29–31
unlicensed broadcast media, 30–31
See also specific country
European Ethnic Broadcasting Association (EEBA), 179
European Union (EU), ethnic media policy, 157–158, 173–174, 176, 179–180, 184
Extra (Chicago), 123–124

Fairchild Radio (Canada), 39
Fairchild TV (Canada), 39–40
Federal Communication Commission (FCC), 180
Feng Hua Yuan, 164
Finland, 29
immigration, 187–188
First Nations (Canada):
ethnic media development, 26, 37–38
ethnic media policy, 182, 187, 193–194
Florida:
El Nuevo Herald, 105, 110
newspapers, 105, 110
radio, 112
Former Yugoslav Republic of Macedonia (FYROM), 238
France:
Beur FM, 245, 246
ethnic media development, 27, 29, 30
ethnic media policy, 194–195
free radio, 195
Gazette de Leyde, 27

immigration, 190–191
Le Monde, 240
minority media, 8
newspapers, 27, 240, 245, 246
radio, 30, 194–195, 245, 246
Témoignage Chrétien, 245, 246
Freedom's Journal (New York), 31, 76, 96–97
Funabiki, Jon, 255
Funkhaus Europa (Cologne), 199
Fusión Latina, 161

Gazette de Leyde (France), 27
General Electric, 102, 111, 152 (table), 172n7
Geo-ethnicity, 11–12
Geo-ethnic media:
challenges of, 223–224
civic engagement, 216–219
collective efficacy, 214
communication ecology, 126–127, 208–214, 225n1, 254–255
community belonging, 214
community health, 219–223, 225n3
community institutions, 214–216
community media sources, 209 (figure), 210, 211 (figure), 212 (figure), 221 (figure)
defined, 207–208
ecological approach, 212–214
neighborhood storytelling network, 215–216
service communities, 207–216
study questions, 210, 213, 222, 224–225
Geo-ethnic storytelling, 208, 215–219, 220–222
German-Americans, newspapers, 35–36
German-Jewish press, 36
German-language media, 35–36
Germany:
Die Tageszeitung, 79–80
Die Zeit, 240
ethnic media, 4
ethnic media development, 28, 29, 35–36
guest workers, 189–190, 196
immigration, 59, 189–190
newspapers, 79–80, 240
Persembe, 79–80
radio, 196, 199, 228, 239
Globalization:
defined, 148–153
determinism, 151–152
economic globalization, 155–156
ethnic media impact, 18, 19
forces of, 153–158
hyperglobalist approach, 148–149
multi-media company headquarters, 152 (table)
regulation, 156–158
skeptic approach, 148, 149–151
technological innovation, 153–155
transformationalist approach, 148, 151–153
See also Ethnic media policy
Golden Hills News, The (San Francisco), 34
Granite Broadcasting, 169
Great Britain:
Afro-Caribbean community, 124–125
Caribbean News, The, 126
Caribbean Times, The, 125, 126, 127, 128
Eastern Eye, 137
ethnic media, 4
ethnic media development, 28, 29, 30, 31
immigration, 58, 60, 64–65, 126, 188–189
Independent, The, 240
Independent Local Radio, 30
Independent Television (ITV), 30
New Nation, 137
New Style Radio, 104
New Vision-The Independent Refugee News and Information Service, 58
newspapers, 124–125, 126, 127, 128, 137, 240
radio, 30, 31, 103–105
television, 28, 30, 64–65
Voice, 125
Greece:
ethnic media development, 29
Ethnos, 141, 155
immigration, 191
newspapers, 141, 155
radio, 5
television, 5
Greek American, The (New York City), 140–146
Greek American Publishing, Ltd., 141–146
Greek-Americans:
newspapers, 44, 45, 82, 140–146, 155
online media, 90n3
population demographics, 144, 146n8
radio, 44–45, 81
television, 44, 45, 81
Greek Beat, 45
Greek-language media:
newspapers, 44, 45, 82
radio, 44–45, 81
television, 44, 45, 81

Greek Media Group (Australia), 44–45
Greek-Press, 145
Gringo Gazette (Mexico), 40
Guest workers (Germany), 189–190, 196

Haitian Times (New York), 5, 160
Hankook Ilbo, 166, 167 (figure)
Hart-Cellar Act (1965), 37
Hawaii media:
  KIKU-TV, 166, 167 (figure)
Herron, Frank, 264
Hispanic-Americans:
  audience trends, 95, 96 (figure), 97, 99, 101–102, 103, 105–108, 109, 110, 111–113
  ethnic identity, 73
  ethnic media competition, 118, 119, 121–122, 123–124, 128, 135–137, 146n1
  ethnic media development, 32–34
  ethnic media ownership, 168, 170–171
  La Nueva (Los Angeles), 20, 234
  La Opinión Contigo (Los Angeles), 123, 124
  La Opinión (Los Angeles), 17, 105, 110, 122, 257
  La Planeta (Boston), 167
  La Prensa (New York), 110, 123, 257
  La Raza (Chicago), 123, 124
  Latina (United States), 241
  magazines, 105–106, 108, 123–124, 241
  newspapers, 17, 20, 32–34, 95, 96 (figure), 99, 105–108, 109, 119, 121–122, 123, 127, 128, 138
  online media, 137, 138, 256–257
  print media circulation, 95, 96 (figure), 97, 105–108
  publications by location (United States, 2005), 106 (figure)
  radio, 20, 102–103, 110, 112–113, 234
  spending power, 19–20
  television, 18, 21, 84–85, 101–102, 135–137, 169–170, 171
  See also Spanish-language media
Historical Black Press Foundation, 97–98
Hoy (New York), 20, 119, 121–122, 123, 138
Huaxia (Australia), 63
Hua Xia Wen Zhai (HXWZ), 154–155, 164
Hurricane Katrina, New Orleans (2006), 62
Hybrid ethnic identity, 74–75
Hypen magazine, 66
Hyperglobalist approach, 148–149
Hyphenated ethnic identity, 72–73

Illinois:
  magazines, 123–124
  newspapers, 123, 124
  radio, 112
Imagined community, 78
Immigration:
  adaptation, 58
  assimilation, 88, 185, 186
  closed policy, 185, 186
  connective media function, 59, 67, 83
  context of reception, 54–58
  culture shock, 63
  defined, 52–54
  18th-19th century, 35
  employment resources, 60
  ethnic enclave, 54–55, 56
  ethnic media development, 26–27, 29–30, 35, 37, 43–45
  ethnic media impact, 54–56, 57 (table)
  ethnic media importance, 51
  ethnic media policy, 157–158, 184–191, 197–198
  ethnic media resources, 58–67
  home-country news, 64–65
  host government policy, 54, 57 (table)
  immigrant media, 9, 23n8
  involuntary immigrant, 52–53
  labor market conditions, 54, 57 (table)
  legal rights, 60–63
  melting-pot theory, 18, 186
  migrant, 52
  migration trends, 26–27
  multiculturalism, 185, 187–189, 190
  new media literacy, 65–66
  online media, 65–67
  open policy, 185, 187, 188, 203n13
  orientation media function, 59, 67, 83
  post-1965, 37
  segregation, 56
  separatists, 56
  settlement community characteristics, 54–55, 57 (table)
  settlement community news, 58–60
  societal attitudes, 55–56, 57 (table)
  sojourner, 52
  study questions, 57, 62, 65, 68
  support systems, 63–64
  symbolic media function, 83
  transnationalism, 64
  voluntary immigrant, 52
  See also specific country
ImpreMedia, LLC, 121, 123–124, 161, 256–257
Independent, The (Great Britain), 240

Independent Communications Authority of South Africa (ICASA), 181
Independent Local Radio (Great Britain), 30
Independent Television (ITV) (Great Britain), 30
Indian-Americans:
 ethnic identity, 74–75
 newspapers, 153–154, 161–162
 television, 162
Indian Country Today, 81, 90n2
Indian Express, The, 153–154, 172n1
Indian Express North American Edition, 161
Indigenous media:
 ethnic media development, 26, 32, 33 (figure), 37–38, 40–43
 ethnic media policy, 182, 187–188, 197–198
 See also Aboriginals (Australia); First Nations (Canada); Native-Americans
Indigenous Public Sphere, The (Hartley), 258
Indonesia, 85
Indonesia Media (California), 158, 159 (figure)
Integrationist policy model, 192–193
Intellectual ghettoization, 230
Interactive One, 136
Intergovernmental organizations (IGOs), 176–178
International Federation of Journalists, 178–179
International Media Group, Inc., 166, 167 (figure)
International nongovernmental organizations (INGOs), 174–175, 178–180
International Telecommunications Union (ITU), 177
Internet. *See* Online media
InterThai/Pacific Rim News (Los Angeles), 159
Involuntary immigrant, 52–53
Ireland:
 immigration, 59, 66–67
 magazines, 66–67, 258
 Metro Eireann, 261
 newspapers, 261
 radio, 104
Italy:
 ethnic identity, 14
 ethnic media development, 29
 immigration, 191
Japanese-Americans:
 ethnic media development, 36
 social institutions, 82
Japanese-language media, 36, 87
Jewish-Americans:
 ethnic identity, 71–72
 German-Jewish press, 36
 social institutions, 82
Johnson-Reed Act (1924), 56
Joong-Ang Ilbo, 166

Kesher (Mexico), 40
KESS-FM (Dallas), 112
KIKU-TV (Hawaii), 166, 167 (figure)
King, Rodney, 81
KLAX-FM, 112
Koori Mail (Australia), 42–43, 89
Korea Central Daily, 155–156, 166
Korean-Americans:
 Hankook Ilbo, 166, 167 (figure)
 newspapers, 5, 155–156, 166, 167 (figure), 232–233, 237–238
 television, 166, 167 (figure)
Korea Times, The (Los Angeles), 5, 155–156, 166, 232–233, 237–238
KSCA-FM (Los Angeles), 112
KSCI-TV (Los Angeles), 166, 167 (figure), 233, 234, 239
KTBK-AM, 110

Language:
 authenticity, 89
 bilingualism, 83–84, 109, 230
 Charter for Regional and European languages, 177, 203n3
 development/maintenance of, 83–84, 87–89
 exclusivity, 88
 multilingualism, 187–188
 See also specific language
Language shift, 83
La Nueva (Los Angeles), 20
La Opinión Contigo (Los Angeles), 123, 124
La Opinión (Los Angeles), 17, 105, 110, 122, 257
La Planeta (Boston), 167
La Prensa (New York), 110, 123, 257
La Raza (Chicago), 123, 124
Latina (United States), 241
Latinoamérica, 161
Latino: *see* Hispanic-Americans

Latino Print Network, 95, 97
Legal rights, 60–63
Le Monde (France), 240
Leonard Green & Partners, L.P., 166, 167 (figure)
Lian Yi Tong Xun, 164
Local media, 10
  community information, 85–87
  policymaking, 182–183
  See also Geo-ethnic media
Locative media, 10
Los Angeles media:
  Channel One TV, 263–264
  El Clasifica, 123–124
  Korea Times, The, 5, 155–156, 166, 232–233, 237–238
  KSCA-FM, 112
  KSCI-TV, 166, 167 (figure), 233, 234, 239
  La Nueva, 20
  La Opinión Contigo, 123, 124
  La Opinión, 17, 105, 110, 122, 257
London media:
  Desi Radio, 104
Louisiana:
  newspapers, 32–34
  El Misisipí, 32–34

Magazines:
  African-Americans, 234
  Asian-Americans, 154–155, 164
  audience trends, 105–106, 108
  California, 123–124, 158, 159 (figure)
  Hispanic-Americans, 105–106, 108, 123–124, 240
  Illinois, 123–124
  Internet Website, 5
  Ireland, 66–67, 258
  online, 66–67, 154–155, 164, 258
  Spanish-language, 123–124
  Sweden, 245, 246
  See also specific publications
Mail & Guardian (South Africa), 240
Mainstream media:
  attrition of, 231–232
  collaboration with, 244–246
  defined, 10–11
  ethnic media acquisitions, 167–168
  versus ethnic media, 10–11, 15, 21
Maryland, newspapers, 96–97, 107, 167
Massachusetts media:
  La Planeta, 167
  Phoenix, The, 167
Media market, 118
Mediam'Rad Project (Paris), 17, 179
Melting-pot theory, 18, 186
Metamorphosis Project (Los Angeles), 11, 13, 158, 208–209
Metro Eireann (Ireland), 261
Metro (Sweden), 245
Mexican American Sun (Los Angeles), 122
Mexico:
  ethnic media development, 40–41
  Gringo Gazette, 40
  indigenous media, 40–41, 78
  Kesher, 40
  newspapers, 40
  radio, 40–41
Miami media:
  WCMQ-FM, 112
Middle East, satellite television, 139
Middle East Broadcasting Center (MBC), 139, 154, 172n2
Mi Ecuador (Spain), 161
Migrant, 52
Migrant Media (Kosnick), 256
Minority Dailies Association (MIDAS), 180
Minority media, 8
Mira Media (Netherlands), 17, 179–180, 181–182, 260
Multiculturalism:
  immigration, 185, 187–189, 190
  shallow multiculturalism, 193–194
Multilingualism, 187–188
Mun 2, 136

National Association of Black Owned Broadcasters (NABOB), 103, 181
National Commission for the Development of Indigenous Peoples (Mexico), 40–41
National Directory of Ethnic Media, 3
National Ethnic and Multicultural Broadcasters Council (NEMBC) (Australia), 181, 182, 247
National Ethnic Press and Media Council of Canada, 182, 203n9
National Expo of Ethnic Media, 167
National Hispanic Television Index (NHTI), 101
National Indigenous Institute (Mexico), 40–41
National Indigenous Media Association of Australia (NIMAA), 43
National Indigenous Radio Service (NIRS) (Australia), 43, 264

Nation-states, 26–27, 150
  ethnic media policy, 174–175, 180–182, 184–191
Native-Americans:
  Cherokee alphabet, 32, 33 (figure)
  ethnic media development, 26, 32, 33 (figure)
  ethnic media ownership, 168
  newspapers, 32, 81
  online media, 81
  radio, 77, 81
  television, 81
Native Public Media (United States), 77
NBC, 111, 152 (table), 170
Netherlands:
  ethnic media, 4
  immigration, 188–189
New America Media (NAM), 98, 103–105, 127–128, 167, 181, 257
New California Media, 165, 172n5
New media literacy, 65–66
New Nation (Great Britain), 137
News Corporation, 152 (table), 156
Newspaper Association of America (NAA), 17
Newspapers:
  advertising revenue, 119, 120 (figure), 121–124
  African-Americans, 31–32, 76, 78–79, 96–97, 107
  Asian-Americans, 109, 128
  audience trends, 94–99, 105–110, 115n15
  Australia, 42–43, 44, 45, 63, 80–81, 89
  Brazil, 240
  California, 5, 21, 34, 36, 66, 105, 108, 110, 122, 123, 138, 147, 155–156, 166, 232–233, 237–238, 241–243, 257
  Canada, 38–39
  cannibalization dilemma, 128, 135
  case study, 140–146
  challenges for, 124–126
  Chinese-Americans, 34–35, 36–37, 257
  Chinese-language, 3–4, 34–35, 36–37, 85
  circulation audits, 94–99, 114n1
  circulation-elasticity of demand, 119, 120 (figure)
  circulation spiral, 119, 121 (figure)
  dual market operation, 109
  ethnic media competition, 119–135, 140–146
  ethnic media development, 27–28, 29, 31–37, 38–39, 40, 42–43, 44, 45, 47n1
  ethnic media ownership, 166, 167
  Florida, 105, 110
  France, 27, 240, 245, 246
  German-Americans, 35–36
  German-language, 35–36
  Germany, 79–80, 240
  Great Britain, 124–125, 126, 127, 128, 137, 240
  Greece, 141, 155
  Greek-Americans, 44, 45, 82, 140–146, 155
  Greek-language, 44, 45, 82
  Hispanic-Americans, 17, 21, 32–34, 95, 96 (figure), 99, 105–108, 109, 119, 121–122, 123, 127, 128, 138
  Illinois, 123, 124
  immigration trends, 126
  Indian-Americans, 153–154, 161–162
  Ireland, 261
  Japanese-language media, 36, 87
  Korean-Americans, 5, 155–156, 166, 167 (figure), 232–233, 237–238
  Louisiana, 32–34
  market dynamics, 119, 121–124
  Maryland, 96–97, 107, 167
  Mexico, 40
  Native-Americans, 32, 81
  New York, 5, 20, 31–32, 34, 36, 76, 82, 96–97, 119, 121–123, 140–146, 155, 160, 257
  online, 66, 90n3, 126–128, 129–130 (table), 134 (table), 135, 256–257
  Pennsylvania, 107
  South Africa, 240
  Spain, 161, 240
  Spanish-language, 4, 17, 20, 32–34, 108, 119, 121–122, 123, 127, 128, 138, 161
  success hypothesis, 124–125
  Sweden, 245
  Syrian-Americans, 56
  Texas, 127, 128, 257
  umbrella competition, 122–124, 146n2
  Vietnamese-Americans, 66, 241–243, 257
  Washington, D. C., 96–97, 107
  See also specific publication
New Style Radio (Great Britain), 104
New Vision-The Independent Refugee News and Information Service (London), 58
New York:
  newspapers, 5, 20, 31–32, 34, 36, 76, 82, 96–97, 107, 119, 121–123, 138, 140–146, 155, 160, 257
  North Star, 32

radio, 70, 112
WFUV, 163
WKCR, 163
WNWK-FM, 163
WNYC, 163–164
WNYE, 163–164
television, 163–164
New York media:
El Diario-Contigo, 123, 124
El Diario, 34, 105, 110, 115n14, 119, 121–122, 123, 257
Freedom's Journal, 31, 76, 96–97
Greek American, The, 140–146
Haitian Times, 5, 160
Hoy, 20, 119, 121–122, 123, 138
La Prensa, 110, 123, 257
Orthodox Observer, 82, 90n3
New York Post, The, 122–123
New York Times, The, 5, 122–123, 160, 234, 240
Nguoi Viet 2 (California), 66
Nguoi Viet Daily (California), 66, 241–243, 257
Nguoi Viet Online, 66
Nielsen Media Research, 99–102, 114n4, 262–263
Nongovernmental organizations (NGOs), 181–182, 183
Nonprofit organizations, 181–182
Norsk Rikskringkasting (NRK) (Norway), 28
North American Free Trade Agreement (NAFTA), 184
North Atlantic Treaty Organization (NATO), 157
North Star (New York), 32
Norway:
ethnic media development, 29
Norsk Rikskringkasting (NRK), 28
television, 28
Nuevo Mundo (San Jose), 108
Nunes, Paulo Rogério, 258

Office of Communications (OfCom) (Great Britain), 180
O Globo (Brazil), 240
Online media:
African-Americans, 136, 137, 138
Asian-Americans, 138
Chinese-Americans, 154–155, 164
ethnic media competition, 126–128, 129–130 (table), 134 (table), 135, 136–137
ethnic media future, 254–258
ethnic media organizations, 164
ethnic media policy, 200–201
Greek-Americans, 90n3
Hispanic-Americans, 137, 138, 256–257
immigrants, 65–67
magazines, 66–67, 154–155, 164, 258
Native-Americans, 81
newspapers, 66, 90n3, 126–128, 129–130 (table), 134 (table), 135, 256–257
online-only media, 137
radio, 136–137
Spanish-language media, 136, 137, 256–257
television, 136–137
Open channels, 199
Open immigration policy, 185, 187, 188, 203n13
Orbit TV (Bahrain), 139
Oriental, The (San Francisco), 34
Orientation media function, 59, 67, 83
Orthodox Observer (New York), 82, 90n3
Ottoman Empire, 28, 47n2
Ownership. *See* Ethnic media ownership

Panos Institute (Paris), 17, 179, 180, 190–191
Pegasus Publishing and Printing, S.A., 141–146
Pennsylvania, newspapers, 107
Persembe (Germany), 79–80
Philadelphia Tribune, The, 107
Philippine News (San Francisco), 21
Philippines, 216–217
Phoenix, The (Boston), 167
Pittsburgh Courier, 78–79
Policy. *See* Ethnic media policy
Polish Peasant in Europe and America, The (Thomas and Znanlecki), 19
Portable people meters, 102–103
Portugal, 29
Preemptive policy model, 195–196
Professional journalism:
agenda setting effect, 236
challenges, 231–234
community advocacy, 238–239
community connections, 229–231
community dissatisfaction, 241–244
contemporary issues, 227–228
elitism, 240–241
employment opportunities, 228–229
ethnic enclave economy, 229
formal standards, 239–240
framing of issues, 236

future role, 246–248
intellectual ghettoization, 230
mainstream media attrition, 231–232
mainstream media collaboration, 244–246
news sources, 232–234, 235 (figure)
objectivity standard, 236–238, 249n4
segregated news conferences, 234
social responsibility, 236–241, 249n3
study questions, 231, 235, 240, 244, 246, 248–249
Proini (New York), 140, 155
Project for Excellence in Journalism (PEJ), 95, 97, 127–128, 138, 165
Proselytism policy model, 196–197
Public access channels, 199
Public service broadcasting, 163–164, 198–199
Public sphere, 191–192

Race, 15
Racial identity, 13–14, 70–71
Radio:
African-Americans, 102–103, 111, 112, 136
African-language, 76
Asian-Americans, 112
audience trends, 99–105, 110, 112–113, 115n19
Australia, 43, 44–45, 63–64, 77, 192–193
Austria, 66
California, 20, 112
Canada, 4, 37–38, 39
Caribbean-Americans, 70
Chile, 196–197
Chinese-language, 63–64
ethnic media competition, 135–137
ethnic media development, 28, 30–31, 37–38, 39–41, 43, 44–45
Florida, 112
France, 30, 194–195, 245, 246
Germany, 196, 199, 228, 239
Great Britain, 30, 31, 103–105
Greece, 5
Greek-Americans, 44–45, 81
Greek-language, 44–45, 81
Hispanic-Americans, 20, 102–103, 110, 112–113, 234
Illinois, 112
Ireland, 104
Mexico, 40–41
Native-Americans, 77, 81
New York, 70, 112
online, 136–137
portable people meters, 102–103
public service broadcasting, 163, 198–199
ratings, 99–100, 101, 102–103
South Africa, 76–77
Spanish-language, 20, 110, 112–113
sustainability models, 103–105
Texas, 112
Wales, 87
See also specific stations
Radio Africa (Austria), 66
Radio Authority (Great Britain), 103–105, 115n9
Radio Bantu (South Africa), 76–77
Radio Beur (France), 30
Radio Bop (South Africa), 77
Radio Eiámpti (Mexico), 41
Radio Faza (Great Britain), 104
Radio 1476 (Austria), 66
Radio Multikulti (Berlin), 199, 239
Radio One, 111, 115n17, 136
Radio 702 (South Africa), 77
Radio Soleil (France), 30
Radio Thohoyandou (South Africa), 77
Radio Tropicale (New York), 70
Radio Uékakua (Mexico), 41
Regulation. *See* Ethnic media policy
Restricted Service Licenses, 199
Roberts Broadcasting, 169–170
Royal Commission on Bilingualism and Biculturalism (Canada), 187, 203n11
Rumbo (Texas), 127, 128, 257

Samsung, 166
San Francisco Bay View, 138
SAT-7, 5, 162
Satellite television:
ethnic media competition, 138–139
Middle East, 139
Schumacher-Matos, Edward, 260
Scotland media:
Awaz FM (Glasgow), 104
Segregation, 56
Sensenbrenner Bill (2006), 218
Separatists, 56
Shallow multiculturalism, 193–194
Sianel Pedwar Cymru (Wales), 88
Sinclair, 170
Sing Tao Daily, 154, 257
Skeptic approach, 148, 149–151
Sojourner, 52
Sotelo, Eduardo, 218

South Africa:
Capital Radio, 77
newspapers, 240
radio, 76–77
South East Europe Media Organization, 178–179
Spain:
Bolivia-Es, 161
El País, 240
ethnic identity, 14
ethnic media development, 29
immigration, 191
indigenous population, 197–198
Mi Ecuador, 161
newspapers, 161, 240
Spanish-language media:
magazines, 123–124
newspapers, 4, 17, 20, 32–34, 108, 119, 121–122, 123, 127, 128, 138, 161
online media, 136, 137, 256–257
radio, 20, 110, 112–113
television, 17, 20, 101–102, 111–112, 135–137, 169–170, 171, 200, 201 (figure), 240
See also Hispanic-Americans
Spanish Radio Association, 103
Special Broadcasting Service (SBS) (Australia), 187, 193
Staats-Zeijung und Herold (United States), 35–36
Starcom MediaVest Group, 101
Sweden:
El Gringo, 245, 246
ethnic media policy, 177, 202n2
immigration, 187–188
magazines, 245, 246
Metro, 245
newspapers, 245
Switzerland, 29
Symbolic media function, 83
Syrian-Americans, newspapers, 56
Syrian World, The (United States), 56

Talentvision (Canada), 39–40
TA NEA (Australia), 44, 45
Tapestry, 101
TeleFutura, 111, 135–136
Telemundo, 102, 111, 136, 137, 200
Television:
African-Americans, 100–101, 110–111, 112
Arab-Americans, 112, 234, 263–264
Arabic-language, 64–65, 138
Asian-Americans, 112
audience trends, 99–105, 110–112
Australia, 43, 44–45
California, 166, 167 (figure), 233, 234, 239, 263–264
Canada, 38, 39–40, 193–194
Chinese-language, 39–40
counter-programming, 135–136
ethnic media competition, 135–137, 138–139
ethnic media development, 28, 30–31, 38, 39–40, 43, 44
ethnic media ownership, 166–171
Great Britain, 28, 30, 64–65
Greece, 5
Greek-Americans, 44, 45, 81
Greek-language, 44, 45, 81
Hispanic-Americans, 17, 20, 84–85, 101–102, 135–137, 169–170, 171
Indian-Americans, 162
Korean-Americans, 166, 167 (figure)
Native-Americans, 81
New York, 163–164
Norway, 28
online, 136–137
open channels, 199
public access channels, 199
public service broadcasting, 163–164, 198–199
ratings, 99, 100–102
Restricted Service Licenses, 199
satellite television, 138–139
Spanish-language, 17, 20, 101–102, 111–112, 135–137, 169–170, 171, 200, 201 (figure), 240
sustainability models, 103
telenovela, 84–85
Wales, 87–88
Welsh-language, 87–88
See also specific station
Television Northern Canada (TVNC), 193–194, 204n15
Telugu Times, 161–162
Témoignage Chrétien (France), 245, 246
Texas:
KESS-FM, 112
newspapers, 127, 128, 257
radio, 112
Rumbo, 127, 128, 257
Thai-Americans, 81–82
Third sector organizations, 175
3CW Radio (Melbourne), 63–64

3XY Radio (Australia), 44–45
Tiempo Iberoamericano, 161
Time Warner Company, 152 (table)
Transformationalist approach, 148, 151–153
Transnationalism:
  immigration, 64
  media, 16
Treaty of Guadalupe Hidalgo (1848), 34
Treaty of Versailles (1919), 35
Treaty of Westphalia (1648), 26
Tribune, 170
Turkey, 29
TVB-Hong Kong, 5
TVBS-Europe, 5
TV Hellas (Australia), 44, 45
TV One, 101, 111, 114n7

Umbrella competition, 122–124, 146n2
United Nations Educational, Scientific, and Cultural Organization (UNESCO), 177–178
United Nations (UN),ethnic media policy, 173–174, 177, 203n4
United States:
  domestic terrorism, 186–187, 237
  early Black press, 31–32
  early Chinese press, 34–35
  early immigrant press, 35
  early Latino press, 32–34
  ethnic media development, 31–37
  immigration, 35, 37, 56, 59–60, 61–62, 66, 67, 186–187
  new immigrant media, 37
  wartime media, 35–37
  See also African-Americans, Hispanic-Americans, Native-Americans
Univisión, 17, 20, 101–102, 111–112, 136, 137, 169–170, 171, 200, 201 (figure)
USA Today, 122

Viacom, 110
Viacom, Inc., 152 (table)
Vietnamese-Americans:
  community health, 222
  newspapers, 66, 241–243, 257
Vivendi, 152 (table)
Voice (Great Britain), 125
Voluntary immigrant, 52

Wales:
  BBC Radio Cymru, 87
  radio, 87
  Sianel Pedwar Cymru, 88
  television, 87–88
Walt Disney Company, 152 (table)
Waringarri, Radio (Australia), 77
Washington, D. C., newspapers, 96–97, 107
WBLS, 102
WCAA, 102
WCMQ-FM (Miami), 112
Welsh-language media, 87–88
WFTD-AM, 110
WFUV (Fordham University), 163
WKCR (Columbia University), 163
WNWK-FM (New York), 163
WNYC (New York), 163–164
WNYE (New York), 163–164
WOJO-FM (Chicago), 112
World Journal, 128, 257
World Trade Organization (WTO), 176, 184
WSKQ-FM (New York), 112
WZUP-FM, 110

XETLA-AM radio (Mexico), 41

Yugoslavia, 29

Zee TV, 162

About the Authors

Matthew D. Matsaganis (Ph.D., University of Southern California) is an Assistant Professor of Communication at the University at Albany, State University of New York. His research addresses issues of ethnic media production and sustainability, neighborhood effects and the role of communication in building civic engagement and community capacity, as well as health disparities and the social determinants of health. His research has been published in the *American Behavioral Scientist, Human Communication Research,* the *Electronic Journal of Communication,* and the *Encyclopedia of International Media and Communications;* he has presented his work at a number of academic and professional conferences. Matthew is also a recovering print journalist. He has worked for a variety of publications in Athens, Greece, and New York City. In November 2001, he received a certificate of recognition from the U.S. Congress for his work as a journalist and for promoting Greek-American friendship and cooperation.

Vikki S. Katz (Ph.D., University of Southern California) is an Assistant Professor of Communication in the School of Communication and Information at Rutgers, the State University of New Jersey. Her research explores issues of ethnic media consumption, particularly the interplay between media content and access to community resources in ethnic minority and immigrant neighborhoods. She has conducted research on the relationship between family decision making around media content and disparities in connecting to health care, schools, and social services; children's translating activities around media content; the viability of ethnic media with second and third-generation audiences; and the role of family communication in civic engagement. Her research has been published in the *Journal of Communication* and the *Journal of Children and Media.* She has also presented her work at academic and professional conferences on topics including ethnic media viability, intergenerational media connection patterns, and immigrant family media use.

Sandra J. Ball-Rokeach (Ph.D., University of Washington) is a Professor of Communication and Sociology in the Annenberg School for Communication and Journalism, at the University of Southern California. She is also the Principal Investigator of the Metamorphosis Project. Sandra is author or editor of six books: *Violence and the Media* (with R. K. Baker); *Theories of Mass Communication* (with M. L. DeFleur); *The Great American Values Test: Influencing Belief and Behavior through Television* (with M. Rokeach & J. W. Grube*); Media, Audience and Society* (with M. G. Cantor); *Paradoxes of Youth and Sport* (with M. Gatz and M. Messner);

and *Technological Visions: The Hopes and Fears that Shape New Technologies* (with M. Sturken and D. Thomas). Her published articles appear in such journals as *Communication Research, Journalism Quarterly, Mass Communication and Society, American Sociological Review, Public Opinion Quarterly, Journal of Communication, New Media and Society, Social Problems,* and *The American Psychologist.* She has been co-editor (with C. R. Berger) of *Communication Research* from 1992 to 1997, a Fulbright scholar at the Hebrew University and a Rockefeller Fellow at the Bellagio Study Center. She currently is a fellow of the Society for the Psychological Study of Social Issues and the International Communication Association. She also serves on the advisory boards of the McCune Foundations, Southern California Public Radio, and the Research and Learning Group, BBC World Service Trust. Her service on editorial boards includes the *Journal Communication, Communication Studies,* the *International Journal of Communication,* the *American Journal of Media Psychology,* and the *Chinese Journal of Communication.*